Worth and Wealth.

WORTH AND WEALTH:

A COLLECTION OF

MAXIMS, MORALS AND MISCELLANIES

FOR

MERCHANTS AND MEN OF BUSINESS.

BY FREEMAN HUNT,

Editor of the "Merchants Magazine," "Lives of American Merchants," etc.

NEW YORK:

STRINGER & TOWNSEND

1856.

PREFACE.

THE reader of these pages will find in them no formal code of Mercantile rules, no systematic treatise on trade. My aim is to present illustrations rather than theories, examples rather than precepts. Yet that there is a true theory of business is as evident as that every art has its science, or, stating the matter more generally and less formally, that there is a good and a bad, a true and a false way of doing every thing. That master of the *theory* of Common Sense, Bacon, has said that "nothing should be put in practice which has not been previously developed in theory." Trade is as universal as the race, as ancient as the first barter, when two men got what both wanted by giving what neither needed, and each gained, while neither lost. In our day, trade has penetrated and gives the key-note to civilized life, and Commerce, which used to hug the coasts of the Mediterranean, and then crept along the shores of the three eastern continents, now ransacks the globe, casts the shadows of its masts in the remotest inlets of the Pacific islands, and wakens Saxon echoes in the loneliest and dimmest forests of Tasmania.

This rich experience of every age, this daily life of trade around us, is full of matter for Mercantile Science. Many a rich waif of thought has been thrown up from the heaving ocean of Commercial life. Some elevating examples of the heroism of mercantile honesty and honor, many dazzling stories of success, are to be found in the annals of trade. Many bright sparks of wit are struck out by the collisions of Commerce.

Out of these it would be no difficult task to compile the Percy Anecdotes of Trade, a sort of Mercantile Lacon, or Hand-Book of Mercantile Practice. It would be still more profitable to arrange this mass of material into something like system, and to construct out of them a true theory of business. And it is strange, that while every profession, every mechanical art has its theory, no one has as yet attempted to construct the Science of Business.

Such a system would embrace a code of business ethics, including the Morals and Manners of Trade, the *rationale* of business management, and a course of business education, including the study of the resources of nations, and Commercial Geography, the processes of production, and the Laws of Wealth, or Political Economy. And it might be studied with advantage by the Merchant's Clerk, just as the law student, or the medical student, studies the elementary books of his profession.

Franklin was the first, I suppose, to bring together with some little attempt at system the rules of business conduct—the maxims of thrift. The influence of his writings, which were full of the true philosophy of business life, in giving tone and direction to the mercantile mind of America, and in a measure of Europe, has been marked and lasting.

Since Franklin's day, while, as we have seen, the materials have immensely increased, nothing has been done towards arranging and digesting them.

The last sixteen years of my life have been devoted to labors and studies, connected with what I have been in the habit of calling the Literature of Commerce: by which terms is indicated that branch of letters, in which Mercantile affairs find voice and utterance, either in books, or the periodical press. How small the space in Literature, Commerce which fills the world, now occupies, is too obvious to need dwelling upon. My time and thought the best products, of which are the volumes of the *Merchant's Magazine,* have been necessarily given to the more practical, material aspects, the facts and figures of Trade. But these dryer studies have often been relieved by lighter and more interesting topics, the anecdote, the happy illustration, the pithy maxim, which are constantly presenting themselves. Nor have I failed, while mainly occupied with the material aspects of Trade, to become daily more impressed with the importance of its social and moral aspects.

This book, as its title indicates, is a somewhat miscellaneous collection, without attempt at strictness of method. The reader may form from it, some idea how rich in anecdote and illustration are business topics; not second in this respect to the Science of Political Economy itself. To selections from various sources, I have added my own contributions and those of several friends. I should do injustice to myself as well as to an honored name, were I to omit expressing my obligations in this particular to John Grigg, Esq., of Philadelphia.

This is a book for the leisure half-hour, those intervals which sometimes occur to the merchant and the clerk; for the fireside, when the mind seeks relaxation, yet would not be unemployed, when the suggestion contained in the pleasant anecdote, or pregnant maxim, finds entrance into a mind prepared, and stamps itself upon the memory.

The reader will, I think, find this volume an appropriate companion to my "LIVES OF AMERICAN MERCHANTS," which furnish noble illustrations of many of the maxims of business life here presented.

FREEMAN HUNT

CONTENTS.

WEALTH AND WORTH:

A COLLECTION

OF MAXIMS, MORALS AND MISCELLANIES.

1.

THE "I CANT'S"—are numerous and ubiquitous. Their numbers are astonishing. A curious statistician estimates that about one-half of the children born into the world, are furnished by Nature with a remarkable lingual facility for the utterance of this brief and cowardly sentence. Neither time or experience enables them to abolish from their vocabulary these fatal words, and from the cradle to the grave, they drag a slip-shod life spent in accomplishing nothing from the fact, that they lack the energy and will necessary to accomplish.

These human drags are recognizable anywhere under any circumstances, and in whatever garb. In the palace, but more often in the prison, especially in such enlightened States as ours, where prisons serve as a welcome refuge to many of them, who are too utterly worthless to get their own living, and therefore force their creditors to get it for them. And with this exception, we can see no other humane purpose in a debtor's prison. Of the regal and ducal "I cant's," history furnishes too many examples to need illustration at our hands. Of titled members of the order, of lower degree, the world is cursed with a less number than formerly, for the reason, that the race is dying of mere inanity; but in the great world, among the masses, it is astonishing what a host of drones share the honey of the bees' gathering. Regarding everything they do as a hardship, looking upon labor as an evil, it seems to be a sort of moral duty with such men to do as little as possible, and get all they can for it. "I can't," is their shibboleth and shield. Propose to them the accomplishment of whatever new work, anything out of the beaten track, any little addition to what they *have done*, and see! how, like trained jack-daws—their *beaks* fly open—without a moments consideration of the possibility or desirability of the doing—and, out it comes! like the "pretty Polly!" of a pet parrot—"*I can't!*"

We have said—you may know them everywhere, in the legislative Halls, on the battle-field, in the council-chamber, at the bar, in the counting-house, in the studio, at the bench, or in the furrow, for they are spawned everywhere; and among all classes of industrials—merchants or mechanics, you may know "I can't"—as well by what he *does*, as by what he will not try to do; and a miserable—mumbling—mealy-mouthed—mountain-raising, and mole-hill moving mummy of a man, will you find him in any of these pursuits. He is always for delay. "He has'nt time, or he has'nt tools; he lacks means; or he must have more help;" you "had better wait," or he knows "it is impossible;" anything rather than *do it*. "I'll try!" never comes into *his* head, as it did into Captain Bragg's; to try being just what he wishes to escape from; while to say "I can't," is the easiest, as well as the meanest method of accomplishing his desire.

"I can't," is a humbug and a nuisance, and society ought to make him sensible of the fact, by kicking him without its pale.

All things are possible—to God! and of the countless things possible to man, through the right use of the gifts He has bestowed upon him, not one in a hundred have yet been accomplished; myriads of failures resulting from the soulless efforts and combinated blunderings of the inanimate host of "I can'ts." A boy, of sound body and mind, ought to be punished every time he uses the phrase, by the adoption of which salutary corrective, the number of the men who will use it can be materially diminished. "Cant," is the most contemptible combination of letters known to the English scholar; and it may be safely assumed that neither Alfred, nor Arkwright; Milton, nor Maury; Washington, nor Whitney; Girard nor Astor, nor any other among the glorious galaxy of determinate industrial stars, ever yet recognized the canting use to which the phrase is put by such as we describe.

2.

WHAT, (asks the Boston *Transcript*,) can be more vexatious than to become involved by endorsements? You meet with a friend who wishes to get a discount at a bank. It is necessary to have an endorser. He asks you to put your name on the back of his note, merely as a matter of form. Out of kindness or good nature you do it, though you reap not the least benefit by so doing. By and by, the note becomes due. It is not paid, and you are forthwith notified that you, being the endorser, must hand over the needful. There is no remedy. Your name is down in black and white, and you cannot erase it. Can any thing be more provoking? Here you have done a good-natured act of disinterested benevolence, and your pocket must suffer for it. A debt accrued by another must be paid by yourself, and all the satisfaction you receive is that you must "pocket the loss," with the best grace you can. Yet, you can learn a lesson of wisdom from such an event, which is, NEVER to do so any more. Such are the benefits of endorsing, and such will they be till the whole system is abolished.

3.

A SACRED regard to the principles of justice forms the basis of every transaction, and regulates the conduct of the upright man of business. He is strict in keeping his engagements; does nothing carelessly, or in a hurry; employs nobody to do what he can as easily do himself; keeps everything in its proper place; leaves nothing undone which ought to be done, and which circumstances permitted him to do; keeps his designs and business from the view of others; is prompt and decisive with his customers, and does not overtrade for his capital; prefers short credits to long ones, and cash to credit transactions, at all times when they can be advantageously made, either in buying or selling, and small profits with little risk, to the chance of better gains with more hazard. He is clear and explicit in all his bargains; leaves nothing to the memory which he can and ought to commit to writing; keeps copies of all important letters which he sends away; and has every letter, invoice, &c., belonging to his business, titled, classed, and put away. He never suffers his desk to be confused by many papers lying upon it; is always at the head of his business, well knowing that if he leaves it, it will leave him; holds it as a maxim, that he whose credit is suspected is not safe to be trusted, and is constantly examining his books, and sees through all his affairs as far as care and attention enable him; balances regularly at stated times, and then makes out and transmits all his accounts current to his customers and constituents, both at home and abroad; avoids, as much as possible, all sorts of accommodations in money matters and law suits, where there is the least hazard; is economical in his expenditures, always living within his income; keeps a memorandum-book with a pencil in his pocket, in which he notes every little particular relative to appointments, addresses, and petty cash matters; is cautious how he becomes security for any person, and *is generous only when urged by motives of humanity.*

4.

PRESERVED FISH commenced life as an apprentice to a blacksmith, and his next situation was that of a seaman on board a whaling-ship. From being a hand before the mast, he rose to be a mate, and finally commander, and in this hazardous pursuit amassed the foundation of his fortune. SAUL ALLEY was bound, when a small boy, apprentice to a coachmaker. During his apprenticeship his father died, and left him totally dependant on his own exertions. The very clothes he wore he was obliged to earn by toiling extra hours, after the regular time of leaving off work had passed. The foundation of his fortune he acquired by the exercise of frugality and prudence while a journeyman mechanic. CORNELIUS W. LAWRENCE, at one time Mayor of New York, President of the Bank of the State of New York, and Collector of the port, was a farmer's boy, and worked many a long day in rain and sunshine on Long Island. There were few lads within twenty miles of him that could mow a wider swath, or turn a neater furrow. These men have been the architects of their own fortunes; they have earned them by the sweat of their brows; and their very wealth, besides the other means of doing good to their fellow-men which it puts in their power, is, in itself, a perpetual stimulus to the mechanic and artisan to earn a similar reward by similar means.

5.

These are questions which all the past have asked, and which all the future will continue to inquire. None ever acknowledge its full attainment. To most the shadow of its approach is never visible. What is it that every individual desires—in some measure, at least; strives for, yet never finds? Is it a reality or a fancy?—the cob of corn fastened by a pole before the donkey, which advances as he advances; just before but never reaches, but to attain which he toils and strives?—or is it an *ignus fatuus*, which deludes by false glare and brightness, and vanishes just when reached?

Man is so constituted that fatigue and disgust come with the object sought. This world conquered, it is thenceforth worthless, and new worlds are longed for. What was once supposed to be success, is found to be of naught. The astronomer enlarges his instruments by his endeavor to examine an indistinct planet; but his double telescope reveals to him new stars and opens to him new systems of which he had not before imagined. There is always something beyond, and discontent in consequence will always be the lot of man.

At times and in certain cases, it is hard to say what is success. Did Milton obtain it? One of the greatest works of man was the result of his labors. Posterity and futurity acknowledged his claims, but the present gave him poverty and neglect, and his fate has been that of many since. Ned Buntline's trash and vulgarity in yellow covers thrives. Is that success? Ik Marvel's high-toned morality and elegant refinement, with fine type and paper, is neglected. How is the question answered?

One very important requisite at the present day is to gain the public attention. All seem aware of this, although some will not descend to forcing it. Still it is indispensable that there be real merit at the bottom, to satisfy after having attracted. Genin must not be content with turning the community by signs and paintings toward his warehouse, or by putting his name and business into the mouths of an entire people. He knows that now that he is universally spoken of, it is of the utmost importance that it be commendingly, that his merchandise be good of its kind, and his character unimpeached.

The theories of to-day have grown up with a mushroom rapidity and are eagerly embraced, but time shows that they lack substance and a true organized vitality, and subsequent analyzation reveals that the thin froth raised up by a rapid yeast contains no substance, is mere air, no better than a soap-bubble which glittered in the light, till the beams of a sun rapidly evaporated it, and showed the emptinest within.

Look at the visions of the past, the theories of great thinkers and the systems of philosophers, once the reverenced opinions of entire nations, and we now wonder how they could have ever been for a moment credited. Was this success?

And it does not require centuries to effect these changes. During the few years that have elapsed since the first part of this, till now forgotten, article was written, the productions of Buntline have returned to the vile dust from which they sprung, while those of Marvel have emerged from their obscurity, and now glitter with a diamond's resplendence in the lap of beauty.

Success is the peace of mind which springs from right impulses and which promises a serene future. Peter Cooper was considered successful when he had accumulated his hundreds of thousands; and when he afterward received the grateful esteem of a city and a nation. But higher than all, his success must be found in his internal sense. Fire, war, and revolution may destroy every trace of his charitable magnificence, but the growth of soul, heightened and stimulated by acts like his, cannot be arrested. This internal conviction is the first shadow of true success, which can only have a profound realization in the Master's words: "Well done, good and faithful servant; thou hast been faithful over a few things: I will make thee ruler over many things; enter thou into the joy of the Lord."

6.

It is stated in Chambers' Continental Tour, that the wealth which now exists in Amsterdam falls much short of what it was previous to the French revolution, or during the period of Dutch commercial pre-eminence. It is not long since strangers, in visiting Amsterdam, were shown the spacious house of a merchant, who, after lavishing much on furniture and painting, actually caused the floor of one of his apartments to be laid with Spanish dollars, set on edge. Whims equally ridiculous, for disposing of an overplus of wealth, appear to have been far from uncommon in former times in Holland. A gentleman of my acquaintance, passing through Arnheim, had his attention directed to an old, fantastical-looking dwelling, concerning which, he gathered the following historical reminiscence:—The original owner was a Jew merchant, and he erected the house out of pure revenge. His coffers were so well replenished that he was at a loss how to employ his superfluous cash. At last he hit upon a fanciful expedient. He determined to make a pavement before his residence, of large massive plates of silver, and to surround it with an ornamental chain, of the same costly metal. Before carrying this plan into effect, it behooved him to obtain the sanction of the authorities. These worthies, however, void of sympathy, set their face against a proposition which might have compelled them to increase the strength of the town-guard. Enraged at their non-compliance, Moses determined to punish them. He ordered his dwelling, situated in the principal street, immediately to be pulled down, and on its site erected the one now standing. It is literally covered with diabolical figures, amounting, it is said, to three hundred and sixty-five.

7.

In the Court of Quarter Sessions, Philadelphia, a jury, which had been out all night, in the case of William H. Simpson, charged with obtaining money from Guthrie & Wess, of that city, by false pretences, returned with a verdict of not guilty, but they directed the defendant to pay the costs. This case illustrates the danger of accomplishing any object, even the payment of a just debt, by a resort to trick; and it would be well to give the principles of law decided in this case, in connection with the verdict, for the information of the trading community. It appeared that Guthrie & West owed Simpson, who is a merchant in New York, about $500; and the latter, in order to obtain payment, sold the former a lot of goods, and agreed to consign them to Philadelphia on a new credit. The boxes supposed to contain the goods were sent on, and the money on the old debt was paid to Simpson; but, on opening the boxes, Guthrie found that they were filled with charcoal. It appears, also, that Guthrie had paid $36 more than he had admitted to be due; and it was for the obtaining of this that the prosecution was entered. The Court, in charging the jury, said that, no matter how dishonorable a trick might be, yet, if it be resorted to for the payment of a just debt, it did not come under the censure of the law—but if the defendant, in resorting to the perilous means of a trick, obtained money not due, or more than was owing, he was guilty under the act of Assembly, and must be convicted.

8.

The following observations are taken from an address delivered by the late Dr. Channing, of Boston, before the Mercantile Library Company of Philadelphia, in May, 1841:—

"Commerce is a noble calling. It mediates between distant nations, and makes men's wants, not, as formerly, stimulants to war, but bonds of peace. The universal intellectual activity of which I have spoken is due, in no small degree, to commerce, which spreads the thoughts, inventions, and writings of great men over the earth, and gathers scientific and literary men everywhere into an intellectual republic. So it carries abroad the missionary, the Bible, the cross, and is giving universality to true religion. Gentlemen, allow me to express an earnest desire and hope, that the merchants of this country will carry on their calling with these generous views. Let them not pursue it for themselves alone. Let them rejoice to spread improvements far and wide, and to unite men in more friendly ties. Let them adopt maxims of trade which will establish general confidence. Especially in their intercourse with less cultivated tribes, let them feel themselves bound to be harbingers of civilization. Let their voyages be missions of humanity, useful arts, science and religion. It is a painful thought, that commerce, instead of enlightening and purifying less privileged communities, has too often made the name of Christian hateful to them; has carried to the savage not our useful arts and mild faith, but weapons of war and the intoxicating draught. I call not on God to smite with his lightnings, to overwhelm with his storms, the accursed ship which goes to the ignorant, rude native, freighted with poison and death; which goes to add new ferocity to savage life, new licentiousness to savage sensuality. I have learned not to call down fire from heaven. But, in the name of humanity, of religion, of God, I implore the merchants of this country not to use the light of a higher civilization to corrupt, to destroy our uncivilized brethren. Brethren they are in those rude huts, in that wild attire. Establish with them an intercourse of usefulness, justice and charity. Before they can understand the name of Christ, let them see his spirit in those by whom it is borne. It has been said, that the commerce of our country is not only corrupting uncivilized countries, but that it wears a deeper, more damning stain; that, in spite of the laws of the land and the protest of nations, it sometimes lends itself to the slave-trade; that, by its capital, and accommodations, and swift sailers, and false papers, and prostituted flag, it takes part in tearing the African from his home and native shore, and in dooming him, first to the horrors of the middle passage, and then to the hopelessness of perpetual bondage. Even on men so fallen, I call down no curse. May they find forgiveness from God through the pains of sincere repentance; but, continuing what they are, can I help shrinking from them as among the most infamous of their race?

"Allow me to say a word to the merchants of our country on another subject. The time is come when they are particularly called to take yet more generous views of their vocation, and to give commerce a universality as yet unknown. I refer to the juster principles which are gaining ground on the subject of free trade, and to the growing disposition of nations to promote it. Free trade!—this is the plain duty and plain interest of the human race. To level all barriers to free exchange; to cut up the system of restriction, root and branch; to open every port on earth to every product; this is the office of enlightened humanity. To this, a free nation should especially pledge itself. Freedom of the seas; freedom of harbors; an intercourse of nations, free as the winds; this is not a dream of philanthropists. We are tending towards it, and let us hasten it. Under a wiser and more Christian civilization, we shall look back on our present restrictions as we do on the swaddling-bands by which, in darker times, the human body was compressed. The growing freedom of trade is another and glorious illustration of the tendency of our age to universality."

9

JACOB BARKER, for some years a practising lawyer in New Orleans, appeared several years since in his own defence and obtained a verdict after a long personal address to the jury, which appears to have made also a vivid impression upon a numerous auditory. In reciting the chequered history of his life—his unrivalled commercial enterprise—"that the canvass of his ships had whitened every sea, and that the star-spangled banner of his country had floated from the mast-heads of his ships in every clime"—his aid in procuring a loan of $500,000 for the government during the last war, &c.,—he said he came to New Orleans poor, and in debt; that he had since made a great deal of money, and spent it in the support of his family and the payment of his debts outstanding in New York; that all these debts were now settled, as was proved; and that he owed nothing in the world at present but one amount (on a note, he believed,) of about $1,000. The *Tropic* says, "His vindication of his reputation for benevolence and veracity was manly and exceedingly eloquent, and fully sustained by the evidence."

10.

COMMERCIAL pursuits are attractive to the ambitious. They offer the hope of wealth, influence, ease, and a high social standing. Consequently, thousands of young men, who ought to remain in the country, and cultivate the ground, enter the cities every year, to engage in trade. There is an unnecessary multiplication of those who come between the producer and the consumer, adding nothing to the value of the commodity. It is not too much to say that a quarter of those now engaged in commerce, in our cities, could do the work which all do. Consequently, the consumer is obliged to support three-quarters of them, who are thus leading an unproductive, if not useless life. A large proportion of those in all kinds of commercial business, are sitting idle behind their counters a great part of the day. Where they attend to fifty customers, they might as easily attend to two hundred. But, as they must be supported, it is necessary for them, somehow or other, to get as much profit out of their fifty customers as they would otherwise do out of more. Hence all the tricks of trade, the thousand deceptions practised upon the ignorance of the purchaser, the arts of puffing, the various devices to attract buyers; which, when not absolutely dishonest, are at least unworthy and degrading. Is it in the order of nature that hundreds of young men, in the prime of life and strength, should stand behind the counter, doing woman's work? Poor women, who depend on their labor, are obliged to toil half the night at the needle, for a miserable compensation, because the situations which they ought to fill, in all kinds of retail business, are taken from them by men who should be ploughing the fields.

11

The skill of a merchant or tradesman is exhibited in the combination of the greatest profit with the least expense; and he will make the most money who calmly looks from the "beginning to the end," rather than to be attracted by any intermediate point, however profitable it may appear.

12

It is very possible for a man to act dishonestly every day, says Dimond, the merchant moralist, and yet never to defraud another of a shilling. A merchant who conducts his business partly or wholly with borrowed capital is not honest if he *endangers* the loss of an amount of property which, if lost, would disable him from paying his debts. He who possesses a thousand dollars of his own, and borrows a thousand of some one else, cannot virtuously *speculate* so extensively as that; if his prospects should be disappointed, he would lose twelve hundred. The *speculation* is dishonest, whether it succeeds or not: it is risking other men's property without their consent. Under similar circumstances it is unjust not to insure. Perhaps the majority of uneusured traders, if their houses and goods were burnt, would be unable to pay their creditors. The injustice consists, not in the actual loss which may be inflicted (for whether a fire happens or not, the injustice is the same,) but in *endangering* the infliction of the loss. There are but two ways in which, under such circumstances, the claims of rectitude can be satisfied—one is by not endangering the property, and the other by telling its actual owner that it will be endangered, and leaving him to incur the risk or not as he pleases.

13

There are some men, whose failure to succeed in life is a problem to others, as well as themselves. They are industrious, prudent and economical; yet, after a long life of striving, old age finds them still poor. They complain of ill luck. They say fate is always against them. But the fact is, they miscarry because they have mistaken mere activity for energy. Confounding two things essentially different, they have supposed that, if they were always busy, they would be certain to be advancing their fortunes. They have forgotten that misdirected labor is but a waste of activity. The person who would succeed in life, is like a marksman firing at a target; if his shots miss the mark, they are a waste of powder; to be of any service at all, they must tell in the bull's eye or near. So in the great game of life, what a man does must be made to count, or it had almost as well been left undone. The idle warrior, cut from a shingle, who fights the air on the top of a weather-cock, instead of being made to turn some machine commensurate with his strength, is not more worthless than the merely active man, who, though busy from sunrise to sunset, dissipates his labor on trifles, when he ought skilfully to concentrate it on some great end.

Every body knows some one in his circle of acquaintance, who, though always active, has this want of energy. The distemper, if we may call it such, exhibits itself in various ways. In some cases, the man has merely an executive faculty, when he should have a directive one: in other language, he makes a capital clerk for himself, when he ought to do the thinking of the business. In other cases, what is done, is either not done at the right time, or in the right way. Sometimes, there is no distinction made between objects of different magnitudes, but as much labor is bestowed on a trivial affair, as on a matter of vast moment. Energy, correctly understood, is activity proportioned to the end. Napoleon would often, when on a campaign, remain for days without taking off his clothes, now galloping from point to point, now dictating despatches, now studying maps. But his periods of repose, when the crisis was over, were generally as protracted as his exertions had been. He has been known to sleep for eighteen hours on a stretch. Second rate men, your slaves of tape and routine, while they would fall short of the superhuman exertions of the great Emperor, would have thought themselves lost beyond hope, if they imitated what they call his indolence. They are capital illustrations of activity, keeping up their monotonous jog-trot forever, while Napoleon, with his gigantic industry, alternating with such apparent idleness, is as striking an example of energy.

We do not mean to imply that chronic indolence, if relieved occasionally by spasmodic fits of industry, is to be recommended. Men who have this character run into the opposite extreme of that which we have been stigmatizing, and fail as invariably of winning success in life. To call their occasional periods of application, energy, would be a sad misnomer. Such persons, indeed, are but civilized savages, so to speak, vagabonds at heart in their secret hatred of work, and only resorting to labor occasionally, like the wild Indian, who, after lying for weeks about his hut, is roused by sheer hunger, and starts off on a hunting excursion. Real energy is persevering, steady, disciplined. It never either loses sight of the object to be accomplished, nor intermits its exertions while there is a possibility of success. Napoleon, in the plains of Champagne, sometimes fighting two battles in one day, first defeating the Russians, and then turning on the Austrians, is an illustration of this energy. The Duke of Brunswick, dawdling away precious time, when he invaded France, at the outbreak of the first revolution, is an example to the contrary. Activity beats about a cover, like an untrained dog, never lighting on the covey. Energy goes straight to the bird.

14

The late Samuel Ward told an elderly lady still living, who questioned him, while yet a lad, as to what he meant to be; his prompt reply was, "I mean to be one of the first bankers in the United States." It is scarcely necessary to add that he succeeded.

15.

The distinction made between the man of business and the business man, by the *Merchant*, (a weekly sheet, published at Philadelphia,) is a good one—a distinction with a difference too palpable to be gainsayed or denied:—

It is a great mistake to confound these two characters as is frequently done, by the thoughtless and unreflecting. The difference between them is the difference between the man who ascends the ladder of fortune with a quick, lithe, and easy step, and he who is always attempting to climb and never gets beyond the first round or two of the ascent. And how many of this latter class do we see—the men of business who are always standing at the bottom looking upward, yet never put their hands and feet to the work. They don't exercise the business talent and energies which they possess, but fold their hands and stand spellbound, while the man of quick, lively, and venturesome parts, takes hold and mounts up, securing a firm grasp upon each round of the ladder as he fearlessly and rapidly advances in the upward way of fortune. But we will endeavor to give a more definite explanation of the difference between these two classes.

The man of business and the *business man* both have business to do; but the *business* man is the one who does it. The business man thinks, moves, acts, and makes himself felt in the world. If a thought comes into his head it is one of breadth and compass—it don't center on self and its narrow world. It reaches away and embraces others. It has a wide range, and does not stop till it touches and affects for good the interests of all. Nor are the thoughts of such men immobile. They become acting, living realities in the wide and busy world. The authors of them make of these business thoughts, actualities—give them "local habitation and a name," and steamboats are built, an ocean is navigated, and distant climes and nations brought together; an electric telegraph springs into being as by enchantment, and lightning becomes garrulous and voluble, and thought out-travels the winged winds; and in a twinkling, the bands and schackles of trade are loosened. Such are the *workings* produced by the *business man.* He awakens the drowsy and helpless multitudes, puts life and thought, energy and action into them, and makes the world leap rejoicing along the path of ages. Where its step before was but a single year, now it strides by scores and fifties.

> " Men of thought, men of action,
> Clear the way."

And they *do clear the way*—their thoughts become tangible, moving, demolishing forces, that break down and crush all opposing barriers, opening a pathway of progress, into which the more sluggish and timid portion of humanity may securely travel. But the *man of business* is emphatically what the name indicates. His business is always on his hands. He don't *do* it. He don't know how to go to work in the right way. His thoughts are all measured and slow. He weighs self-made doubts and supposed contingencies, and before he moves the *business man* gets up and runs away from him and wins the race. The man of business won't go ahead, he only eddies round and round—he don't "progress"—his path is a circle. He don't find himself at night many miles on his journey's way, but like the hour hand of a clock just where he started. He is not clear and decided in what he does, but often stands hesitating and puzzled. He ventures and falls back; has a stout heart in *fancy,* but none in *fact.* Such a man may get a living—he may even help others to live, but the throbbing heart of the great world will not be accelerated by his presence nor his work. Thus you will perceive that a man of business is not necessarily a business man.

> "Act—act in the living present,
> Man within, and God o'er head."

16.

There is no greater mistake that a business man can make, than to be mean in his business. Always taking the half cent, and never returning a cent for the dollars he has made and is making. Such a policy is very much like the farmer's who sows three pecks of seed when he ought to have sown five, and as a recompense for the leanness of his soul only gets ten when he might have got fifteen bushels of grain.

Everybody has heard of the proverb of "penny wise and pound foolish." A liberal expenditure in the way of business is always sure to be a capital investment. There are people in the world who are short-sighted enough to believe that their interest can be best promoted by grasping and clinging to all they can get, and never letting a cent slip through their fingers.

As a general thing, it will be found—other things being equal—that he who is most liberal is most successful in business. Of course we do not mean it to be inferred that a man should be prodigal in his expenditures; but that he should show to his customers, if he is a trader, or to those whom he may be doing any kind of business with, that, in all his transactions, as well as social relations, he acknowledges the everlasting fact that there can be no permanent prosperity or good feeling in a community where benefits are not reciprocal.

We know of instances where traders have enjoyed the profits of hundreds of dollars' worth of trade, and yet have exhibited not the slightest disposition to reciprocate even to the smallest amount. Now, what must necessarily follow from such a course? Why, simply the loss of large profits per annum, in the loss of trade, which, under a more liberal system, might have been retained.

The practice of some men seems to be, to make as little show in the way of business as possible. Such a one, if a trader, takes no pains with the appearance of his store. Everything around him is in a worn-out, delapidated, dirty condition. To have it otherwise it would cost a dollar for whitewash, and perhaps five for painting, and a few dollars besides for cleaning up and putting things in order. And so he plods on and loses hundreds of dollars' worth of custom for the want of attention to these matters, while his more sagacious neighbor, keeping up with the times, and having an eye to appearances, does a prosperous business.

Another will spend no money in any way to make business for fear he should not get it back again. Consequently he sends out no circulars, distributes no handbills, publishes no advertisements; but sits down croaking about the hard times—moaning over the future prospect of notes to pay, no money, and no trade; and comes out, just where he might expect to come—short, while his neighbor, following in a different track, doing all that is necessary to be done to make business, has business; isn't short, but has money to loan; and it would be just like him to get twelve per cent, perhaps more, for the use of it; and we should not blame him for so doing.

The fact is, times have changed. The manner of doing business is different now, from what it used to be. It would be just as foolish to insist upon doing business now, in the old-fashioned way, as it would be to insist upon traveling with an ox-team instead of by railroad; to get news by old-fashioned stages instead of having it brought by the lightning telegraph. The times demand men of enlarged, liberal, energetic souls—men who will keep up with the world as it goes; men of hearts too, who not only desire to go ahead themselves, but take pleasure in seeing others succeed; and who have public spirit enough to do something for, and rejoice in the prosperity of the people.

17.

In the first place, make up your mind to accomplish whatever you undertake; decide upon some particular employment and persevere in it. All difficulties are overcome by diligence and assiduity. Be not afraid to work with your own hands, and diligently too. "A cat in gloves catches no mice." Attend to your own business, and never trust it to another. "A pot that belongs to many is ill stirred and worse boiled." Be frugal. "That which will not make a pot will make a pot lid." Be abstemious. "Who dainties love shall beggars prove." Rise early. "The sleeping fox catches no poultry." Treat every one with respect and civility. "Everything is gained and nothing lost by courtesy." Good manners insure success. Never anticipate wealth from any other source than labor. "He who waits for dead men's shoes may have to go for a long time barefoot" And, above all things, "*Nil desperandum,*" for "Heaven helps those who help themselves." If you implicitly follow these precepts, nothing can hinder you from accumulating.

18.

A Merchant ought to acquire and maintain an easiness of manner, a suavity of address, and a gentlemanly deportment; without which the finest talents and the most valuable mental acquirements are often incapable of realizing the brilliant expectations which they induce their possessor to form.

19.

The following notice of a distinguished merchant of Boston, was furnished by J. S. Sleeper, Esq., an old shipmaster in the employ of "Billy Gray," as he was familiarly called, and afterwards editor of the "*Mercantile Journal.*"

William Gray, by his successful mercantile career, well illustrated the truth of the homely adage, "Honesty is the best policy." His ships were found in every sea, deeply laden with the products of every country. Although bold in his speculations, he was prudent in his calculations—and fortune smiled upon his undertakings. But William Gray was, emphatically, *an honest man.* Not a dollar of his immense wealth was acquired by violating, directly or indirectly, the laws of any country. Having, on a number of occasions, had charge of large amounts of property belonging to him, we have had abundant opportunities of knowing the manner in which he transacted his commercial operations—and we have often had occasion to admire the *stern integrity* which formed a prominent feature in his character.

"The agents or shipmasters whom he employed, were always cautioned, in the plainest language, against infringing, in the slightest degree, upon the revenue laws of any nation—and if it came to his knowledge that his orders, in this particular, had not been strictly obeyed, even if the departure from the straight line of rectitude had been dictated solely by the desire of the captain or supercargo to promote the interest of his employer, the offender was promptly dismissed with disgrace from his service. And this was but a part of the system of integrity which entered into *all* his actions—and which should always constitute the basis of the character of a mercantile man."

20.

In giving *credit*, there should be caution without mistrust; and when debts are contracted with parties that become embarrassed in their circumstances, it is often of great importance for the creditor *to be indulgent without negligence, and firm without rigor.* When a tradesman is in the habit of giving credit to any extent, and his capital is limited, it follows, of necessity, that he must also take credit himself. Here we see the evil of the system. To preserve his own character, he must, of course, make good his payments on the *very day* whereon they become due; whereas, his customers only pay their debts when it suits them, and very frequently not at all! It is not my intention to go fully into the question of the pernicious system of credit, seeing that, in some cases, it must be given; but I warn all tradesmen from trusting any but those whom they *know* to be respectable and honorable people. A man who does "a cash" business to the amount of five hundred dollars per annum, is doing better than he who sells on credit five thousand dollars at the risk of losing one half of the amount by bad debts.

21.

It is essential to the success of a retail tradesman, to establish himself in some leading thoroughfare. A store with a spacious double window is very desirable, if it can be obtained, as it admits of variety and display. In selecting a house, always bear in mind that "a rolling stone gathers no moss." Hundreds of tradesmen have been wrecked upon the postulate, "this will do for THE PRESENT." The "present" is always the golden moment of your life. Clutch it with a firm grasp. Fix upon premises in which you may stay as long as you live. Recollect there is much truth in the assertion, that "three removes are as bad as a fire."

Having obtained the store you want, do not put an article

into it, until you have secured a lease of it. No one should be a tenant at will. If by care and attention to business, you make a stand more valuable than before, it will be the "will" of the landlord that you turn out—and unless you are pretty certain of doing this, you can have no object in taking a store at all. Steady improvement in a *retail* business is invariably *local.* He who employs years of his time in forming and consolidating a valuable connection, would be esteemed a madman to remove from the situation that gave birth to it to another where it would be lost; and yet the non-possession of a lease of the place you occupy, will very frequently accomplish the same end. In a word, if your business depends upon customers, get them and keep them by staying where you are. Do not listen to the advice which certain officious friends and foolish people are continually in the habit of offering without consideration. "Don't *hamper* yourself with a lease," say they; which, being interpreted into anything intelligible, means—"Don't, secure the only means of security." A lease to a tradesman, is what an anchor is to a ship—the only *hold fast* to be relied on.

22.

The Hon. Edward Everett, in his memoir of the late Peter Chardon Brooks (in "*Lives of American Merchants, eminent for Integrity, Industry, Energy, Enterprize and Success in Life,*") thus portrays the character of the wise merchant and the upright man :—

"Mr. Brooks was eminent among that class of men, who, without playing a dazzling part on the stage of life, form the great conservative element of society; men who oppose the modest and unconscious resistance of sound principle and virtuous example to those elements of instability, which are put in motion by the ambitious, the reckless, the visionary, and the corrupt. His conservatism, however, was liberal and kindly; it partook in no degree of bigoted attachment to the past; it was neither morose nor dictatorial. On the contrary, Mr. Brooks moved gently along with the current of the times, fully comprehending the character of the age in which he lived, and of the country of which he was a citizen. Personal experience had taught him that it was an age and a country of rapid improvement and progress. He recognized this as the law of our social existence, and did all in the power of a man in private life to promote it. He was never heard to speak of the present times in terms of disparagement as compared with former times; and notwithstanding his great stake in the public prosperity, he always looked upon the bright side, in those junctures of affairs which most severely affected the business of the country. His equanimity was never shaken, nor his hopeful spirit clouded. He was never care-worn, taciturn, or austere; but always discreetly affable, cheerful himself, and the source of cheerfulness to others.

"Moderation was perhaps the most conspicuous single trait in his character, because practised under circumstances in which it is most rarely exhibited. Possessing the amplest facilities for acquisition, he was moderate in the pursuit of wealth. This moderation was founded on a principle which carried him much farther than mere abstinence from the licensed gambling of the stock exchange. He valued property because it gives independence. For that reason, he would neither be enslaved to its pursuit, nor harassed by putting it at risk. At the most active period of life, he never stepped beyond the line of a legitimate business. He often, with playful humility, said that "he preferred to keep in shoal water," not because the water was shallow, but because he knew exactly how deep it was. The same

3

moderation which restrained him in the pursuit, contented him in the measure. As we have seen above, he retired from active business in the prime of early manhood, with what would be thought at this day a bare independence for a growing family. His written memoranda show that he did this, with no plans for the increase of his property, by other courses of business ;—but from a feeling that he had enough for the reasonable wants of himself and family, and the apprehension that, in the event of his sudden decease, their interests would be greatly endangered by the continued expansion of his affairs. These surely are not motives which usually actuate a man of ardent temperament—for such he was by nature—at the age of thirty-six, and with all human prospects of a long and successful career.

"Born and brought up in straightened circumstances, frugality was a necessity of his early years; and, as far as his personal expenditure was concerned, continued to be the habit of his life. For this he had many reasons, besides the force of second nature. He had no leisure for the wasteful pleasures which consume time; no taste for luxurious personal indulgences. Health he considered too costly a blessing to be fooled away. Temperate in all things, but rigidly abstaining from none of which the moderate use consists with virtue and health, he passed through life without imposing upon himself ascetic restraints;—a stranger to the pains or languor of disease. He was an early riser throughout the year. A great friend of cold water inwardly and outwardly, before hydropathy or total abstinence were talked of, he did not condemn a temperate glass of wine after they became the ruling fashion of the day.

"Though exact in the management of his property and in all business relations which grew out of it, (and without this, large fortunes can neither be accumulated nor kept,) he was without ostentation liberal, and on proper occasions munificent in its use. The passion for accumulation is in its nature as distinct and strong as its rival political ambition, and like that is very apt to increase with its gratification, and especially with years; but the reverse was the case with Mr. Brooks. His willingness to impart increased as he advanced in life. His donations to others, in no way connected with himself, exceeded, for a long course of years, his expenditure in the support of his family, and this without reckoning large sums given for single public objects. He was a liberal and discriminating supporter of every benevolent institution, and every public-spirited object; and often gave time and counsel when they were more important than money. He gave, however, as he did everything else, without parade; and, as appears from his books, annually expended considerable sums known at the time only to Him that seeth in secret.

"And this remark leads, by natural transition, to the last with which we shall detain the reader, viz.: that his liberality, like the other traits of his character, was connected with an unaffected sense of religious duty. Although sparing of outward demonstration in all things, he embraced, with a lively and serious conviction, the great truths of the Christian revelation. He was a punctual and respectful observer of the external duties of religion; an unfailing attendant on public worship; a regular communicant; an habitual and devout reader of the Bible. He had a general knowledge of doctrinal distinctions; but took no interest in the metaphysics of theology. His faith was principally seen in his life; and even his business journal is interspersed with reflections, which show a mind deeply impressed with a sense of religious duty to God and man."

23.

The maxim "all is not gold that glitters," if not purely English in its origin and application, is at all events not recognized in France. In the latter kingdom the reputation of a man for wealth is about in proportion to his display of it. A showy house of business, and an elegant style of living, indicating that the proprietor has abundance of wealth himself, are essential perquisites to his being intrusted with the property of others. The contrast which prevails to this state of things in England, is strikingly illustrated by an incident related in the *Edinburgh Review.* A retired merchant of enormous fortune, living in great seclusion, is said to have kept his account with a banking firm headed by a baronet. His balance in the bank was generally from thirty to forty thousand pounds, and the baronet deemed it only a proper attention to so valuable a customer to invite him to dinner at his villa in the country. The splendor of the banquet, to which the old man reluctantly repaired, impelled him on his entrance to apologize to his host for subjecting the latter to so much inconvenience. The baronet replied that, on the contrary, it was incumbent on him to apologize, for taking the liberty of asking his guest to partake of a family dinner. Nothing further passed, but the next morning the customer drew his whole balance out of the bank.

24.

The Hon. Charles Sumner, by invitation of the Mercantile Library Association of Boston, delivered on the evening of the 13th of November, 1854, an introductory address to one of the annual courses of lectures of that Association. The address gives Mr. Sumner's views in regard to the "*Position and Duties of the Merchant,*" but is mainly devoted to "the career of a remarkable man (Granville Sharp) whose simple life, beginning as the apprentice to a linen draper, and never getting beyond a clerkship, shows what may be accomplished by faithful humble labors, and reveals precisely those qualities which, in this age, are needed to crown the character of the Good Merchant."

In the paragraphs we transfer to our "*Maxims, Morals, and Miscellanies*," we do not tread on forbidden ground.

"'Every man owes a debt to his profession,' was a saying of Lord Bacon, repeated by his cotemporary and rival, Lord Coke. But it does not tell the whole truth. It restrains, within the narrow circle of a profession, obligations which are broad and universal as humanity. Rather should it be said that every man owes a debt to mankind. In determining the debt of the merchant, we must first appreciate his actual position in the social system; and here let us glance at history.

"At the dawn of modern times trade was unknown. There was nothing then like a policy of insurance, a bank, a bill of exchange, or even a promissory note. The term "chattels," so comprehensive in its present application, yet when considered in its derivation from the Latin *catalla*, reveals the narrow inventory of personal property in those days, when 'two hundred sheep' were paid by a pious Countess of Anjou for a coveted volume of homilies. The places of honor and power were then occupied by men who had distinguished themselves by the sword, and were known under the various names of knight, baron, count, or—highest of all—Duke, *Dux*, the leader in war.

"Under these influences the feudal system was organized, with its hierarchy of ranks, in mutual relations of dependence and protection; and society for a while rested in its shadow The steel-clad chiefs, who enjoyed power, had a corresponding responsibility; and the mingled gallantry and gentleness of chivalry often controlled the iron hand. It was the dukes who led the forces; it was the counts or earls who placed themselves at the head of their respective counties; it was the knights who went forth to do battle with danger, in whatever form, whether from robbers or wild beasts. It was the barons at Runnymede —there was no merchant there—who extorted from King John that Magna Charta which laid the corner-stone of English and American liberty.

"In America feudalism never prevailed, and our revolution severed the only cord by which we were connected with this ancient system. It was fit that the Congress which performed this memorable act should have for its President a merchant. It was fit that, in promulgating the Declaration of Independence, by which, in the face of kings, princes, and nobles, the new era was inaugurated, the education of the counting-house should flaunt conspicuously in the broad and clerkly signature of John Hancock. Our fathers "builded wiser than they knew;" and these things are typical of the social change then taking place. And by yet another act, fresh in your recollection, and of peculiar interest in this assembly, has our country borne the same testimony. A distinguished merchant of Boston, who has ascended through all the gradations of trade, honored always for his private virtues as well as public abilities—I may mention the name of Abbott Lawrence—has been sent to the Court of St. James as the ambassador of our republic, and with that proud commission, higher than any patent of nobility, has taken precedence of the nobles of that ancient realm. In this circumstance I see the triumph of personal merit, but still more, the consummation of a new epoch.

Yes, sir! say what you will, this is the day of the merchant. As in the early ages, war was the great concern of society, and the very pivot of power, so is trade now; and as the feudal chiefs were the "notables" placed at the very top of their time, so are the merchants now. All things attest the change. War, which was once the universal business, is now confined to a few; once a daily terror, it is now the accident of an age. Not for adventures of the sword, but for trade do men descend upon the sea in ships, and traverse broad continents on iron pathways. Not for protection against violence, but for trade, do men come together in cities and rear the marvelous superstructures of social order. If they go abroad, or if they stay at home, it is trade that controls them, without distinction of persons. And here in our country every man is a trader. The physician trades his benevolent care; the lawyer trades his ingenious tongue; the clergyman trades his prayers. And trade summons from the quarry the choicest marble and granite to build its capacious homes, and now, in our own city, displays warehouses which outdo the baronial castle, and salesrooms which outdo the ducal palace. With these magnificent applicances, the relations of dependence and protection, which marked the early feudalism, are reproduced in the more comprehensive feudalism of trade. Even now there are European bankers who vie in power with the dukes and princes of other days, and there are traffickers every where, whose title comes from the ledger and not the sword, fit successors to counts, barons, and knights. As the feudal chief allocated to himself and his followers the soil, which was the prize of his strong arm, so now the merchant, with a grasp more subtile and reaching, allocates to himself and followers, ranging through multitudinous degrees of dependence, all the spoils of every land, triumphantly won by trade. I would not press this parallel too far, but, at this moment, especially in our country, the merchant, more than any other character, stands in the very boots of the feudal chief. Of all pursuits or relations, his is now the most extensive and formidable, making all others its tributaries, and bending at times even the lawyer and the clergyman to be its dependent stipendiaries.

"Such in our social system is the merchant; and on this precise and incontrovertible statement I found his duties. Wealth, power, and influence are not for self-indulgence merely, and just according to their extent are the obligations to others which they impose. If, by the rule of increase, to him that hath is given, so in the same degree new duties are superadded; nor can any man escape from their behests. If the merchant be in reality our feudal lord, he must render feudal service; if he be our modern knight, he must do knightly deeds; if he be the baron of our day, let him maintain baronial charity to the humble—ay, sir, and baronial courage against tyrannical wrong, in whatsoever form it may assume. But even if I err in attributing to him this peculiar position, I do not err in attributing to him these duties; for his influence is surely great, and he is at least a man bound by his simple manhood to regard nothing human as foreign to his heart."

25.

There is not a more honorable or a more useful member of society than a Good Merchant. And there is, perhaps, no occupation in life which has been more exalting in its influences, ever since the time when, of old, "Merchants were Princes"—as princes they still are, in character and station, at least, though not in name or rank. To what of a secular nature do we owe any thing like the same amount of obligation as to Commerce? Where else should we have obtained all those vast resources which are building us up as a great people, and which are enabling us to maintain, even as we do, our position as a Christian people, and to spread abroad those Christian influences which are due from us a prosperous people—where, but from Commerce, and at our merchants' hands? There is an elasticity too, —a power of expansion in Commerce, which enables it to adapt itself to the increasing exigencies of a country, as our own case has so signally shown.

"A well-regulated Commerce," says an eminent moral philosopher, "is not like law, physic, or divinity, to be overstocked with hands; but, on the contrary, flourishes by multitudes, and gives employment to all its professors." Fleets of merchantmen are so many squadrons of floating stores, that vend our wares and manufactures in all the markets of the world, and find out chapmen under both the tropics.

It is evident, then, how much we owe to Commerce, and how greatly we depend upon our merchants, for our means both of social progress and religious effort. And if it be true, as a distinguished sage has recorded that it is, that "the prosperity of a people is proportionate to the number of hands and minds that are fully employed," we see further how, mainly contributing as he does to this, the merchant is not only a motive power, as it were, in the social system, but a responsible agent in its whole economy.

And if the merchant be thus responsible, how important that he should ever remember and fulfil his responsibility. In a word, of how much moment is it that he should be the *Good Merchant.*

Appropriately, then, and opportunely, did Charles Sumner, lately select this as the subject of his eloquent address before the Mercantile Library Association of Boston, which we rejoice to find is published and put into circulation—pretty extensively, let us hope, throughout the mercantile community of the Union. He has sought therein to set forth "what this age requires from the mercantile profession, or rather, since nothing is justly required which is not due, what the mercantile profession owes to this age." There is such a thing, he shows, as "an account current" between it and humanity—he might have said, also, between it and religion; for to the merchant, with his gains—with his "goods laid up in store"—the principle will forcibly apply which is involved in the divine precept; "of him to whom much is given will much be required."

The remarkable man whom Mr. Sumner has exhibited as an example to the young merchants of Boston, was one whose conduct, he declared, "reveals precisely those qualities which, in this age, are needed to crown the character of the Good Merchant." This was Granville Sharp—whose case, however, has so close an identity with a question on which we do not wish to enter, that we must refrain from touching upon it, however slightly, now—though we might do so with the best effect, and not without advantage. But, confining ourselves strictly to the subject in hand, when it is acknowledged—as acknowledged it must be—that, "of all pursuits or relations, his is now the most extensive and formidable, making all others its tributaries, and bending at times even the lawyer and the clergymen to be its dependent stipendiaries"—there is conveyed therein a weight of importance, in its bearings upon our social and our religious interests, which indeed deserves to be carefully and conscientiously considered.

The man who was thus forcibly held up as a model for the mercantile character and conduct of this age and country, boldly and successfully asserted the principle: "that every public ordinance contrary to reason, justice, natural equity, or the written Word of God, must be promptly rejected." And it is in him, the eloquent expositor of so much virtue and philanthropy, he told this Mercantile Association—"it is in him that the merchant, successor to the chivalrous knight, who aims to fulfil his whole duties, may find a truer prototype than in any stunted though successful votary of trade, while the humble circumstances of his life seem to make him an easy example. In imitating him," it is added, "Commerce would thrive none the less, but goodness more. Business would not be checked, but it would cease to be pursued as the 'one idea' of life. Wealth would still abound, but there would be also that solid virtue, never to be moved from truth, which you will admit, even without the admonition of Plato, is better than all the cunning of Dœdalus, or all the treasures of Tantalus. The hardness of heart engendered by the accursed greed for gain, and by the madness of worldly ambition would be overcome; the perverted practice, that *policy is the best honesty*, would be reversed; and *merchants would be recalled, gently but irresistibly, to the great practical duties of this age*, and thus win the palm of true honesty, which trade alone can never bestow.

> 'Who is the honest man?
> He who doth still and strongly good pursue,
> To God, his neighbor, and himself most true.'"

Surely, then, this were a salutary and seasonable admonition to a mercantile community, and its delivery does Mr. Sumner infinite credit and honor. Yet it is but the repetition of what the church catechism teaches in its answers to the two important questions:—"What is thy duty toward God?" and "What is thy duty toward thy neighbor?" And were that teaching but more general, and more effectual than it is, we should see very many bright examples among us of the GOOD MERCHANT.

26.

The same authority which requires man to be "fervent in spirit," also commands us to be "diligent in business." Religion and business, therefore, are both right, and may essentially serve each other. A truly religious man will give proper attention to business; and a man who conducts business as he ought, will do it on religious principles. But for a man to join a church, attend the sacrament, or perform any religious service, thereby to secure confidence among men, that he may obtain their custom in trade, it is serving mmamon and not God. When men attend meetings to advertise their goods, for the purpose of speculation, they evidently belong to the church of Judas, rather than that of Christ. We once knew a case like this:—"A father and a son, lived near each other in a new settlement. The old gentleman invited preachers to the neighborhood, and entertained them freely, opening his doors for religious meetings. The son took alarm and advised his father to discontinue the practice, or he would surely ruin himself and come to want. The father took no notice of his son's worldly minded caution, and instead of coming to poverty he grew wealthy fast. The son, seeing how things went, concluded he would try the same method to obtain property. So when the preachers came again he invited them to his house, supposing it would add to his property, as he concluded it had to his father's.

It is easy to see that, in this case, the young man's God was the world. Another way of developing the same spirit, is discovered in the way a man in Providence explained his belief in the existence of a Deity. In an evening's meeting, while exhorting, he remarked:—"Brethren, I am just as confident that there is a Supreme Being, as I am that there is flour in Alexandria; and that I know for certain, as I yesterday received from there a lot of three hundred barrels of fresh superfine, which I will sell as low as any other person in town."

Here is a strange mixing of religion and business which cannot strike one very agreeably.

Some years since we were well acquainted with a yonug minister in Maine, who mixed up prayer with everything, and on all occasions. Here is one instance in a hundred we might give: —he called one evening on a brother minister, just as the family were sitting at the tea-table.

"Good evening," said the Rev. Mr. M., "sit up and take some tea with us."

"No!" said the new comer, Mr. R., "I will pray while you eat."

"There is another room you can go into to do that."

"No, I will pray here," said R., and down he got on his knees and commenced praying.

Mr. M. having another gentleman at the table, with whom he was in conversation about a set of Clarke's Commentary, concluded he would continue his conversation, notwithstanding the by-play of the prayer. But Mr. R. kept his ear well open to the conversation, while he conducted his devotions. Finally he turned his head to the speakers at the table, and said:—

"Brother M., I will give you seven dollars for those books," and then turned back to his prayers for a few minutes. Then turning again, he continued, "brother M., you had better take what I offered you." After going on with his prayer a little longer, he once more broke out, "you can't do better." Then once more to prayer.

If that was not religion and business, we know not what

is; and as objectionable as it may seem in this case, there are a great many persons who evidently try to serve God and mammon on the same principle, if not exactly in the same manner. But good advice is, "Let everything be done decently and in order."

27.

James Holford has risen step by step up the ladder of fortune until he stands securely at the summit, with fame, wealth, and honors surrounding him. Some twenty years ago this same James Holford was at the very foot of the ladder pondering how he should rise. The ladder was very curious to contemplate, and still more curious was it to hear what the world said about it.

"It is all luck, sir," cried one, "nothing but luck; why, sir, I have managed at times to get up a step or two, but have always fallen down ere long, and now I have given up striving, for luck is against me."

"No, sir," cried another; "it is not so much luck as scheming; the selfish schemer gets up while more honest folks remain at the foot."

"Patronage does it all," said a third, "you must nave somebody to take you by the hand and help you up, or you have no chance."

James Holford heard all these varied opinions of the world, but still persisted in looking upward, for he had faith in himself.

"The cry of luck's all, what does it amount to in reality," thought he, "but that some people are surrounded by better circumstances than others; they must still, however, take advantage of these circumstances permanently to succeed; and I, having very indifferent circumstances around me, have the more need to use great exertion in order to better them; and when reverses come I will not despair as some do, but persevere on to fortune. I want no friend to take me by the hand, and do that for me which every healthy man can do better for himself. No. I will rise by myself alone."

The resolution was earnestly made, and faithfully carried out. From the humblest office in a store, to the post of the highest trust, James Holford rose in a few years. He placed his affections on one alike to him in sympathies and in fortune, and wedded happiness with her. He became a trader for himself, having from his income laid by sufficient to start with. His probity, his courtesy and his application, commended him to all his customers, and every year saw him advancing higher in the world's estimation. Not only did he devote his energies to his business, but his leisure hours were given to the cultivation of his mental faculties, so that his neighbors soon began to look upon him as an authority in public matters, and again and again confided offices of trusts to him, in which he invariably won golden opinions. Independent in spirit as he is now also independent in fortune, and still in the vigor of health and life, with a fine troop of children around him, James Holford looks with hope and serenity to the future, while in his every action he still offers a model to the world.

His counsel is much sought by the young and aspiring, and he thus discourses to them concerning the ladder of fortune:—

"The steps from the foot to the summit are not many, but each has a name which must be distinctly known by all who would seek to climb. The first step is faith, and without this, none can safely rise; the second, industry; the third, perseverance; the fourth, temperance; the fifth, probity; and the sixth, independence. Having obtained thus high a position on the ladder, the future rise is easy, for faith will have taught the climber never to doubt or despair; industry will have kept him from vice either in thought or deed; perseverance will have shown him how easily difficulties are surmounted when calmly met; temperance will have preserved both health and temper; probity will have ensured respect and given stability to the character; and independence of spirit, while it will give dignity to the man, will certainly gain the admiration of the world. One step more has to be acquired, which is experience—the only true knowledge of life, and then the summit of the ladder is surely reached."

Young men, the ladder of fortune can be mounted by all of you, if you learn the moral of James Holford's life Say, who is the first to profit by it?

28.

Mr. John McDonogh, the millionaire of New Orleans, has engraved upon his tomb a series of maxims, which he had prescribed as the rules for his guidance through life, and to which his success in business is mainly attributable. These rules would undoubtedly secure riches and honor; and as a whole are worthy of being accepted:—

"Remember always that labor is one of the conditions of our existence. Time is gold; throw not one minute away, but place each one to account. Do unto all men as you would be done by. Never put off till to-morrow what you can do to-day. Never bid another to do what you can do yourself. Never covet what is not your own. Never think any matter so trifling as not to deserve notice. Never give out that which does not first come in. Never spend but to produce. Let the greatest order regulate the transactions of your life. Study in your course of life to do the greatest amount of good. Deprive yourself of nothing necessary to your comfort, but live in an honorable simplicity and frugality. Labor, then, to the last moment of your existence.

"Pursue strictly the above rules, and the Divine blessing and riches of every kind will flow upon you to your heart's content; but, first of all, remember that the chief and great study of our life should be to tend, by all means in our power, to the honor and glory of our Divine Creator. The conclusion to which I have arrived is, that, without temperance, there is no health; without virtue, no order; without religion, no happiness; and that the aim of our being is to live wisely, soberly, and righteously."

To the above maxims of McDonogh we would add one more, which comes to us opportunely in the columns of the Philadelphia *Daily Reporter*. It is a rule of rules—the complement of all the rest—the keystone of the arch of mercantile character. For what most men lack is not rules, but the energy to apply them at the right moment; not moral principles, but *moral presence of mind*—and this is SELF-POSSESSION, SELF-RELIANCE. "Wo unto him that is faint-hearted," says the son of Sirach.

"We have just received the following letter," says the *Reporter*, "from one of Philadelphia's best and noblest merchants." The letter is as follows:—

"I send you the extract I spoke a few days since. It contains more real truth of what my long experience has been in the great battle of life, (having commenced at the first round of the ladder,) than any article I have ever seen in print, and I do hope that every newspaper in our country will republish it, for the benefit of all young men who are about commencing business, and who, are now in business, for it will do much good, if they will be governed by its precepts."

The extract referred to appeared originally in the Richmond *Post*, and is as follows:—

"When a crisis befals you, and the emergency requires moral courage and noble manhood to meet it, be equal to the requirements of the moment, and rise superior to the obstacles in your path. The universal testimony of men whose experience exactly coincides with yours, furnishes the consoling reflection that difficulties may be ended by opposition. There is no blessing equal to the possession of a stout heart. The magnitude of the danger needs nothing more than a greater effort than ever at your hands. If you prove recreant in the hour of trial, you are the worst of recreants, and deserve no compassion. Be not dismayed or unmanned, when you should be bold and daring, unflinching and resolute. The cloud whose threatening murmurs you hear with fear and dread is pregnant with blessings, and the frown whose sternness now makes you shudder and tremble, will ere long be succeeded by a smile of bewitching sweetness and benignity. Then be strong and manly, oppose equal forces to open difficulties, keep a stiff upper lip, and trust in Providence. Greatness can only be achieved by those who are tried. The condition of that achievement is confidence in one's self."

We certainly do not often meet with a piece of better sentiment or sounder morality. This confidence in one's self, in a world where every man appears to be striving against his fellow, is as necessary to a successful career as is breath to physical existence. Or it may be likened to the healthful action of the heart, whose steady pulsations direct and keep in harmony every movement of the animal economy. This once lost, and the consequences are as calamitous as those that follow any disorder of the great human engine. In order to maintain intact this self-confidence, one must respect himself, which can only be done by pursuing a uniform life of honor and integrity. There are those who quail and shudder before every breath of adverse fortune.

Their timidity is their stumbling-block, if not their ruin, while they have the additional mortification of witnessing the rapid advance and ultimate success of those who, commencing life with themselves have placed and retained self-confidence at the helm of their adventurous bark. The writer of the letter inclosing us this extract is a most admirable specimen of the results of this sound philosophy, and the eminent position he now occupies in the affection and respect of the community, and, indeed, of the country, must be abundant reward for the trials and difficulties he so nobly battled in his earlier career.

29.

In November, 1841, the mercantile house of Shelton, Brothers & Co., of Boston, found it necessary to suspend payment of their debts, and to close up the business of the firm. Their creditor, after an investigation of their concerns, agreed to receive fifty per cent of the amount of their respective demands, and release the house entirely from their obligations. This agreement was entered into by all the creditors, the stipulated per centage was paid, and the demands cancelled. Some time after the failure of the house, Mr. Henry Shelton, one of the partners, died. Mr. Philo. S. Shelton, the surviving partner, proceeded, with undaunted and persevering energy, to wind up the concerns of the old firm, and to commence business anew, on his own account. In his enterprise he has been prosperous, and soon made a new dividend of twenty-five per cent among all his creditors, upon the full amount of their cancelled demands against the original house, paying out to them the aggregate sum of forty thousand dollars, for which they had no legal claim upon him whatever. This payment was entirely voluntary on his part; and it has been made not only to individual creditors, but, in some instances, to rich corporations, by whom the loss would not have been felt.

30.

It is an awkward thing to begin the world without a dollar—and yet hundreds of individuals have raised large fortunes from a single shilling. We know a gentleman, a builder, in an extensive way of business, now well worth one hundred thousand dollars, who was a bricklayer's laborer some six years ago, at one dollar per day. He became rich, by acting upon principle. He has frequently assured me that even when he was in ill-paid employment he continued to save fifty cents per day, and thus laid up one hundred and eighty-two dollars the first year. From this moment his fortune was made. Like the hound upon the right scent the game sooner or later won was sure to become his own. Another very extensive firm, one of which has since died, and left behind him an immense property, the other is still alive, has realized as much, and yet both these men came to New York without a cent, and swept the very shop wherein they both afterwards made their fortunes. Like the builder whom we have just mentioned, they possessed an indomitable spirit of industry, perseverance and frugality, and the first dollar became in consequence the foundation of a million more.

The world at large would call these individuals fortunate, and ascribe their property to good luck; but the world would be very wrong to do so. If there was any luck at all in the matter, it was the luck of possessing clear heads and active hands, by which means multitudes of others have carved out their own fortunes, as well as those instances we have above cited. But the word *business* means *habit.* Parodoxical as it may seem at first sight, business is nothing in the world except habit—the soul of which is regularity. Like the fly-wheel upon a steam engine, this last keeps up the motion of life steady and unbroken, thereby enabling the machine to do its work; without this regularity, your motions as a merchant may be capital, but never will be profitable.

31.

Examples of the fatal effects of an inordinate love of speculation are unfortunately too numerous. The earliest recorded instances of this hurtful speculative spirit occurred in Holland in 1634, and is known under the name of the Tulip Mania. In that year the principal cities of the Netherlands were seized with a desire to possess certain descriptions of tulips; and this engaged them in a traffic which encouraged gambling to a ruinous extent. The avarice of the rich was inflamed by the prospect of boundless wealth, and the poor imagined their troubles at an end, and fortunes within their grasp. The value of a flower rose to more than its weight in gold. And this period, like all others of a similar character, ended in enriching a few by the impoverishment of the many. Tulips were not more highly prized nor sought after more eagerly in 1634 than railway scrip in 1845. A similar principle, or rather the want of all principle, was as noticeable in the one case as in the other. Contracts were entered into for the delivery of certain roots, which were never seen by broker, by buyer, or by seller. At first all appeared to flow smoothly. Congratulations and revelings were general. Bargains were confirmed at costly banquets; and a man one day pinched with poverty, astonished his neighbors the next by the display of boundless magnificence. The desire to trade in flowers took hold of all ranks; and the drowsy Hollander, with little of the romantic in his character, believed that a veritable golden age was approaching. This feeling was not confined to one class or profession of the people, it spread to all. To obtain cash, property of every description was sold at ruinous prices. When, too, it became known that London and Paris were seized with this tulipomania, it was thought that the wealth and commerce of both hemispheres would centre in Holland, and that want and wretchedness would become a tale of the past. Perhaps there are no greater instances of human folly on record than the prices given for these bulbs. Goods to the value of two thousand five hundred florins were given for one root. Another kind usually sold for two thousand florins; and a third was valued at a new carriage, two grey horses, and a complete harness; and twelve acres of land were given for a fourth. But this unnatural state of things could not last. The panic came, confidence was destroyed, agreements, no matter how solemnly entered into, were broken, and every city in the Netherlands had its bankrupts. The gay visions of wealth which had dazzled thousands dissolved, and left not a rack behind. The possessors of a few tulips, which a few days before were valued at many thousands of pounds, were astounded when the truth appeared that they were worth absolutely nothing. The law would not regard the contracts entered into as legitimate trade, but looked at them as gambling transactions. Actions for breach of contract were therefore void. So extensive was the evil, that it occupied the attention of the Deliberative Council of the Hague, who were, however, quite unable to find a remedy. Its effects were seen for many years in a depressed commerce abroad and a wide spread distress at home.

32.

THE *Philadelphia Merchant* says that nine-tenths of the failures in the commercial world are traceable to a want of the insolvent's acquaintance with the details of business. This may appear to many an unwarrantable conclusion, but to the intelligent business man no argument need be addressed to convince him of its obviousness.

Fast living and extravagant family establishments, are the

causes alleged by the superficial reasoner, for the insolvent's downfall; but to the observant business man these are only the superinducing cause to a hasty disruption of the short-sighted insolvent's affairs. But few men start business and fast living at the same time; and most of that few have but a short-lived existence in the credit market, and consequently do but little either good or harm in a commercial point of view. Nor is the number great who, upon entering business, erect princely establishments for the expenditure of their own profits and their creditors' principal. Fast living and extravagant family outlays "creep on apace" with the free and easy habits of the merchant, who presumes that he is doing well when he is doing a large and extensive business. With large sales he counts on large profits, and pauses not to reflect upon his increasing expenditures and probable augmentation of bad debts. Did he consult his "trial balance" monthly, not merely to inform himself whether or not his bookkeeper had got the credit side of the ledger to balance with the debit side to the very cent, but with a view of ascertaining the condition of every account, both representative and personal, he would then see not only the amount of his purchases and sales, but who had paid and who had not, what amount of notes had been taken up, and what amount was necessary to provide for those maturing—how his expenses had augmented and bad debts accumulated; and the consideration of these would suggest measures to be adopted for the securement of claims of a dubious or doubtful character. And what is more, they would suggest, besides many important details of a business character, whether or not his business will warrant the drain made upon it for family and other expenses. If it will not, he can explain his condition to his wife and family, who have an equal interest with him in sustaining his reputation and standing, as an honorable business man, and they will join with him in all those retrenchments necessary to enable him to maintain a proud position among his fellows, on the change or in the mart.

There are none so sensitive to the blameless standing of the merchant, as the "loved ones at home," and there is no sacrifice they would not make to sustain the high calling of the husband and father.

He who acquaints himself with the duties of his business, will guard its every interest, and, if need be, will apprise his wife and family with what it will allow for the necessaries and luxuries of life; and his family will be content therewith. He is not a good business man who keeps his wife and family in ignorance of his ability to indulge their fancied requirements.

33.

It is an evil of the intense competition in great mercantile communities that it drives many from the walks of legitimate business into schemes of speculation with reference to sudden and extravagant gains. The history of frauds teaches that they originate chiefly in the attempt to grow rich rapidly by financiering, rather than by diligence in business. Financiering has its place in legitimate business. Some men have a talent for this, which is as true a mark of genius as is poetry or art. But it is not a talent that every man can acquire; and it is fortunate that this is so; for if all the world should turn financiers, the earth itself would soon go into bankruptcy. Now the calamity of a great city is, that every one who gains a little money takes to financiering as a readier mode of increasing it than by regular business. Wall street, the focus of financiering, gives a tone to the whole business community.

But financiering is a deep game; and he who leaves an honest toil in a business that he does understand, for calculations of chance in matters where he has no skill, is very apt to become the loser; and as in all lotteries, to grow desperate in the attempt to make up his losses. We do not speak of investments in stocks as property, but of the spirit of speculation; and we have no doubt that a just verdict upon many cases of fraud would be, "This man lost his capital and his character by speculation in stocks." Keep, therefore, to honest toil in a legitimate business, and do not aspire to become a *financier*. "Be content with such things as ye have."

34.

THE advice of FRANKLIN to a young tradesman, given more than a century ago (1748) may be followed with advantage by the rising generations of merchants and tradesmen in all time:—

As you have desired it of me, says Franklin, I write the following hints, which have been of service to me, and may, if observed, be so to you.

Remember that *time* is money. He that can earn ten shillings a day by his labor, and goes abroad or sits idle one-half that day, though he spend but six-pence during his diversion or idleness, ought not to reckon *that* the only expense; he has really spent, or rather thrown away, five shillings besides.

Remember that *credit* is money. If a man lets his money lie in my hands after it is due, he gives me the interest, or so much as I can make of it, during that time. This amounts to a considerable sum where a man has good and large credit, and makes good use of it.

Remember that money is of a prolific generating nature. Money can beget money, and its offspring can beget more, and so on. Five shillings turned is six, turned again it is seven and three pence, and so on till it becomes an hundred pounds. The more there is of it, the more it produces every turning, so that the profits rise quicker and quicker. He that kills a breeding sow destroys all her offspring to the thousandth generation. He that murders a crown destroys all that it might have produced, even scores of pounds.

Remember that six pounds a year is but a groat a day. For this little sum (which may be daily wasted either in time or expense unperceived) a man of credit may, on his own security, have the constant possession and use of a hundred pounds. So much in stock, briskly turned by an industrious man, produces great advantage.

Remember this saying, "the good paymaster is lord of another man's purse." He that is known to pay punctually and exactly to the time he promises may at any time, and on any occasion, raise all the money his friends can spare. This is sometimes of great use. After industry and frugality, nothing contributes more to the rising of a young man in the world than punctuality and justice in all his dealings; therefore, never keep borrowed money an hour beyond the time you promised, lest disappointment shut up your friend's purse forever.

The most trifling actions that affect a man's credit are to be regarded. The sound of your hammer at five in the morning, or nine at night, heard by a creditor, makes him easy six months longer; but, if he sees you at the billiard table, or hears your voice at a tavern, when you should be at work, he sends for his money the next day, demands it before he can receive it in a lump.

It shows, beside, that you are mindful of what you owe; it makes you appear a careful as well as an honest man, and that still increases your credit.

Beware of thinking all your own that you possess, and of living accordingly. It is a mistake that many people who have credit fall into. To prevent this, keep an exact account, for some time, both of your expenses and of your income. If you take the pains at first to mention particulars, it will have this good effect; you will discover how wonderfully small trifling expenses amount up to large sums, and will discern what might have been and may for the future be saved, without occasioning any great inconvenience.

In short, the way to wealth, if you desire it, is as plain as the road to market. It depends chiefly on two words, *industry* and *frugality;* that is, waste neither *time* nor *money*, but make the best use of both. Without industry and frugality nothing will do, and with them everything. He that gets all he can honestly, and saves all he gets (necessary expenses excepted), will certainly become *rich*—if that Being who governs the world, to whom all should look for a blessing on their honest endeavors, doth not in his wise providence, otherwise determine.

35.

THE Rev. Dr. ADAMS, of New York, delivered a lecture before the Young Men's Christian Association of Newark, in which he portrayed the mercantile profession in its brighter features, without touching the darker sides of the picture. He commenced with a happy allusion to the motto on the seal of the letter inviting the lecture, "*Res, non verba*"—actions, not words—which was worthy the imitation of every young man. Our republic was not founded by poets and theorists, but by surveyors, merchants, mechanics, and others, whose principle was *Res, non verba.* In commencing his theme—*the ideal of a merchant*—he noticed Shakspeare's description of Shylock and Antonio;

while we stigmatize one as an avaricious man, believing strongly in law, but not in mercy, we are won by the sublime heroism of the merchant's self-sacrifice. The world is a great mart, where riches, fame, and luxurious ease are striven for; but he would protest against the idea that to attain these we must devote all our energy, discarding everything else. He mentioned prominent merchants of the Old World who had done much for literature as well as business; there was no incongruity between habits of thought and action. The merchant should not write over his mind the inscription of his counting-room—"No admittance, except on business." The idea that mercantile life was one of ease and exemption from labor, had poisoned the prospects and advancement of many a boy, and spoiled a good farmer or mechanic in a poor merchant. There is no more respectability in wielding a pen in broadcloth, than in following a plow or welding an ax. As much worth, interest, and honor as a man puts in his business, so much will he derive from it.

In mercantile life, honesty will be severely tried, and will either decline or be strengthened so that it will be steadfast ever after. He then dwelt upon *credit*—its beautiful derivation *credo*, I believe—men trusting in fellow-men ; and this surrounded them like the halo that old painters throw around everything divine. The nice sense of honor in their code was more binding than statutes, and helped them in adversity. What expanding ideas crowd the merchant's mind as he views the great panorama of Commerce! Who knows so well as he the civilizing effects of Commerce? Their exchange forms a sort of court to which every nation sends its representatives, and nature seemed to have distributed her products for their benefit. He spoke strongly in favor of early and discreet marriages, which should not be deferred till they could vie with the opulent ; and paid a high tribute to Mrs. John Adams, who he regarded as the cause of her husband's advancement. Her gentle influences, which lay about the roots of his character, stimulated and strengthened its growth. Wealth adds nothing to intelligence or real enjoyment, our capacity for happiness being in our nature, and not in our means. Simplicity and industry are the most beautiful ornaments of successful merchants ; and the world looks more hopefully and trustfully to them than to its legislators.

36.

A VERY pleasant commotion was caused in one of the towns in the vicinity of Boston, by a singular instance of sticking to the Contract, related to us by a friend. A sea captain was about to start on a long voyage, and entered into a contract with a builder to erect him a handsome and commodious house during his absence. Every thing was to be done according to the contract, which the captain had had drawn up with great care. A large sum was to be forfeited by the builder if he should fail to observe any of the stipulations, or attempt to put in his notions where the contract made no provision for them. The captain sailed and returned. His house stood in ample and imposing proportions before his sight, and he confessed himself delighted with the exterior. But when he entered and attempted to ascend to the second floor of the building, he found *no stairs*, and no means of ascent were to be had till ladders were sent for. The captain felt that he was trifled with and a bit of a gale seemed brewing. But this was soon quieted by the opening of the written contract, and there was found *not the least provision for stairs in any part of the house !* "*Give me your hand, sir !*" said the noble captain at once. "*All right ! you've stuck to the contract, and I like it.*"

The stairs were subsequently, at a great extra expense, put in, and the captain often remarked that one of the pleasantest things about his elegant residence was, the remembrance of one man who *could* stick to the very terms of a contract.

Now "such a getting up stairs" as was involved by this fidelity to a contract few would like, but it is, after all, one of the best checks on want of care in business arrangements. Nine tenths of the trouble growing out of building operations arise from violations of the terms of the contract, on the ground that such and such things were omitted—such and such alterations will give great satisfaction when they are executed—this omission being put over against that addition, and both the builder and the property owner looking, for the time, only on that side of the transaction which favors them individually. When the settlement comes, lo, a bill of items longer than Jacob's ladder is brought forth in addition to the sum specified in the contract, and the property owner is asked to pay for every whim and carelessness of the builder. The only remedy for these evils, which so often lead to vexatious law-suits, is, to specify every intended variation from the contract as carefully as the first arrangement was drawn up; and when this is not done, *stick to the contract*, though it impels to "such a getting up stairs" as was never seen before.

37.

All men are liable to the ups and downs of business, and those who are engaged in commerce or trade, though they may be cautious and prudent, are sometimes caught in a tight place and are obliged to stop. It has been stated that considerably over seventy-five per cent of those engaged in trade, fail in the course of their career. It must be very disagreeable to be obliged to call a meeting of creditors; but when circumstances render it necessary, *it should be done ere it is too late to* retrieve one's failing fortunes. No honest creditor will ever treat an honest debtor hardly, who is frank and open, the community at large, have respect for that man, who shows his hand fairly and makes a truthful statement.

Recent occurrences show the folly which some men will resort to, in order to retrieve their position,—and who, in hopes of avoiding a failure, commit a thousand times greater evil, and not only sacrifice their credit, but their honor. How often do we hear on 'change, of this or that man failing, who, the day previous, victimized an intimate friend by exchanging checks, or borrowing a few thousand dollars. This robbing Peter to pay Paul, is a greater sin by far, than allowing a note to be protested, which has been given in exchange for goods. It is not a rare case either, to find that a merchant will sometimes enter into rash speculations, to raise money to relieve himself from embarrassments, which proves only temporary, and only tends to bury him deeper in the mire. We are aware that some men commit these errors, in the hope of better times dawning, but where one is favored by a freak of fortune, twenty find themselves more involved than before.

These evils arise in a great measure from the fear that some men have of facing trouble. To put off from to-day, that which must inevitably happen to-morrow, the vilest schemes are resorted to, and men raise money at a sacrifice of principle, integrity and character. If such a prolongation of misery brought relief, it could not be wondered at, but it is an exception, rather than a rule, that it only renders more certain, that ruin which stares them in the face. Instead of standing on the brink of the precipice, and saying, "Here, gentlemen, are my books, here is my statement, such and such causes have brought me here," and commencing anew, they plunge into the vortex, and, having lost the confidence of their fellow men, find it impossible to rise again.

The haste to be rich, is urged as the primary cause of half the failures. A resort to speculation will probably take the balance. A desire to be considered smart, induces many young men to dabble in stocks, but the chances are about equal to the faro table. A legitimate business closely attended to rarely fails to secure a profit. It will rarely fail to secure wealth, if that profit is not wasted by extravagance or profligacy. It is in Boston as elsewhere, that young merchants live up to their incomes so closely that they have nothing to fall back upon, and thus barter years of happiness for a few years of mistaken gentility.

38.

It is stated by Boeck, in his "Economy of Athens," that commercial occupations were never in great esteem among the ancient Greeks. No person of ancient nobility ever condescended to them, although conversely a manufacturer might raise himself to the head of public affairs, such as Cleon, Hyperbolus, and others. The early statesmen, however, encouraged industry, especially Solon, Themistocles, and Pericles, partly with the intention of improving the condition of the lower classes, and partly of increasing the population of the city; as well as advancing the cause of commerce, and of manning the numerous fleets by which, after the time of Themistocles, the Athenians held the mastery of the sea. And it was this circumstance that rendered the resident aliens indispensible for Athens, who carried on manufactures and commerce to a great extent, and were bound to serve in the fleet. It even appears that the useful arts were encouraged by honorary rewards, though even by these means they could not gain in the public estimation. There were prizes for the common people, for which the higher ranks did not compete with them. At the same time, the respectable citizens, who had none of the higher aristocratical notions, like Pericles, Alcibiades, or Callias, the son of Hipponicus, whose pride yielded in nothing to the haughtiness of the modern nobility, were not ashamed of superintending extensive manufactories, worked at their own expense. The inferior citizens were as much reduced to the necessity of manual labor as the poor aliens and slaves. It was not until after the balance had been turned in favor of the aristocracy, that measures of severity were brought forward; as, for example, Diophantus proposed that all the manual laborers should be made public slaves. There was again another reason why no restriction should have been imposed upon the freedom of industry, viz.: the little importance that was attached to it. An alien was allowed to carry on any trade, although he was prohibited from holding any property in land. With regard, indeed, to the sale in the market, strangers were on a less advantageous footing than natives, as they were obliged to pay a duty for permission to expose their goods there. The law of Solon, that men should not deal in ointments, was only founded on principles of education, in order to withdraw men from womanish labors—subsequently, however, it became a dead letter, for Eschines, the philosopher, had a manufactory of ointments

39.

A GENUINE scoundrel is a man who, by his sanctity, has obtained credit; and, through religious professions, keeps back property from his legitimate creditors.

40.

An English merchant of the name of C——, resided in Canton, and Macao, where a sudden reverse of fortune reduced him from a state of affluence to the greatest necessity. A Chinese merchant, named Chinqua, to whom he had formerly rendered service, gratefully offered him an immediate loan of ten thousand dollars, which the gentleman accepted, and gave his bond for the amount. This, the Chinese immediately threw into the fire, saying, "When you, my friend, first come to China, I was a poor man—you took me by the hand; and, assisting my honest endeavors, made me rich. Our destiny is now reversed—I see you poor, while I am blessed with affluence." The bystanders had snatched the bond from the flames. The gentleman, sensibly affected by such generosity, pressed his friend to take the security, which he did, and then effectually destroyed it. The disciple of Confucius, beholding the increased distress it occasioned, said he would accept of his watch, or any little valuable, as a memorial of their friendship. The gentleman immediately presented his watch; and Chinqua, in return, gave him an old iron seal, saying, "Take this seal—it is one I have long used, and possesses no intrinsic value; but, as you are going to India, to look after your outstanding concerns, should fortune further persecute you, draw upon me for any sum of money you may need, sign it with your own hand, and seal it with this signet, and I will pay the money."

41.

Self-reliance, to the merchant, and indeed to all who would succeed in the accomplishment of a laudible purpose or pursuit, is indispensable. It was this trait, perhaps, more than any other, that enabled an Astor, a Girard, a Gray, in our own country, to work out for themselves vast fortunes—to accumulate millions. An eminent writer has somewhere said, if our young men miscarry in their first enterprise, they loose all heart. If the young merchant fails, men say he is ruined. If the finest genius studies in one of our colleges, and is not installed in an office in one year afterwards, it seems to his friends and to himself that he is right in being disheartened, and in complaining the rest of his life. A sturdy Yankee who in turn tries all the professions, who teams it, farms it, peddles, keeps a school, preaches, edits a newspaper, goes to Congress, buys a township, and so forth, in successive years, and always, like a cat, falls on his feet, is worth a hundred of these city dolls. He walks abreast with his days, and feels no shame in not studying a profession, for he does not postpone his life, but lives already. He has not one chance! Let a stoic arise who shall reveal the resources of man, and tell men they are not leaning willows, but can and must detach themselves; that, with the exercise of self-trust, new powers shall appear; that a man is the word made flesh, born to shed healing to the nations; that he should be ashamed of our compassion; and that the moment he acts from himself, tossing the laws, the books' idolatries and customs, out of the window, we pity him no more, but thank him and revere him—and that teacher shall restore the life of man to splendor, and make his name dear to all history. It is easy to see that a greater self-reliance—a new respect for the divinity in man—must work a revolution in all the offices and relations of men: in their religion; in their education; in their pursuits; their modes of living; their association; in their property; in their speculative views.

42.

THE honor of an honest man, as far as dollars and cents goes, dies when he dies—therefore, honorable conditions in writing.

43.

"A FRIEND stepped into our den," says the editor of the Philadelphia *United States Gazette*, "to have a good hearty grumble at the times, and to predict future difficulties." Now, we know very well all the difficulties of the times; but we know they might be worse, and despondency will make them so. We feel for, indeed, we feel *with*, those who suffer, and therefore understand the grievances of our neighbors. We inquired of our friend how he was situated—whether he was inextricably involved; and learned with pleasure that, foreseeing, he had forearmed; and though he was making little—perhaps rather outliving his net profits—yet he was comfortable, because safe. Still he exclaimed, "What *are* we all to do?"

"Why, what *have* you all to do?"

"There are," said he, "to be paid, not less than six millions of dollars!"

"Awful! What! all in one day?"

"Oh no! not in one day, but in this season; and where is the money to come from?"

"Really, I do not know; but I imagine that the same water which floats the steamboat at Market-street, is used by the vessels at the navy-yard. Let me tell you a story, very old and very common, but tolerably applicable to the subject which occupies your mind. One day there was trouble at the great house-clock. All *hands* had come to a dead stand. The whole works had stopped. This excited the surprise of the long minute-hand, who was in the habit of bustling about at a rapid rate. He, therefore, put his finger down, opened the little door in front, and asked the cause of the delay. He found the pendulum in the dumps, quite gloomy, and at a stand still.

"'What is the matter below?' asked the minute-hand.

" 'I am disheartened,' said the pendulum, 'at the gloomy prospects. I have been looking into my year's engagements, and find, to my astonishment, that I have upwards of thirty millions of beats to make this year, and there is no aid to be obtained. I must do it all myself.' " 'That is bad, sure enough,' said the minute-hand, 'but what then?'

" 'Why,' said the pendulum, 'finding that it would be impossible for me to get through all this, I determined to stop.'

" 'Yes,' said the minute-hand despondingly, 'and all the rest of us must stop in consequence of your troubles.'

"This dialogue was overheard by the hour-hand, which was at rest among 'the little ones above,' and so he called down to the pendulum:—

" 'You are quite too fearful,' said the hour-hand. 'It is neither just to us, nor politic with regard to yourself, to take an *aggravated* view, as you have done, of your labors in advance. You may have more to do than some of the rest of us, but you have no more in proportion; and you will find that, whatever number of beats you have to make in a year, you have only one to make in a second, and that is what all large pendulums have to perform. The wheels need a little oiling, and I think the works want winding up; but then you see that, in the hardest strain we have, each wheel shares with the other the extra force; and I expect every day to hear that some oil has been applied to ease the operation, and it is probable that the door will be kept a little closer, to keep out foreign substances that clog the movements. Courage and perseverance, with a little co-operation, and all will go well. Do you start below, we above will keep all hands moving, and put the best face possible upon the affairs; and, in a very short time, we shall give *striking* evidence that our movements are right.' "

44.

"The Vale of Caldere; or, The Past and Present;" by William Dearden, author of the "Star Steer," etc., is a work having many merits. "Among Mr. Dearden's favorites," says the *London Economist*, "we can see that Thomas Carlyle, Emerson, and Longfellow, are particularly distinguished; and that of itself indicates a mind imbued with many just and noble sentiments, which nothing that he says absolutely belies." "The picture I have drawn of commerce," says Mr. Dearden, "exhibits, I am aware, its harsher features; but, in thus delineating and holding up these to view, I hope no one will blame me—for, as a wise man well observes, 'it is in general more profitable to reckon up our defects than to boast of our attainments.'" There can be no doubt as to what the "wise man" says being a good rule of individual conduct; but it is no justification for a man of genius, education, and taste, writing a whole book, (and not a small one,) about the evils and vices which attend society in its progress towards civilization, and leaving it to be inferred, as far as he knows, that nothing but evil and vice attends it.

The poem of Mr. Dearden is in "six books." At the end of Book II., after taking a rather harsh, but perhaps just view of the labors of a factory, as they exist in England, he apostrophizes trade as follows:—

"Genius of Trade! such are the sounds that cheer—
Go where thou wilt—thy leaden heart and ear!
Look at thy trophies!—thousands made to chew
The bread of pain, to feed a pampered few,
Whom thou hast raised—because to thee they sold
Conscience and virtue, for the meed of gold—
Far, far above the common herd, to shine
Immaculate, adopted sons of thine!"

And again, we have at page 163 of Mr. Dearden's poem, the following :—

"Oh Trade! where are the blessings in thy train,
Which thy fond votaries laud in vaunting strain?
What though we view, where'er our eyes we turn,
Rich bounties showered from thy too partial urn;
For every boon thou hast conferred, we find
A thousand evils poured on human kind!

* * * * * *

Why is the owner of yon mansion made
To lord o'er others whom he once obeyed?
Is his plebian blood, like gold that's tried
Thrice in the fiery furnace, purified
From all alloys that taint the lowly born,
Whom his proud heart, forsooth, affects to scorn?
Did lofty talents, and superior sense,
This mushroom lordling raise to eminence?
Did he become a magnate in the land
By means that would not make him blush to stand,
With soul unscathed by conscience' withering ban,
In the dread presence of an honest man?
Ah no!—a *little* care and cunning, joined
With *little* necessary frauds, that find
Free toleration by the liberal law,
Which all, who please, from Trade's great Koran draw:
A lucky turn of fortune; a *discreet*
And frugal husbandry of all the sweet
Gold-droppings from her copious honeycomb;
A *little* schooling of the Rib at home
In economic arts and trade-finesse;
A *little* leaning to the wrong, to bless
The eager pocket, though it stings the soul;
A *little* alms to *any* creed—in cowl
Or cassock clad—if, in return, 'twill win
A *golden* unction for the *trifling* sin:

A *little* dabbling in young orphans' blood ;
A *little* pinching of the scanty food
Earned by the wo-worn widow ; a *complete*
Forgetfulness of crippled Eld, unmeet–
Now that his days of usefulness are o'er–
To beg a pittance at his master's door.
These are the means by which this upstart came
To wealth, importance, and commercial fame !"

This view of trade is not very flattering ; but it is well to view matters in which we are deeply interested from all points, or all sides of a "look-out."

45

GOYDER, in his work entitled "*Acquisitiveness, its Uses and Abuses*," pays a just tribute to the Society of Friends :—"If I wished to point to a model where wealth seems to have been accumulated for the sole purpose of doing good, I would hold up to admiration the people called Quakers. They are wealthy to a man ; and where, throughout Christendom, in its varied ramifications, is there a body of people who have done so much good, and with so much disinterestedness ? not choosing their own connection as the sole recipients of their bounty, but extending it to every shade of religious creed. In the proper and legitimate uses of wealth, I present this people as a model worthy of general imitation. The late venerated Richard Reynolds, of Bristol, who had amassed a princely fortune in the iron trade, looked upon himself merely as the steward of the Almighty. His entire income, after deducting the moderate expenses of his family, was devoted to benevolence ; and he thought his round of duty still incomplete, unless he devoted his time likewise. He deprived himself of slumber to watch beside the bed of sickness and pain, and to administer consolation to the heart bruised with affliction.

On one occasion, he wrote to a friend in London, requesting to know what object of charity remained, stating that he had not spent the whole of his income. His friend informed him of a number of persons confined in prison for small debts. He paid the whole, and swept the miserable mansion of its distressed tenants. Most of his donations were enclosed in blank covers, bearing the modest signature of 'A Friend.' A lady once applied to him in behalf of an orphan, saying, 'When he is old enough, I will teach him to name and thank his benefactor. 'Nay,' replied the good man, 'thou art wrong. We do not thank the clouds for rain. Teach him to look higher, and to thank Him who giveth both the clouds and the rain. My talent is the meanest of all talents—a little sordid dust; but as the man in the parable was accountable for his one talent, so am I accountable to the great Lord of all.'"

46.

EDWARD COLSTON, at the age of forty years, became a very eminent East India merchant, prior to the incorporation of the East India Company, and had forty sail of ships of his own, with immense riches flowing in upon him. He still remained uniform in his charitable disposition, distributing many thousand pounds to various charities in and about London, besides private gifts in many parts of the kingdom. In the year 1708, he instituted a very magnificent school in St. Augustine's-back, in Bristol, which cost him eleven thousand pounds in the building, and endowed the same with between one thousand seven hundred and one thousand eight hundred pounds per annum, forever. He likewise gave ten pounds for apprenticing every boy, and for twelve years after his death ten pounds to put them into business. It has been frequently reported that his private charities far exceeded those in public. "We have heard," says the *Bristol* Eng.) *Journal*, "that one of his ships trading to the East Indies had been missing upwards of three years, and was supposed to be destroyed at sea, but at length she arrived, richly laden. When his principal clerk brought him the report of her arrival, and of the riches on board, he said, as she was totally given up for lost, he would by no means claim any right to her; therefore he ordered the ship and merchandise to be sold, and the produce thereof to be applied towards the relief of the needy, which directions were immediately carried into execution. Another singular instance of his tender consciousness for charity was at the age of forty, when he entertained some thoughts of changing his condition. He paid his addresses to a lady, but being very timorous lest he should be hindered in his pious and charitable designs, he was determined to make a Christian trial of her temper and disposition, and therefore, one morning, filled his pockets with gold and silver, in order that, if any object presented itself in the course of their tour over London bridge, he might satisfy his intentions. While they were walking near St. Magnus church, a woman in extreme misery, with twins in her lap, sat begging; and, as he and his intended lady were arm-in-arm, he beheld the wretched object, put his hand in his pocket, and took out a handful of gold and silver, casting it into the poor woman's lap. The lady, being greatly alarmed at such profuse generosity, colored prodigiously; so that, when they were gone a little further towards the bridge-foot, she turned to him, and said, 'Sir, do you know what you did a few minutes ago?' 'Madame,' replied Mr. Colston, 'I never let my right hand know what my left hand doeth.' He then took his leave of her, and for this reason never married to the day of his death, although he lived to the age of eighty-five."

47.

In November, 1844, the Hon. Thomas G. Cary, an eminent merchant of Boston, delivered a lecture before the Mercantile Library Association of that city, in which, besides inquiring into the causes of frequent failure among men of business, he endeavored to show that the encouragement of the fine arts, in a republic, depended on the security of property. The extracts below refer to a merchant of New York, who has done something for the fine arts in this country, and who bequeathed a beautiful example in his life, for the imitation of the Man of Trade, and, indeed, all who grow up under a government like ours.

"Instances can be adduced to show that, even in countries where the arts have been brought to the highest degree of perfection, genius has been compelled to struggle with harassing want; and others can be found which indicate that, even among *us*, the taste, the liberality, and the ability that are necessary for the reward of the artist, have already made their appearance, and given promise of vigorous growth. One instance on each side will serve as an illustration.

"It is said that the celebrated painter, Coreggio, in Italy, received but forty ducats for the picture of Night, (or Dawn,) which forms, now, one of the chief attractions in the great gallery at Dresden; and that such was his disappointment and grief at the inadequate price, and the inconvenient mode of payment which he was forced to accept for another of his greatest productions, that he died, shortly afterward, in misery.

"About twelve years since, a favorite American artist who was then pursuing his studies in Italy, received from Mr. Luman Reed, a grocer in New York, the dimensions of a room in the house which he was then building for himself, with a request that he would prepare to fill the panels with such paintings of his own as he should design, for the sum of three thousand dollars. The painter was just then perplexed by accounts of pressing want from those who were dependent upon him at home, and had found himself obliged, with deep regret, to prepare for an immediate return to this country. The magnitude of the commission which he then received, and the liberality of the terms, at once relieved him from difficulty, and enabled him to remain in Italy as long as he had intended, for the purpose of studying the models of the great masters there; and when the work which he was then desired to undertake, was completed, the three thousand dollars had been extended to five thousand. Here, then, was an instance of such support to the fine arts as they are likely to receive in the United States.

"It is very probable that for the same sum of money, pictures of greater merit, and certainly of more celebrity, might have been purchased from the works of the old masters. But here was vital succor to the living artist, encouragement to continue his efforts, when it was most acceptable. It was such aid as would have gladdened the heart of Coreggio; perhaps have prolonged his life, and enlarged the number of the treasures which he left to the world. It was an act corresponding to what is called patronage in other countries; and yet it was not patronage. It was free from all claim of the irksome deference that is usually felt to be due to the patron. It was performed in the spirit which cordially acknowledges a full equivalent, in the work, for the price paid; and which leaves the spirit of the artist unshackled by dependence. It was the act, too, of one whose life, as I know, from personal acquaintance and observation, was in keeping with the spirit of it; and I avail myself of this opportunity to bear testimony to his worth, and to present his character for imitation.

Mr. Reed was a native of Connecticut, but engaged in business in New York. By industry, perseverance, and steady adherence to sound principles of action, he became one of the foremost in the highly respectable class to which he belonged. He grew gradually rich; and was, at length, enabled to build for himself an expensive house in an eligible situation, and to indulge the taste for beauty that seemed natural to him, in ornamenting it. His interest in the arts, as it grew, was accompanied by sympathy for the artist. I had known him well, myself, during a residence of ten years in New York, and was surprised one day by a visit from him in Boston. After a cordial greeting, I inquired after the state of the tea-market, which had been the great field of his success. He told me, with a smile, that, although he was as active there as ever, he had come on other matters; and that he wanted my aid to procure for a young artist whom he wished to encourage, permission to copy, at the Athenæum, the original sketch by Stuart of the head of Washington, which is preserved by the trustees with particular care; meaning, he said, to present the copy to a public society in New York. The permission was readily obtained, and I have since understood that, after that was arranged, he went into the tea-market here with sufficient advantage to provide a liberal compensation for the young artist while he was at work; thus making trade subservient to taste. He died shortly afterward, in the prime of life, leaving a collection of paintings, engravings, shells, and other objects of beauty and interest, altogether so valuable, that it is proposed to make them the commencement of a public gallery in New York; and leaving, too, an establishment in business conducted on principles so secure that it has been the school of industrious success to younger men, who owe their prosperity mainly to him.

"We have much to do, no doubt, before we can raise the standards of taste among us to the highest elevation; but, whatever may be the comparative merit of the collection that I speak of, it serves as proof of the point that we wish to establish. As the powers of the artist are confined to no one class, but are occasionally developed in all, so the love of beauty in color, in proportion, and expression, exists everywhere among us, and seeks gratification as the means of indulging it are found. Its strength will depend on the preference that we may cherish for objects really deserving of admiration, over the indulgences of coarse and sordid inclinations. But its culture has commenced, and with good promise. Beside the readiness with which the works of Allston and other artists have been purchased, we have recently had additional evidence of this in our own community.

"Owing to the growth of Boston, and change of character in some parts of it from that of quiet residence to the bustle of business, it lately became necessary to raise seventy-five thousand dollars, in order to remove the Athenæum from where it is, to a more eligible situation. As the capitalists among us had made large donations to the institution heretofore, it was thought but just to make an appeal to the *public* now, and ascertain whether a spirit exists, in the community at large, to support such an institution; and it was decided that no further donations should be asked for, but that shares should be offered for sale. They have all been taken. The money was provided with ease, by the subscriptions of various classes, comprising the mechanic as well as the man of fortune; and an intimation is given that more can be had, if desired, from those who are willing to receive payment for what they advance, in the right of access to books, and to a gallery of paintings and statuary.

"The fine arts, then, are likely to receive such support among us, that no egregious failure in respect to them will be eventually charged upon us, if we are likely to have the means to encourage them."

48.

THE impressions made on our boyhood are the strongest we ever receive, and remain with us even to old age as fresh and vivid as at the first. During our clerkship we form opinions of men and things which no after circumstances can eradicate. A boy when he sees any inconsistency of character in another, makes no allowance for circumstances; he judges only the naked fact, and condemns or approves accordingly. I never knew a man who stood well in the community, of whom his clerks thought meanly, and hence I would rather have the good opinion of my clerk than a stranger's, for if less critical, it is more honest and true. I recollect being made a confidant in the secrets of two individuals when a boy, which gave me a contempt for their characters that I could never get rid of, and if brought in contact in business with them now, I should always suspect their honesty. They were heated politicians, with so hearty a contempt for John Bull, that taking their own word for it, they would not so much as eat with a knife and fork of English manufacture, if they could avoid it. During the war, the English had possession of Castine, at the head of Penobscot Bay, and smuggling English goods from that place into the country was extensively practised. The temptation was too great for the cupidity of our two republicans, and fairly overcame all their scruples. I lived at that time in an eastern town, and one bitter cold night in February, I was called from my bed by two men whom I never knew before, at two o'clock, to go and receive several sleigh loads of smuggled goods, which, by direction of my employer, I took into the cellar, through a back way, in the store where I was a clerk, and secreted them carefully.

One of the sleighs was loaded with hardware, and in crossing the ferry over the Kennebeck, they met with a sad accident. The only ferry-boat was a large flat gondola. When they arrived on the opposite side, intending to stop for some refreshments, they drove the sleighs out of the gondola, except the hindmost one, which being loaded with the hardware was very heavy and tipped the boat very much. This was permitted to remain, and while they were regaling themselves, the tide rose, overflowed the sides of the boat, and sank it. The goods were of course wet. Among them was a package of sewing needles, and being accustomed to handling such goods, our republicans employed me to open, dry, and re-pack them in emery, which I did very carefully, at the expense of several days' labor. Needles were five times as dear then as now, so that the case was valued at some hundreds of dollars, which but for my care and industry would have been spoiled entirely. And one day when a custom-house officer came into the store to search for smuggled goods, I showed him every place in the store except where they were. The goods were delivered out again and sent in small parcels to Boston and New York for sale. The part I had taken and the value of my services led me to expect a generous reward, and I congratulated myself with the anticipated profits of fidelity to the trust reposed in me. When the last package of goods was removed, one of the smugglers came to me and said· "You are a capital little fellow;

if I had you in my store you would be worth your weight in gold. Always be as faithful, and you will always be trusted."

Expectation was now on tiptoe; I would not have given a sixpence to insure a twenty dollar bill in my hand the next moment, but like all high worldly hopes mine were doomed to disappointment. The republican smuggler put his hand in his pocket and solemnly drew forth an American half-dollar. "That," said he, "is the real coin, the true American eagle; keep it, and be sure you always avoid an Englishman as you would poison." He took his valise in his hand and walked towards the stage office—I looked after him till he was out of sight; and his gait, form, and figure, to the smallest outline, are as fresh in memory now as at that moment, and the contempt I then felt for him has never been effaced. I have met him often in the streets of New York; he does not know me, but I never passed him without laughing, though I have kept his secret to this day.

The morals which I would draw from this short story, are, first, always make a bargain for your services beforehand; never expect a sense of justice in a man whom you know to be dishonest in anything; never trust a man's patriotism who talks loudly in politics.

49.

WHERE sails the ship? It leads the Tyrian forth,
For the rich amber of the liberal North.
Be kind, ye seas—winds, lend your gentlest wing,
May, in each creek, sweet wells restoring spring!
To you, ye gods, belongs the merchant! O'er
The waves, his sails the wide world's goods explore;
And, all the while, wherever waft the gales,
The wide world's goods sails with him as he sails!

50.

The Hon. Robert C. Winthrop in an address delivered in 1846, before the Mercantile Library Association of Boston, illustrated the importance of mercantile asssociations, which are so admirably adapted to prepare their members for the future merchants of the country; "those, who in the progress of time, are to take the places of the intelligent, the enterprising, the wealthy and honorable men, who now carry on the vast foreign and domestic trade" of our great commercial cities.

"If there be a class of institutions more important than any or all others, to the moral character of our community, it is that which furnishes entertainment and employment during the evenings—the long winter, and the short summer evenings, too—for young men; and more especially for those, who either have no homes to which they may resort, or for whom the influences of the paternal roof have been in any way paralized. Libraries and reading-rooms for the merchants' clerks and the mechanics' apprentices of our city, numerous enough and spacious enough to accommodate them all, and furnished with every temptation which the amplest endowments can supply; these are among the most effective instruments which can be devised, for advancing our highest moral and social interests, and are entitled to the most liberal encouragement of all true philanthropists. It is not enough that the tippling shops and gambling tables are broken up. There is mischief still for idle minds to devise, and for idle hands to do. Innocent entertainment and useful occupation must be supplied, and supplied with some circumstance of interest and attraction, and fascination, if possible, or you have only driven dissipation and vice from the public haunt to the private hiding place, where they will lose nothing of their grossness or their guilt, by losing all their apprehension of exposure. And when the cheering spectacle is exhibited of the young men of the city, associating themselves for this great end of their own self-defence; organizing themselves not into a company, like that recently instituted by the merchants' clerks of London, for making up to their employers out of a common stock, the losses which may result from their own annual, ascertained, average of fraud and roguery, but into a company to insure themselves against the vices and immoralities and idleness from which those losses and those frauds flow as from their fountain—what heart can refuse them its sincerest sympathy, what tongue its most encouraging word, what hand its most efficient aid?

"If there be an appeal for sympathy and encouragement which no patriotic philanthropic breast can resist, it is that of young men struggling against the temptations which beset their path, and striving to prepare themselves, intellectually and morally, for discharging the duties which are about to devolve on their maturer life. And if there be a spectacle calculated to fill every such breast with joy, and to reward a thousand fold those who may have contributed in any way to the result, it is that of young men who have thus striven and struggled with success. There is a name in history. It is associated with some of the proudest achievements of the proudest empire of the world. It has been shouted along the chariot-ways of imperial Rome on occasions of her most magnificent triumphs. Whole volumes have been filled with the brilliant acts which have illustrated that name in three successive generations. But there is a little incident which takes up hardly ten lines on the historic page, which has invested it with a charm higher and nobler than all these. The Sybils, we are told, had prophesied that the *Bona Dea* should be introduced into Rome by the best man among the Romans. The senate was accordingly busied to pass judgment

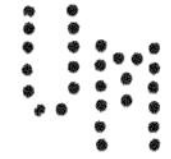

who was *the best man in the city.* And it is no small tribute to the Roman virtue of that day, that all men are said to have been more ambitious to get the victory in that dispute, than if they had stood to be elected to the highest and most lucrative offices and honors within the gift of the Senate or the people. The Senate at last selected Publius Scipio; of whom the only record is, that he was the nephew of Cneus, who was killed in Spain, and that he was a *young man,* who had never attained to that lowest of all the public honors of the empire, for which it was only necessary for him to have reached the age of two-and-twenty years. We may admire—we must admit—the resistless energy, the matchless heroism, of those two thunderbolts of war—Scipio, the conqueror of Hannibal, and Scipio, the destroyer of Carthage. But who does not feel, that this little story has thrown around that name a halo of peerless brilliancy; yes, one

Which shall new luster boast,
When Monarch's gems and victors' wreaths
Shall blend in common dust!"

51.

Elihu Burritt, the Learned Blacksmith, furnishes some important statements in relation to the expenses of war, that, to say nothing of its morality or humanity, should be sufficient to deter governments and men of common sense from ever engaging in it.

In 1835, a year of great commercial prosperity, the value of all the British and Irish produce and manufactures exported from the United Kingdom, was two hundred and eight millions two hundred and thirty-seven thousand nine hundred and eighty dollars. The appropriations for the payment of the interest of the British war debt, and for the support of the Army, Ordnance, and Navy, during the current year, amount to two

hundred and twenty-five millions four hundred and three thousand five hundred dollars ! ! Think of that ! The war-expenses, in the time of peace, exceeding by nearly twenty millions of dollars per annum, all that the human and iron machinery of that great kingdom can produce beyond its home consumption ! ! And now there is to be a famine there, and the guilty policy that taxes the very air breathed by the poor, to pay these war expenses, has locked up British ports against the Egyptian granaries of the world, leaving those hungry millions to covet swine's food in the sight of interdicted abundance.

The mercantile shipping of the civilized world amounts to about eight millions of tons, which is worth, new and old, thirty dollars per ton, and netts, clear of interest, insurance, etc., ten per cent., or twenty-four millions of dollars per annum. *The appropriation to the British Navy for the current year is* thirty-three millions six hundred and twenty thousand two hundred dollars ! ! Is not this a sober fact ? that the annual expense of the nation's navy exceeds the nett profit of all the mercantile shipping owned by the civilized world ?

The war-debts of the European nations amount to ten thousand millions of dollars. It would require the labor of *four millions* of men, at one hundred and fifty dollars per annum for each man, to pay the *interest* of this sum at six per cent. To pay the principal, it would be necessary to levy a tax of at least TEN DOLLARS on every inhabitant of the globe ! Another fact, rendering this more impressive, may be found in the "scrap of curious information," that no heathen nations are in arrears for the butcheries they have perpetrated on the human race. They pay cash down for all that is done for the devil under their hands. Christian nations alone "go on tick" for that kind of service.

From March 4th, 1789, to June 30th, 1814, our government expended on the War Department six hundred and sixty-three millions four hundred and thirty-eight thousand eight hundred and fifty-one dollars. The interest on this sum, at six per cent, would build Whitney's great railroad from the lakes to the Pacific, two thousand five hundred miles in length, at fifteen thousand dollars per mile; and thus erect a highway for the commerce and communion of the family of nations, which should be reckoned in all coming time one of the greatest enterprises that ever blessed the race.

52.

Mr. —— followed up his business with an energy and an ardor which were remarkable, even among the merchants of London. The seas were covered with his ships; the whole earth was embraced in his speculations. His name was familiar among merchants over all the globe; and his signature to an obligation was as current in value as the coined money of a crowned king. His income more resembled the revenue of a state than the income of a private gentleman; and by the influence of his wealth, he was a power in himself, to which the governments of kingdoms paid deference, and to whom they applied in their pecuniary emergencies as to one whose decision was able to precipitate or prolong the war or peace of empires. With all this, instead of growing hard and covetous with the increase of wealth—an effect which it is sorrowful to observe riches too often produce—he became more kindly and affable; his heart grew more compassionate towards the wants and necessities of his fellow creatures; his benevolence increased with his means of doing good; so that it is no wonder that he was as popular among the poor as he was reverenced by the rich, and esteemed by the wise and good.

53.

A MAN of business should be able to fix his attention on details, and be ready to give every kind of argument a hearing. This will not encumber him, for he must have been practised beforehand in the exercise of his intellect, and be strong in principles. One man collects materials together, and there they remain, a shapeless heap; another, possessed of method, can arrange what he has collected; but such a man as I would describe, by the aid of principles, goes farther, and builds with his materials.

He should be courageous. The courage, however, required in civil affairs, is that which belongs rather to the able commander than the mere soldier. But any kind of courage is serviceable.

Besides a stout heart, he should have a patient temperament, and a vigorous but disciplined imagination; and then he will plan boldly, and with large extent of view, execute calmly, and not be stretching out his hand for things not yet within his grasp. He will let opportunities grow before his eyes until they are ripe to be seized. He will think steadily over possible failure, in order to provide a remedy or a retreat. There will be the strength of repose about him.

He must have a deep sense of responsibility. He must believe in the power and vitality of truth, and in all he does or says, should be anxious to express as much truth as possible.

His feeling of responsibility and love of truth will almost inevitably endow him with diligence, accuracy and discreetness—those common-place requisites for a good man of business, without which all the rest may never come to be "translated into action."

54.

Almost every merchant has been rich, or at least prosperous, at some point of his life; and if he is poor now, he can see very well how he might have avoided the disaster which overthrew his hopes. He will probably see that his misfortunes arose from neglecting some of the following rules:—

Be industrious. Everybody knows that industry is the fundamental virtue in the man of business. But it is not every sort of industry which tends to wealth. Many men work hard to do a great deal of business, and, after all, make less money than they would if they did less. Industry should be expended in seeing to all the details of business—in the careful finishing up of each seperate undertaking, and in the maintenance of such a system as will keep everything under control.

Be economical. This rule, also, is familiar to everybody. Economy is a virtue to be practised every hour in a great city. It is to be practised in pence as much as in pounds. A shilling a day saved, amounts to an estate in the course of a life. Economy is especially important in the outset of life, until the foundations of an estate are laid. Many men are poor all their days, because, when their necessary expenses were small, they did not seize the opportunity to save a small capital, which would have changed their fortunes for the whole of their lives.

Stick to the business in which you are regularly employed. Let speculators make their thousands in a year or day; mind your own regular trade, never turning from it to the right hand or the left. If you are a merchant, a professional man, or a mechanic, never buy lots or stocks unless you have surplus money which you wish to invest. Your own business you understand as well as other men; but other people's business you do not understand. Let your business be some one which is useful to the community. All such occupations possess the elements of profits in themselves, while mere speculation has no such element.

Never take great hazards. Such hazards are seldom well balanced by the prospects of profit; and if they were, the habit of mind which is induced is unfavorable, and generally the result is bad. To keep what you have, should be the first rule; to get what you can fairly, the second.

Do not be in a hurry to get rich. Gradual gains are the only natural gains, and they who are in haste to be rich, break over sound rules, fall into temptations and distress of various sorts, and generally fail of their object. There is no use in getting rich suddenly. The man who keeps his business under his control, and saves something from year to year, is always rich. At any rate, he possesses the highest enjoyment which riches are able to afford.

Never do business for the sake of doing it, and being counted a great merchant. There is often more money to be made by a small business than a large one; and that business will in the end be most respectable which is most successful. Do not get deeply in debt; but so manage as always, if possible, to have your financial position easy, so that you can turn any way you please.

Do not love money extravagantly. We speak here merely with reference to getting rich. In morals, the inordinate lov· of money is one of the most degrading vices. But the extravagant desire of accumulation induces an eagerness, many times, which is imprudent, and so misses its object from too much haste to grasp it.

55.

Credit or confidence given to men of doubtful integrity, is an injustice done to all who hold on to their honesty.

56.

It is stated in a foreign paper, that a merchant, in prosecuting his morning tour in the suburbs of Edinburgh, found, as he walked along, a purse containing a considerable sum of money. He observed a lady at a considerable distance, who, he thought, would be the owner and loser. Determined to be correct in the party to whom he delivered it, he fell upon a strange, yet ingenious plan to effect this. He resolved to act the part of a "poor distressed tradesmen," and boldly went forward, hat in hand, and asked alms. This was answered with a polite "Go away! I have nothing to give you." The *poor* man, however, persisted in his entreaties until he had got assistance for his "famishing wife and children," the lady, from reasons, no doubt, similar to Mrs. Maclarty's, at last condescended; but, to her dismay, found that the wherewith was gone. The merchant, now satisfied that he was correct, with a polite bow returned the purse, with an advice that in future she would be more generous to the distressed and destitute.

57.

The following picture, we cannot say how correctly drawn, of the British merchant, is abstracted from Chronicles of "The Fleet," by a Peripatician, which contains two interesting stories, the "Ruined Merchant," and the "Turnkey's Daughter."

There certainly is no character on the face of the earth more estimable than that of the British merchant. His enlarged intercourse with the world leads to an enlarged and liberal spirit of dealing with mankind; his necessary avocations exercise his mind in a wholesome activity; his daily experience of the value of character and of a good name, stimulates him to preserve them, and trains him and fixes him in habits of truth and of fair dealing. Liberality is his motto, charity his virtue, generosity his practice. He is always ready to lend a helping hand to the weak, an assisting one to the unfortunate, and to look with indulgence on the errors of the head, when not accompanied by vices of the heart. His vocation, at the same time that it is one of the most honorable in itself, is also one of the most useful to society. He is one of the connecting links of nations; he is the great agent in the interchange of the products of various lands, and of the commodities and manufactures of different and distant countries—the distributor of the wealth of the world. He is one of the prime promoters and conservators of peace on earth; for no one feels more strongly than he how much the good-will, and the civilization, and the inestimable benefits which enlightened commerce brings, are marred and thrown back by the evil effects of war. He is the friend and the protector of the rights of the laboring poor, because he knows that by their labor all wealth is created.

58.

INATTENTION to business is not always the effect of a pressure in the money-market, but is induced, sometimes, by a variety of causes. If a merchant wishes a clerk to be faithful, and attentive to his interest, he should take some care of the welfare of those in his employ. Any act of kindness, by which gratitude will be awakened, will go farther towards making a good clerk, than a thousand severe, and sometimes irksome business precepts. A display of passion towards those who, by the nature of their situation, can make no defense, is not only galling to a sensitive mind, but it often leads to future evils, which no opposite influence can counteract.

59.

Commerce brings into the market almost every thing that has a being in the water, on the earth, and in the air; from the whale that spouts and foams in the great deep to the smallest insect that exists in the land. A late writer remarks with great justice that "the importance of insects to commerce is scarcely ever treated of. Great Britain does not pay less than a million of dollars annually for the dried carcasses of a tiny insect—the Cochineal. Gum Shellac, another insect product from India, is of scarcely less pecuniary value. A million and a half of human beings derive their sole support from the culture and manufacture of silk, and the silk-worm alone creates an annual circulating medium of between one hundred and fifty and two hundred millions of dollars. Half a million of dollars is annually spent in England alone for foreign honey; ten thousand hundred weight of wax is imported into that country each year. Then there are the gall-nuts of commerce, used for dyeing, and in the manufacture of ink, etc., whilst the cantharides, or Spanish fly, is an important insect to the medical practitioner. In this way we see the importance of certain classes of the insect race, whilst in another view, the rest clear the air of noxious vapors, and are severally designed by nature for useful purposes, though we in our blindness, may not understand them."

60.

The judgment of all the great moral writers of the age has condemned the practice of imprisonment for debt; all experience is against it; there is not a jailer or a turnkey that ever closed the door on a prisoner who will not confess its inefficacy; we will say nothing of the denunciations of the Scriptures against those who oppress and trample on the poor and the unfortunate, because in this so-called Christian country, Christian-principles are always disregarded when any question relating to the making of money is to be considered; but we will speak of it only as a matter of expediency; not as a matter of religion, or of charity, or of justice, or of humanity, but merely as a matter of expediency; and we contend that, viewed only in respect to its unprofitable operation on the community, inasmuch as it prevents a vast number of people from adding by their labors to the general wealth of the country, imprisonment for debt is statistically an inexpedient practice. It cannot be defended as a punishment, because, when plainly stated in that light, it cannot be allowed that punishment should be inflicted before crime be proved, and no one can have the hardihood to say that the bare circumstance of a person not being able to pay his debt makes his failure criminal; because if he were to be considered criminal, it would follow that because the default of A prevented B from paying C, that therefore B, who was prevented, not by his own fault, but by the default of A, from paying C, was a criminal deserving of punishment! a conclusion which, when thus stated, is too absurd for any sane man to assent to. But the actual operation of the law is to punish the innocent man B, for the failure of the other man A: an injustice so monstrous, that, from its injustice alone, it is a matter of amazement how such a law can be persevered in, as it still is, in several of our democratic States!

But, seeing the sure and certain progress of reform, we are led to hope that men will be wise at last, and place the question upon its proper footing; and come, in the end, to see that it is exceedingly prejudicial to the community at large, to strip one of its members of all that he possesses, and to turn him houseless, naked, and friendless, into the streets!

61.

PERCY, in his anecdotes, gives an instance of generosity on the part of a Chinese merchant, of the name of Shai-king-qua, who had long known a Mr. Anderson, an English trader, and had large transactions with him. It appears that Mr. Anderson met with heavy losses, became insolvent, and at the time of his failure owed his Chinese friend upwards of eighty thousand dollars. Mr. Anderson wished to come to England, in the hopes of being able to retrieve his affairs; he called on the Hong merchant, and in the utmost distress, explained his situation, his wishes, and his hopes. The Chinese listened with anxious attention, and having heard his story, thus addressed him: "My friend Anderson, you have been very unfortunate; you lose all; I very sorry; you go to England; if you more fortunate there, you come back and pay; but that you no forget Chinaman friend, you take this, and when you look on this, you will remember Shai-king-qua." In saying these words, he pulled out a valuable gold watch, and gave it to Anderson.

Mr. Anderson took leave of his friend, but he did not live to retrieve his affairs, or to return to China. When the account of his death, and of the distress in which he had left his family, reached Canton, the Hong merchant called on one of the gentlemen of the factory who was about to return to Europe, and addressed him in the following manner: "Poor Mr. Anderson dead! I very sorry; he good man; he friend, and he leave two childs; they poor—they have nothing—they childs of my friend; you take this for them; tell them Chinaman friend send it!" And he put into the gentleman's hand a sum of money for Mr. Anderson's children, amounting to several hundred pounds.

62.

There is embodied in a little work, entitled "Illustrations of the Law of Kindness," by the Rev. G. W. Montgomery, more of the spirit and genius of Christianity, than in the ponderous tomes of many learned theologians, since the days of the Reformation. The perusal of this volume has almost, if not quite, convinced us "that there never yet was an instance in which kindness has been fairly exercised, but that it has subdued the enmity opposed to it." Among the many well-authenticated anecdotes adduced in illustration of the law of kindness, or of "overcoming evil with good," nothing, we think, could more effectually enforce this doctrine, than the effect of such facts as the following:—

"The brothers Cheeryble of the novelist are, as is well known, scarcely overcharged portraits of two real English merchants; one of whom, we regret to know, is now no more. Of these men, the following story was originally told in a Manchester paper:—The elder brother of this house of merchant princes amply revenged himself upon a libeler, who had made himself merry with the peculiarities of the amiable fraternity. This man published a pamphlet, in which one of the brothers (D.) was designated as 'Billy Button,' and represented as talking largely of their foreign trade, having travelers who regularly visited Chowbent, Bullock Smithy, and other foreign parts. Some 'kind friend' had told W. of this pamphlet, and W. had said that the man would live to repent of its publication. This saying was kindly conveyed to the libeler, who said that he should take care never to be in their debt. But the man in business does not always know who shall be his creditor. The author of the pamphlet became bankrupt, and the brothers held an acceptance of his which had been endorsed by the drawer, who had

also become bankrupt. The wantonly-libeled men had thus become creditors of the libeler. They now had it in their power to make him repent of his audacity. He could not obtain his certificate without their signature, and without it he could not enter into business again. He had obtained the number of signatures required by the bankrupt laws, except one.

"It seemed folly to hope that the firm of brothers would supply the deficiency. What! they who had been cruelly made the laughing-stock of the public, forget the wrong, and favor the wrong-doer? He despaired; but the claims of a wife and children forced him at last to make the application. Humbled by misery, he presented himself at the counting-room of the wronged. W. was there alone, and his first words to the delinquent were, 'Shut the door, sir!' sternly uttered. The door was shut, and the libeler stood trembling before the libeled. He told his tale, and produced his certificate, which was instantly clutched by the injured merchant.

"'You wrote a pamphlet against us once!' exclaimed W. The supplicant expected to see his parchment thrown into the fire; but this was not its destination. W. took a pen, and writing something on the document, handed it back to the bankrupt. He, poor wretch, expected to see there, 'Rogue, scoundrel, libeler!' inscribed; but there was, in fair round characters, the signature of the firm! 'We make it a rule,' said W., 'never to refuse signing the certificate of an honest tradesman, and we never heard that you were anything else.' The tear started into the poor man's eyes.

"'Ah!' said W., 'my saying was true. I said you would live to repent writing that pamphlet. I did not mean it as a threat; I only meant that some day you would know us better, and would repent you had tried to injure us. I see you repent

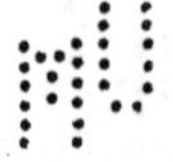

of it now.' 'I do—I do;' said the grateful man. 'Well, well, my dear fellow,' said W., 'you know us now. How do you get on? What are you going to do?' The poor man stated that he had friends who could assist him when his certificate was obtained. 'But how are you off in the meantime?'—and the answer was, that, having given up everything to his creditors, he had been compelled to stint his family of even the common necessaries, that he might be enabled to pay the cost of his certificate. 'My dear fellow,' said W., 'this will never do; your family must not suffer. Be kind enough to take this ten pound note to your wife from me. There, there, my dear fellow—nay, don't cry—it will be all well with you yet. Keep up your spirits, set to work like a man, and you will raise your head yet.' The overpowered man endeavored in vain to express his thanks—the swelling in his throat forbade words; he put his handkerchief to his face, and went out of the door, crying like a child."

63.

All legislation is founded on an erroneous notion, which, until people clear their heads of it, will always infect and mar all legislation in respect to the laws of debtor and creditor. That erroneous notion is, that there is an innate disinclination in all men to pay their debts; whereas it is precisely the contrary principle that prevails. We never knew a man, except in a case here and there where the man was a rascal, and it is not on exceptions but on generalities that legislation ought to be founded—we say we never knew a man who was not only desirous but anxious to pay his debts. But the legislature has ever proceeded on the contrary supposition; so that all the laws relating to debtor and creditor have been made with a view to force the debtor to do that which he is willing enough to do if he could. Now if the legislature, instead of racking its invention to devise all sorts of pains, and penalties, and tortures, to wrench from the debtor what he has not got—had directed its attention to devise facilities for enabling the debtor to pay as far as he can, and not to break him down so utterly and irremediably as forever depriving him of the power of paying his debts, all would be the gainers to an incalculable degree. For the creditor would have a chance of his money, which now he has not; the debtor would have a chance of retrieving his position, and of fulfilling his obligations, which every man in his heart longs to do, which now he has not; and society would not be put to the expense of all the apparatus of the law and of its huge prisons for confining unfortunate debtors; which ought to be regarded only as ingenious inventions for furthering the revengeful feelings of the vindictive creditor, and for preventing the debtor, most effectually, from ever paying him.

64.

THERE is an unapproachable perfection of cant in the annexed advertisement, which we take from a Manchester (Eng.) paper:—

TO DRAPERS, HABERDASHERS, WAREHOUSEMEN, ETC.

"Wanted, towards the latter end of April, by an eminently pious young man of Scotland, who has been regularly bred to the above branches, and considerably experienced generally, a situation as assistant clerk, manager, salesman, or traveler. The advertiser is twenty-one years of age, possessed of excellent health, an amiable disposition, good ability, extensive knowledge of the great scriptural doctrine, strictly evangelical, and would be found to be of immense advantage in assisting to advance the claims and reign of the Messiah's kingdom, amidst all the civil and ecclesiastical opposition so prevalent among the nations of the earth, in these latter agitating times. Testimonials and references to several eminent evangelical ministers and members of the Gospel, as well as to former and present employers, of the most strict and satisfactory tendency as to character and ability, with portrait, may be had on application. No objections to town or country, and would be willing to conform to the rules of a liberal church or dissenting family, holding evangelical principles, and make himself generally useful. A house favorable to Evangelical, Presbyterian, or Independent Church principles, affording permanent employment, and progressive advancement of salary, preferred."

65.

THAT evil results, in many instances, from wealth, is sufficiently manifest; but it is not certain, on this account, that virtue is only safe in the midst of penury, or even in moderate circumstances. Nor, because the wealthy are often miserable, is it certain that happiness dwells chiefly with the humble. It may be quite true that no elevation such as riches bring about, insures perfect purity and amiableness of character, and that content is found nowhere; and yet there may be a more steady connection between virtue and easy circumstances, also between content and easy circumstances, than between the same things and poverty. The poor escape many temptations and many cares which beset the rich; but, alas! have they not others of a fiercer kind, proper to their own grade? Let the statistician make answer. It is only, indeed, to be expected, that an increasing ease of circumstances should be upon the whole, favorable to moral progress, for it is what industry tends to; and industry is a favored ordination of heaven, if ever anything on earth could be pronounced to be such.

66.

The following remarks, though intended for England, are not without application to the retail trade of our commercial cities. They are from a little work, recently published in England, entitled "The Evils of the Late Hour System, by Ralph B. Grindrod, L.L. D."

"The unreasonable conduct of a numerous class of purchasers makes the employment of assistant drapers, in particular, and of all engaged in the traffic of goods, more wearisome and fatiguing than it would be under more favorable circumstances. Every hour, nay, every minute, requires constant attention to the same monotonous round of minute and uninteresting details. To this, is too frequently superadded those perpetual trials of the patience and temper, which those alone can realize who have been subjected to the unreasonable demands of inconsiderate customers. It matters not how often the drawers and shelves may have been arranged during the night. They must again and again be disarranged to accommodate the whims of customers, who too often, after almost endless trouble, make but slight purchases. The young men of our mercers' shops, however minute the order, are required, under all circumstances, to exhibit the same bland and obsequious attention to those upon whom they wait.

"An assistant draper, of long experience, informs the writer that after customers have, late in the evening, so pulled about various articles of dress, the after arrangement of which would give employment for a considerable portion of time, it is generally the case that they conclude by a remark to the following effect:—'it is impossible to tell what sort of color it may be by daylight; so I will call again in the morning.' This wonderful discovery, unfortunately for the poor assistant, is only made after a tedious trial of the patience and temper, although probably the light of day had given place to that of gas at least an hour previously.

"The modern spirit of competition has induced a numerous class of tradesmen to adopt a plausible but fictitious appearance of traffic—a practice which, we may readily suppose, does not diminish the hard lot of assistants. No leisure moments, consequently, must be devoted to other than the business of the shop—no intervals of rest are permitted in the absence of persons to purchase. An *appearance* of business is enforced; the hurry and bustle of a thriving trade is exhibited; in lack of other duties, articles must be packed and repacked; ribbons again and again rolled—every specious means, in short, is put into operation to impress the public with an opinion of extensive traffic. The already overtasked assistants suffer the penalties of this system of delusion."

67.

THE following passage on this subject occurs in the letter of the Hon. Thomas G. Cary, a merchant of Boston, to a lady in France, who wrote to a lady here, to inquire "what ground there could possibly be for the dreadful accusations which she hears against us everywhere abroad," in consequence of the supposed failure of a national bank, the supposed delinquency of the national government, the debts of the several States, and repudiation. Mr. Cary explains these matters very satisfactorily, and in answer to the superficial statements in the books of English travelers in the United States, he thus summarily disposes of the sneer cast upon the Americans for their reputed love of money:—

"When it is said, as it often is, with scorn, that our conversation, in this country, relates too much to money matters, that we *talk* about dollars, etc., it is but fair to remember that, notwithstanding all that some of our own writers have thought proper to concede, money is regarded here as the *means* of progress, rather than the end in view. It is power in any part of the world; and where difference of rank is abolished, and the highest places are open to the competition of every one, it is *great* power, since it enables a man to raise those who depend on him to the enjoyments and advantages of which he may have felt the want. Probably there is no part of the world where the character of the miser is more uncommon than here; and I have often thought, in noticing the ways of foreigners who come here, that, if we *talk* more about dollars than they do, they *think* more of them than we do by far."

68.

In no way, perhaps, can a young man destroy his business character more effectually than by obtaining the reputation of one who breaks his promises. The mercantile world, in placing under its ban the individual who suffers his note to be protested, is less unjust than is popularly supposed. Instances of hardship, we are willing to concede, do occasionally arise under the operation of this rule; but they are less frequent than is generally believed, and not more cruel than in similar exceptional cases. Nine men out of ten who fail owe their insolvency either to having traded beyond their means, to a careless management of their affairs, or to criminal speculations. That is, they have undertaken more than they could perform, and this while knowing at the time of the promise that there was great doubt whether they could meet their engagements. Perhaps, indeed, they had no deliberate intention of violating their promise. But they either were more ignorant than they should have been of their ability to perform, or they trusted too confidently to the chances of the future, or they took heavier risks subsequently than was consistent with their liabilities. The innocent, therefore, suffer but rarely by this species of mercantile proscription. On the other hand, the rule is absolutely necessary to the commercial world, for, without it, payments could scarcely ever be depended on, and financial distress would frequently be alarmingly increased.

Strict business integrity, in this particular, depends much on the general character. A person who pays little regard to slight promises, usually is somewhat careless of greater ones also. Defects of this kind, like flaws in machinery, never lessen, but always grow worse, until finally, under the strain of a powerful temptation, they often break down a man's career forever. The most punctual men in keeping a trivial engagement, we have always found to be the exactest in their business transactions. Washington was a memorable example of particularity in small things as well as great, and his strict probity in the latter, was unquestionably the result, in a considerable degree, of his fidelity in the former.

In our experience also, the men who never kept an engagement to the moment, the men who were proverbially always "behind time," have been, mostly, those who have failed subsequently in business. We have learned too, to be cautious of those who are over-ready to promise. It is the individual who carefully considers before he makes a pledge, who can be most surely depended on to keep it. A multiplicity of promises necessarily prevents the promiser from observing them all, for one conflicts with the other, and disables even the best-intentioned. A disregard of promises, finally, is like a fungus, which imperceptibly spreads over the whole character, until the moral perceptions are perverted and the man actually comes to believe he does no wrong, even in breaking faith with his warmest friends.

69.

Success in life mainly depends upon perseverance. When a man has determined to follow a certain line of business, he must at the same time resolve to persevere until success crowns his efforts. He must never be cast down by the difficulties which may beset his path—for whoever conquers difficulty, conquers a weakness of his own frail nature likewise. How many men have commenced business under the most favorable auspices, and yet when a cloud has momentarily overshadowed their path, have lost all command over themselves and fled before the temporary gloom, instead of persevering on until the cloud has been dispersed, and sunshine once more smiled upon their efforts. Others, more fickle, have thought their business, in some minor departments, unworthy of their perseverance and energy, and forgetting the golden maxim that, "whatever is worth doing is worth doing well," have ceased to persevere in small matters, until sloth has entered deeply into their minds, and their whole business greatly neglected.

We are too apt to attribute success in business to good fortune, instead of great perseverance. This is a great evil, and should be eschewed, as it leads many to suppose that Dame Fortune will do that for them which they are unwilling to do for themselves.

The history of every great success in business is the history of great perseverance. By perseverance the mind is strengthened and invigorated, and the difficulty that once seemed so formidable is a second time surmounted with ease and confidence.

Energy and great perseverance are never thrown away on a good cause, or left unrewarded; and to every man of business, perseverance should be his motto, and then he may look with confidence to fortune as his reward.

70.

"I'M but a gatherer and distributer of other men's stuff," said Isaac Walton. This would have constituted him a merchant, although he had traded like Daniel Dowlas, in small wares down to wooden nutmegs. The poorest pedler is an itinerant merchant; and since man is the only trading animal on earth, he is bound to qualify himself *thoroughly* for whatever branch he embraces. As an accomplished linguist is familiar with foreign characters, using them only in the tongue to which they belong, so an individual, with a sound mercantile education, when addressing another, cautiously employs the technical terms known to his correspondent. Errors arising from neglect of this rule have frequently occurred, which we will illustrate by a story from a contemporary which may not be generally known:—A brewer once employed a brickmaker to manufacture a quantity of bricks, the latter having agreed, wrote for two or three loads of *Spanish*—the technical term for ashes or laystal stuff to mix with clay, instead of which he received from the brewer a dozen hogsheads of molasses! Such want of knowledge is likely to produce serious delay. In the above instance it only incited merriment; but it plainly shows that a thorough business man is familiar with the general peculiarities of other trades as well as his own. He is posted up in manufacturers' prices, the best markets for barter, rate of duties, etc. A mind well stored with essential data is not likely to be alarmed at the deceptions published by speculatoris in daily journals; it only perceives the laws that regulate supply and demand, as all fluctuations are considered matters of course.

We might dilate on this subject on two accounts, deprecating those unprincipled news-mongers who pander to stock-jobbers, and lamenting the superficial instruction too many of our traffickers receive, which is painfully evident, when rogues can raise panics with impunity—each one more alarming than the last—until our poor novices "lose the sense of action," like a certain visionary who remained transfixed in a sepulchral vault, all night dreading to move, under the supposition that something supernatural pulled his gown tail, which had hitched on a hook. The terrors of imagination, like a fog-cloud, magnify every danger.

Judgment—good common sense—is the motive power that raises a utilitarian to the summit of success. During the smoke of battle, skilful generals direct the motions of their army with the same dexterity as they would shift draftsmen on a chequer board, because they are versed in mathematics, and every position on the field presents a problem, which is familiar with Euclid's disciplinarians. Thus are merchants schooled in the game of life, and no "weak invention of the enemy" can discompose their equanimity. The diurnal methodical routine continues, whether public banks expand or contract, and their best friend—capital—is treated as a friend. They know well how to invest a surplus capital, and where a good mercantile security is to be found;—want of such necessary knowledge too often occasions sad embarrassment. Of fixed or floating capital, the latter is most profitable; the former is too fluctuating and precarious, arising from rents or interest, while "all commodities, the entire cost of which is replaced out of the current income, are floating capital. The former are stationary, yielding only income, and slow of transfer; the latter are constantly circulating." The mutations of traffic render it important that a reserve fund should be convertible into cash at any time. How many men have been ruined by making advances on growing crops, vaguely anticipating the profits or produce that has to pass through a manufacturing process before it is marketable. Innumerable cases might be cited of errors in judgment, committed by mercantile men, from not having been rigidly trained "in the way they should go." A visionary boasted of having driven a nail into the sky, and another replied, "but I clenched it." An ignoramus drives at random, but one who is regularly disciplined will, by judicious management, fix what an unskilled neighbor fails in.

71.

ALTHOUGH the Spaniards have a dislike, as we are told, to foreigners and foreign productions, yet the latter necessarily find their way into Spain, because she has no productions of her own, and must have them. But they hate custom-houses and custom-house officers as much as they do foreigners; and they also prefer a smuggled article, even if it is a foreign production; hence it is that there is no scene in Spanish life without a smuggler, at least so say the English. The peasant smuggles through necessity, the rich man through avarice, or the pleasure of cheating the revenue. Even the queen, we are told, robs her own exchequer, by wearing contraband finery. The whole southern coast, says a writer in the *Foreign Quarterly*, from Barcelona to Cadiz, is perpetually transformed, at night, into a strand for the loading of contraband goods. It is estimated that there are not less than four hundred thousand smugglers hovering perpetually about the mountains near the sea-cost, who descend at night to hold communion with proscribed foreign smugglers, and receive from them the materials for rendering millions of the Spanish population comfortable, free of duty. The annual amount of cotton goods smuggled into Spain, if we may believe Marlioni, a Spanish senator, is more than thirteen millions of dollars.

72.

"Can you loan me two thousand dollars to establish myself in a small retail business?" inquired a young man not yet out of his teens, of a middle aged gentleman, who was pouring over a pile of ledgers in the counting-room of one of the largest establishments in Boston. The person addressed turned toward the speaker, and regarding him for a moment with a look of surprise, inquired :—

"What security can you give me, Mr. Strosser?"

"Nothing but my note," replied the young man promptly.

"Which I fear would be below par in market," replied the merchant, smiling.

"Perhaps so," said the young man, "but Mr. Barton, remember that the boy is not the man; the time *may* come when Hiram Strosser's note will be as readily accepted as that of any other man."

"True, very true," replied Mr. Barton, mildly, "but you know business men seldom loan money without adequate security —otherwise they might soon be reduced to penury."

At this remark the young man's countenance became deathly pale, and, having observed a silence of several moments, he inquired in a voice whose tones indicated his deep disappointment—

"Then you can not accommodate me, can you?"

"Call upon me to-morrow, and I will give you a reply," said Mr. Barton; and the young man retired.

Mr. Barton resumed his labors at the desk, but his mind was so much upon the boy and his singular errand, that he could not pursue his task with any correctness; and, after having made several sad blunders, he closed the ledger, and took his hat, and went out upon the street. Arriving opposite the store of a wealthy merchant upon Milk street, he entered the door.

"Good morning, Mr. Hawley," said he, approaching the proprietor of the establishment, who was seated at his desk, counting over the profits of the week.

"Good morning," replied the merchant, blandly; "happy to see you; have a seat? Any news? how's trade?"

Without noticing these interrogations, Mr. Barton said:

"Young Strosser is desirous of establishing himself in a small retail business in Washington street, and called this morning to secure of me a loan of two thousand dollars for that purpose."

"Indeed!" exclaimed Mr. Hawley, evidently surprised at this announcement; "but you do not think of loaning that sum, do you?"

"I do not know," replied Mr. Barton. "Mr. Strosser is a young man of business talent and strict integrity, and will be likely to succeed in whatever he undertakes."

"Perhaps so," replied Mr. Hawley, doubtfully; "but I am heartily tired of helping to re-establish these young aspirants for commercial honors."

"Have you ever suffered any from such a course?" inquired Mr. Barton, at the same time casting a roguish glance at Mr. Hawley.

"No," replied the latter, "for I never felt inclined to make an investment of that kind."

"Then here is a fine opportunity to do so. It may prove better than the stock in the bank. As for myself, I have concluded that, if you will advance him one thousand dollars, I will contribute an equal sum."

"Not a single farthing would I advance for such a purpose;

and if you make an investment of that kind, I shall consider you very foolish."

Mr. Barton observed a silence of several minutes, and then arose to depart.

"If you do not feel disposed to share with me in this enterprise, I shall advance the whole sum myself."

Saying which, he left the store.

* * * * * *

Ten years have passed away since the occurrence of the conversation recorded in the preceding dialogue, and Mr. Barton, pale and agitated, is standing at the same desk as when first introduced to the reader's attention. As page after page of his ponderous ledger was examined, his despair became deeper and deeper, till at last he exclaimed:

"I am ruined—utterly ruined!"

"How so!" inquired Hiram Strosser, who entered the counting-room in season to hear Mr. Barton's remark.

"The last European steamer brought news of the failure of the house of Perleh, Jackson & Co., London, who are indebted to me in the sum of nearly two hundred thousand dollars. News of the failure has become general, and my creditors, panic-stricken, are pressing in my papers to be cashed. The banks refuse me credit, and I have not the means to meet my liabilities. If I could pass this crisis, perhaps I could rally again, but it is impossible; my creditors are importunate, and I can not much longer keep above the tide," replied Mr. Barton.

"What is the extent of your liabilities?" inquired Strosser.

"Seventy-five thousand dollars," replied Mr. Barton.

"Would that sum be sufficient to relieve you?"

"It would."

"Then, sir, you shall have it," said Strosser, as he stepped up to the desk, and drew a check for twenty thousand dollars. "Here, take this, and when you need more, do not hesitate to call upon me. Remember that it was from you I received money to establish myself in business."

"But that debt was canceled several years ago," replied Mr. Barton, as a ray of hope shot across his troubled mind.

"True," replied Strosser, "but the debt of *gratitude* that I owe has never been canceled, and now that the scale is turned I deem it my duty to come up to the rescue."

At this singular turn in the tide of fortune, Mr. Barton fairly wept for joy.

His paper was taken up as fast as it was sent in, and in less than a month he had passed the crisis, and stood perfectly safe and secure; his credit increased and his business improved, while several other firms sunk under the blow, and could not rally, among whom was Mr. Hawley, alluded to at the commencement of this article.

"How did you manage to keep above the tide?" inquired Mr. Hawley of Mr. Barton, one morning, several months after the events last recorded, as he met the latter upon the street, on his way to his place of business.

"Very easily, indeed, I can assure you," replied Mr. Barton.

"Well do tell me how," continued Mr. Hawley; "I lay claim to a good degree of shrewdness, but the strongest exercise of my wits did not save me; and yet, you, whose liabilities were twice as heavy as my own, have stood the shock, and have come off even bettered by the storm."

"The truth is," replied Mr. Barton, "I cashed my paper as soon as it was sent in."

"I suppose so," said Mr. Hawley, regarding Mr. B. with a look of surprise, "but how did you obtain the funds? As for my part I could not obtain a dollar credit, the banks refused to take my paper, and my friends even deserted me."

"A little investment that I made some ten years ago," replied Mr. Barton, smiling, "has recently proved exceedingly profitable."

"Investment!" echoed Mr. Hawley—"what investment?"

"Why, do you not remember how I established young Strosser in business some ten years ago?"

"O, yes, yes," replied Mr. Hawley, as a ray of suspicion lit up his countenance "but what of that?"

"He is now one of the heaviest dry goods dealers in the city, and when this calamity came on, he came forward, and very generously advanced me seventy-five thousand dollars. You know I told you, on the morning I called to offer you an equal share of the stock, that it might prove better than an investment in the bank."

During this announcement, Mr. Hawley's eyes were bent intently upon the ground, and, drawing a deep sigh, he moved on, dejected and sad, while Mr. Barton returned to his place of business, with his mind cheered and animated by thoughts of his singular investment.

73.

"HONESTY *is* the best policy;" and aside from the consideration of a solemn reckoning hereafter, it is the surest way to worldly thrift and prosperity. But to honesty there must be added a great degree of caution and prudence. Many a young man has been led by the consciousness of his own integrity to place such confidence in mankind as to render him an easy prey to knaves and swindlers.

74.

The best delineation of the credit system, or the best illustration of its operations, showing the results that may arise, and the number of individuals that may, without even knowing each other, be affected by the act of a single individual, we find in the following imaginary dialogue which we quote from the Mobile *Tribune.* It contains, childish as it may seem, a lesson of import, and may be profitably read by old and young. It purports to be a conversation between a cotton dealer and his child, and runs as follows :—

Pa.—(Reading a newspaper, mutters) "No rise in the rivers —never going to rise again, I believe, wife."

Little Daughter.—"I wish the rivers would rise."

Pa.—"Why, what have you got to do with the river's rising?"

Little Daughter.—"A great deal, papa, for then the boats would run."

Pa.—"And what have you to do with the boats running my child, hey?"

Little Daughter.—"They would bring the cotton down."

Pa.—(Looking over his spectacles)—"And what have you to do, pet, with cotton bales?"

Little Daughter.—"Why, if the cotton was down, pa, you would be able to sell it you know, dear papa," smilingly.

Pa.—"And what then?"

Little Daughter.—"You would have plenty of money."

Pa.—"Well?"

Little Daughter.—(Laying her little hand on his shoulder, and looking into his face)—"Then you could pay ma that gold twenty dollar piece you borrowed of her, you know, papa."

Pa.—"And what then, minx?"

Little Daughter.—"Then mamma could pay Aunt Sarah that ten dollars she owes her."

Pa.—"Ay, indeed! And what then?"

Little Daughter.—"And Aunt Sarah would pay sister Jane that dollar she promised to give her on New Year's, but didn't, 'cos she didn't have no cotton, I mean money, pa."

Pa.—"Well, and what else?" (Pa lays down the paper and looks at her curiously, with a half smile.)

Little Daughter.—"Cousin Jane would pay brother John his fifty cents back, and he said when he got it he would give me the half dime he owes me, and two dimes to buy marbles, and this is what I want the rivers to rise for, and the big boats to run! And I owe nurse the other dime, and must pay my debts."

Pa looked at ma. "There it is," he said, "we are all, big and little, like a row of bricks. Touch one, and *presto!* away we all go, down to my little Carrie. She has, as a child, as great an interest in the rise as I have. We are all, old and young, waiting for money to buy marbles."

75.

George Davidson, the author of "*Trade and Travel in the East,*" spent twelve months in Hong Kong, and thus speaks of its advantages as a place of trade. The morality of his remarks as to the opium trade, are rather questionable:—

"A decisive proof of the eligibility of Hong Kong as a place of trade, and of its importance in the eyes of the Chinese themselves, is afforded by the immense sums paid by some of them for ground on which to build *Hongs,* where they can deposit their goods with safety, beyond the reach of their grasping mandarins. This advantage to a Chinaman is something so new, and so far beyond any thing he ever dreamed of enjoying, that I conceive the benefits likely to accrue from it, to Hong Kong, to be incalculable.

"Goods stored in Canton or Macao, the property of a Chinaman, were never safe in the event of their owner getting into trouble with the Chinese authorities; and, if the property of foreigners, they could not be insured against fire, the risk arising from the universal carelessness of the Chinese, and the consequent very frequent occurrence of extensive conflagrations, being considered too great by the underwriters. Both these difficulties are completely obviated in Hong Kong, and every substantially built house and warehouse, together with the property in them, were insured against fire, previously to my quitting the island. One Chinaman had, in March last, completed buildings for the storage of property collected from the different ports on the coast, on which upwards of forty thousand dollars had been laid out, and what is more, they were already well filled.

"As a convenient and safe *depot* for opium, (a trade, in my opinion, quite as legitimate and honorable as that in brandy, gin, and other spirits,) Hong Kong is admirably situated. The purchaser from the western ports as well as from the north-eastern, finds the distance he has to travel moderate, and, on his arrival, has no one to dread, no mandarin daring to show his face on shore. The ships that bring the drug from India here find a safe and commodious harbor, where they can unload their cargoes in open day, without hindrance or molestation, and where they are not driven to the necessity of carrying on their operations in the dark. Were the opium trade actually one of mere smuggling, I would be as ready as any one to condemn it, and to raise my voice against those concerned in it; but when one considers that not a hundredth part of the quantity sold annually is really smuggled—that ninety-nine chests out of every hundred pay a heavy duty (miscalled a bribe,)—that the Chinese government derives from it, indirectly, but not the less certainly, a very considerable revenue—and finally, that large quantities of it are known to be consumed within the walls of the imperial palace at Pekin, I confess I see no reason for the clamorous indignation with which the traffic has of late been assailed by European moralists."

76.

North American and French whalers have, for several years, been frequent visitors to San Carlos, Peru, as they can there provide themselves, at a cheap rate, with provisions for the long fishing season. All the captains bring goods which they smuggle on shore, where they sell or exchange them at a high profit. A custom-house officer is, indeed, sent on board every vessel to examine what is to be unshipped; but a few dollars will silence him, and make him favor the contraband operations, which are carried on without much reserve. A French captain brought to Chiloe a quantity of water-proof cloaks and hats, made of a sort of black waxed cloth, and sold them to a dealer in San Carlos. To evade the duty, he sent his men on shore, each wearing one of these hats and cloaks, which they deposited in the dealer's store, and then returned on board the ship, dressed in their sailor's garb. This was repeated so often, that at length it was intimated to the captain, that if his men had a fancy to come on shore with such hats and cloaks, they would be permitted to do so, but it must be on condition of their returning on board dressed in the same costume.

77.

THE calling of the Merchant acquires a new importance in modern times. Once, Nations were cooped up, each in its own climate and language. Then, WAR was the only mediator between them. They met but in the battle-field, or in solemn embassies to treat for peace Now, TRADE is the Mediator. They meet on the Exchange. To the Merchant, no man who can trade is a foreigner. His wares prove him a citizen. Gold and silver are cosmopolitan. Once, in some of the old governments, the magistrates swore, "I will be evil-minded towards the *People*, and will devise against them the worst thing I can." Now, they swear to keep the laws which the People have made. Once, the great question was, How large is the standing army? Now, What is the amount of the national earnings? Statesmen ask less for the Ships of the Line, than for the Ships of Trade. They fear an over-importation oftener than a war, and settle their difficulties in Gold and Silver, not as before, with Iron. All ancient States were military; the modern, mercantile. War is getting out of favor as property increases and men get their eyes open. Once, every man feared Death, Captivity, or at least Robbery, in War; now, the worst fear is of Bankruptcy and Pauperism. This is a wonderful change. Look at some of the signs thereof. Once, Castles and Forts were the finest buildings; now, Exchanges, Shops, Custom-Houses, and Banks. Once, men built a Chinese Wall to keep out the strangers—for stranger and foe were the same; now, men build Railroads and Steamships to bring them in. England was once a stronghold of Robbers—her four seas but so many castle-moats; now, she is a great Harbor, with four Ship-Channels. Once, her chief must be a bold, cunning Fighter; now, a good Steward and

Financier. Not to strike a hard blow, but to make a good bargain, is the thing. Formerly, the most enterprising and hopeful young men sought fame and fortune in deeds of arms; now, an army is only a common sewer, and most of those who go to the war, if they never return, "have left their country for their country's good." In days gone by, constructive Art could build nothing better than Hanging Gardens, and the Pyramids—foolishly sublime; now, it makes docks, canals, iron roads, and magnetic telegraphs. Saint Louis, in his old age, got up a crusade, and saw his soldiers die of the fever at Tunis; now, the King of the French sets up a Factory, and will clothe his people in cottons and woollens. The old Douglas and Percy were clad in iron, and harried the land on both sides of the Tweed; their descendants now are civil-suited men who keep the peace. No girl trembles though "all the blue bonnets are over the border." The warrior has become a Shop-keeper.

"Lord Stafford mines for coal and salt;
The Duke of Norfolk deals in malt,
The Douglas in red herrings;
And noble name and cultured land,
Palace, and park, and vassal band,
Are powerless to the notes of hand
Of Rothschild or the Barings."

78.

COMMERCE, as well as life, has its auspicious ebbs and flows, that baffle human sagacity, and defeat the most rational arrangement of systems, and all the calculations of ordinary prudence. Be prepared, therefore, at all times, for commercial revulsions and financial difficulties, by which thousands have been reduced to beggary, who before had rioted in opulence, and thought they might bid defiance to misfortune.

79.

By every variety of commentary, has almost every fibre of the character of that extraordinary man, George Washington, been illustrated. His military talent has, in all its phases, been brought to the notice of the world—weighed, analyzed, reviewed—until it has come out of its fierce ordeal, established, as of the very first order of judgment, energy, bravery. His reputation as a statesman has been blazoned abroad with a vigor, derived alike from the truth and its forcible use. Men have honored themselves by giving the power of their intellect to the history of his devotion to his country. All his movements in war—all his acts in the cabinet, are on record; and he is one of the very few men that ever trod the earth, of whose reputation it is safe, that the knowledge of it should be thorough.

But George Washington was a great man, in other departments of life than those blended with the army and state; and it is to a feature in his character, less prominently before the world, but one of the most valuable, of which we would speak in this article. It is the order, regularity, method, punctuality, and, above all, the rectitude—the unsullied and unchangeable devotion to his engagements, which distinguished him, and which, combined, are the very qualities that make up the merchant. In all these, the example of Washington may fittingly be urged upon the consideration of the merchants of the Union. The old merchants of the colonies were the very men who periled the most in arraying themselves on the side of a separation from England. Theirs was no cheap patriotism—no offering of words; but the severing of a profitable mercantile connection—the riving asunder of relations that involved sacrifices alike keen and costly. From among those merchants, some of the most valued and useful of the officers and soldiers of the revolution were taken, and they proved themselves as active in the trade of war, as they had ever been vigilant in the war of trade.

The education of Washington was purely a practical one. All that he added to this was the result of efforts in maturer life, generally made, as events demonstrated the particular necessity of the study. This was a business foundation, early laid; and though at a time of life when boyhood is usually in its recklessness, the various parts of a business education were thoroughly built up in his character.

At the age of thirteen, he studied the intricate forms of business with an ardor which showed what was in him—with a method which demonstrated how that was to be developed. He copied out bills of exchange, notes of hand, bills of sale, receipts, and all the varieties of the class, which he denominated "Forms of Writing," and these are remarkable for the precision and the elegance with which they are copied. His manuscripts, even then, were of the utmost neatness and uniformity; the diagrams always beautiful; the colums and tables of figures exact, and in unstained and unblotted order. Old Tim Linkinwater would have looked most approvingly over *his* work, and admitted "George" to the awful books of "Cheeryble, Brothers." His excellent historian, Mr. Sparks, who has given us that rarest of all books, a reliable biography, remarks, that these excellent habits of method and order, thus early formed, continued throughout life. His business papers, ledgers, day-books, in which none wrote but himself, were models of exactness. The description of them might apply to those of the most careful bookkeeper in our metropolis. Every fact had its place, and was recorded in a plain, clear handwriting, and there was neither interlineation, blot, or blemish! Frank Osbaldistone's father could have asked no more. Is it any wonder that with such ideas of what the methods of a business man should be, we should find as one of his "Rules of Behavior,"—a code of laws drawn up for his own government, when at the immature age to which we have already referred, and wonderful in their fitness—the following :—

"12th. Let your discourse with men of business be short and comprehensive."

In the 46th. "Undertake not what you cannot perform, but be careful to keep your promise."

These rules—this manifestation of a "business talent,"—were not merely the development of some temporary purpose, but firmly fastened rules of life, which were made to mould his life, and their value to him soon became manifest. He left school at the age of sixteen; and such was his reputation for probity and habits of business—for diligence and habits of dispatch—that several eminent Virginia gentlemen were anxious to secure his services; and he soon became busied in laborious duties, the cares of which found an agreeable relief by the society of his cherished brother Lawrence, at Mount Vernon, a name, whose associations were thereafter to be rendered so glorious. With that brother, in 1751, he left the soil of his country for the first and last time, and made a visit of four months to the West Indies. Throughout all this tour, the traits of character, of which this article is particularly designed to speak, were constantly manifesting themselves. He daily copied the log-book, noted every thing, looked at every thing, and was never idle. When at Barbadoes, the commerce of the Island was one of the subjects, concerning which, he made investigation, and about which, he made appropriate records in his journal.

The time soon came for him to be the actor in the greater scenes of life, and were it within the design of this article to follow his steady advance from one station of usefulness and honor to another, it would only be to point to the same unchanging rectitude, and fidelity to every engagement—the same precise order—the same undeviating exactness. The boy, who had with such care collated and prepared the details of an exercise at school, brought into like order the statistics necessary to be studied before a campaign could be wisely commenced. Every thing that could illustrate the duty of the soldier—the province of the commander—the plan of attack or defence—the topography of the field of battle—was, by his indomitable industry, his steadfast method, brought into a condensed form, that it might be easily grasped by the mind—that "the business" of the war might be well done.

Nor was it in war alone, that the man of order developed himself. We quote, in full, what Mr. Sparks says upon the subject of his conduct in this respect, when President of the United States :—

"During the presidency, it was likewise his custom to subject the treasury reports and accompanying documents to the process of tutuler condensation, with a vast expenditure of labor and patience ; but it enabled him to grasp, and retain in their order, a series of isolated facts, and the results of a complicated mass of figures, which could never have been mastered so effectually by any other mode of approaching them."

From 1759 to 1764, Washington was, in some measure, an acting merchant ; for, in that calmest period of his life—after the brief, but brilliant episode of the Braddock campaign, most honorable to himself, however disastrous to one whose name was more prominent, and before the great drama of the revolution—

he regularly exported to London the product of his large estate on the Potomac. The shipments were made in his own name, and to his correspondents in Bristol and Liverpool, to which places his tobacco was consigned. Are there none of those precious bills of lading yet in existence? They would be valued by many of us, on this side of the water, at least, as evidences of the attention which he gave to all his business.

In return for the articles exported, it was his custom, twice in each year, to import, at that period, from London, the goods which he desired to use; and Mr. Sparks thus delineates how accurately he fulfilled his duties as an importer :—

"He required his agent to send him, in addition to a general bill of the whole, the original vouchers of the shopkeepers and mechanics, from whom purchases had been made.

"So particular was he in these concerns, that he recorded with his own hand, in books prepared for the purpose, all the long lists of orders, and copies of the multifarious receipts from the different merchants and tradesmen who had supplied the goods. In this way, he kept a perfect oversight of the business; ascertained the prices; could detect any imposition, mismanagement, or carelessness, and tell when any advantage was taken of him; of which, if he discovered any, he did not fail to remind his correspondents."

And all this, we must remember, was while he had the charge of the vast estate of Mount Vernon, and while he was dispensing a large and generous hospitality.

When the French war had ended, it became his duty to attend to the settlement of the complicated military accounts of the colony of Virginia, a task arduous enough, but, like all the other duties of his life, faithfully performed.

The war of the revolution left him no leisure for persona.

attendance on his private business, but yet it was never neglected. He could not be personally present; but while the noises of the camp, the preparations for battle, the deliberations of councils, were all shared in to the utmost, his correspondence about his home affairs, were as thorough and minute, as though he had been an absentee of leisure.

His accounts, while engaged in the service of his country, were so accurately kept, that to this hour they are an example held up before the nation. His habits of business enabled him, amidst the tumult of the revolution—its fierce contests—its sufferings and disorders, to so methodize and record all the business incidents of each day, that the end of the war found him prepared to lay before Congress the exact statement of his expenditures. There was about him a pervading principle of order, not of a lifeless, sluggish cast, but life-like and energetic; so that, while every thing was well done, it was done in time and in earnest.

Let any one read his will, and they will rise up from the perusal with the conviction, that a more thorough man of business never lived. There have been many documents of a similar kind, drawn up with wonderful care and labor, and at vast remuneration, by gentlemen learned in the law, but none where every incident is so carefully attended to—not in the spirit of fearfulness of flaws and evasions, and all the thousand munitions of attack to which they resort who "break" wills—but in the orderly, sound, business-like manner, in which a Gresham might have written his projection of an exchange.

But we need point to no isolated instance. His whole life establishes the fact, that a more perfect man of business never lived than was George Washington.

Valueless, indeed, in the comparison, had they stood alone,

would all this method, and order, and industry be. A merchant may have all these, and yet be but sagacious and—unprincipled; but of this man, a nobler record is left to us. I quote only what Thomas Jefferson has said, and *he* spoke certainly with no improper bias:—

"HIS INTEGRITY WAS MOST PURE."

To the merchant of the United States, the example of *Pater Patriæ* has not been, and will not be lost. So prompt to do—so exact in doing—so wise to know what was to be done—so prudent as to what should *not* be done—such unsullied honesty—such pure integrity. These are the qualities that, combined, make up the good and great merchant; and as they were eminent in George Washington, may he not be claimed as well by the merchants, as by the soldiers, or farmers, or statesmen?

80.

A MAN who has any feeling of honor, would rather die outright than become a bankrupt, and any reasonable sacrifice he would willingly consent to. Misfortune is one thing—imprudence another—and knavery the climax. When a man is unfortunate, he is deservedly an object of sympathy. To such, I would say, the moment you find yourself in embarrassed circumstances, and perceive that you cannot extricate yourself, without speculating with what does not belong to you, call a *private* meeting of your creditors, and lay before them the entire state of your affairs. Make a proposition of what you think you will be able to pay, towards the liquidation of their claims, and trust to their generosity to accept it. You will then be taken by the hand by your creditors—get a release—and perhaps, with their kind assistance and advice, become a better man of business than ever you were,—*but keep nothing back.*

81.

In the ports upon our coast engaged in that important branch of American commercial enterprise, the whale fishery, the arrival of a ship from its long voyage to the South Atlantic, or Pacific Oceans, is an exciting event, that often gives rise to scenes of thrilling interest. Sometimes, a ship that has not been heard from for several months, makes its appearance; and of course, the anxiety of those interested is intense, to ascertain her success, and if all her crew have returned in safety.

THE Spring, the quickening Spring's sweet voice,
Runs whispering o'er the ground;
Streams gushing from their chains rejoice,
Young buds breathe sweetness round.
Why pace those groups the sunny shore?
Why climb yon hill-top o'er and o'er?
What wanderers on the dark blue main,
Will Spring's soft breath bring back again?

They linger on the beach—they gaze,
And sigh, as at their feet
The breaking billow moans and plays,
Half sorrowful, half sweet.
A speck appears—"A sail! a sail!
Swelling before the landward gale!
She's large—how high that mast ascends!
A ship! a ship!—our friends! our friends!"

Strain every eye; look long, look far—
She comes, deep laden—low;
The first, full ship—the morning star—
Why move her wings so slow?
Hearts rise, hearts sink—'tis hope, 'tis fear;
The joyous shout, the trembling tear.
What hath time done, on sea or shore?
Will all that parted meet once more?

Her cannon speaks, her streamers swell,
  Abroad her signals fly;
All's well!—she's standing in! *All's well!*
  A hundred voices cry.
How bold, how giant-like her state!
That deep-sunk keel bears costly freight—
Those thunders quick and loud declare
Success and health are regent there.

They land, and meet the long-worn clasp
  Of friendship's welcome hand;
The loud acclaim, the hearty grasp,
  Of hundreds on the strand;
The bursting questions and replies,
Half said, half answered; tears and cries;
The rush for home, the long embrace—
O who such glowing scenes can trace?

Another sail!—no cannon roars.
  No pendants strike the air;
How hushed, how sad she nears the shore!
  Death's angel has been there.
Boats float around—no shouts are heard,
No echoes with rejoicing stirred.
That low flag casts a gloomy shade
O'er decks where death his pall hath laid.

A mother watched the treacherous main
  Long for that ship's return;
A maiden's heart is rent in twain,
  The dismal truth to learn;
Oft on the star-light beach she strayed,
And for the wandering seaman prayed;
Or chid the winds and waves that brought
No tidings of the friends she sought.

Vain was the maid's or mother's tear—
  His lot was bold and brief;
His comrades land, and give no cheer,
  For they have lost their chief.
Thus sounds of mirth, and sounds of wo,
From heart to heart together flow;
And boundless joy and anguish stern
Are mingled when the ships return.

Yet still to *Thee* our souls we raise,
  O Lord of land and sea!
In bliss or wo, the wings of praise
  Shall still mount up to thee.
The wife's glad smile, the mother's tear,
The funeral wail, the welcome cheer,
All rising from the heart's bright urn,
Shall praise Thee for the ship's return.

82.

The time has been, when a verbal contract between two parties would be considered binding. The world since then has changed, and in order to be perfectly safe from loss or injury, I advise my readers to deal with every man and woman, so far as business is concerned, as if they were rogues. They may start, but I state no more than what is necessary to be done. As for friends—with them, still greater precautions are needful. Let nothing of any moment whatever be undertaken without its being first penned down in black and white, and signed in the presence of a witness. You have then some data to go upon, and can right yourself, in case of necessity, in a court of law. A want of attention to these points in early life, cost me some thousands. I paid dearly for my experience, but if I may yet be serviceable to my fellow-tradesmen, the money will not have been altogether thrown away.

83.

THE following is an extract of a letter from the Rev. Mr. Hume, missionary at Bombay, to the editor of the "*Dayspring.*" Mr. Hume says there are about twenty-five thousand Parsees, or followers of Zoroaster, resident in Bombay, and that they consti tute the most intelligent, enterprising and wealthy class of the native population. Our own favored Christendom, (we say it reverently,) is not without its praying merchants, who know how to drive a good bargain :—

"A few days since, I had occasion to go into the shop of a Parsee, with whom I am considerably acquainted. It was in the afternoon, and I found him standing on the steps of his shop, with his face toward the setting sun, busily engaged in repeating his prayers. Many people were passing along the street just before him; but this seemed to cause him no concern, unless when he had occasion to bow to some acquaintance. When I turned to enter his shop, he gave me a very cordial salutation, bowing and waving his hand for me to enter, but all the time repeating his prayers as rapidly as ever. Perceiving that no one was present in the shop to attend to me, he clapped his hands several times, making a loud noise, the object of which seemed to be well understood by the family, as his son, a young man of about twenty years of age, came running into the shop.

"I asked him the price of the article which I had come to purchase; when he, being in doubt, went and inquired of his father, who, with the fore-finger of the right hand, wrote upon the palm of the other the price to be charged. The young man then came back and told what his father had said; but the price being extravagant, I objected to it, and told him what I would give. The young man, not feeling at liberty to act on his own responsibility, went and reported my offer to his father, who shook his head, and again wrote on his hand, as before, a sum considerably less than the first mentioned. The young man again came and stated the price now asked; which being still very unreasonable, I was about to leave, but said I would give him the sum offered at first if he chose to take it. The young man again hastened to his father with my offer, and, as he shook his head at this, I passed out at another door, leaving him repeating his prayers as busily as ever. While I remained, he appeared much interested in what was passing in the shop; and although praying with his face in an opposite direction, he every moment turned so far about as to catch a glance of us, and observe what we were doing.

"The person here mentioned is an intelligent, shrewd business man; but, alas, how blind in regard to spiritual matters! He readily acknowledged that we are indebted to God for every thing; but I have often seen him, early in the morning, bowing reverently in succession to the different articles in his shop, muttering over something at the same time. This is done from a superstitious belief that it may secure him good prices and prosperous business."

84.

The following instance of the unexampled liberality of an English merchant, towards an absconding fraudulent debtor, which originally appeared in the Boston *Post*, is well worth recording in a volume of "*Maxims, Morals and Miscellanies,*" illustrating, as it does, in some degree, the divine principle of "overcoming evil with good":—

"In March, 1846, Andrew V. Leeman, mahogany dealer, London, finding himself embarrassed in his affairs, proceeded to collect all the debts that were due to him, without paying off any. In a short time, he raised full fifty thousand dollars, or over ten thousand pounds sterling. With this sum in his pocket, he took passage for Boston, in the Britannia, in May. His creditors, as soon as his flight was known, attached his effects, and had him decreed a fraudulent bankrupt. Then Mr. W. B. Winter, one of the principal creditors, provided with a record of the judgment against Leeman, started in the Caledonia in pursuit, and upon arriving in Boston, traced him, through Mr. Henshaw, the broker, to whom he had offered some English money for sale. Deputy Sheriff Freeman arrested Leeman, who at once gave up the ten thousand pounds, in Bank of England notes and sovereigns; but in consequence of his former good standing and honorable course as a man of business, Mr. Winter restored to him one thousand pounds, nearly five thousand dollars, and promised to give his wife two hundred and fifty pounds more, when he returned to England."

85.

SYREEN, a custom-house officer at Liverpool, apprehended a woman named Eliza Smith, a passenger on board an American vessel, on suspicion of having smuggled tobacco in her possession. Upon examining her dress, seventeen pounds of tobacco were found concealed under it; but the most remarkable of the expedients which had been resorted to for the purpose of deceiving the lynx-eyed deputies of the customs, was that of giving to the contraband leaf the resemblance of a loaf. A quantity of cut tobacco had been pressed into a tin, over which a thin layer of dough was spread, which, being baked, had the appearance to the eye of a veritable loaf. The quantity of tobacco which the woman had contrived to secret in this, and other modes, amounted to no less than seventy pounds.

86.

"A Sermon of Merchants, preached at the Melodeon, on Sunday, November 22d, 1846, by Theodore Parker, Minister of the Twenty-Eighth Congregational Church in Boston," was published at the time by request. The text, or rather motto, as it has very little to do with the character of the discourse, from Ecclesiasticus xxvii. 2, "*As a nail sticketh fast between the joinings of the stones, so doth sin stick close between buying and selling*," tells a truth, which scarcely loses any of its force, although derived from a portion of the Bible that has been rejected by orthodox authority, as forming no part or parcel of the inspired writings. Mr. Parker points out, in his usual manly, candid, and forcible manner, what he conceives to be the Position, Temptations, Opportunities, Influence and Duty of Merchants. He distributes men into four classes. 1. The men who create new material for human use, either by digging it out of mines and quarries, fishing it out of the sea, or raising it out of the land, as Producers. 2. Men who transform this material into other shapes, fitting it for human use; men that make grain into flour and bread, cotton into cloth, iron into needles or knives, and the like. These indirect producers are classed as Manufacturers. 3. The third class, who simply use these things when thus produced and manufactured, are the Consumers. We come now to the fourth class, the Merchants, who are described by Mr. Parker, as—

"Men who buy and sell; who buy to sell, and sell to buy the more. They fetch and carry between the other classes. These are Distributors; they are the Merchants. Under this name I include the whole class who live by buying and selling, and not merely those conventionally called Merchants to distinguish them from small dealers. This term comprises traders behind counters and traders behind desks; traders neither behind counters nor desks.

"There are various grades of Merchants. They might be classed and symbolized according as they use a Basket, a Wheelbarrow, a Cart, a Stall, a Booth, a Shop, a Warehouse, Counting-room, or Bank. Still all are the same thing—men who live by buying and selling. A Ship is only a large Basket, a Warehouse, a costly Stall. Your Pedler is a small Merchant going round from house to house with his Basket, to mediate between persons; your Merchant only a great Pedler sending round from land to land with his Ships, to mediate between nations. The Israelitish woman who sits behind a bench in her stall on the Rialto at Venice, changing gold into silver and copper, or loaning money to him who leaves hat, coat, and other *collaterals* in pledge, is a small Banker. The Israelitish man who sits at Frankfort-on-the-Maine, changes drafts into specie, and lends millions to men who leave in pledge a mortgage on the States of the Church, Austria, or Russia, is a Pawnbroker and Money-changer on a large scale. By this arithmetic, for present convenience, all grades of Merchants are reduced to one denomination—men who live by buying and selling.

"All these four classes run into one another. The same man may belong to all at the same time. All are needed. At home, a Merchant is a mediator to go between the Producer and the Manufacturer—between both and the Consumer. On a large scale, he is the mediator who goes between continents—between producing and manufacturing States—between both and consuming countries. The calling is founded in the state of Society, as that is a compromise between Man's permanent nature and transient condition. So long as there are Producers and Consumers, there must be Distributors. The value of the calling depends on its importance; its usefulness is the measure of its respectability. The most useful calling must be the noblest. If it is difficult, demanding great ability and self-sacrifice, it is yet more noble. A useless calling is disgraceful; one that injures mankind—infamous. Tried by this standard, the Producers seem nobler than the Distributors; they than the mere Consumers. This may not be the popular judgment now, but must one day become so, for Mankind is slowly learning to judge by the natural Law published by Jesus—that he who would be greatest of all, must be most effectively the Servant of all.

"There are some who do not seem to belong to any of the active classes, who are yet Producers, Manufacturers, and Distributors, by their Head more than their Hand; men who have fertile Heads; Producers, Manufacturers, and Distributors of Thought; active in the most creative way. Here, however, the common rule is inverted: the Producers are few—men of Genius; the Manufacturers many—men of Talent; the Distributors—men of Tact; men who remember, and talk with tongue or pen. Their name is legion."

87.

The Scripture speaketh not in vain in saying, that "the love of money is the root of all evil," for there is not an evil under the sun, to the commission of which men are not prompted by the love of money; and yet, notwithstanding all the light on this subject given in the Scriptures, and confirmed by general experience, men everywhere are occupied in the constant and keen pursuit of wealth, and the prime object with the many is to obtain it, and to push their families forward in the unhappy race of avarice and aggrandizement. For money, men sacrifice domestic comfort, health, character, and even hazard life itself; for it they are guilty of fraud, deception, and robbery. For money, they sacrifice friendship, gratitude, natural affection, and every holy and divine feeling. For money, man becomes a creeping, crawling, obsequious creature, instead of walking erect as the offspring of man. Mammon and Manhood are incompatible. Why all this anxiety about money? Why this constant fever, this pushing and driving in order to obtain it? Even because men form a false estimate of *Life* and its elements. "A man's life consisteth not in the abundance of the things which he possesseth." He who would live, must stir up the divine fire that is in him, to consume selfishness, and to dispense the light and heat to all around. Money he may seek in moderation, as a means, not as an end; and in order to preserve his manhood, he must learn to practise self-denial and economy, and to be contented with small things; above all, he must remember that God has set honor upon his labor, by appointing man to live by labor; labor is truly honorable, and however mean the occupation may be, if honest, it is never disgraceful. Instead, therefore, of sinking Manhood in the pursuit of Mammon, by creeping, crawling, and bending to every one whom you may imagine can help you forward in the race of worldly advancement, stand *erect*, determine in the strength of God to be a MAN, to buy the truth at whatever cost, and never sell it for any price; to labor at any work, if needful, to speak what is in thy heart, and never to creep, and crawl, and mutter. God helps those who help themselves.

88.

WEALTH is desirable, if honestly acquired, and is blessed by contentment.

89.

In all free countries, the merchants have played a distinguished part. In old Venice they were already dukes and princes at a period when the nobility of other lands were military chieftains. Florence owed her wealth and power to her merchants. It was commerce that raised Amsterdam to greatness. The merchants of England sit in her House of Lords, and hold the destinies of the realm in their potent hands. In fact, as civilization advances, commerce asserts her rightful claims to superior consideration over the rude and often unlettered military chieftain; and the men who develop the resources of a nation, and increase intelligence, as well as add to its physical comforts, are deservedly ranked highest as benefactors of mankind. It would be a curious study to trace, if we had time, the struggle in England between the mercantile interest and the landed aristocracy, the one seeking to obtain its due weight in government, the other laboring to keep down its aspiring rival. But the merchant, in the end, conquered the feudal baron. And had it not been for her merchants, England would long since have succumbed in one or another of her foreign wars. But for their gigantic resources, freely placed at the service of the State, Napoleon would have burnt her dock-yards and pulled down Westminster Hall.

The character of the *true* merchant deserves all of this eulogium. But in speaking of the merchant, we allude to the liberal and intelligent commercial man, not to the mean and narrow-minded. A merchant of enlarged views, like the late Abbott Lawrence, of Boston, has no superior in any walk of life; and there are men of the same stamp in other cities, though, perhaps, it would be indelicate to name them here. Such a man, especially if engaged in a foreign trade, is really better informed for all the higher purposes of legislation, and has altogether more comprehensive views, than most of our professed statesmen. His business relations force him to keep up with the changes in other countries. He must know the settled and unsettled condition of their governments, their native products and manufactures, the habits and mode of life of the people, else he cannot make shipments with any prospect of success. In the late difficulty with Brazil, when all persons begun to inquire respecting that empire—and we must say that the general ignorance regarding Brazil, considering its immense resources, and the fact that it is the United States of South America, is very reprehensible—the shipping merchants were the only class of our citizens who could furnish any correct account of the people and government there. We would give more for the opinion of an able merchant on any affair relating to our foreign relations, than for that of all the lawyers, politicians, and professed statesmen we have, if we except one or two illustrious names.

So of our merchants of intelligence engaged in the Western trade. They do not confine themselves to the mere acquisition of a fortune, to the amassing cent per cent, but enlarge their minds by a knowledge of the peculiarities and resources of the great West. Their business frequently calling them abroad, they have opportunities to compare the social condition of Europe with that of America, the relative progress of inventions in each, the spread of intelligence, the extension of liberal principles, and all those other great questions in which every generous and observing mind may be presumed to take an interest. Unfortunately, all do not avail themselves of these advantages. There are, and we speak it with regret, merchants who neglect those occasions for improving the mind and heart, who make money their god, and who spend a long life with every energy devoted solely to acquiring that gold which is only to be a subject of quarrel among their descendants. Such persons are like crazed wanderers, passing through a pleasant country, and taking no note of the beautiful scenery around, so intensely are they absorbed in their childish and foolish thoughts ; or, like the man in the Pilgrim's Progress, who raked among dust and ashes for dross, while an angel overhead vainly offered him a golden crown. For nothing is more true, than that an undivided attention to the acquisition of wealth stifles our social sympathies, debases the intellect, and lays up, as the scriptures solemnly express it, "much store of sorrows" for after days. The man who makes himself a slave to money, wins for his prize the Dead Sea apple—"golden without, but ashes within."

90.

There is no economy like that which saves interest, nor loss like that which pays it at high rates. Let a man owe a few thousand dollars at interest at two or three per cent. a month, and it imperceptibly uses him up. He labors and finds the load returning with increased force. It almost always turns out with money borrowers much worse than they expected. The reason is, that now, things are so managed by having monthly or short payments of interest, that it is constantly compounded. Whether the man who receives it compounds it or not, it is compounded to the borrower. We have frequently watched the silent crushing weight of this invisible compound. What is building up Wall street, New York, State street, Boston, and Third street, Philadelphia, with the massive private banking houses with which all those streets are ornamented? What built up the mighty fortune of the Rothschilds, and all the other great bankers of the world? Per cent. did it. The insignificant, as it looked, one per cent., or half per cent. exchange, with the et ceteras, like clustering drops, fed the stream which poured its millions into their treasuries. Per cent. is the controlling business of the age, and if allowed to creep on will own the world. Let a man worth one hundred thousand dollars borrow twenty-five thousand at three per cent. per month for two years—we have heard of even worse than this—he pays the interest monthly, and thus is deprived of the use of the money. It is the same as if compounded, for if he pays two per cent. the interest money would be worth that to him, too. Then at the end of two years he has paid out in usance a sum about equal to the whole capital borrowed. What business, with losses incident to trade, will bear such a drain? Such a thing is scarcely possible. Bankruptcy is almost its inevitable end. The same is true to a greater or less degree as the rate may be higher or lower. The injunction can not be too frequently impressed on individuals as well as on cities and States, to avoid debt and all large rates of interest. They almost invariably end in ruin.

91.

Two dry goods merchants, one in Cedar and the other in Chatham street, both of whom had failed some six or eight years since, and compromised with their creditors for about fifty or sixty cents to the dollar; having been since then doing a successful business, at the close of the old year they waited on their old creditors, unexpectedly to them, with checks for the whole deficiency, with interest, in one instance; and for one-half the deficiency, with interest, in the other. The dry goods merchants, in the above cases, only acted in accordance with the principles of true moral honesty.

92.

John Grigg, of Philadelphia, began his career as Bookseller and Publisher in the house of Benjamin Warner, which was engaged in a very extensive business.

A biographical sketch of Mr. Grigg in the "*Merchant's Magazine*," gives some interesting details of his marked life, and furnishes pertinent commentary and illustration for our "*Maxims and Morals.*"

"Mr. Warner," says his biographer, "seems to have been a man of quick appreciation of character. He at once conceived a high opinion of Mr. Grigg's character and abilities. Mr. Warner was a *Friend*, and a friend, indeed, in every sense, he proved to his young clerk, who at once entered his house, and justified the flattering opinion of his employer, by the characteristic energy and clearness of head which he brought to bear upon his new pursuit. Versatility is said to be an American characteristic, and few men have possessed it more strongly than Mr. Grigg. The readiness of adaptation to new pursuits, situations and emergencies, which made him efficient in each of the varied callings with which within a few years he had already made himself familiar, marked his career through life. It was his favorite opinion that all difficulties can be overcome by perseverance—that no man or boy can tell what he can make of himself until he tries. He made it a rule of life when difficulties appeared, to clap on double energy, and like Hercules, to rely upon the strength of his own shoulders to get the wagon out of the ditch.

He had need of all his own resources of character in the calling which he had adopted. But it was the last change of pursuit he was to make. He had found a business whose range of operations suited his abilities and ambition. The difficulties of the bookselling business are said to be peculiarly great. This is the consenting opinion of those familiar with it; and it is obvious how much tact and discrimination, sagacity and careful study of the public taste, it requires. So connected is it with Literature, that a mistaken literary judgment may involve the most serious business consequences. Dazzling projects, which on paper give assurance of brilliant results, when put in execution prove worse than failures. It was not, however, until a few years later, when he had worked his way up to the higher walks of his business, that these qualities were called out into most active exercise. But the same energy which was displayed in the more responsible station to which he soon attained marked his performance of the humbler duties of a clerk. This devotion, this determination to do "whatever his hands found to do" "with all his might," whether as clerk, or as principal, as Banker, Manufacturer, Clerk of Court, or Publisher, is the secret of his success —of all success in business. The late William Gray, of Boston, in his days of opulence, was tauntingly reminded that he had once been a drummer. His quick retort contains volumes of the practical philosophy taught by such lives as his and Mr. Grigg's. "Didn't I drum well, though."

Mr. Grigg has always been remarkable for strength of memory. One of his feats at this time, was to learn the name of every book in the store, its price, and the place where to find it, so that he was able, at once, to lay his hand upon it when called for. It was thus he commenced his clerkship. In a few days, this readiness and aptness began to excite the jealousy of an older clerk, since deceased, who was nominally above the last comer; and his own emulation was chafed at a superiority in position in the establishment of those who were inferior to him in fact. To avoid these unpleasant feelings, Mr. Warner proposed a journey to Virginia, for the purpose of settling the affairs of a firm in that State, with which his house was connected, and which had been dissolved by the death of one of the partners. This commission Mr. Grigg gladly undertook. How successfully he performed this duty, every duty belonging to the new calling which was to be the business of his life is best shown by the testimony left by Mr. Warner, on his death, a few years after. A memorandum was found attached to his will, which contained a legacy more valuable than gold, a legacy of *golden opinion.* Taking into view the possibility of his business being continued after his death, he thinks "one or two young men in whom confidence can be reposed" might be found to take charge of it, and adds, "I consider John Grigg as possessing a *peculiar* talent for the bookselling business. *Very industrious*, and from three years observation, (the time he has been employed in my business,) I have found nothing in his conduct to raise a doubt in my mind of his possessing correct principles." Praise like this is the noblest of rewards, the most stirring of incentives.

The executors of Mr. Warner could not do otherwise than confide to one in whom he expressed such high confidence, and so explicitly pointed out as his successor, the settlement of the affairs of the firm. Nor was this a slight undertaking. The business of the house had been immense: connected with it were numerous agencies and branches, it had dealings with various houses at the South and West, and the settlement of it rendered frequent journeyings necessary. During one of those journeys, an incident occurred which is too characteristic of the days of stage-coach traveling, and of the determined energy of Mr. Grigg's character to be omitted. He was at Charleston. It was the latter part of December, 1825, and by Christmas day he must be in Philadelphia. He pushed forward, traveling day and night; at Baltimore, the steamboat which usually connected was found to have left off running, and the travelers were forced to take to the mail-coach. But every seat was full when Mr. Grigg arrived; there was no alternative for the determined traveler, weary and excited as he was by incessant journeying for seven long days and sleepless nights, but to ride outside with the driver. The day, or rather the night, was cold, the air was full of sleet, the road miry. But to the driver's seat he mounted and pushed on. At Havre de Grace another driver took the reins, who was unacquainted with the road; it was long after dark, and the "insides," who began to be fearful of their necks as the coach plunged and tossed in the mire, grew clamorous for putting back until morning. But Mr. Grigg was determined that the stage should go a-head and be in Philadelphia by Christmas day, and besides, they carried the mails, and a public conveyance must not be delayed! So he procured a lantern, and going before the coach, piloted the travelers through the darkness and mire, for about two miles. Finally mounting the box again, he took the reins into his own hands, and daylight saw the delighted travelers, arrived at Elkton, and well on their way. They at once admitted him to a seat inside, upon their knees. And early on Christmas morning Mr. Grigg *was* in Philadelphia.

On another of these journeys Mr. Grigg was suddenly taken very sick at Lexington, Kentucky. He was staying at the house of a friend, on his way home. He was too sick to stand, but not, as he thought, or was determined to think, too sick to travel. His will was stronger than disease, and no dissuasion could turn him from his fixed purpose of going forward. So he was carried from the house to the stage-coach, at his *express* request, laid on the bottom of the coach, and in this rough sort of ambulance, he pushed on to Philadelphia with soldierly fortitude. There is something too much like rashness in such zealous devotion to business, to make it altogether a safe example; but it will be appreciated by every merchant whose spirit has been vexed and patience wearied by the delays, the loiterings on the road for which their traveling agents and clerks are fond of making a pretext out of the slightest illness, and in which they are oftentimes ready to indulge, without the decency of any pretext at all.

It is with such energy that Mr. Grigg has performed the journey of life. At the end of the first year a statement of the business of the firm, as conducted by him, was exhibited to H. C. Carey, Esq., who had been appointed by the parties in interest to advise with the executor. Mr. Carey, whose undoubted ability as a Political Economist is combined with the practical ability of the business man, also, on examining the balance exhibited by the statement, expressed the unqualified opinion that no business had ever been managed with more tact and skill than this complicated estate. As early as November, 1823, Mr. Grigg succeeded in completely settling up the affairs of the firm.

He was now once more without fixed occupation, but not, as before, without means; above all, not without experience, which is better than money. He had not only saved something, but had mastered the details of a difficult branch of business. For an instant, however, Mr. Grigg seems to have been undetermined what course to pursue. Conversing at this time with a friend, Joseph Cushing, Esq., of Baltimore, he explained his situation, and laid before him his prospects. "Rely on yourself," said his friend, "you cannot fail to succeed. You will yet astonish yourself and the book trade of the whole country." The next day

Mr. Grigg hired a store, with lodging apartments back of it, and commenced the business of book selling on his own account.

Thus prudently and carefully did he set about the fulfillment of this prophesy. How brilliantly it has been verified, the entire book trade of the country can testify. Upon the same spot where he began, Mr. Grigg conducted his business with ever increasing success and widening range of operations. The genius and enterprise of its head pervaded the house, and all its operations were conducted with that unity of aim and effect, which a commanding mind knows how to give to the most multifarious details, and to impress upon all who come within its range. Nor was the influence of this almost military promptness and efficiency of operation confined to his own house. Mr. Grigg became noted among his brethren for his peculiar faculty. A nervous energy, a rapidity of calculation and resolution, a promptness to act marked his entire course.

He possessed, in short, a kind of *mercantile intuition.* In a very recent letter, from Lebanon, Ohio, where, as we have seen, Mr. Grigg passed many of his early years, another of the friends of his youth, whose friendship, like Mr. Corwin's, has been life-long, presents, in a very striking manner, these traits of his character. "He comprehends at the first glance," writes A. H. Dunlevy, Esq., of Lebanon, "business matters in all their bearings, direct and remote, and astonishes you with the quickness with which his opinion is formed, and that, not to be changed. The judgment thus formed almost always proves correct," and he is thus enabled to "dispose of his affairs as they come up without their accumulating on his hands, and by this means has been able through life to dispatch a greater amount of business than almost any other man, without any apparent severe labor. Another prominent trait in his character has been his open candor and unwavering integrity. He was ever faithful to himself and to others *in avowing his opinions or fears in relation to their business*, and hence he made fewer bad debts, in his extended business than almost any one else in like circumstances."

The change which Mr. Grigg effected in the book trade of the country, has been described as nothing less than a revolution. Constable, the famous bookseller of Edinburgh, Sir Walter Scott's publisher and partner, was fond of calling himself the "Napoleon of the realms of print," a compliment to himself hardly justified, except by the boldness, bordering on rashness, of his operations. Mr. Grigg's friends had better reason, in many respects, for bestowing, as they were sometimes in the habit of doing, the same honor upon him, for to boldness and rapidity he united cool and clear judgment, the quick eye to look *a-head before going a-head.*

Through the financial tempest of 1836 and 1837, Mr. Grigg steered his course safely and successfully, and although engaged in a business of vast extent during the whole perilous financial period from 1833 to 1840, was among the few, who suffered little by the revulsions of the times. He was largely interested in stocks and other species of property most liable to be affected. But he saw from afar the dangers which were threatening the business of the country, and his quick foresight early anticipated the inevitable issue of the unequal contest between the Government and the United States Bank. He promptly took measures to change his investments from stock to real estate, and became the owner of large properties in Mississippi and Illinois, as well as in Philadelphia. When the shock of the crisis came, his foot was on the *ground*, and, he stood firm.

Mr. Grigg has not, we thus see, entirely confined himself to the line of his peculiar business. Men of wealth never show a truer public spirit, than when they step forward to aid with hand and purse a great public enterprise in its infancy. Public works are, for the most part, anything but attractive investments, at the outset, and it is oftener a case of self-sacrifice than of self-interest to invest money in new projects of this kind. Mr. Grigg was an early and prompt friend and large subscriber to the stock of the Pennsylvania Railroad, a work of the same interest and importance to Pennsylvania, as the Erie Railroad is to the State of New York, and the national value of all these great works connecting the sea-board with the West, need not to be enlarged upon. We have already referred to the circumstances under which Mr. Grigg was induced to invest largely in real estate. Philadelphia is indebted to him for numerous elegant dwellings which adorn her beautiful streets. Besides the real estate investments in Mississippi, in 1836, he entered extensive tracts of the public lands in the Sangamon country, Illinois, of which he has from time to time sold large portions. In his dealings with the numerous purchasers of his land, Mr. Grigg's uniform fairness and liberality have made him universally popular, an exception to the general rule as to non-resident land-owners, who are by no means favorites at the West.

93.

Property purchased on credit is a deposit place in your hands, which it would be fraudulent for you to use in any manner so as to endanger the interests of your creditors. Flattering prospects of gain in this way sometimes occur; but they too often prove delusive, and leave the rash adventurer under an insupportable load of responsibility. Debts are sacred, and every honest man will do every thing in his power to discharge his obligations, with punctuality and honor.

94.

THE following eloquent passage is from a speech of the Hon. Reverdy Johnson, of Maryland, at the complimentary dinner given in 1847, to the Hon. Mr. King, of Georgia, by the New York merchants.

"Commerce, in every age of the world, has been the chief pioneer in the march of man's civilization. Unlike the achievements of war, the track of commerce is ever to be traced by the blessings which follow its footsteps. It travels over no blood-stained fields to secure its noble ends; it brings man not into deadly strife with man, but into friendly and harmonious association. Its conquests are not heralded by tidings of fierce, and deadly, and demoniac conflict; no blood stains its triumphs; no human agony has it to answer for. It works by far different and immeasurably better means. It removes local prejudices—breaks down national antipathies—and binds the whole family of man together by the strong ties of association, and of mutual and dependent interests.

"In all the elements, then, of true greatness, how inexpressibly superior are the peaceful and social influences of commerce to all that is generally accomplished by the pride, pomp and circumstances of war. The one showers upon the world wealth and felicity—humanizes and civilizes man; the other riots in blood, misery and desolation. War is, to be sure, at times inevitable; but man's wickedness makes it so. There have been occasions, and may be again, when it becomes a virtue. A nation's freedom is sometimes only to be secured by it. Our own history furnishes a noble and glorious example of this. We had a warrior, chosen by Heaven, to fight for and to win our freedom; and in doing so, he won for himself an immortality of fame. The name of Washington will continue to live, as long as there remains upon earth a vestige of virtue and knowledge. But such struggles are of rare occurrence; and, for the most part, how limited is the number of those whom war has rendered immortal!

> "Of all the bones have whitened battle fields,
> How very few live in the chronicle?"

95.

A MERCHANT should be an honorable man. Although a man cannot be an honorable man without being an honest man, yet a man may be strictly honest without being honorable. Honesty refers to pecuniary affairs; honor refers to the principles and feelings. You may pay your debts punctually, you may defraud no man, and yet you may act dishonorably. You act dishonorably when you give your correspondents a worse opinion of your rivals in trade than you know they deserve. You act dishonorably when you sell your commodities at less than their real value, in order to get away your neighbor's customers. You act dishonorably when you purchase at higher than the market price, in order that you may raise the market upon another buyer. You act dishonorably when you draw accommodation bills, and pass them to your banker for discount, as if they arose out of real transactions. You act dishonorably in every case wherein your external conduct is at variance with your real opinions. You act dishonorably if, when carrying on a prosperous trade, you do not allow your servants and assistants, through whose exertions you obtain your success, to participate in your prosperity. You act dishonorably if, after you have become rich, you are unmindful of the favors you received when poor. In all these cases there may be no intentional fraud. It may not be dishonest, but it is dishonorable conduct.

96.

Our views have become so completely identified with the commercial matters of the age, that on taking up a new book, especially of travels, we run our eye over its pages to see if we can find anything that will be likely to interest the mercantile reader; and our estimate of the value of a work is apt to depend very much upon the information it contains pertaining to subjects connected with trade and commerce. Running over the pages of Mrs. Butler's (formerly Fanny Kemble) "Year of Consolation," published in 1847, we find a few passages of her experience of the morality of shopkeeping, &c., in Rome. Mrs. B. says:—

"English people are the only honest trades-people that I am acquainted with, and I say it advisedly; for Americans are unpunctual, and an appointment is a contract with time for its object, and they are as regardless for the most part, of that species of contract, as of some others of a different kind. I have now been six months in Rome, and have had leisure and opportunity to see something of the morals of retail trade; at any rate, in matters of female traffic, among the shopkeepers here. In the first place, the most flagrant dishonesty exists with regard to the value of the merchandise, and the prices they ask for it of all strangers, but more particularly of the English, whose wealth, ignorance, and insolence, are taxed by these worthy industrials without conscience or compassion. Every article purchased in a Roman shop, by an English person, is rated at very nearly double its value; and the universal custom here, even among the people themselves, is to carry on a haggling market of aggression, on the part of the purchaser, and defense, on that of the vender, which is often as comical as it is disgusting. In Nataletti's shop, in Rome, the other day, I saw a scene between the salesman and a lady-purchaser, an Italian, that would have amazed as well as amused the parties behind and before the counters of Howell & James, Harding's, etc. The lady, after choosing her stuff and the quantity she required, began a regular attack upon the shopman ; it was *mezza voce*, indeed, but continuous, eager, vehement, pressing, overpowering, to a degree indescribable ; and the luckless man having come for a moment from behind the shelter of his long table, the lady eagerly seized him by the arm, and holding him fast, argued her point with increasing warmth. She next caught hold of the breast of his coat, her face within a few inches of his, her husband meanwhile standing by and smiling approvingly at the thrift and eloquence of his wife ; I think, however, she did not succeed. The shopman looked disgusted, which I am afraid is a consequence of their having adopted the English mode of dealing in that house, as they themselves informed me, to signify that they did not cheat, lie, or steal, but dealt like honest people. I felt proud of his manner of speech : 'Madame, nous avons adopte la maniere Anglaise ; nous vendons au prix juste, nous ne surfaisons pas, et nous ne changeons pas nos prix,' so that to deal in the English fashion is synonymous to dealing justly. It pleases me greatly, and it is true ; for, in France, too, they have abandoned the abominable system of prices for the English ; and it delights me to think that integrity, justice, truth, cleanliness, and comfort, follow in the footsteps of my own people wherever their wandering spirit leads them through the world. It is very fit and just that they should bring such compensations to the foreign people, among whom they so often introduce, also, habits of luxury, of ostentation, and that basest habit of bartering for money the common courtesies and amenities of life, the civilities and the serviceableness which are priceless, which the continental people have, and our own have not, and which we should have learnt to imitate rather than taught them to sell. I may as well mention here, that I have found Nataletti's shop the best in Rome, in every respect. In one morning's shopping, the other day, we had two or three curious instances of the shopkeeping morality here: going into Gagiati's, in the Corso, the great omnium gatherum, or, as the Americans would call it, variety store, they first attempted to cheat my sister upon the change due to her for some gold she gave them; I was looking at some fans which were being shown to an Italian purchaser at the same time; I had taken up one, which the shopman told me was worth eighteen scudi; the Roman buyer took up another, which had been shown me at the same price, and with sundry 'nods and becks and wreathed smiles' at the shopkeeper, said, in an under tone, 'Dunque quindici?' the latter nodded, returned the significant pantomime, and adding, 'Eh! capite.' I capited too, and, perceiving that I was attentively observing what was going on, the salesman took the fan I had in my hand, and without uttering a syllable, said, 'Ebbene, Signora, seidici scudi;' 'but,' said I, 'a moment ago, you told me the price was eighteen.' 'Oh!' exclaimed he, with the most dauntless impudence, 'se piace a lei di pagar dieci otto va bene e padrona.' I was so utterly disgusted, that I laid the commodity down without another word. Further on, we bought some tin pails and water-buckets for our bed-rooms in the country. At one shop, I was made to pay nearly three scudi for that which my sister purchased immediately after for a scudo and a half a little distance further on, and she no doubt paid, as an Englishwoman, much more than the goods were worth. We then proceeded to a perfumer's for some hair pomatum—we had already repeatedly purchased the same thing at the same place. On this occasion, however, we were charged an additional paul upon each small article, and upon remonstrating, and stating that we had repeatedly bought the same thing at the same place, and always paid such a sum for it, the shopman replied, 'Yes, that was true, but now they had altered the price;' a sort of *ad libitum* mode of dealing, which may be pleasant and mournful to the souls of the venders, but is mournful alone to those who buy. Of truth, and its inviolable sacredness, the Italians generally seem to have as little perception as the French; and dishonesty and falsehood are so little matters of shame, that detection in either of them only excites a shrug and a grin on the part of the offender."

97.

During the "panic" in the money market some few years ago, a meeting of merchants was held in the Exchange, to devise ways and means to extricate themselves from their pecuniary difficulties. The great hall was crowded, addresses were made, resolutions passed, committees appointed, and everything done that is usual and necessary. After all this, one of the company moved that the meeting stand adjourned until some future day, when up jumped a little jobber, in a great state of excitement, and requested the merchants to linger a moment, as he had something of the greatest importance to communicate. The jobber was known to be a very diffident person; and, as he never ventured on the responsibilities of speaking on any former public occasion, all were anxious to hear what he had to say.—"Gentlemen," said he, with evident emotion, and in the most emphatic, feeling and eloquent manner, "what's the use of talking of some *future* day? We want relief, I tell you!—*immediate* relief!" and down he sat amidst a universal roar of laughter. *The next day he failed!*

98.

See now ascending, amid the overwhelming plaudits of the andience and the orchestra, a young man of pale and interesting countenance, with an immense profusion of uncombed black hair, lending romantic disorder to an appearance in every way peculiar. This is young Lostiswitz, and he turns towards the immense assemblage which greets him, while he gracefully endeavors to remove the hair out of his eyes in order to survey them. Still he ascends and they applaud, and still he labors to behold them through the struggling curtain of dark hair maze. But at length he has reached the rostrum of the conductor. All is at once as still as death. On him, the hero of that evening, every eye is bent. Many already have poured forth the soul tribute of tears. His modest demeanor wins all hearts. And now he waves his baton, and the breathless silence is broken by the first stroke of the orchestra, (the chord of .he 1-2-3-4-5-6-7-8-9-0,) struck by the whole band *staccatissimo Fiff*, with the unity of a single gun.

A pause ensues. Then there begins a plaintiff, warbling strain on the oboe, accompanied by the ophicleides and one gong. This marks the first entrance of the boy-man into mercantile life. The lingering remembrances of his boyish sports and pleasures (graphically depicted by the touching accents of the oboe in E major) are brought effectively into contrast with the rough rebukes and reproaches of the senior clerk, conveyed by the bassos in C minor. Want of punctuality and inaccuracy in the details of business are now sharply urged against him by the violins, in staccato passages *contretemps*. He submits with becoming modesty to this censure, in a holding note on the second bassoon. But his mind presently rallies; he girds himself up for his daily task; he is sensible of a divine energy; and now a strict fugue is led off by the tenors, and grows upon the ear through all the forms of harmonic proportion, self-evolving, infinite, yet regular. This proclaims new habits of business, exactness in accounts, well-kept books, and general exemplary conduct. Years roll on, accompanied by the violoncello; the youth wins the approbation of his superiors—the man is a partner in the firm! Vainly, my dear friend, should I endeavor to convey to you the least adequate conception of the exquisite and finely-preserved graduations by which the picture poem, sculpture music expresses to the sense of the spectator, auditor, *crescendo poco a poco*, the commercial progress of its youthful hero. With this noble climax the first movement concludes.

After a short pause, needed alike by the audience and the performers to recruit their spirits, exhausted by excitement, a grateful *Pastorale* movement commenced, indicating that degree of comfortable independence and rural excitement which are the fruits of well-regulated industry, when the time-earned blessings of competence have placed within reach of the successful partner a small house and grounds in the suburbs, unfurnished, with other conveniences. Every morning at nine o'clock, after a moderate, but excellent breakfast, we see him driving into town in G major, *allegro* two fours. Every evening at five we see him returning to dinner on the dominant.

I observed more than one commercial man in the room, who had passed through all the usual stages of mercantile life, yielding himself up to the delusion of the moment, and reveling in associations rekindled among the embers of existence by the spell of the spirit ruler. Every mind was conscious of a secret regret when the last note of this movement expired. It was to them as the going down of an autumnal sun—bright, but prophetic of no genial return.

Now followed an *adagio no poco prestissimo, piano quasi forte, senza tempo,*—by far the most sui-general and future-age-anticipating portion of this divine work. Lostiswitz has here displayed that deep insight into the principles of instrumentation which gives him the extraordinary superiority he at present enjoys over contemporary composers as a combinationist.

This movement commences with a trio for two serpents and an octave flute, indicative of extensive commercial embarrassment, and so skilfully has the composer applied the resources of his genius to the subject before him, that, with this simple machinery, the whole process of what appears a complicated bankruptcy is brought before the mind with startling reality, insomuch, that it may be doubted if in a country like England, this portion of the symphony would not require considerable modification, in the event of its performance there. The failure of correspondents, the blockade of the Mexican ports, rumors of the plague at Alexandria, the consternation of clerks and accountants, the presentation of bills for payment, the impetration of renewal, the galling insolence of minacious creditors,—all these things told, and were told with such effect that a powerful sensation of alarm pervaded the whole house, in the midst of which Herr ——, of the firm of —— & Co., was carried out in a state of suspended animation. At length a calm ensues; the assets are found sufficient to prevent injury to credits, confidence revives, orders pour in, and all again is harmony and prosperity. Then comes the grand finale.

A brisk *Allegro* in triple time denotes the accumulation of money in the three per cents; but this movement gradually assumes a statelier style and loftier measure, as honors succeed to riches; and at length, the freedom of the city having been presented in a complimentary *Andante* of four horns, not without a neat and appropriate reply from the double bass, and a prince of the blood royal having proposed for the sixth daughter in a subsequent bar, the whole of this prodigious work is brought to an end on a sustained dominant, equally remarkable for the novelty of its sequences and the perfect propriety of its matrimonial arrangments.

99.

"A VERY elegant tea-service, of rich plate, was presented, on New Year's day, in 1840, with appropriate ceremony, to a merchant in New York, who had been unfortunate in business; but, on his return to prosperity, paid off his creditors, principal and interest. The inscription on the tea-urn, as follows, records the honorable testimony:—

"Presented to WILSON G. HUNT, by John Haggerty, William Adee, and Joseph Corlies, in behalf of themselves and his other creditors; who, in the year 1832, (satisfied that his insolvency was occasioned by misfortunes in trade,) accepted a compromise of their claims, and gave him a complete release from all legal liability; as a testimonial of their high respect for his just sense of the *moral obligation of contracts*, as evinced by the payment, in the year 1839, of the balance of their respective claims, principal and interest; an act reflecting honor on himself as a merchant, and proving him one of the noblest of the Creator's works—an *honest man*."

What honest man would not prefer the "tea-service," with its honest inscription, to the gains of trade "kept back" from the creditors, although the debtor was released from the *legal* discharge of his indebtedness?

100.

We find the following interesting account of the mode of conducting business arrangements in a dry-goods store in Philadelphia, in the columns of a Southern Journal. Precision in such matters begets thrift and prosperity, and we hope the precepts of the annexed article may be universally carried out in business communities :—

The amount of sales made at this store, is about three hundred thousand dollars annually ; each department in the store is alphabetically designated. The shelves and rows of goods in each department are numbered, and upon the tag attached to the goods, is marked the letter of the department, the number of the shelf and row on that shelf to which such piece of goods belongs. The cashier receives a certain sum extra per week, and he is responsible for all worthless money received. Books are kept, in which the sales of each clerk are entered for the day, and the salary of the clerk cast, as a per centage on each day, week and year, and, at the foot of the page, the aggregate of the sales appears, and the per centage that it has cost to effect these sales, is easily calculated for each day, month or year. The counters are designated by an imaginary color, as the blue, green, brown, etc., counter. The yard-sticks and counter-brush belonging to it, are painted to correspond with the imaginary color of the counter ; so, by a very simple arrangement, each of these necessaries is kept where it belongs ; and should any be missing, the faulty clerks are easily known.

All wrapping paper coming into the store is immediately taken to a counter in the basement, where a lad attends with a pair of shears, whose duty it is to cut the paper into pieces to correspond with the size of the parcels sold at the different departments, to which he sees that it is transferred. All pieces too small for this, even to the smallest scraps, are by him put into a sack, and what is usually thrown away by our merchants, yields to this systematic man some twenty dollars per year. In one part of the establishment is a tool-closet, with a work-bench attached ; the closet occupies but little space, yet in it we notice almost every useful tool, and this is arranged with the hand-saw to form the center, and the smaller tools radiating from it in sun form ; behind each article is painted, with black paint, the shape of the tool belonging in that place.

It is, consequently, impossible that anything should be out of place except through design ; and if any tool is missing, the wall will show the shadow without the substance. Such is the salutary influence exerted by order, that those who enter this employ habitually careless and reckless, are reformed entirely ; and system, which before was irksome, has become to them a second nature. The proprietor's desk stands at the farther end of the store, raised on a platform facing the front, from which he can see all the operations in each section of the retail department. From this desk run tubes, connecting with each department of the store, from the garret to the cellar, so that if a person in any department, either porter, retail or wholesale clerk, wishes to communicate with the employer, he can do so without leaving his station. Pages are kept in each department to take the bill of parcels, together with the money paid ; and return the bill receipted, and change, if any, to the customer. So that the salesman is never obliged to leave the counter ; he is at all times ready either to introduce a new article, or watch that no goods are taken from his counter, excepting those accounted for.

His peculiar method of casting the per centage of a clerk's salary on his sales, enables him at all times, (coupling it with the clerk's general conduct, and the style of goods he is selling,) to form a just estimate of the relative value of the services of each, in proportion to his salary. By the alphabetic arrangement of departments, numbering of shelves, and form of the tools, any clerk, no matter if he has not been in the store more than an hour, can arrange every article in its proper place, and at any time, if inquired of respecting them, or referred to by any clerk, the proprietor is able to speak understandingly of the capabilities and business qualities of any of his employees. He has brought up some of the best merchants at present engaged in the trade, who do honor to the profession as well as their tutor.

101.

What caused his failure? THIS is the first interrogatory propounded by both friend and creditor, when the Insolvent's misfor tune becomes noised abroad.—The answer given to this one question, by a warm hearted friend may be as different from the one given by a suffering creditor as light is from darkness. But the answer of neither friend nor creditor may explain the cause—the cause must be explained by one who has neither friendship to bias nor loss to influence his opinion. Then, what is the cause of his failure? or rather, why did he fail? That which has been the cause of the failure of the man or firm now in the mind's eye, has been the cause of the failure of nine-tenths of the Insolvents in every Commercial City in the world. The cause may be succintly stated by the employment of a commercial phrase; he did not "post up" himself, in the matters and details of his business, as a good Accountant would Journalize and Post the transactions of the firm.

A good Accountant can turn to his Ledger and inform him

self, or employer, of the amount of stock on hand at the date of the last "stock taking," the amount purchased since taking account of stock, the amount sold, and the balance, that should be, in amount, of the stock on hand, (less, as a matter of course, the amount of gross profits made on the amount sold;)—the amount of Cash on hand at stock taking, the amount since received, the amount expended, and the balance on hand;—The amount of Bills Receivable on hand at stock taking, the amount since received, the amount paid in, on account of said Bills, together with the amount that has passed in payment of the firm's indebtedness, and the balance remaining on hand;—The amount of Bills Payable, (which must, as a matter of course, include accepted drafts,) running at the time of stock taking, the amount since given in liquidation or on account of the firm's indebtedness, (or for accommodation) the amount expended in the redemption of said Bills, and the amount (balance) still running:—The amount paid for Expenses since stock taking, (such as rents, salaries, gas, fuel, etc.)—The amounts paid and received for Discounts, Interest, etc., and the balance against or in favor of the firm:—The amount of losses sustained since stock taking, the amount received on account of debts that had previously been charged to Profit and Loss, and the balance against or in favor of the firm:—And lastly, the amounts of Debit and Credit, of Individual balances, the former of which, if not looked to with an earnestness that shall lead to the adoption of measures for the securement of every cent, will lead to failure, sooner or later.

These ascertainments can be given by a good Accountant, monthly, fortnightly, or even weekly, in a weekly, fortnightly, or monthly "Trial Balance," which should be so prepared as to give the head of the firm a "birds-eye" view of every unbalanced account on his Ledger.—This should be taken home by the business man, to be read and pondered over, when his mind is free from the perplexities of pressing calls on his attention to this and that and the other minutiæ of active business life.

To be thus kept apprized of his affairs, the business man must employ a competent Bookkeeper, if he is not one himself and has leisure to attend to that part of his business—this will cost him from one thousand to fifteen hundred dollars a year, but that amount may be more than saved by the head of the firm being made better qualified to direct each branch of his affairs, in a business like manner.

It is for the want of correct information of their own standing, and consequently of the qualifications necessary to direct business operations, THAT SO MANY FAIL.

102.

A GENTLEMAN of Charleston, (S. C.,) who was unfortunate in business thirty years ago, and consequently unable, at that time, to meet his engagements with his creditors, after more than twenty years of toil, succeeded in paying every creditor, (except one whose residence could not be ascertained,) the whole amount due them. He has, in that twenty years, brought up and educated a large family, but he still owed one of his former creditors. He was not satisfied to keep another's property—he made inquiry, and received information that the party had died some years since. He again pursued his inquiry respecting the administrator, and ascertained his name and residence, wrote him, acknowledged the debt, and requested him to inform him of the manner he would receive the money. A few weeks since, he remitted the whole amount, principal and interest.

103.

THERE are few propositions respecting which mercantile men are more unanimously agreed than that which affirms the inexpediency and folly of what are called the usury laws; and the tenacity with which our different legislatures adhere to their interdict of the freedom of trade in this article of money, is a striking instance of the propensity of our legislators to trammel trade with laws which it must either violate or sink under.

The argument against the propriety of legislative interference to regulate the rate of interest appears to us so conclusive and unanswerable, and has been so repeatedly and clearly set forth, not by money-lenders so much as by money-borrowers, who may be presumed to have understood what the interests of trade demand, that we are amazed that the whole system of usury laws has not long since been blotted from the statute-books of every State in the Union.

It has been justly urged, that it is plainly in no respect more desirable to limit the rate of interest than it would be to limit the rate of insurance, or the prices of commodities. And though it were desirable, it cannot be accomplished. The real effect of all legislative enactments having such an object in view, is to increase, not diminish, the rate of interest. When the rate fixed by law is less than the customary or market rate, lenders and borrowers are obliged to resort to circuitous devices to evade the law; and as these devices are always attended with more or less trouble and risk, the rate of interest is proportionably enhanced.

Fixed rates of interest are absurd, because the value of money is constantly varying, being subject to the same law that regulates other articles. Everybody who notices the daily newspaper reports can see for himself that no market is more fluctuating than the money market. At one period and in one state of things money is worth twice as much as at another time and in another state of things. Unless the legislature can stay *all* the fluctuations of trade, it is idle to think of singling out the article of money, and insisting that that shall command a uniform price.

Other considerations enter into the contract between the borrower and lender affecting the just premium for the use of money. The rate will of course depend, in a measure, upon the security given. In proportion as that is doubtful, should the premium rise. The lender must be compensated for the risk he incurs, as well as for the use of his funds, and it is right and reasonable that he should be.

In short, the laws to which we are objecting are destitute of all sound basis. They are unreasonable, impracticable, oppressive to those whom they profess to protect, embarassing to legitimate trade, and an unwarrantable restriction upon every man's freedom. For these and other reasons they ought to be abolished.

104.

In a lecture by the late Judge Hopkinson, of Pennsylvania, delivered before the Mercantile Library Associations of Philadelphia and New York, in 1839, and originally published in the *Merchant's Magazine*, at the time, occurs the following passage :—

"As a summary of the doctrines I desire to impress upon you, let me add, that debts contracted in the indulgence of extravagant and unbecoming luxuries, or in the pursuit of rash and desperate adventures, are a violation of the sound principles of mercantile integrity ; that the true merchant will thoroughly qualify himself for his business by a patient and systematic preparation, and will depend upon the regular operations of legitimate commerce for his profits, which, though more slow, are finally more sure and lasting than the fluctuating gains of speculation ; that if misfortune and bankruptcy should fall upon him, he will meet them promptly and manfully, and not attempt to gain a few lingering, anxious days of credit, for himself, by drawing his friends into the vortex of his ruin, and extending it to others, who may, unwittingly, continue to trust him. He will rather at once surrender into the hands his creditors shall choose to hold the trusts for them, all the property in his possession or power, unencumbered by selfish stipulations for his own benefit, undiminished by any concealment, or by assignments or transfers to favorites of any description."

105.

The late William Oliver, of Dorchester, Mass., who died in 1847, left the whole of his property, valued at not less than *a hundred thousand dollars*, to be divided equally between the Perkins Institution for the Blind, at South Boston, and the McLean Assylum for the Insane, at Somerville. One-third of this sum was to be paid over immediately, and the remainder at the decease of his two sisters. Mr. Oliver commenced life as a poor boy, and acquired his property by his prudence and energy in mercantile pursuits. One hundred thousand dollars was the amount he fixed upon as the extent of his wishes in early life ; and when he had made that sum, he retired to his country residence in Dorchester, and passed the summer and autumn of his days in unceasing, but unostentatious benevolence.

106.

One of the most important lessons to be impressed upon business men, says the "*Independent*," and especially upon young men who are seeking their fortune, amid the intense competition of city life, is a sober estimate of the value of character above wealth. It is natural to men to create factitious distinctions in society. In every form of political society, except the republic, such distinctions exist by birth or in permanent civil and ecclesiastical orders. Pride is nurtured and vanity gratified by blood, or family, or title, or inherited rank. But such distinctions are precluded in a republic, by its very constitution. Hence, there remains but one basis of social distinction, namely, wealth. In limited circles, indeed, there may be an aristocracy of talent, of education and refinement, of literature or science, but in society at large, gradations of social position are measured by stock-certificates, rent-rolls, and bank-accounts. In the old world a patent of nobility holds good, though there is no income adequate to sustain it; and a penniless count stands higher in the social scale than the untitled millionaire. Here the appearance of wealth is the passport from circle to circle. Office is uncertain, and does not always dignify the holder. It cannot be retained for life, much less transmitted to descendants. Hence, wealth has gained an importance far beyond that which belongs to it where it is used only to keep up an estate, to display rank, to enjoy life, to procure the advantages of education and of travel. Here it creates rank; it gives social position, even without antecedent respectability or correct education; and hence pride and vanity, that in other countries have so many and various outlets, here crowd into this one channel, and either fill it to its utmost level, or agitate it with eddies and contentious waves. In this city, especially, the feeling is universal, that to be anybody, or to do anything, one must have wealth. New York is as full of idols as Athens was when it was easier to find a god there than a man; nor do the objects worshipped in the two cities differ except in form. For what do men here worship if it be not *stocks* and *stones*? With wealth in view as the one great object in life, upon which every thing else depends, it is not strange that many grasp at the prize without any scruple as to the means.

In the upper circles of fashionable life no questions are asked how one came by his money, if he only shows that he has money, or appears to have it. If he lives in a fine house, keeps a good carriage, gives splendid parties, no questions are asked as to whether all this is honestly paid for. With such a standard before them, it is not surprising that aspiring men, who feel themselves in other respects the equals, if not the superiors of their wealthy neighbors, should find some short road to wealth. The passion for riches, the idea that success in life depends mainly upon wealth, is fruitful in temptations to dishonor. "For they that *will be* rich fall into temptation and a snare, and into many foolish and hurtful lusts, which drown men in destruction and perdition; for the love of money is the root of all evil; which while some coveted after, they have erred from the faith, and pierced themselves through with many sorrows."

This is the maelstrom of character in our city. Men will be rich, they must be rich; they put forth on the sea of speculation, they reach after every floating straw of prosperity, they give themselves to the giddy passion of money-getting, and are whirled everywhither by its power. Smoothly they ride at first on the giddy outskirts of dishonesty, till infatuated with the pursuit, they dive deeper and deeper, and are sucked into the mighty vortex—a wreck of character, fortune, hope, and life. The only safeguard is to hug the shore of honesty. Make *character* supreme.

So strong is the infatuation of wealth among us, such the glare of wealth above character, such the imputed disgrace of poverty, that even feminine delicacy will come out from the retirement of private life to resent the imputation of poverty before marriage as a greater grief than a husband's fraud; and the newspapers must publish to the world that, whatever robberies a man may be charged with, his wife was never guilty of the stupendous crime—or being "a *poor* girl." We transgress no rule of propriety in thus adverting to what is matter of public advertisement. We offer no censure upon individuals. But is it not pitiable to see from such volunteer exposures of high life, how wealth and character stand respectively in the estimation of many who make our society? The influence of such false pride is baleful in the extreme. Is it not worth to any woman more than gold to say, "However poor I or my family may have been, my husband is an honest man!"

107.

In every transaction, let the terms and conditions of the bargain be understood BEFOREHAND; and if important, put in writing; and in cases at all doubtful, insist on a guarantee.

Be not afraid to ask this; it is the best test of responsibility; for, if offence be taken, you have in all probability escaped loss. He who is in fact responsible, will like you the better for being thus guarded; for he knows he is dealing with a man of prudence, who looks to the end of things, and may therefore expect to be well served. You may always protect yourself by simply insisting on security. "Once well begun is twice done."

108.

WITHOUT this distinguishing mark of true manhood, we fail in securing either the happiness of ourselves or others. Without ENERGY, a man becomes a drone in society, a nonentity in the world. There are special occasions in the life of every man, when he needs to fall back upon the natural energy of his nature. Do afflictions, sad and grievous, weigh him down and seem to crush him to the earth? Let him remember that this is but the "cup" which his Divine Master has given him—the "furnace" which is to purify his soul, and fit him for the heavenly rest hereafter. Rise then! afflicted man! Put forth the energy you possess, and soar above your sorrows. Perhaps your business cares are such as to cause you many anxious days and sleepless nights. The times are hard, money is almost out of the question, and you feel like folding your arms and giving up in despair. We hear of such cases every day. Don't look upon the *dark* side of the picture! Keep moving! If you fail of success in one place—try another, and give yourself no rest till you triumph.

The world is large enough for us all, and as the song goes—

> "Uncle Sam is rich enough
> To give us all a farm."

Remember that the world does not contain a briar or a thorn, that divine mercy could have spared. These very briars and thorns which encompass you, are the instruments which will try the energy of your character, and settle your capacity to fulfil the mission of life. To all then, we say, suffer no feeling of despondency to weigh you down. Rise triumphantly above all your sorrows and troubles, and you will make the world better and happier for having been born into it.

109.

It affords us pleasure to call the attention of the readers of our "*Maxims*" to a treatise on Moral Philosophy, that exhibits the principles and enforces the obligations of morality in all their perfection and purity—a work that furnishes a true and authoritative standard of rectitude—by an appeal to which the moral character of human actions may be rightly estimated. Such, in our opinion, is the character of "*Essays on the Principles of Morality, and on Private and Political Rights and Obligations of Mankind.*" Jonathan Dymond, the author, was a member of the Society of Friends, or Quakers, and wrote these essays whilst engaged in active business as a linen draper, in London. He died quite young, in the spring of 1828, leaving in manuscript three essays on the above subject.

Rejecting what he considered the false grounds of duty, and erroneous principles of action, which are proposed in the most prominent and most generally received theories of moral obligation, he proceeds to erect a system of morality upon the only true and legitimate basis—the WILL OF GOD. He makes, therefore, the authority of the Deity the sole ground of duty, and His communicated will the only ultimate standard of right and wrong; and assumes that, "wheresoever this will is made known, human duty is determined; and that neither the conclusions of philosophers, nor advantages, nor dangers, nor pleasures, nor sufferings, ought to have any opposing influence in regulating our conduct."

The attempt to establish a system of uncompromising morality must necessarily bring the writer into direct collision with the advocates of the utilitarian scheme, particularly with the celebrated Dr. Paley; and, accordingly, it will be found that he frequently enters the lists with this great champion of expediency. In thus attempting to controvert a system of moral philosophy, dubious, fluctuating, and inconsistent with itself, into a definite and harmonious code of ethics, the author undertook a task for which, by the original structure of his mind, and his prevailing habit of reflection, he was, perhaps, peculiarly fitted. He had sought for himself, and he endeavors to convey to others, clear perceptions of the true and the right; and, in maintaining what he regarded as truth and rectitude, he shows everywhere an unshackled independence of mind, and a fearless, unflinching spirit. The work is evidently the result of a careful study of the writings of moralists, of much thought, of an intimate acquaintance with the spirit and genius of the Christian religion, and an extensive examination of human life in those spheres of action which are seldom apt to attract the notice of the meditative philosopher.

The author, in proceeding to illustrate his principles, evidently sought as far as might be, to simplify the subject, to disencumber it of abstruse and metaphysical appendages, and rejecting subtleties and needless distinctions, to exhibit a standard of morality that should be plain, perspicuous, and practicable. On the subject of Insolvency the work discourses after this manner:—

"Why is a man obliged to pay his debts? It is to be hoped that the morality of a few persons is lax enough to reply—Because the law compels him. But why, then, is he obliged to pay them? Because the Moral Law requires it. That this is the primary ground of the obligation, is evident; otherwise the payment of any debt which a vicious or corrupt legislature resolved to cancel, would cease to be obligatory on the debtor. The Virginian statute, which we noticed in another essay, would have been a sufficient justification to the planters to defraud their creditors.

"A man becomes insolvent and is made a bankrupt: he pays his creditors ten shillings instead of twenty, and obtains his certificate. The law, therefore, discharges him from the obligation to pay more. The bankrupt receives a large legacy, or he engages in business and acquires property. Being then able to pay the remainder of his debts, does the legal discharge exempt him from the obligation to pay them? No: and for this reason, that the legal discharge is not a moral discharge; that as the duty to pay at all was not duty founded primarily on the law, the law cannot warrant him in withholding a part.

"It is, however, said, that the creditors have relinquished their right to the remainder by signing the certificate. But why did they except half their demands instead of the whole? Because they were obliged to do it; they could get no more. As to granting the certificate, they do it because to withhold it would be only an act of gratuitous unkindness. It would be preposterous to say that creditors relinquish their claims voluntarily; for no one would give up his claim to twenty shillings on the receipt of ten, if he could get the other ten by refusing. It might as reasonably be said that a man parts with a limb voluntarily, because, having incurably lacerated it, he submits to an amputation. It is to be remembered, too, that the necessary relinquishment of half of the demand is occasioned by the debtor himself; and it seems very manifest that when a man, by his own act, deprives another of his property, he cannot allege the consequences of that act as a justification of withholding it after restoration is in his power.

"The mode in which an insolvent man obtains a discharge, does not appear to effect his subsequent duties. Compositions, and bankruptcies, and discharges by an insolvent act are in this respect alike. The acceptance of a part instead of the whole is not voluntary in either case; and neither case exempts the debtor from the obligation to pay in full if he can.

"If it should be urged that when a person entrusts property to another, he knowingly undertakes the risk of that other's insolvency, and that, if the contingent loss happens, he has no claims to justice on the other, the answer is this; that whatever may be thought of these claims, they are not the grounds upon which the debtor is obliged to pay. The debtor always engages to pay, and the engagement is enforced by morality; the engagement, therefore, is binding, whatever risk another man may incur by relying upon it. The causes which have occasioned a person's insolvency, although they greatly affect his character, do not affect his obligations: the duty to repay when he has the power, is the same whether the insolvency were occasioned by his fault or his misfortune. In all cases, the reasoning that applies to the debt, applies also to the interest that accrues upon it; although with respect to the acceptance of both, and especially of interest, a creditor should exercise a considerate discretion. A man who has failed of paying his debts ought always to live with frugality, and carefully to economize such money as he gains. He should reflect that he is a trustee for his creditors, and all the needless money which he expends is not his, but theirs.

"The amount of property which the trading part of a commercial nation loses by insolvency, is great enough to constitute a considerable national evil. The fraud too, that is practised under cover of insolvency, is doubtless the most extensive of all species of private robbery. The profligacy of some of these cases is well known to be extreme. He who is a bankrupt to-day, riots in the luxuries of affluence to-morrow; bows to the creditors whose money he is spending, and exults in the success and impunity of his wickedness. Of such conduct we should not speak or think but with detestation. We should no more sit at table, or take the hand of such a man, than if we knew he had got his money last night on the highway. There is a wickedness in some bankruptcies to which the guilt of ordinary robbers approaches but a distance. Happy, if such wickedness could not be practised with legal impunity! Happy, if public opinion supplied the deficiency of the law and held the iniquity in rightful abhorrence!

"Perhaps nothing would tend so efficaciously to diminish the general evils of insolvency, as a sound state of public opinion respecting the obligation to pay our debts. The insolvent who, with the means of paying, retains the money in his own pocket, is, and he should be regarded as being, a dishonest man. If public opinion held such conduct to be of the same character as theft, probably a more powerful motive to avoid insolvency would be established than any which now exists. Who would not anxiously (and therefore, in almost all cases, successfully) struggle against insolvency, when he knew that it would be followed, if not by permanent poverty, by permanent disgrace? If it should be said that to act upon such a system would overwhelm an insolvent's energies, keep him in perpetual inactivity, and deprive his family of the benefit of his exertions—I answer, that the evil, supposing it to impend, would be much less extensive than may be imagined. The calamity being foreseen, would prevent men from becoming insolvent; and it is certain that the majority might have avoided insolvency by sufficient care. Besides, if a man's principles are such that he would rather sink into inactivity than exert himself in order to be just, it is not necessary to mould public opinion to his character. The question, too, is not whether some men would not prefer indolence to the calls of justice, but whether the public should judge accurately respecting what those calls are. The state, and especially a family, might lose occasionally by this reform of opinion—and so they do by sending a man to New South Wales; but who would think this a good reason for setting criminals at large? And after all, much more would be gained by preventing insolvency, than lost by the ill consequences upon the few who failed to pay their debts.

"It is cause of satisfaction, that, respecting this rectified state of opinion, and respecting integrity of private virtue, some examples are offered. There is one community of Christians which holds its members obliged to pay their debts whenever they have the ability, without regard to the legal discharge.* By this means, there is thrown over the character of every bankrupt who possesses property, a shade which nothing but payment can dispel. The effect, (in conjunction we may hope with private integrity of principle) is good—good, both in instituting a new motive to avoid insolvency, and in inducing some of those who do become insolvent, subsequently to pay all their debts.

* "Where any have injured others in their property, the greatest frugality should be observed by themselves and their families; and although they may have a legal discharge from their creditors, both equity and our Christian profession demand, that none, when they have it in their power, should rest satisfied until a just restitution be made to those who have suffered by them. And it is the judgment of this meeting, that monthly and other meetings ought not to receive collections or bequests for the use of the poor, or any other services of the society; of persons who have fallen short in the payment of their just debts, though legally discharged by their creditors; for until such persons have paid the deficiency, their possessions cannot in equity be considered as their own."—*Official documents of the yearly meeting of the Society of Friends.*

"Of this latter effect many honorable instances might be given: two of which having fallen under my observation, I would briefly mention. A man had become insolvent, I believe, in early life; his creditors divided his property amongst them, and gave him a legal discharge. He appears to have formed the resolution to pay the remainder, if his own exertions should enable him to do it. He procured employment, by which, however, he never gained more than twenty shillings a week; and worked industriously and lived frugally for eighteen years. At the expiration of this time he found he had accumulated enough to pay the remainder, and he sent the money to his creditors. Such a man, I think, might hope to derive, during the remainder of his life, greater satisfaction from the consciousness of integrity, than he would have derived from expending the money on himself. It should be told that many of his creditors, when they heard the circumstances, declined to receive the money, or voluntarily presented it to him again. One of these was my neighbor; he had been but little accustomed to exemplary virtue, and the proffered money astonished him; he talked in loud commendation of what to him was unheard-of integrity; signed a receipt for the amount, and sent it back as a present to the debtor. The other instance may furnish hints of a useful kind. It was the case of a female who had endeavored to support herself by the profits of a shop. She, however, became insolvent, paid some dividend, and received a discharge. She again entered into business, and in the course of years had accumulated enough to pay the remainder of her debts. But the infirmities of age were now coming on, and the annual income from her savings was just sufficient for the wants of her declining years. Being thus at present unable to discharge her obligations without subjecting herself to the necessity of obtaining relief from others; she executed a will, directing that at her death the creditors should be paid the remainder of their demands: and when she died they were paid accordingly.

"A young man under twenty-one years of age purchases articles of a tradesman, of which some are necessary and some are not. Payment for unnecessary articles cannot be enforced by the English law—the reason with the legislature being this, that thoughtless youths might be practised upon by designing persons, and induced to make needless and extravagant purchases. But is the youth who purchases unnecessary articles with the promise to pay when he becomes of age, exempted from the obligation? Now it is to be remembered, generally, that this obligation is not founded upon the law of the land, and therefore, that law cannot dispense with it. But if the tradesman has actually taken advantage of the inexperience of a youth, to cajole him into debts of which he was not conscious of—the amount or the impropriety, it does not appear that he is obliged to pay them; and for this reason, that he did not, in any proper sense of the term, come under an obligation to pay them. In other cases, the obligation remains. The circumstance that the law will not assist the creditor to recover the money, does not dispense with it. It is fit, no doubt, that these dishonorable tradesmen should be punished, though the mode of punishing them is exceptionable indeed. It operates as a powerful temptation to fraud in young men, and it is a bad system to discourage dishonesty in one person by tempting the probity of another; the youth, too, is of all persons the last who should profit by the punishment of the trader. He is reprehensible himself: young men who contract such debts are seldom so young or so ignorant as not to know that they are doing wrong."

110.

The world is too apt to judge of men by their success or failure in their business relations, and in this, the world again shows that "its wisdom is foolishness." It is and must be evident to the most unobserving—we mean those whose hearts and very souls are not bound up in money, who do not worship Mammon, who have not bent the knee to the golden image of themselves, (the calf) who know no relative distinction between man and man, except the bare possession of wealth, obtained from success in business, that the preponderance of good qualities, those which bring a man sympathizingly nearer to his fellow being, that make him a better citizen, neighbor, parent and friend, are possessed in a greater degree by the unsuccessful, than by those who have met with no reverses of fortune.

Of course, our remarks are not intended to apply to those who have failed in life, from being addicted to vicious courses and idle, dissolute pleasures ; but we mean those who have been unsuccessful, from a lack of the requisite boldness, tact and perseverance in business pursuits, which generally arise from a spirit of covetousness and an overpowering desire to amass wealth.

How often do we not observe men, who possess every ennobling qualification, talented, intellectual, humane, brave and kind, that are beset by pecuniary difficulties and surrounded by poverty ; while others, who are not fit to untie the latchets of their shoes, are rolling in wealth, like the hog in his mire ! How often do we not hear the trite old proverb repeated, of "a fool for luck." These men amass money, they hoard and lay up thousands on thousands, they die, rot and are forgotten. They know not the use of the means God gave them, the time, health and opportunity to acquire. They seemed not to be aware that it was the rightful property of the Great Master of the Universe, of whom they were only stewards. They understood not, that it was merely put under their care for noble and great uses; but hugged the flattering unction to their souls, that it was gained and achieved by their own personal wisdom and untiring industry; that to them is due the praise of having exhibited a superior shrewdness and deeper cunning in its attainment; and with their hands thrust deep into their pockets, they strut their brief career on this petty scene of existence, arrogating to themselves, as they look with scornful eye upon their poorer brother, the Pharasaical conceit, "I am better than thou."

Could these men but know and feel how really pitiful they were; how they have thrown away and trampled upon the nobler qualities of the soul, how they have lost time and converted talent to the ignoble purpose of the mere amassing of that dross, the bare possession of which causes a silent, but fervent aspiration for the termination of their mortal careers; they would not be so apt to pride themselves on the result of their toil.

We cannot do better than to close this essay with the following truthful and telling sentences, uttered by Mr. Geo. Hilliard, of Boston, before a large and intelligent audience. They are worthy of being stored up in the memory and garnered in the heart.

"I confess that increasing years bring with them an increasing respect for men, who do not succeed in life, as those words are commonly used. Heaven has been said to be a place for those who have not succeeded upon earth; and it is surely true that celestial graces do not best thrive and bloom in the hot blaze of worldly prosperity. Ill success sometimes arise from a superabundance of qualities in themselves good—from a conscience too sensitive, a taste too fastidious, a self-forgetfulness too romantic, a modesty too retiring. I do not go so far as to say with a living poet, that 'the world knows nothing of its greatest men,' but there are forms of greatness, or at least of excellence, which 'die and make no sign;' these are martyrs that miss the palm, but not the stake; heroes without the laurel, and conquerors without the triumph."

111.

Having taken possession of your premises, let your first care be to insure them, as well as your stock in trade, against fire. This is one of the duties most incumbent upon a young tradesman. If the house which he inhabits, as well as all the goods in his shop, were positively his own, (that is to say, were actually paid for,) it would be one of the most absurd things upon earth to neglect the means of providing a remedy against the overwhelming consequences of fire, more especially when such remedy is attainable without the slightest difficulty or trouble. But in the other, and more common case, where the goods are not *morally* his own, inasmuch, as his creditors have not been paid for them, the neglect of this precaution becomes absolutely *criminal*. If a tradesman who has obtained goods upon *credit*, hesitates or neglects to insure them against fire, and they should afterwards be consumed, and he be unable to pay for them in consequence, however much others may mince the matter, the simple fact will be, that he has negatively robbed those who confided in him. Neglect this precaution, and I should feel no pity for you if your stock and furniture were all destroyed by fire!

112.

NOT many years ago, the father, in placing his son at school, used such language as this: "I wish my boy to learn arithmetic and writing; but I do not care about his studying any foreign language, or to take up his time with history; for I am going to make a merchant of him." The lad, intended for the store, did spend his time on the multiplication and interest tables; he did learn to write and read, and these, many merchants can bear testimony, closed his school career. How many a man can recollect when he bade adieu to his schoolmates for the last time, and felt he was committing but a frail bark to the tempestuous world, as the school door closed behind him forever. Just at the time that he was beginning to feel some interest in his studies, because he was beginning to understand them, he was cut short of any further instructions, and turned into the counting-house, to sigh for the green play-ground, his merry school-fellows, and perhaps, for daily tasks which, when completed, made his mind spring with elastic joy. But his easy dress must undergo a change also. The round jacket must give place to a premature long-tailed coat; the easy shoe to the high-heeled boot; the open shirt collar to the starched cravat. With the feelings of a boy, but the dress of a man, he is forced, at the tender age of fourteen, to lay aside his affections and assume ceremony; to be polite where he wishes to love; to smile when he longs to laugh; to walk consequentially, when he longs to run and shout. His tastes, too; what a sacrifice! He loved flowers, the fragrant hay, the breath of spring, the noise of the spring freshet, which told him that the snows were melting on the hill-sides. Instead of these, he has the smell of tar, docks, and foreign spices. Perhaps his employment is in a store where South American hides are stored for sale. Here, he holds his nose, at first, in deep disgust; but habit is second nature, and he, after a while, can face even this like a man; but, as he opens the store of a warm, summer morning, he is forced to say to himself, "This being a merchant is not what it is cracked up to be, after all." Poor boy! thy education is just begun. Many years of dry, profitless toil are before thee; many long walks with heavy bundles, wearying thy arms, unused to any weights but thy light bat and ball, or gaily painted fish pole; perchance thy curiously ornamented gun, stored away in charge of thy fond mother, now far from thee in thy dear, rural home—you will survive all this, and, by and by, forget those thoughts that now bring thy heart almost into thy throat, and to repay thee, thy own name will stand in gilded letters over the door from which thou now sweepest the blinding dust of commerce. Courage!

We know it is easy to pick flaws in almost any system of education; but we appeal to all thinking men if the training young boys receive, who intend to follow trade as their occupation, it is not necessarily incomplete and shallow? To begin with: very many are obliged to resort to the city writing master, after they have commenced their clerkship, to make up for deficient practice at school. Not a few get their knowledge of accounts and book-keeping by sad experience of errors, which cost their employers much more than tuition fees. But these are slight matters, compared with others we have to mention. The lad, fitting for the store, is only taught those branches which will enable him to perform the duties of his place. His intellectual powers, his tastes, his habits of mind, are viewed as of little consequence. It seems to be forgotten, that he must have leisure hours to employ; times when, unless he is doing something good, he will find something evil to occupy him. It is forgotten that he is a tender, impressible being, open to all influences about him, and, as a youth, liable to be caught with syren songs and gilded baits. If he reads will he turn to history or biography? No, he has no taste for such studies; he was educated to be a merchant. What will be his reading? Most probably, some highly-wrought novel, which will inflame his passions and give him a romantic turn. Does he read Latin or French in his leisure hours? Oh no, these are forbidden books to the young clerk; dead languages to him, paying no interest, teaching nothing about buying and selling, taking his attention from the solid branches, the useful branches. Alas! what can he do in such a case but read novels or go to the play, or learn practical geometry on a billiard table? At this last employment he learns *angles* with a vengeance, and forgets often, on his way home from such a resort, the mathematical principle, "that a straight line is the shortest distance between two points."

It is rather remarkable that so much of human effort is bestowed upon reforming evils which might have been prevented in the outset. After an alarming conflagration, that burns down a large part of the city, an efficient fire police is established. After an epidemic has got strong hold of the citizens, the mayor looks carefully to the cleansing of the streets. Churches are built, and ministers are fed, to reclaim the vicious man whose early youth was neglected; and finally a system of public lectures is going on in all our cities, to teach men and women the elements of history and science, which they ought to have learned at school. And, in this last specific, the solid food has been given in moderate doses, well disguised in declamation and flowery language, for fear of nauseating the patients, weak with long fasting.

The fact to which we allude is strikingly illustrated in the whole course of education. We send our children to cheap schools, sometimes to the district school, where teachers are hired for about the wages of the man who sweeps the streets, where they are taught bad pronunciation, slovenly reading, and riddles in arithmetic, and then, if they set about obtaining anything like a complete education, much time and labor must first be spent in unlearning, reforming, and getting a fair start. But little care and expense is bestowed upon the lad who is destined for the store, because the parent hopes that his education will some how or other be completed by running of errands, doing up parcels, and going to the post office.

And, strange enough to tell! it is finished in this hap-hazard way; and the young man, after a few years, returns to the home he left—a raw country lad, a polished gentleman. His dress is faultless, his manners are easy, his conversational powers quite the wonder of the village maidens. How is this? Where did he acquire his language, his fund of information, his ready wit and store of sparkling anecdote? In the world, to be sure; by mixing with his fellows, talking, walking the streets, keeping his eyes open, and learning to observe.

Was it ever your good fortune, kind reader, to fall in with a city-bred lawyer, merchant, doctor or mechanic, in a stage-coach, on a long journey? and did he not enliven your otherwise tedious ride, and appear to you like a being from another world, by the side of silent country squires, who stand so much upon their dignity? If such has been your luck, you can readily understand how a free intercourse with men of all ranks and professions, how the rude bustle of the city streets, their noise and life, educate and inform, and give life to the mind.

It is no wonder that city folks and city clerks are so bright and amusing, for they are forced to employ their faculties, if i:

be for nothing else, to keep out of the way. Here is no stagnation, no apathy, no time for castle-building ; it is all reality, life, action, and self-preservation. Where else in England, than in busy London, could Charles Lamb have found materials for his inimitable essays ? How happens it that our best poets, Sprague and Bryant, live in the very din of the world's noise, unless there is a kind of inspiration in it ?

It may seem that we argue against ourselves in showing the valuable education of city life ; in stating that men, with little book learning, in a few years become polished, agreeable, and amusing. This is the bright side of the picture—the shading will come presently. It is not stating the truth too strongly to say that America is proud of her merchants. In fact it is another name for gentlemen among us. Whether in the church, the legislative hall, the drawing-room, the home, they suffer not in comparison with any men in the land. We are a mercantile people, a trading nation, and why should not our merchants stand first and foremost in every enterprise ? But—we are bound in conscience to speak the truth—many young men are ruined in our cities yearly, for lack of a better early training of the intellect and the heart. Thousands fall a prey to dissipation and vice, because they have no taste for quiet and studious pursuits. Their business being over for the day, they seek that relaxation, in forbidden pleasures, which the fireside, the library, the literary circle should furnish. And the error is, that young lads intended for mercantile life, are not well educated. We have as good as acknowledged that they can get along very well, as far as business and appearance and social intercourse are concerned without a very complete education, but there is something more concerned besides these. There is a moral nature at stake—a soul, a heart, affections and habits.

The literary societies in the city are doing an immense deal of good, and remedy, in part, the evil to which we allude. But it will not be questioned that something more may be done, away back of the period when these are brought to bear upon the young mind. To reap the advantages of the fine libraries now open to the young merchant, he must receive an early training which will fit him to appreciate and enjoy the books that otherwise will be dead letter to his eyes. Who could read and enjoy Milton as his first book of poetry? Who would understand Silliman's Journal, that had not paid any attention to the natural sciences? Will the lyceum, the lecture-room, the debating-hall, furnish their full advantages to him who begins his education in places designed to polish, perfect, and keep fresh the mind? The answer to these questions grants the point we would urge—a better primary education for those intended for mercantile life.

113.

The Life and Times of Jacques Cœur, the French Argonaut, was published in London in 1847. It contains the only notice, we believe, in English, of the great French merchant and financier of the middle ages, during the reigns of Henry V. and VI., in England. The London *Examiner* thus states the leading facts in the life of Jacques Cœur:—

"It was the money of Jacques Cœur which enabled the French to profit by the genius and enthusiasm of Joan of Arc; and it was his honest sympathy, and steady, manly counsel, which seems to have sustained the tender and brave heart of the noblest of royal mistresses, Agnes Sorel, in her efforts to save the king. On her death, she selected him for her executor. He had sprung from the people, and raised himself, by successful commercial enterprise, to a level with the princes of his age. He found French commerce behind that of every other nation, and left it prosperous and increasing. Direct and speedy communication with the East seems to have been his great idea. Modern Europe is still contending for it. He had at one time, in this employment, three hundred factors; and the rest of the merchants of France, with the whole of those of Italy, are not supposed to have equaled this one man in the extent of their commercial dealings. *As rich as Jacques Cœur*, became a proverb It was even rumored and believed that he had found the philosopher's stone. And he proved worthy of his wealth by giving it noble uses. He raised three armies for Charles at his own cost; and he repaired and re-established, in his office of *Argentier*, the deranged finances of the kingdom. But his weakness seems to have lain in the direction of personal magnificence and splendor, and to this we may trace his fall. He did not allow sufficiently for the prejudices of his age, and at last armed them for his ruin. He is described to have far transcended, in his personal attendance and equipments, the chiefs of the most illustrious families of France; and when Charles made his triumphal entry into Rouen, the merchant, Jacques Cœur, was seen by the side of Dunois, with arms and tunic precisely the same as his. His destruction was planned by a party of the nobles, and an indictment of all sorts of crimes preferred against him; among them the charge of having poisoned Agnes Sorel. He narrowly escaped torture and death; and only this by confiscation of his treasures (which his judges divided among them) and perpetual banishment. The latter resolved itself ultimately into a sort of strict surveillance in a French convent, which he at last escaped by the fidelity of one of his agents, who had married his neice. He was again characteristically engaging in active pursuits, and beginning life anew as the Pope's captain-general, on the coast of Asia Minor, when illness seized him in the Island of Scio. He left, in his death, another example of the world's treatment of its greatest benefactors."

From the memoir, we make a single extract in regard to the commercial enterprise of the great French merchant:—

"In the course of twenty years, Jacques Cœur had more commercial power than all the rest of the merchants of the Mediterranean put together. Three hundred of his agents resided at the different ports, not only of Europe, but of the East, and in all the nations contiguous to France. Everywhere his vessels were respected, as though he had been a sovereign prince; they covered the seas wherever commerce was to be cultivated, and from farthest Asia, they brought back cloths of gold and silk, furs, arms, spices, and ingots of gold and silver, still swelling his mighty stores, and filling Europe with surprise at his adventurous daring, and his unparalleled perseverance. Like his great prototype, Cosmo de Medici, who, from a simple merchant, became a supreme ruler, Jacques Cœur, the Medicis of Bourges, became illustrous and wealthy, and sailed long in the favorable breezes of fortune, admired, envied, feared, and courted by all.

"His wealth gave rise to a proverb, long retained by the citizens of his native town: 'As rich as Jacques Cœur,' expressed all that could be conceived of prosperity and success. Popular tradition asserts that, so great was the profusion of the precious metals that he possessed, that his horses were *shod with silver*; a common reputation, even at the present day, enjoyed by persons of singular wealth. The adornment of Bourges, where he was born, was not one of the least projects of the great merchant; and having, with a large sum, purchased a considerable tract of land in the town, he began, in 1443, to build that magnificent mansion which still remains a noble relic of his taste and wealth."

114.

It was not six o'clock, yet I was already pacing my room with hasty and anxious strides, and my fellow lodgers must certainly have regretted my vicinity, in that I was the indiscreet disturber of their morning repose. Was ever poor author, through unforseen circumstances, betrayed into a more vexatious dilemma than was I at that moment, in the free Hanse Town of Hamburgh? My exchequer was exhausted, and my departure yet to be effected, with not a red cent left in my pocket. Mr. Marr, my friendly host, is good and kind-hearted, and not the man to cut an unpaid account immediately from one's skin; but the Prussian Schellpost takes no passengers on credit, and on the next day, without fail, I must forth to Berlin. For the twentieth time had I rummaged through my letter-case, in the hope that some shrinking treasure-certificate, some modest letter of credit, might have crept into a corner, but in vain! Stop! what paper is that? It is a letter which a well-wishing patron has given me, and which I have negligently omitted to present. The address is quite simple—"Herr Mohrfeld, Deich-street." I breathed aloud, "Perhaps this is the man from whom help is to reach me." I remembered that my patron had described him as the head of a very eminent mercantile house, whose acquaintance would greatly advantage me. Speedily did I come to a decision—dressed myself, and with the stroke of eight left the hotel for Deich-street, where I expected my rescuing angel to appear to me. Stop! here, at the hop-market, I must pause a moment. Yonder is a short, thick-set man, in a blue overcoat, with badly combed brown hair, and whose ruddy face has a blunt and taciturn expression. He has bought a good fish, sent a porter away with it, and pursues his walk. He has his hands crossed behind him—his eyes cast upon the ground—and with a low humming, turns into the Deich-street. Without his taking any notice of me, we strode together, and at last both stood still before the same house. There he recovered from his thoughtful manner, and looking steadily at me, asked in a suppressed tone, "Do you wish to speak with any one here?" Vexed that so ordinary-looking man should address me with so little ceremony, I answered with some haughtiness, "I have business with the house of Mohrfeld." He smiled, and then said earnestly, "I am Mohrfeld!" What! and from this man, who buys his own fish, and appears in a threadbare coat, am I to expect help? Is this mean-looking personage the only dependence, in respect of his purse, of his novel-writing guest? But he was the only anchor of hope to which I could cling. With lightning haste I removed my hat, and said, with a most respectful air, "Pardon me! I had till now not the honor—I have"—here I drew the letter from my pocket—"a commission to deliver this letter." Herr Mohrfeld interrupted me, "Not now; by and by I will speak with you in the counting-room; you must, however, wait awhile. Come"—he stepped into the house, and I followed. In the great hall, all was activity. There were two great scales, on which workmen were weighing coffee, as a clerk stood by with his memorandum book. Mr. Mohrfeld looked on silently for a few moments, and was passing on, when a laborer threw down a bag of coffee in a manner to burst it, and scatter the berries upon the floor. "What gross carelessness!" tartly exclaimed the merchant; and stooping to collect the scattered coffee, continued, "Gather it all up, and put it again in the sack. Then have it properly mended, and you, Mr. Moller, see that the bag is weighed afterwards, and if there is a loss, charge the amount to this improvident man. It shall be deducted from his week's pay."

"That is hard," said the man. "Only a little coffee"—

"Only a little coffee!" answered the merchant, quickly. "He who despises trifles, is not worthy of great things; out of eight-and-forty shillings is composed a thaler; and to one good vintage many warm days are necessary. So! not worth the trouble? Negligence is a great failing, and ruinous to ordinary business. Mr. Moller, when this man again, even in the smallest particular, displays his carelessness, discharge him on the spot. I make you answerable."

"Great God!" thought I, "for a handful of coffee, will he deprive a man of his bread? How hard! how cruel! how will it go with me?"

A young man, dressed with great elegance, came now out of the office, bowed to the merchant, and was about to pass out of the door, but at a look from his employer, stood still.

"What an appearance you make," said Mohrfeld, disdainfully. "Is there to be a ball in my counting-house? and where were you yesterday evening? If I am not in error, you were curvetting on a palfry out of the Damn Door, and had no time to observe your employer, who passed you on foot."

"I beg a thousand pardons," answered the young man, turning blood-red in his face. "I"—

"So good!" interrupted Mohrfeld. "I have nothing to do with that which my people do out of business hours, if they perform their duties punctually. But with you it is different. You have a poor mother who suffers for necessaries; three uneducated brothers; two of whom I met yesterday barefoot, and that at a time of life when they should be in school. It would be more honor to you to attend to that, and to take care of your brothers, instead of dressing in the latest fashion, and capering upon a saddle-horse. Go to your business, sir."

The young man became purple in the face, withdrew himself backwards like a crab, and vanished through the door. The merchant strode through the store, and entered the counting-room, where I followed him. What a sight! a long and rather gloomy hall presented itself, with numerous desks, behind each of which stood a person busily writing or reckoning, and of whom I counted thirty. In an adjoining room sat many more. Not far from the door sat a rather elderly man at a counter, and near him stood several iron chests, and the association drew from me a deep sigh.

"Well, Mr. Casten," said the merchant, as he approached his cashier, "what news?" "But little," answered he, quietly. "There is a demand for bills. We have, however, nothing to spare. In Livonia we have nothing, and on Genoa and Venice we have not more than our three ships loading for those ports require. Two value on New York, and one on Havana, that will be wanted, and I have notified them. Can you use any Copenhagen or Swedish paper at the current rates?" "No! there must be as little funds as possible locked up in paper. I shall need a large cash balance. Remember that." He passed on, and stood before a desk. "Were the goods sent yesterday on board the Artemisia, Mr. Kohler?" he asked. "Are the policies for the Pleil taken out, and has Captain Heysen got his papers?" "It is all attended to," said the clerk. "Here is the bill of lading; here the policy, and the receipt of the captain." "Good; your punctuality pleases me. Go on, method is the soul of business. Take care of that sand, however. It has a slovenly appearance to see it so scattered as on your desk."

Mr. Mohrfeld had now arrived at his desk, which was secluded from the main hall by a rail. He pointed me to a chair, and began to examine some letters that had waited his coming. A deep silence now pervaded the room, which was broken only by the monotonous scratching of many quills. No loud word was spoken, and seldom a suppressed whisper was heard. No notice was taken of me; not a word was addressed to me, nor was a curious glance directed towards me. The merchant read through his letters, and called several young men to him, giving directions, but receiving no answers. "At one o'clock, all must be ready for signature. You, Mr. Becker, must take care that no more errors creep into your French letters. You are too quick, too hasty. Take example of Mr. Hart—his English letters are a master correspondence. Above all, I observe lately in your letters a worthless innovation. You use a pompous, verbose style, and employ three lines where three words are sufficient. Abandon that. A flowery style is always a folly, and especially so in mercantile letters; but it comes from the senseless novels and romances that you are eternally reading, and which will yet incapacitate you for every useful employment. I have warned you—take care for the future."

This was a brilliant prospect! What reception could a novel-writer expect from a man possessed of such views? At this moment Mohrfeld turned to me, and said rather short, "Well, sir, about our business!" "At your service," I stammered, and reached him my letter; but he had not opened it ere we were again interrupted. "See there! good morning, Captain Heysen," said the merchant, with animation. "You come, probably, to take leave; a lucky voyage to you, and bring yourself and crew back in good health. Pay good attention to ship and cargo, and make me no 'general average.' Your wife, say you? why, in any circumstances let her apply to me at once. If you have a good opportunity, and avail yourself skilfully of it, you may be back by Christmas. Well, adieu, Captain, you have"—here he glanced at the almanac—"no time to lose. It is now high water, you may lose the tide, and I am not pleased to have the ship anchored at Blankenese. Lucky voyage." The captain vanished, and another man took his place. "Good morning, Mr. Flugge, what have you to say?" asked the merchant; "I am well pleased with that last purchase of wood. You earned your commission with honor. When you have such another lot on the same terms, let me know. My ships must be employed. There are already three lying idle. As soon as the new stock arrives, let me know. Adieu." "I beg your pardon, sir,"—this was directed to me—"that I keep you so long waiting, but the current business takes precedence." "Good morning, Pilot! Already back. Is my 'Hope' gone to sea safely?" "All as you wish, Mr. Mohrfeld," answered a robust Elbe pilot. "The ship is a fast sailer, and not afraid of a breeze. Here is a letter from the captain. But I must to-day on board another vessel. Perhaps I can take my pilotage with me? "That's of course, Pilot; and for the quick pilotage, ten thalers more. Go to my cashier, he will make it all right." "What do you want!" This was addressed to a meagre-looking little man, with a bald head and snuffy nose, who, in a threadbare black coat, and stooping posture, stood before the wealthy merchant.

"I beg a thousand pardons," he answered, "I am Doctor Eck, from Frankfort. I have for a long time had in consideration the peculiar procreation of mankind, and at last have succeeded in the formation of a brilliant theory, that I intend to promulgate in a series of lectures; and I would therefore solicit"—

"I am sorry," interrupted the merchant, "but I am opposed to all theories that cannot be promptly applied to the concerns of life. Away with your air-castles, fog-projects and chimeras! I am very sorry."

The poor doctor perspired with anxiety; and scarcely able to speak, he looked pitiably at the subscription list in his hand, and stammered out something of patrons and down-trodden sons of Minerva; but his voice faded into an indistinguishable murmur. The merchant regarded him for a moment with a sarcastic smile, then took the list and wrote a line. It must have been a very important line, for the face of the doctor brightened with a heartfelt laugh as he busied himself to lay more papers upon the desk. The merchant motioned him away, saying, "No matter! It is a pleasure to me when my signature can be of use to a meritorious and learned man, even if personally I derive no profit from his talents. Your theory and my practice are very different; an interchange of ideas that are so directly opposed, leads only to endless confusion. Farewell!"

The doctor retired, and made room for a man who pressed close up, and without further ceremony began: "Mr. Mohrfeld, your 'Fortuna' is quite ready, and can be launched at any moment. I wish to know what time you will appoint?"

"Monday morning, Mr. Reich," answered the merchant. "I am well pleased with your prompt and efficient mode of business. Now, as young beginners should be encouraged, you may lay the keel of a new ship on my account. Try yourself at that. I passed your yard yesterday, and observed the order and industry with which it is conducted. Persevere in that manner. Well! remember Monday morning. Farewell! Who are you?"

This was addressed to a poorly-clad woman, with pallid cheeks and eyes red with weeping, who now stood before him. At this nearly harsh address of the merchant, she looked anxiously up, and answered, "I am the wife of Bodmer, the man who was so unfortunate as to fall from the loft and break his leg."

"Shocking! very shocking! I am very sorry for Bodmer; he was an orderly man, and ever cheerfully performed his duties But my surgeon visited him; what did he say?"

"He gives the best hope of saving my husband's life, but it will be a tedious sickness; and who knows if the poor man will ever again be able to work? What then, shall we, with our five poor children, do?"

"Have confidence in the man in whose service you have met the misfortune," answered the merchant. "What the patient needs of wine and strengthening food, shall be furnished from my kitchen. The weekly wages you will receive regularly on Saturday. Now go home, and remember me to your husband, whom I will soon visit."

The woman through her tears rendered speechless thanks, and the merchant began reading my letter.

"Your letter has rather an old date," said he suddenly; I have long expected it. Your circumscribed time has probably prevented an earlier call?"

I stammered out a lie, something about my indisposition to disturb so active a business man, and that at the moment I was in great necessity. He did not let me finish, but went on.

"You are here highly recommended to me. If I can do any thing for you, speak freely. Persons away from home, frequently stand in need of aid."

This was the moment to speak of the deep ebb of my purse; but oh! the false shame—the words would not leave my lips.

"Nothing?" he proceeded. "Well, on another occasion, perhaps. Come, however, on Sunday to my cottage before the Damn Door, and take a spoonful of soup with me. Men of business have on week-days but small leisure to bestow on mere conversation."

Here was my dismissal; but without money, however, I could not go. I was completely cleaned out, and must travel. At this moment there came to my rescue a clerk, who handed between the desk and myself a letter brought by an express, addressed to Mr. Mohrfeld. It was instantly opened and read, and was probably of a favorable nature, as a pleasing smile played round the lips of the merchant; but suddenly, as if betraying a weakness, it again vanished, and he laid the letter with accustomed unconcern on one side. As he did so, his glance again fell on me.

"Anything further to command, sir?"

Now must I speak, cost what it will. I stepped close to his chair, bowed my lips to his ear, and poured forth a multitude of words, among which the most emphatic where, "want of money." To an elegant construction of sentences at such a moment would even Demosthenes have given no thought. The merchant stared at me with wondering eyes, then took my letter in hand and again read it through with close attention; after which, he wrote a line under it and handed it to me, saying, "Here, sir, have the goodness to hand this to my cashier. I shall depend on seeing you at my table on Sunday; for the present you will excuse me."

I bowed silently, and soon stood before the man surrounded with iron chests. He took the letter, and said, "you have to receive one hundred marks courrant. Will you please give a receipt? Here is the money."

"And here, sir, is your receipt," cried I with a lightened heart, as I thrust the fifty-one thalers, nineteen and two-thirds shillings into my pocket, hurried out of the office into the free air of heaven, and turned towards the Alster Hall, in the elegantly-decorated rooms of which I speedily enjoyed a substantial breakfast.

115.

In Prussia, as well as in Holland, captains in the merchant service, of small property, which generally consists of a little vessel commanded by themselves, make the ship their home, and live there constantly, with their families, who accompany their head in all his voyages. One of the Prussian captains, M. Hesser, was recently navigating his galliot Minerva, from Konigsberg to Riga. On board his vessel was his young wife, with three small children, and his crew, composed of a mate and four sailors. In the Baltic, during a violent storm in the night, while Hesser and his men were on deck, the galliot was run into by the English merchant ship Star, Capt. Robson. The shock of the two vessels was so great that Capt. Hesser and one of his sailors were thrown against the prow of the Star, to which they clung, and from whence they crawled on board that ship.

The three other sailors fell into the sea and disappeared immediately, so that there remained on the galliot only Mrs. Hesser, her three children and the mate—the later, unfortunately, during the accident, had met with a severe fall, by which he was so seriously wounded that he was unable to work. In this state of things Mrs. Hesser had the courage to take upon herself the charge of navigating the ship. By turns, captain, mate and sailor, using the little nautical knowledge she had been able to acquire in her former voyages, this intrepid young woman succeeded, by incessant labor, for eighteen hours, in gaining, with her vessel, the port of Riga. The native and foreign sailors at Riga, having learned the courageous conduct of Mrs. Hesser, caused a medal to be struck in her honor, and the corporation of seamen at Riga presented her with one thousand effective rubles —(four thousand francs.) Capt. Hesser and his sailors, who were saved on board the Star, were carried by that vessel to Rostock, in the Grand Duchy of Mecklenburgh, whence they arrived safe and sound at Riga.

116.

The astronomer who would accurately trace the wonders of the firmament, must take his views from an observatory that is not liable to be shaken. His stand should be immovable. No outward passing influence should jar it, or cause the least vibration or tremor. The slightest motion of his observatory will produce errors of immense magnitude. The object at which he is gazing may be thrown out of its true position millions of miles by a hair-breadth error at the point of observation. All this is easily and generally understood, as it relates to astronomical observations.

But it is not always considered that an analogous rule applies to every kind of observation and knowledge; and that in no case can we accurately judge of things, unless we view them from the right stand point, as the Germans phrase it. Before we pronounce confidently in reference to any event yet future, we must be quite sure that our observatory is firm, solid, standing on a rock—that it is shaken by no wind of selfish interest, or gust of blinded passion—that it is surrounded by no mist of prejudice, or error—in short, that it is the true point from which to see things as they are, in their real place and just proportions.

How often is the mercantile world thrown into confusion and chaos, by disregarding this simple common-sense principle! Mercantile success, we all know, depends very much upon a sagacious calculation of the probabilities of the future. The young merchant looks to the future for that competence which is the object of his labors; and his hope is realized in proportion as he is skilful in anticipating the phases and wants of that future. The sagacious merchant infers from certain appearances of the present, that such and such will be the condition and wants of the coming season, and he prepares himself to meet that condition and those wants, and prosperity is the reward of his foresight and care. He judges, from information which he has carefully collected, and from appearances which he watchfully noted, that a certain crop will be short, or a particular description of goods scarce; he estimates the demand, and the prices which a short supply will occasion; he takes care, in good season, to obtain the control of as much of the article to be supplied as he can dispose of; and, this done, he can coolly count his gains weeks or months before they are realized, with as much confidence as if they were already in his hands.

The two principal conditions of success in mercantile calculations appear to be a sound and well-informed judgment, and a regulated and reasonable desire of gain. The inordinate, grasping anxiety of wealth, which characterizes many men, is, in a large proportion of cases, a passion fatal to their success. It blinds the judgment, and misleads it into visionary schemes and ruinous speculations; and an ample experience shows that men of the coolest, most deliberate habits, when they have once yielded to the passion for wealth, are no longer capable of reasoning wisely. Of the other qulifications—namely, correct information, as a condition of mercantile success, it seems hardly necessary to speak. "Knowledge is power," says the great master of English philosophy. Not less in mercantile life than elsewhere is this maxim true. The language of every merchant should be, "give us light," increase and multiply the means of information. What is capital, energy, enterprise, sagacity, without accurate knowledge, extensive information? An ignorant merchant may happen to succeed, even in this day, but every one must see that it is a most improbable peradventure.

A single fact is worth a folio of argument, and we have one just to the point—it is this: that one of the leading causes of the late financial crisis and panic in England, was the want of true information respecting the amount of flour and grain which this country could supply. A number of the English corn merchants proceeded on the belief that our surplus was exhausted, when such was not the fact. They made their contracts upon that false assumption, and were ruined.

There is no one subject in which the whole mercantile community have deeper interest than that of the vast modern increase of the facilities for diffusing and obtaining full and correct information on everything pertaining to trade, so that all can enjoy its advantages; and no man need hope to compete successfully with his neighbor, who shuts himself out from a participation in these facilities. The time has come when it is no longer in the power of the few to monopolize; and every day tends more and more to equalize the condition and advantages of business men, and to throw wide open to all, the door to wealth, respectability, influence, and honor. Nor is there any necessity for the frequent failures in the mercantile life, which have distinguished the past. The young merchant who commences on the broad and sound moral basis of integrity, and nice mercantile honor, and who conducts his business with intelligence and judgment, and without undue eagerness and haste to be rich, will generally meet with success, as he will certainly deserve it. It is true this is a day of ardent competition ; but it is not less true, that it is a day when manly, honorable enterprise buckles on its armor under auspices the most cheering, and hopes the most encouraging.

117.

Many young and talented persons miss the road to fortune by the want of humility and patience. They think everything must depend on "a good start," and unless they can make "a good engagement," they will remain out of employment for weeks and months. They miss three things—support for that time, the practice that keep talents improving, and the furnishing of the best evidence that they are willing to work.

A man is far more likely to be called from an humble to a more advantageous position, than from idleness to the place he desires. Even in prison Joseph made himself useful by labor, and thus showed what he was fitted for, and built the ladder that led him out of obscurity. But now there are many young men who if they cannot have "good situations" will not do anything They forget that any situation of honest toil is good when compared with idleness ; and that it is better to labor where they can receive only a sufficiency for the time, than to remain out of employment ; and besides the daily expense of living thus, they are in danger of forming *habits* of indolence and ruinous expenditure.

The trouble with many young men is a foolish pride which seems to say that idleness is more honorable than work. They have very delicate *feelings*—it goes "*against their feelings*" to do this and that, when there is nothing whatever of immorality or debasement connected with the employment. To give an instance, we will repeat a dialogue which took place recently.

A young man, nicely brushed up and very genteel, entered an office, and with a polite air addressed the gentleman there with, "Sir, you want a young man here, I believe?"

"Yes," was the reply.

"Here are my recommendations," said the young man as he handed a paper certifying that he was worthy of confidence, etc.

The gentleman read the paper, and looked up, remarking, "We should be glad to do your friends the compliment of engaging you, and therefore you will please let me say something in regard to fitness."

"What shall I be expected to do?" asked the young man.

"To aid in the office as opportunity may present, and to pay notes, and collects drafts, etc.," was the answer.

"I don't think collecting drafts would agree with my feelings," replied the young man.

"Well," quietly responded the gentleman, "I would not advise you to do anything against your feelings. Good morning."

Here it is how they miss it. A certain fastidiousness of feeling is set up where there is nothing dishonorable, nothing that should be repulsive to the most conscientious. What can be less against all true and worthy feeling than the collection of *drafts*? What is there to soil glove or fingers, sensibility or conscience? But this is only a specimen of the scores of ways in which "my feelings" are brought into collision with virtuous labor, and honorable industry. What sphere in life is there where the education and discipline of the feelings is not of first importance? Early attention to this would prevent a foolish fastidiousness from springing up, and it would avoid a thousand volcanic eruptions in counting-houses where feelings in one member and another cross each other, like the sea crossing into the central fires of the earth and bidding Vesuvius to spout up its eruptions.

Strength of feeling is good. It is not necessarily an evil. It is the source of energy, promptness, and power. It aids quickness of thought, readiness of apprehension, and concentration of abilities. But *undisciplined* it is injurious. It is constantly bringing a man into painful contact unnecessarily with his fellows; and it erects false barriers to usefulness and fortune. Strength of feeling belongs to all great men. The calmness and dignity of Washington only showed that divinity of principle that ruled the storm. How perpetually through the struggle for independence did things come up "not agreeable to his feelings," but he curbed and disciplined those feelings, and instead of permitting them to be a wild horse to bear him in seeming retreat from the battle-field of Freedom, they were as the war-horse on which he rode grandly from victory to victory.

118.

In the *Merchants' Magazine*, for November, 1847, we reviewed at length the admirable address of Judge James Hall, before the "Young Mens' Mercantile Library Association of Cincinnati," in celebration of its eleventh anniversary, in 1846; embodying, in that article, all that relates to the topic selected by the author for the occasion, viz: "The Dignity and Usefulness of Commerce, as Illustrated by the History of the Commercial Greatness and Growth of the West." At the close of the address, Judge Hall touches upon a very important point, and one of paramount importance to the merchant. It presents itself in the form of a question, thus: "What should be the character of those who act so important a part in the business of the country, who control its resources, direct its energies, and, in a great degree, form the moral standard which regulates the transactions of the whole people?" The mercantile mind of our people is sufficiently keen. But enough: the learned judge answers the question briefly, but pertinently, as follows:—

"The pursuit of wealth, attracting as it does intellects of every grade, includes among its votaries many of the most aspiring and most capable minds; and gives to them that constant and healthy exercise, which is calculated to sharpen the faculties; and, if united with reading and reflection, produces a high degree of refinement. The merchant should cultivate his mind, and acquire knowledge as an element of power. Dealing in the products of various climes, and of all the arts, and engaged in an intercourse, personally or by correspondents, which extends to all the marts of traffic throughout the world, he should be well acquainted with the geography of the globe, and with the productions, resources, habits, financial systems, and commercial usuges of all nations. He should know thoroughly the composition and history, the mode of production, cost, and all other incidents, connected with every article in which he deals; and should be versed especially in the moneys and measures, the exchanges, the commercial laws and regulations, of the various places to which his business relations extend. This much we insist upon, as actually necessary to the respectability of the mercantile character, and to enable the merchant to wield his capital to advantage. But the intelligent merchant should aspire to something more than this. His position in society demands that he should place himself upon an equality with the most cultivated of his fellow citizens. As a class, the merchants are the most wealthy men of our country. In social intercourse they mingle with the most refined, with those who are highest in intellectual standing, and official position. There is no place in society, no post in the government, from which the merchant is excluded. On the contrary, his command of money, and the facilities afforded by his relations of business, place him in a prominent position, give him the control of the various commercial and moneyed institutions, and render him the fit and active director and agent in the whole circle of public charities, and in the numberless endowments for literary and liberal purposes. Having thus opened to him a wide sphere of usefulness, he should enter upon it with a consciousness of its dignity and importance, and qualify himself for the discharge of its various duties, by an assiduous and a liberal cultivation of his mind and morals.

"The merchant should be a patron of the arts, a promoter of education, a friend to literature and science, an active agent in all public improvements; because his habits of business, his wealth, his connection with moneyed institutions, and with fiscal concerns, enable him to render efficient aid to enterprises of patriotism and benevolence. He should be forward in every good word and work, also, as a means of blunting that vulgar prejudice, which supposes that the men who possess or control wealth, enjoy exclusive privileges; and should show a willingness to pay liberally for the advantages of his position, whether real or imaginary, by using those advantages freely for public good.

"There is another point, in regard to the commercial character, of great delicacy, but which I do not feel at liberty to pass untouched, as it is most essential to the honor and the prosperity of the mercantile class as well as of the community to which they belong. The most precious possession of the merchant is his *credit.* And here allow me to draw a distinction: the credit of the merchant does not consist simply in his wealth, or in his ability to borrow money by means of his connections, or of the securities he may be able to offer. It is a gross fallacy to suppose that what is termed an "undoubted standing," requires nothing for its support but the possession of *facilities* for raising money. The credit of a merchant depends mainly on his character for integrity, capacity, and industry. The true merchant is a man whose morality is as inflexible as the rules of arithmetic: his honesty is as invariable as the result of a correct balance-sheet. He should be not only honest, but strictly honorable, so that the confidence reposed in him should be unlimited. Such a man is trusted, not merely on account of his wealth, but in consideration of his personal character.

The commercial virtues are so essential to the well being of society, that their cultivation should be an object of sedulous care to the whole mercantile body, who should exercise a conservative influence by frowning upon every infraction of the laws of fair trading. Punctuality should be insisted upon as an indispensable requisite, and no man should be trusted or tolerated, who would forfeit his word or violate his engagements. Society has a right to demand of all its members the observance of good faith, and it is only by insisting on this right that a wholesome public opinion is established.

Especially should the merchants of a city like ours, endeavor to establish a high tone of commercial character. They should set up a standard of strict and elevated morality, which every regular dealer and fair merchant would acknowledge to be just, and to which all should be required to adhere. They should patronize those virtues which adorn the individual character, which promote success in business, while they render its transaction safe and agreeable, and which are as beneficial as they are honorable to the community in which they flourish—industry, honesty, temperance, and prudent economy; while, by inflexible rules, and strict observances, they should discountenance fraud, deception, trickery, and bad faith.

When we speak of the rapid advancement of our country to its present high state of prosperity, we are easily led by national vanity into the employment of high sounding words which do not always lead us to satisfactory conclusions. Patriotism, public spirit, benevolence—liberty, education, the freedom of the press, our liberal institutions, the benign and pacific policy of our government, are referred to as causes of our national growth and aggrandizement. I shall not dispute the happy influence of all these principles. But there is one element in the national character, one principle of action animating the entire mass of our people, which is greater than any other; nay, I will be bold enough to assert, more powerful than all others united. Whether it be called avarice, or the love of money, or the desire of gain, or the lust of wealth, or whether it be softened to the ear under the more guarded terms, prudence, natural affection, diligence in business, or the conscientious improvement of time and talents—it is still *money-making* which constitutes the great business of the majority of our people; it is the use of money which controls and regulates everything.

Whether the propensity for money-getting is beneficial or otherwise, depends upon circumstances. Industry is an admirable quality; its exercise is directly useful to the public as well as to individual interests, and it is accompanied by temperance, prudence, morality, and other virtues. But the desire of wealth, for its own sake, is far from being a virtue. Where money is greedily sought, without regard to the means of acquisition, and without liberality in its expenditure, the passion which directs its pursuit is base and sordid. The miser is a wretched man, a worthless citizen, a dishonor to the dignity of human nature.

I am happy to believe that the acquisition of wealth does not necessarily, nor as I hope usually, blunt the sensibilities, nor destroy the manliness of a generous character—that it is not always a selfish and mercenary occupation. If money be sought with moderation, by honorable means, and with a due regard to the public good, no employment affords exercise to higher or nobler powers of mind and heart. And such should be the character of the merchant. He should guard his heart against the seductive influence of money; he should carefully shield his mind against the narrow precepts of avarice. Money should be regarded as the agent and representative of the good it may be made to perform—it should be sought as an instrument of self-defence against the evils of poverty; of parental love, enabling us to provide for those dependent on us; of public spirit, in affording the means of promoting the public good.

118.

Never talk of your designs till they have been accomplished, and even then, the less you say the better. This is a very important caution for the merchant or man of business. Some persons are naturally so talkative that they no sooner form a design of entering into a speculation, or following some particular branch of trade or commerce, than they take the earliest opportunity of acquainting all their friends with it. By giving way to this weakness, you put it in the power of others to forstall you, and those whose interest interferes with yours, will do all they can to disappoint you for their own advantage. In this respect, the example of GIRARD, the Napoleon of commerce, is worthy of all imitation. No man ever heard him boast of *what he would do.* He remained quiet and silent till the time came for action, and then he struck the blow with an unerring aim which insured him success. As a merchant, he was inquisitive, active, prompt, and sagacious: studious to learn all he could from others, and as careful to impart nothing in return.

119.

THE day was dark, the markets dull,
The 'Change was thin, gazettes were full
  And half the town was breaking;
The countersign of cash was "Stop,"
Bankers and bankrupts shut up shop;
  And honest hearts were aching.

When near the 'Change my fancy spied
A faded form, with hasty stride,
  Beneath grief's burthen stooping;
Her name was Credit, and she said
Her father, Trade, was lately dead,
  Her mother, Commerce, drooping.

The smile that she was wont to wear
Was withered by the hand of care,
  Her eyes had lost their lustre;
Her character was gone, she said,
For basely she had been betrayed;
  And nobody would trust her.

That honest Industry had tried,
To gain fair Credit for his bride,
  And found the lady willing.
But ah! a fortune-hunter came,
And Speculation was his name;
  A rake not worth a shilling.

The villain was on mischief bent,
He gained both dad and mam's consent;
  And then poor Credit smarted.
He filched her fortune and her fame,
He fixed a blot upon her name,
  And left her broken-hearted.

While thus poor Credit seemed to sigh,
Her cousin, Confidence, came by,
(Methinks he must be clever;)
For when he whispered in her ear,
She check'd the sigh, she dried the tear,
And smiled as sweet as ever.

120.

Several years since, Capt. Penny, the master of an English whaling ship, conceived the project of establishing a resident whale fishery on the shore of Davis's Straits. The idea originated in the circumstance that the crew of an American whaler, which was wrecked there, had succeeded in killing during their brief stay at Kumsooka, some eight or nine whales. Captain Penny proposed that an English commercial company under a royal charter should engage in the enterprise of forming the resident fishery. His plan, so far as government was concerned, fell through; but he was supported by several commercial gentlemen, and the Lady Franklin and Sophia, Arctic exploring ships, were purchased and fitted out in Aberdeen for the expedition last year. Both ships were supplied with tanks for the oil, and the necessary arrangements were made for encountering a winter's residence in the Straits, in order to be ready for the first opportunity of getting at the fish in the spring. The ships sailed in July, 1853, and nothing was heard of them until towards the latter part of August, 1854, when advices were received in England stating that the speculation had proved eminently successful, forty thousand dollars worth of oil having been procured, and ten or twelve tons of bone. The Lady Franklin has returned to England with a full cargo, at last accounts.

121.

"WELL," said Major Henry, an affluent citizen of Auburn, to his amiable lady, one morning after his faultless cup of coffee, and his usual glance at the morning news, "Mary, we will for the present trade with young Williams & Co., in Walnut street. Please send the servants there."

"What! leave Simpson & Co., where we have traded so long to our entire satisfaction? What can have occurred to offend you?"

"Nothing, my dear; they are truly honorable men and politely attentive to their customers."

"And so respectable, Major; such an old, well established firm. Why, all the *élite* trade there," said Mrs. H.

"There is no reason in the world, Mary, why we should leave them, but that I have an object in bestowing our patronage elsewhere."

"Please explain yourself," said she, "for you are perfectly inexplicable at present."

"Well, my dear, Williams & Co. are worthy men just established in business, and I suspect the sweet breezes of popular favor do not blow any too strongly. Perhaps we can aid in giving proper direction to the current."

"Nonsense!" exclaimed Mrs. H. with petulence; they can take care of themselves, as other firms do. Surely, we are under no obligations to exchange friends for strangers; you are capricious."

"We are not obliged, in the sense you use the term," said he. "Heaven is under no obligation to earth that calls for the bestowal of the daily and unceasing blessings ever vouchsafed. —But, Mary, listen to a chapter in my early history that will illustrate the question:

"My parents, you know, were in limited circumstances, and I commenced life dependent on my own exertions. I accepted a clerkship in a firm, with a small salary. By conscientious devotion to business, this was gradually increased, until, with frugality, I was enabled to accumulate a sum that I thought would warrant commencing for myself. I opened a store in Pearl street, with a limited stock in trade, but with large hopes for the future. But customers did not throng my counters. Day after day I spent wistfully looking at the crowds that hurried by, yet scarcely deigning a passing look within. It was a new arrangement, and few cared to patronize the novelty. All had other places to trade.

"All this continued until trouble rose up before me. Rent, and payment for stock yet on my shelves, were coming due. Visions of bankruptcy hovered before my eyes daily, and dreams of ruin and disgrace tortured me nightly. All the fruits of my past years of toil and self-denial would be consumed. I became so nervous that the entrance of a customer was painful instead of cheering. I could not meet my acquaintances with habitual cheerfulness, and their friendly inquiries concerning my business were like daggers to my sensibility. I shall never lose the taste of that bitterness of feeling that swelled up from my breast, with forced replies. But the crisis—the pay day came. Stock all on hand, but no cash. With little faith in success, but as drowning men catch at straws, I determined to state my case to a certain wealthy citizen, well known for his eccentric acts of benevolence, and request a loan. I did so.

"'Humph! I'll see about that; call again,' was his only reply, and he resumed the reading that my entrance interrupted.

"I was already forgotten, thought I, as I departed in no very enviable state of mind.

"The next morning I received a note from a bank, stating that the cashier had been requested to notify me that two thousand dollars had been deposited to my credit there. I was saved, temporarily, at least. I well knew my benefactor. How earnest my vow some day to prove it, it is vain to attempt to describe. I drew the amount, met my obligations punctually, and established an unlimited credit, which, by the way, I very sparingly used. Again I rejoiced in hopes. But I have yet to tell you of the greatest favor that worthy man conferred upon me.

"A few days after the grant of the timely loan, a carriage drove up to the store, and in the lady that alighted I recognized with joy the amiable wife of my benefactor. She made a large bill, and I augured well from it. I prided myself upon my taste in selecting goods, and had some exquisitely beautiful patterns. Mrs. Chedell, for that was the lady's name, your very good friend, Mary, was a fashionable example, even to the ton, in those days, and she took particular care to associate our name with her purchase.

"The consequence was, when my next pay day came, my cash account was in such a favorable state that I met my engagements easily; and henceforth the road to my present position was natural and easy. I am indebted to Mr. and Mrs. C., under Providence, for my fortune, I fully believe. In that day, when good and evil seemed so equally balanced, favor thrown into the financial scale decided the question. Since that I have sympathized with young aspirants for the favors of trade, and extended, when I could, the helping hand. Now, my dear, am I capricious?"

The expressive countenance of his listener replied eloquently and well.

At that moment Mr. Chedell himself entered the room, and was warmly welcomed. But the reception he met could not remove from his countenance marks of trouble plainly perceptible there.

"Major Henry," said he, with an effort, "I did you a favor once. Have you forgotten it?"

"Never! my dear sir," said he emphatically, and smiling confirmation to his word, while no trace of discontent at the remainder detracted from his sunny expression.

"Now I am in trouble," exclaimed Mr. C. "My son is seriously embarrassed by the state of the money market, and some heavy demands unexpectedly made upon him through the imprudence of a foreign agent. We cannot meet those drafts, and accommodation is denied at the banks. Hence I came to you."

"I am glad to have an opportunity of proving to you how grateful I am for that old favor," said the Major, proceeding to his desk for the purpose of complying with his request. He hastily attached his signature to a blank check, which he requested Mr. C. to fill with the required amount.

"Come again," said the kind-hearted Major; "come again; if this be insufficient, command my utmost means."

"How short-sighted," said Mr. C., feelingly, "in reference to their true interest, are those who neglect opportunities of doing good. I have never yet performed a trivial act of kindness, in a judicious way, that did not eventually overwhelm me with returning benefits."

"Then you think all your benevolence good policy! and the disposition to do all the good you can, evidence of shrewdness rather than virtue, do you?" said the Major, jokingly.

Happy-hearted man. The rewards of virtue are many and

great. The lowering clouds of care that of late hung so darkly over the spirits of the one, were suddenly dispelled by the sunlight of the other's gratitude.

The world is not all selfishness—the usury of kindness not always ingratitude.

Mrs. Henry was deeply affected by what she had seen and heard, and thenceforth she needed no persuasion to induce her to join her husband in his plans of charity and benevolence.

Nor will any one who reads aright the moral of this tale, be slow to follow in the pleasant life-path to which it is a guide.

122.

We were conversing lately with a gentleman of very extensive business relations, says the Philadelphia *Merchant*, and found he had filed away all his bills for twenty years in a very methodical manner. Every one was folded to the same size, and then indorsed with the name of the person, the amount, what for, and when paid, so that at a glance the story of each bill was told. It was really amusing to see what a combination of business affairs was thus brought before us by glancing from bill to bill through one of the neat bundles thus indorsed. In addition to this, our friend had entered into a book a copy of those indorsements, to which he could make reference, and from which he could select the amounts of various bills more easily than otherwise, and by which he had a security against the loss of a bill in any manner. How much of trouble and loss of time might be prevented in many places of business by the presence of a like order and method! It should be imposed as an essential to good clerkship, and the habit thus induced will operate in other matters where order and method are the essentials of good management.

123.

CITIES are, to the dwellers in the country, very like what lights at night are to flies—brilliant and attractive, but certain ruin. They see the blaze from a distance; they long to warm themselves in the genial glow; they hear of its manifold excitements, and they begin to despise the dull routine of their inland homes. In a little while, they have disposed of what little they possessed in the country, imbibed perhaps from ancestors whose memory is a blessing to them, and they hurry off to commence a new life in an untried sphere of existence. They plunge headlong into all manner of dissipation; they resort to desperate speculations, and even some questionable modes, to keep their expenses; and the upshot of the experiment is, that, in a few months, they are bankrupt, and what little their families once possessed is lost, along with their respectability and reputation. All that they have gained is extravagant habits and tastes, which can no more be gratified. This is a frequent and melancholy experience. We are led to these remarks by reading the following statement in Cist's Cincinnati *Advertiser*; and a similar statement might be made of every city in the nation:—

"The avidity with which young men crown those avocations in life in which there is a chance of making money with rapidity, or of acquiring political or social distinctions and eminence, is the more remarkable, when it is apparent, on the very surface of the subject, that they are venturing in a lottery in which there are many blanks to one prize. A few acquire the object of their pursuit—the mass sink into obscurity and insignificance.

Take, for example, many pursuits. It is the experience and observation of intelligent persons in our Eastern cities, that there is hardly a firm in existence now, which did business twenty years ago; and that nine out of ten in mercantile life, in the long run, amidst the fluctuations of its pursuits, are broke.

Let me, however, bring the subject nearer home. I had prepared a list of the principal active business men, who were in trade twenty years ago, in Cincinnati, of which a brief extract is all that I have space for in this volume. In place of giving names, I shall distinguish the firms by numbers:—

No. 1, Broke; afterwards resumed business; has since left Cincinnati.

2, Broke; resides now in Indiana.

3, Broke, and now engaged in collecting accounts.

4, Died.

5, Now captain of a steamboat.

6, Left merchandising to put up pork, which business he also quit in time to save his bacon; independent in circumstances.

7, Dead.

8, Broke; resides now in St. Louis.

9, A firm; one of the partners died, the other out of business; both insolvent.

10, Partners; both dead.

11, Partners; broke; one now a book-keeper, the other dead.

12, Became embarrassed, and swallowed poison.

13, A firm; broke.

14, A firm; broke; one of the partners died a common sot, the others left the city.

15, A firm; broke, and left the city.

16, A firm; all its members out of business.

17, A firm; senior partner dead.

18, A firm ; senior partner dead, junior resides at Toledo.

19, Is now a clerk, and left Cincinnati, after becoming intemperate.

20, A firm ; two of the partners dead, one of whom died intemperate ; the other is now engaged in other business.

21, A firm ; senior partner died intemperate, junior now pastor of a Presbyterian church.

22, Died of Madeira wine.

23, do. do. do.

24, A firm ; one of the partners dead, the other now in business in Pearl-street.

25, A firm ; junior partner in business in Pearl-street.

26, A firm ; broke ; one of the partners in other business, one removed to New York, and the third a clerk.

27, Broke, and drowned himself in the Ohio.

28, Broke, became intemperate, and died of delirium tremens.

29, Broke ; resides in Baltimore.

30, Removed to Baltimore.

31, A firm ; senior partner dead, the other partners dealing in real estate.

32, Out of business, having broke three times.

33, Broke ; now dealing in flour.

34, Died of cholera.

35, A firm ; senior partner dead, junior gone to New Orleans.

36, Broke ; removed to New Orleans.

37, Broke ; removed to Illinois.

38, Broke ; removed to Missouri.

My list comprehends some four hundred business men, of which the above is a sample. I know of but five now in business, who were so twenty years since. Such is mercantile success."

124

In another part of this book we gave an extract from Mr. Parker's "*Sermon of Merchants*," touching the position of the Merchant. From this position, he proceeds to point out certain peculiar temptations, as follows :—

"One temptation is to an extravagant desire of Wealth. They see that money is Power, the most condensed and flexible form thereof. It is always ready ; it will turn any way. They see that it gives advantages to their children which nothing else will give. The poor man's son, however well born, struggling for a superior education, obtains his culture at a monstrous cost ; with the sacrifice of pleasure, comfort, the joys of youth, often of eyesight and health. He must do two men's work at once—learn and teach at the same time. He learns all by his Soul, nothing from his circumstances. If he have not an iron body as well as an iron head, he dies in that experiment of the cross. The land is full of poor men who have attained a superior culture, but carry a crippled body through all their life. The rich man's son needs not that terrible trial. He learns from his circumstances, not his Soul. The air about him contains a diffused element of thought. He learns without knowing it. Colleges open their doors ; accomplished teachers stand ready ; Science and Art, Music and Literature, come at the rich man's call. All the outward means of educating, refining, elevating a child, are to be had for money, and for money alone.

"Then, too, Wealth gives men a social position, which nothing else, save the rarest genius, can obtain, and which that in the majority of cases is sure not to get. Many men prize this social rank above everything else, even above Justice and a life unstained.

"Since it thus gives Power, Culture for one's children, and a distinguished Social Position, Rank amongst men, for the man and his child after him, there is a temptation to regard money as the great object of life, not a means but an End ; the thing a man is to get even at the risk of getting nothing else. It 'answereth all things.' Here and there you find a man who has got nothing else. Men say of such an one, 'He is worth a million!' There is a terrible sarcasm in common speech, which all do not see. He is 'worth a million,' and that is all ; not *worth* Truth, Goodness, Piety ; not worth a Man. However, I must say, I cannot think there are many such amongst us. Most men, I am told, have mainly gained wealth by skill, foresight, industry, economy, by honorable pains-taking, not by trick. Still there is a temptation to count wealth the object of life—the thing to be had if they have nothing else.

"The next temptation is to think any means justifiable which lead to that end,—the temptation to fraud, deceit, to lying in its various forms, active and passive ; the temptation to abuse the power of this natural Strength, or acquired Position, to tyranize over the weak, to get and not give an equivalent for what they get. If a man get from the world more than he gives an equivalent for, to that extent he is a beggar, and gets charity, or a thief, and steals ; at any rate, the world is so much the poorer for him. The temptation to fraud of this sort, in some of its many forms, is very great. I do not believe that all trade must be gambling or trickery ; the Merchant a knave, or a gambler. I know some men say so ; but I do not believe it. I know it is not so now ; all actual trade, and profitable, too, is not knavery. I know some become rich by deceit. I cannot but think these are the exceptions ; that the most successful have had the average honesty and benevolence, with more than the average industry, foresight, prudence, and skill. A man foresees future wants of his fellows, and provides for them; sees new resources hitherto undeveloped, anticipates new habits and wants; turns wood, stone, iron, coal, rivers and mountains to human use, and honestly earns what he takes. I am told the Merchants of this place rank high as men of integrity and honor, above mean cunning, but enterprising, industrious and far-sighted. Still, I must admit the temptation of fraud is a great one; that it is often yielded to. Few go to a great extreme of deceit—they are known and exposed; but many to a considerable degree. He that maketh haste to be rich is seldom innocent. Young men say it is hard to be honest, to do by others as you would wish them to do by you. I know it need not be so. Would not a reputation for uprightness and truth be a good capital for any man, old or young?

"This class owns the machinery of society, in great measure,—the Ships, Factories, Houses, Shops, Water-Privileges, and the like. This brings into their employment large masses of working-men, with no capital but Muscles or Skill. The law leaves the employed at the employer's mercy. Perhaps this is unavoidable. One wishes to sell his work dear, the other to get it cheap as he can. It seems to me no law can regulate this matter, only Conscience, Reason, the Christianity of the two parties. One class is strong, the other weak. In all encounters of these two, on the field of battle, or in the market-place, we know the result; the weaker is driven to the wall. When the earthen and iron vessel strike together, we know beforehand which will go to pieces. The weaker class can seldom tell their tale, so their story gets often suppressed in the world's literature, and told only in outbreaks and revolutions. Still, the bold men who wrote the Bible, Old Testament and New, have told truths on this theme which others dare not tell—terrible words, which it will take ages of Christianity to expunge from the world's memory.

"There is a strong temptation to use one's power of Nature or Position, to the disadvantage of the Weak. This may be done consciously or unconsciously. There are examples enough of both. Here the Merchant deals in the labor of men. This is a legitimate article of traffic, and dealing in it is quite indispensable in the present condition of affairs. In the Southern States, the Merchant, whether Producer, Manufacturer, or Trader, owns men and deals in their labor, or their bodies. He uses their labor, giving them just enough of the result of that labor to keep their bodies in the most profitable working state. * * * * * Here it is possible to do the same thing: I mean, it is possible to employ men and give them just enough of the result of their labor to keep up a miserable life, and yourself take all the rest of the result of that labor. This may be done consciously or otherwise, but legally, without violence, and without owning the person. This is not Slavery, though only one remove from it. This is the Tyranny of the Strong over the Weak; the Feudalism of money; stealing man's work, and not his person. The merchants, as a class, are exposed to this very temptation. Sometimes it is yielded to. Let me mention some extreme cases; one from abroad, one near at home. In Belgium the average wages of *men* in manufactories are less than twenty-seven cents a day. The most skilful women in that calling can only earn twenty cents a day, and many very much less. In that country almost every seventh man receives assistance from the public; the mortality of that class, in some of the cities, is ten per cent a year! Perhaps that is the worst case which you can find on a large scale even in Europe. How much better off are many women in Boston, who gain their bread by the needle? yes, a large class of women in all our great cities? The Ministers of the Poor can answer that; your Police can tell of the direful crime to which Necessity sometimes drives women whom honest labor cannot feed!

"I know it will be said, buy in the cheapest market and sell in the dearest; get work at the lowest wages. Still there is another view of the case, and I am speaking to men whose professed religion declares that men are Brothers, and demands that the Strong help the Weak. Oppression of this sort is one fertile source of Pauperism and Crime. How much there is of it I know not, but I think men seldom cry unless they are hurt. When men are gathered together in large masses, as in the manufacturing towns, if there is any oppression of this sort, it is sure to get told of, especially in New England. But, when a small number is employed, and they isolated from one another, the case is much harder. Perhaps no class of laborers in New England is worse treated than the hired help of small proprietors.

"Then, too, there is a temptation to abuse their political power to the injury of the nation; to make laws which seem good for themselves, but are baneful to the people; to control the Churches, so that they shall not dare rebuke the actual Sins of the Nation, or the Sins of trade, and so the churches be made apologizers for lowness, practising infidelity as their sacrament, but in the name of Christ and God. The ruling power in England once published a volume of Sermons, as well as a Book of Prayers, which the clergy were commanded to preach. What sort of a gospel got recommended therein, you may easily guess."

125.

As important as financial solvency in a mercantile community, is that strict integrity of purpose which guarantees reliance in the word, as well as the bond of the merchant. Were it necessary in all the transactions which take place between men of business to pass written guaranties, legally constructed and attested by witnesses, trade would be sadly hampered. The wheels of commerce would be clogged, and important time would be lost in gathering together the means requisite to guard against breaches of faith. Indeed, honor and policy both dictate that the word of those with whom we are often brought in business contact should be implicitly relied on, and that verbal assurances should often be taken as guarantees as sacred as would be legally attested instruments of engagement. In every great commercial mart, this confidence happily obtains, and comparatively few are the instances in which it is signally abused. Yet in California, as almost everywhere else, there *are* occasional instances where men, disregarding the most solemn pledges, violate their word, and entail consequent loss upon those who had confided in their honor.

The species of breach of faith alluded to has of late most glaringly taken form in the violation of verbal compacts in regard to rates at which merchandise should be disposed of. A consignee receives one of a series of cargoes of goods, for which he is naturally anxious to find a market. Owing to a variety of causes, he alone may be cognizant of the fact that other cargoes of a similar character are on the way from the same or similar ports, and he alone may know that the amount of such goods likely to come to hand within a short period is greater than the immediate requirements of the market demand. That he should endeavor to dispose of his consignment as speedily as possible, and at prices as remunerating as possible, it will be conceded is consistent with his duty to his consignor, always providing that he resort to no unworthy means of accomplishing his object.

Honor may not require of him that he should take especial pains to inform the business world that he expects an early glut of the market, but honor *does* require that he should not labor to create an impression inconsistent with what he knows to be true. More especially does it require, that after his assurances that a scarcity is at hand, and after he has disposed of a portion of his merchandise at prices below which he has promised his customers that he will not sell within a given period, he should not enter the market at lower rates, and undersell those who had reposed confidence in his integrity. It is true, that by pursuing an opposite course, the returns he may make will prove more satisfactory to the shipper, and in view of the uncertainty of law, even should law be resorted to, he may enjoy legal immunity; but in the estimation of those who duly appreciate mercantile integrity, he stands branded as one unworthy the name of a merchant.

126.

The following letter was written by a distinguished New England merchant to his son, who is in business in New York city, on the occasion of his coming of age. The advice it contains may be read with profit by a good many young men who are in similiar circumstances with the gentleman to whom it was written:—

My Dear Son:—Your letter of the 16th, I read with great pleasure. We did not forget your birth-day, which ushers you into *manhood.* An important event; truly so—not merely because it brings with it to you *legal* rights and capacities, but also because twenty-one attracts attention, confidence, and expectations from friends and business men. You are a citizen, to all intents. Responsibilities devolve on the man of twenty-one, as he reaches that long, longed for bourne. He is expected to be, in the best sense, a *man*. "When the brisk minor pants for twenty-one," he is not apt to reflect on, nay, he does not conceive the obligations and responsibilities that gather upon him. He takes a part in the great business of life. His moral obligations—it is not easy to say how they are affected by birthday of twenty-one. He is a voter, and has new political rights; and hence result certain moral duties which he is to carefully guard. Respecting your salary for the future, I would remark it ought to be liberal. I think you have served a good apprenticeship. How good a business capacity you have achieved, it is not for me to say. My opinion is decidedly favorable. One remark, in this connection, I cannot help making. There is a habit of extravagant expenditure among all classes of society in New York, that borders on insanity. It is at war with general health, morals and prosperity. It is, indeed, nearly allied to, if not the fruitful parent of, the mighty frauds, peculation, forgeries, which are almost daily uncovered in the great city. This personal and social extravagance will soon lead to ruinous failures throughout all classes of people. Mark that! It is natural and expedient that I should earnestly exhort my sons to beware of the tendencies of the times in this behalf. I feel extremely desirous that they should moderate their expenditures. Wisdom, prudence and honor alike demand it. 'Tis honorable to acquire property—by honorable and honest means, however. I freely say, I think my sons in New York are energetic, upright business men. Let them go ahead thus, and rely on the favor of a good Providence for success.

127.

ADVERTISERS will do well to ponder the following sensible remarks, contained in a cheap little book, entitled "How to get money."

"Whatever your occupation or calling may be, if it needs support from the public, advertise it thoroughly and efficiently, in some shape or other that will arrest public attention. I freely confess, that what success I have had in my life, may be attributed more to the public press than to nearly all other causes combined. There may possibly be occupations that do not require advertising; but I cannot well conceive what they are. Men in business will sometimes tell you they have tried advertising, and that it did not pay. This is only when advertising is done sparingly and grudgingly. Homeopathic doses of advertising will not pay perhaps; it is like half a portion of physic, making the patient sick but effecting nothing. Administer liberally and the cure will be permanent. Some say they cannot afford to advertise. They mistake: they cannot afford *not* to advertise. In this country, where every body reads the newspapers, it will be seen that these are the cheapest and best media through which persons can speak to the public where they are to find their customers. Put on the *appearance* of business, and generally the *reality* will follow. The farmer plants his seed, and while he is sleeping, his corn and potatoes are growing. So with advertising. While you are sleeping, or eating, or conversing with one of your customers, your advertisement is being read by hundreds and thousands of persons who never saw you or heard of your business, and never would, had it not been for your advertisement appearing in the newspapers.

128.

THE late ITHIEL TOWN, a celebrated architect of New Haven, Connecticut, had a very fine library of expensive books. Being in London some twenty-five or thirty years ago, he saw a large illustrated folio which he wished to possess, but it was not for sale. He, therefore, left a commission with the late Mr. Evans, a book and print seller, to procure the best copy that turned up, if it could be had for twenty pounds sterling. Some years passed, during which Mr. Town renewed his commission, extending his price to twenty or thirty guineas. At length Mr. Evans wrote to say he had procured the much coveted work at the price of four pounds, and sent it to Mr. Town at that rate. Mr. Evans knew very well that Mr. Town would as willingly have paid twenty or thirty as four pounds, but he was a man of sterling integrity. He has been dead some years, and his son Edward succeeded to the business, and inherits the same honorable principles as his father. The writer of this lately commissioned him to try and procure a beautiful work after Sir Joshua Reynold's if it could be had for five or six pounds. He has just received a first impression on India paper for two pounds. Such instances of honorable fair dealing deserve notice, and any gentleman requiring works of art or illustrated books would do well to apply to Mr. Evans, No. 403 Strand, London.

A few years ago a gentleman of New York, having occasion to change his residence, sent for the late Mr. Royal Gourley, the auctioneer, to value and purchase a lot of books. He came, and after inspection, said he thought they might net about one hundred dollars after paying commission. The gentleman was perfectly satisfied ; Mr. Gourley gave his check for one hundred dollars, and the gentleman considered the matter settled ; but he was somewhat surprised to receive a letter from Mr. Gourley in about three weeks, saying the books were sold and had netted more than his valuation, and as he desired nothing more than his commission, he had great pleasure to enclose his check for fifteen dollars. Surely such instances of pure and upright integrity deserve mentioning in these times.

129.

THERE is no truth of human character so potential for weal or wo, as firmness. To the merchant it is all important. Before its irresistible energy the most formidable obstacles become as cobweb barriers in its path. Difficulties, the terror of which causes the pampered sons of luxury to shrink back with dismay, provoke from the man of lofty determination only a smile. The whole history of our race—all nature, indeed—teems with examples to show what wonders may be accomplished by resolute perseverance and patient toil.

It is related of Tamerlane, the celebrated warrior, the terror of whose arms spread through all the Eastern nations, and whom victory attended at almost every step, that he once learned from an insect a lesson of perseverance, which had a striking effect on his future character and success.

When closely pursued by his enemies—as a cotemporary tells the anecdote—he took refuge in some old ruins, where, left to his solitary musings, he espied an ant tugging and striving to carry a single grain of corn. His unavailing efforts were repeated sixty-nine times, and at each several time, so soon as he reached a certain point of projection, he fell back with his burden, unable to surmount it—but the seventieth time he bore away his spoil in triumph, and left the wondering hero re-animated and exulting in the hope of future victory.

How pregnant the lesson this incident conveys! How many thousand instances there are in which inglorious defeat ends the career of the timid and desponding, when the same tenacity of purpose, would crown it with triumphant success.

Resolution is almost omnipotent. Sheridan was at first timid, and obliged to sit down in the midst of a speech. Convinced of, and mortified at, the cause of his failure, he said one day to a friend, "It is in me, and it shall come out." From that moment he rose, and shone, and triumphed in a consummate eloquence. Here was true and moral courage. And it was well observed by a heathen moralist, that it is not because things are difficult that we dare not undertake them. Be then bold in spirit. Indulge no doubts, they are traitors. In the practical pursuit of our high aim, let us never lose sight of it in the slightest instance; for it is more by a disregard of small things, than by open and flagrant offences, that men come short of excellence. There is always a right and a wrong; and if you ever doubt, be sure you take not the wrong. Observe this rule, and every experience will be to you a means of advancement.

130.

Pick up that pin—let that account be correct to a farthing—find out what that ribbon costs before you say "you will take it"—pay that half dime your friend handed you to make change with—in a word, be economical, be accurate, know what you are doing—be honest and then be generous; for all you have or acquire thus belongs to you by every rule of right, and you may put it to any good use if you acquire it justly and honestly, for you have a foundation, a back ground which will always keep you above the waves of evil. It is not parsimonious to be economical. It is not selfish to be correct in your dealings. It is not small to know the price of articles you are about to pur chase, or to remember the little debt you owe. What if you do meet Bill Pride decked out in a much better suit than yours, the price of which he has not learned from his tailor, and he laughs at your faded dress and old-fashioned notions of honesty and right, your day will come. Franklin, who from a saving boy, walking the street with a roll under his arm, became a companion for kings, says, "Take care of the pennies, and the dollars will take care of themselves." La Fitte; the celebrated French banker, leaving the house to which he had applied for clerkship, was not too proud or careless to pick up a pin. This simple pin laid the foundation of his immense wealth. The wise banker saw the act, called him back, and gave him employment, convicted by the seeming small circumstance of his ability and honesty. Be just and then be generous. Yes, be just always and then you can always be generous. Benevolence is a great duty, a heaven given privilege, by which you not only benefit the object, but feel a sensation of joy in your own soul which is worth more, far more, than gain. But you may not give your neighbor's goods. Your own just earnings you should always share with the needy, but generosity can never be measured by the amount you lavish on a fine dress, or that you spend with your friends to satisfy the requirements of vanity and folly. What if they do pat you on the shoulder? They would do as much to any dog that would serve them. It is the service, not yourself, that gets the flattery, or you spend your money for nought, certainly. Well, let the girl say you are small, rather than spend that dollar you need for a book. Get the book, if it is a good one, it will tell you that no girl worth having ever selected a man for a husband for his long tailor and livery-stable bill more than for his long ears.

131.

"The hour, the appointed hour,
But at your post."

MANY persons who are in the habit of making visits of business commit a sad error in not stating their object *at once* and in as few words as possible. They hesitate, introduce some subject altogether foreign, occupy much precious time, and all to little purpose. Instead of proceeding to the matter in hand directly, they apologize for the intrusion, intimate that *another* time may prove more acceptable, explain and prevaricate, until at last the real object is absolutely forced from them. All this is exceedingly annoying to persons who are constantly engaged and who have no time to waste upon mere prosers. We may mention the case of one individual who invariably states his object in a roundabout way, and introduces at least one other subject preparatory to that which he really desires to converse upon. He does so, too, in the politest manner; forgetful, however, that time is precious and that there are other people in the world besides himself. A visit strictly of business should be brief, direct, and to the purpose. When, moreover, a comparative stranger enters a room and finds two others confidentially engaged, he should have the good sense either to withdraw at once or to ask for an interview aside. It often happens, however, that such intruders sit down quietly, with their ears outstretched, and thus they not only listen, but, at the first opportunity, they volunteer their opinions and advice.

There are, moreover, certain periods of the day in which most individuals are actively employed. At such seasons, therefore, they should not be intruded upon except by intimate friends, unless the necessity arises out of a business urgency. Sometime since we observed an experienced and enterprising merchant passing rapidly up Chestnut street, the time being a few minutes of three o'clock. Just above Third street he was stopped by one of the idlers of the town, who commenced a silly conversation. The merchant manifested impatience, but the other seemed determined to persist. The merchant "stood it" for about five minutes, and then broke away, evidently irritated. The fact is, he was about to take up one or two notes in bank, and the interruption under the circumstances was quite annoying. An anecdote in point may be mentioned: Douglass Jerrold, the celebrated writer, was one day hurrying through a leading street in London, evidently immersed in thought, when he was interrupted by a *quidnunc*, who exclaimed, "Well, Jerrold, what is going on to-day!" The reply was quick and petulent, but pithy and pointed. "I *don't* know," said Jerrold, "but *I* am!" and on he went.

Another:—Some years since a distinguished lawyer of Philadelphia, on passing up Walnut street, saw an intimate friend held closely by the button by an inveterate proser, whose designation we will give for the present as Mr. S. The lawyer immediately stopped and observed to his friend, "When you have done with Mr. S., I would like a few moments conversation with you." He then fell back a few steps and waited. The effect was as anticipated, and the proser immediately took his departure. The lawyer then stepped up to his friend and remarked, "When *you* find *me* in a like dilemma be good enough to afford *me* the relief that I have just given *you*. Good day." It should be remembered that punctuality in the fulfilment of engagements is a matter of the utmost importance with men of business; and yet it is quite difficult for them to be punctual under some of the circumstances that we have described. A day or two since a friend was stopped in the street for only five minutes to hear a story that turned out of very little importance, and yet he lost his passage to New York. He arrived at the wharf *just one minute too late!*

Another anecdote in point:—In the year 1842, two most eminent physicians, had an appointment together for the purpose of consultation. The hour was four o'clock in the afternoon. Dr. R. arrived at the designated time, and, with watch in hand, walked up and down the parlor. Five minutes elapsed and Dr. W. had not yet made his appearance. At the expiration of ten minutes, he came. Dr. R. then complained bitterly, and said in consequence of the delay his entire business for the afternoon had been deranged. Dr. W. apologised, and promised to do better next time. The other shook his head with incredulity, and said that, unfortunately, the case was not the *first* of the kind. They then visited the patient and made another engagement for ten o'clock the next morning. Dr. W. was on *this* occasion five minutes in *advance*, whereas Dr. R. made his appearance *exactly* as the clock was striking ten. The other, as he saw his approach, exclaimed with exultation, "Ah! Doctor, *who* is the punctual man this time?" "*I* am," retorted Dr. R. with considerable spirit. "I am here *at* the appointed time, neither before nor after, and that, according to *my* view of the subject, is punctuality. And he was right.

Still another:—A leading lawyer of Philadelphia, now among the departed, carried his notions of punctuality to a very remarkable extent. At the time designated for a meeting in his office he would remain five minutes to allow for any possible difference in watches, and then, should the other party fail to appear, he would invariably go out. At first the plan was regarded as novel and eccentric; but soon the effect was salutary, for all who made engagements with him knew that they must be punctual or were prepared to take the consequences. The subject is one that might be followed up to almost any extent. How many members of our public bodies are in the constant habit of keeping their colleagues waiting, and thus delaying and postponing the transaction of important business. Such a course is not only discourteous and ungentlemanly, but is unjust and unfair. No man has a right wantonly to waste the time of his neighbor, while the individual who makes an engagement not intending to fulfil it, exhibits a sad want of gentlemanly propriety, and is in fact, guilty of a meanness as well as an insult.

132.

"The good Merchant tells the Truth and thrives by that; is upright and downright; his word, good as his Bible-oath. He pays for all he takes; though never so rich, he owns no wicked dollar; all is openly, honestly, manfully earned, and a full equivalent paid for it. He owns money and is worth a man. He is just, in business with the strong; charitable, in dealing with the weak. His Counting-Room, or his Shop, is the sanctuary of fairness, justice—a school of uprightness, as well as thrift. Industry and Honor go hand in hand with him. He gets rich by industry and forecast, not by sleight of hand and shuffling his cards to another's loss. No man becomes the poorer because he is rich. He would sooner hurt himself than wrong another, for he is a man, not a fox. He entraps no man with lies, active or passive. His Honesty is better capital than a Sharper's Cunning. Yet he makes no more talk about Justice and Honesty, than the Sun talks of light and heat; they do their own talking. His profession of Religion is all practice. He knows that a good man is just as near Heaven in his shop, as in his church ; at work, as at prayer ; so he makes all work sacramental ; he communes with God and Man in buying and selling —communion in both kinds. He consecrates his week-day and his work. Christianity appears more divine in this man's deeds than in in the holiest words of Apostle or Saint. He treats every man as he wishes all to treat him, and thinks no more of that than of carrying one for every ten. It is the rule of his arithmetic. You know this man is a Saint, not by his creed, but by the letting of his houses, his treatment of all that depend on him. He is a Father to defend the weak, not a Pirate to rob them. He looks out for the welfare of all that he employs ; if they are his help, he is theirs ; and as he is the strongest, so the greater help. His private prayer appears in his public work ; for in his devotion he does not apologize for his sin, but asking to outgrow that, challenges himself to new Worship and Piety. He sets on foot new enterprises, which develop the nation's wealth, and help others while they help him. He wants laws that take care of Man's Rights, knowing that then he can take care of himself and of his own, but hurt no man by so doing. He asks laws for the weak ; not against them. He would not take vengeance on the wicked, but correct them. His Justice tastes of Charity. He tries to remove the causes of Poverty, Licentiousness, of all crime, and thinks that is alike the duty of Church and State. Ask not him to make a Statesman a Party Man, or the churches an apology for his lowness ; he knows better—he calls that Infidelity. He helps the weak help themselves. He is a moral educator—a church of Christ gone into business—a Saint in trade. The Catholic Saint who stood on a pillar's top, or shut himself into a den and fed on grass, is gone to his place—that Christian Nebuchadnezzar. He got fame in his day. No man honors him now ; nobody even imitates him. But the Saint of the nineteenth century is the Good Merchant; he is wisdom for the foolish, strength for the weak, warning to the wicked, and a blessing to all. Build him a shrine in Bank and Church, in the Market and the Exchange, or build it not: no Saint stands higher than this Saint of Trade. There are such men, rich and poor, young and old; such men in Boston. I have known more than one such, and far greater and better than I have told of, for I purposely under-color this poor sketch. They need no word of mine for encouragement or sympathy. Have they not Christ and God to aid and bless them? Would that some word of mine might stir the heart of others to be such—of you young men. They stand there clean amid the dust of commerce and the mechanic's busy life; they stand there like great square Pyramids in the desert, amongst the shifting tents of the Arabs. Look at them, ye young men, and be healed of your folly. Think—it is not the calling which corrupts the man, but the men the calling. The most experienced will tell you so. I know it demands manliness to make a man, but it is that work God sent you here to do."

133.

THERE is much of enlightened judgment in the following quotation from the late Dr. CHALMERS, and it is so exactly applicable to England at the present time that we copy it:—"In opposition to the maxim that the spirit of enterprise is the soul of commercial prosperity, do we hold that it is the excess of this spirit beyond the moderation of the New Testament, which, pressing on the natural boundaries of trade, is sure at length to visit every country, where it operates, with the recoil of all these calamities, which, in the shape of beggared capitalists, and unemployed operatives, and dreary intervals of bankruptcy and alarm, are observed to follow a season of overdone speculation."

134.

The good merchant is scrupulously just and upright in all his transactions. Integrity, good faith, exactness in fulfiling his engagements, are prominent and distinctive features in his character. He is a high-minded and honorable man; he would feel a stain upon his good name like a wound, and regards with utter abhorrence everything that wears the appearance of meanness or duplicity. Knowning that credit is the soul of business, he is anxious to sustain the integrity of the mercantile character. Accordingly, his word is as good as his bond. He stands to his bargain, and is faithful to his contract. He is like the good man described by the Psalmist,

> "Who to his plighted vows and trust
> Hath ever firmly stood;
> And though he promise to his loss,
> He makes his promise good."

He would rather at any time relinquish something of his lawful rights, than engage in an irritating dispute. He would rather be the object than the agent in a dishonorable or fraudulent transaction. When one told old Bishop Latimer that the cutler had cozened him in making him pay two pence for a knife not worth a penny, "No," said Latimer, "he cozened not me, but his own conscience."

The good merchant is not in haste to be rich, observing that they who are so, are apt to "fall into temptation and a snare," and often make shipwreck of their honor and virtue. He pursues commerce as his chosen calling, his regular employment. He expects to continue in it long, perhaps all his days, and is therefore content to make small profits and accumulate slowly. When he first entered into business, he was determined not to be a drudge, nor be chained to the desk like a galley-slave, nor make his counting-room his home. He recollects that he is not merely a merchant, but a man ; and that he has a mind to improve, a heart to cultivate, and a character to form. He is therefore resolved to have time to develop and store his intellect, to exercise his social affections, and to enjoy in moderation the innocent and rational pleasures of life. He accordingly sets apart and consecrates a portion of his time, his evenings at least, to be spent at home, in the bosom of his family. He will not, on any account, deny himself this relaxation ; he will not, for any consideration, rob himself of this source of improvement and happiness. He is willing, if need be, to labor more years in order to obtain the desired amount of wealth, provided he can improve himself in the mean time, and enjoy life as he goes along.

The good merchant, though an enterprising man, and willing to run some risks, knowing this to be essential to success in commercial adventure, yet is not willing to risk everything, nor put all on the hazard of a single throw. He feels that he has no right to do this—that it is morally wrong thus to put in jeopardy his own peace and the comfort and prospects of his family. Of course he engages in no wild and visionary schemes, the results of which are altogether uncertain, being based upon unreasonable expectations and improbable suppositions. He is particularly careful to embark in no speculation out of his regular line of business, and with the details of which he is not familiar. He is aware, that although he knows all about the cost of a ship, and can determine the quality and estimate the value of a bale of cotton, he is not a good judge of the worth of wild lands, having had no experience therein. Accordingly, he will have nothing to do with any bargains of this sort, however promising they may appear. He will not take a leap in the dark, nor purchase upon the representations of others, who may be interested in the sale; fearing lest what is described to him as a well-timbered township may turn out to be a barren waste, and what appears, on paper, a level and well-watered district, may be found, on inspection, a steep and stony mountain, of no value whatever. He therefore deems it safest for him to keep clear of these grand speculations, and to attend, quietly and regularly, to his own business. Above all, he makes it a matter of conscience not to risk in hazardous enterprises the property of others intrusted to his keeping.

The good merchant, having thus acquired a competency, and perhaps amassed a fortune, is liberal in dispensing his wealth.

At the outset, he is careful to indulge in no extravagance, and to live within his means, the neglect of which precaution he finds involves so many in failure and ruin. Simple in his manners, and unostentatious in his habits of life, he abstains from all frivolous and foolish expenditures. At the same time, he is not nigardly or mean. On the contrary, he is liberal in the whole arrangement of his household, where everything is for use and comfort, and nothing for ostentation and display. Whatever will contribute to the improvement and welfare of his family, or whatever will gratify their innocent tastes, be it books, or engravings, or pictures, he obtains, if within his means, though it cost much; knowing that at the same time he may foster the genius and reward the labors of our native authors and artists, an estimable class of men, whose works reflect honor upon their country, and who consequently merit the patronage of the community. But whatever is intended for mere parade and vain show, he will have none of, though it cost nothing. He thinks it wise and good economy to spend a great deal of money, if he can afford it, to render home attractive, and to make his children wise, virtuous, and happy. Above all, he never grudges what is paid to the faithful schoolmaster for their intellectual and moral training; for a good education he deems above all price.

Having thus liberally provided for all the wants of his household, the good merchant remembers and cares for all who are related to him, and who may in any way stand in need of his aid. And this aid is administered in the most kind and delicate manner. He does not wait to be solicited; he will not stop to be thanked. He anticipates their wishes, and by a secret and silent bounty removes the painful sense of dependence and obligation. He feels it a pleasure, as well as a duty, to help them; he claims it as his privilege to do good unto his brethren. He would feel ashamed to have his needy relatives relieved by public charity or private alms.

But our good merchant feels that he has duties, not only to his immediate relatives and friends, but to a larger family, the community in which he lives. He is deepily interested in its virtue and happiness, and feels bound to contribute his full share to the establishment and support of all good institutions, particularly the institutions of learning, humanity, and religion. He is led to this by the expansive and liberalizing spirit of his calling. It is, unfortunately, the tendency of some occupations to narrow the mind and contract the heart. The mere division of labor, incident to, and inseparable from, many mechanical and manufacturing pursuits, though important and beneficial in other respects, yet serves to cramp and dwarf the intellect. The man who spends all his days in making the heads of pins, thinks of nothing else, and is fit for nothing else. Commercial pursuits, on the other hand, being so various, extensive and complicate, tend to enlarge the mind, and banish narrow and selfish feelings. The merchant looks abroad over the world, puts a girdle round the earth, has communications with all climes and all nations, and is thus led to take large and liberal views of all things. The wealth which he has acquired easily and rapidly, he is consequently disposed to spend freely and munificently. It has been beautifully said of Roscoe, the distinguished Liverpool merchant, "Wherever you go, you perceive traces of his foot-steps in all that is elegant and liberal. He found the tide of wealth flowing merely in the channels of traffic ; he has diverted from it invigorating rills to refresh the gardens of literature. The noble institutions for literary and scientific purposes, which reflect such credit on that city, have mostly been originated, and have all been effectually promoted, by him." In like manner, our good merchant encourages learning, and patronises learned men. He is particularly liberal in endowing the higher seats of education, whence flow the streams that make glad the cities and churches of our God.

The good merchant is, likewise, a munificent benefactor to all institutions which have for their object the alleviation of human wretchedness, and the cure of the thousand ills which flesh is heir to. He lends, too, a substantial support to the institutions of religion. He feels the need of them himself, and he understands their unspeakable importance to the peace, good order, and virtue of society. He thinks that he sleeps sounder, and that his property is more secure, in a community where the sanctions of religion are superadded to the penalties of the law ; where the stated inculcation of religious principles and sentiments diffuses a healthy moral atmosphere, which, though unseen, presses like the weight of the surrounding air, upon every part of the body politic, and keeps it in its place. Accordingly, he contributes cheerfully and liberally to the support of public worship, and, moreover, as Fuller says of the good parishioner, "he is bountiful in contributing to the repair of God's house, conceiving it fitting that such sacred places should be handsomely and decently maintained."

Such we conceive to be the character of the good merchant. It may, perhaps, be thought by some that the character is a visionary one; and that, amidst the competitions of trade, the temptations to unlawful gain, the eager desire of accumulating, and the natural unwillingness to part with what has been acquired with much labor and pains, there can be no place for the high-minded and generous virtues which we have described. We might have thought so too, if we had never seen them exhibited in actual life. The portrait which we have attempted to draw is not a fancy sketch, but a transcript from nature and reality.

135.

"I WISH I had his money!" said a young, hearty-looking man, as a millionaire passed him in the street. And so has wished many a youth before him, who devotes too much time to wishing, that too little is left for working. But never does one of these draw a comparison between their several fortunes. The rich man's money looms up like a balloon before them, hiding uncounted cares and anxities, from which they are free: keeping out of sight those bodily ills that luxury breeds, and all the mental horrors of *ennui* and satiety; the fear of death that wealth fosters, the jealously of life and love from which it is inseparable. Let none wish for unearned gold. The sweat by which 'tis gathered is the only sweet by which it is preserved for enjoyment, for in too literal a sense is it true, that "'tis easier for a camel to pass through the eye of a needle, than for a rich man to enter the kingdom of Heaven."

Wish for no man's money.

The health, and strength, and freshness, and sweet sleep of youth are yours. Young Love, by day and night, encircles you. Hearts unsoiled by the deep sin of covetousness, beat fondly with your own. None—ghout-like—listen for the death-tick in your chamber ; your shoes have value in men's eyes—only when you tread in them. The smiles no wealth can purchase greet you—living ; and tears that rarely drop on rose-wood coffins, will fall from pitying eyes upon you—dying. Be wise in being content with competency. You have, to eat, to drink, to wear, enough ? then have you all the rich man hath. What though he fares more sumptuously ? He shortens life—increases pains and aches, impairs his health thereby. What if his raiments be more costly ? God loves him none the more, and man's respect in such regard comes ever mingled with his envy.

Nature is yours in all her glory : her ever varying and forever beautiful face smiles Peace upon you. Her hills and vallies ; fields and flowers ; and rocks, and streams, and holy places—know no desecration in the step of Poverty ; but welcome ever to their wealth of beauty—Rich and Poor alike.

Be content ! The robin chirps as gaily as the gorgeous bird of Paradise. Less gaudy is his plumage, less splendid—his surroundings. Yet no joy that cheers the Eastern beauty, but comes upon his barren hills to bless the nest that Robin builds. His flight's as strong, his note as gay ; and in his humble home, the light of happiness shines all as bright, because no cloud of envy dims it. Let us then, labor and be strong—in the best use of that we have ; wasting no golden hours in idle wishes for things that burthen those who own them, and could not bless us if we had them, as the gifts already bestowed by a Wisdom that never errs. Being content, the poorest man is rich : while he who counts his millions, hath little joy if he be otherwise.

136.

"Owe no man anything," was the injunction of a Christian Apostle, whose lessons were seldom if ever unworthy of attention. If we were to express the sentiment, we should prefer the motto of John Randolph, "pay as you go." The politician compassed the idea better than the Apostle. Owe men we must, in all the courtesies and kindnesses which belong to and grace humanity; it is a debt collateral with our being—an obligation of our nature; therefore the Apostle was not definite enough; but Randolph hit the mark when he confined his maxim to debts pecuniary, which men, under the present order of things, are liable to incur. He touched with a true and noble philosophy one of the commonest and greatest of society evils.

We take it for granted that, as a general rule, debts pecuniary are contracted to be paid, sooner or later. As a general rule, their burthen is least the sooner they are paid. Interest, usury, dependence, law-suits, and costs of all kinds that hang over standing and litigated debts add, if we could but get at their total for a single year in this country, millions of dollars to the original obligations. Friendships are broken over debts; forgeries and murders are committed on their account; and however considered, they are a source of cost, annoyance and evil—and that continually. They break in everywhere upon the harmonious relations of individuals and society; they blunt sensitiveness to personal independence; and, in no respect that we can fathom, do they advance the general well-being.

Well, as debts are incurred to be paid, and as the saving all lies on the side of the earliest payment, why not manage to pay as we go, and thus avoid all debts, duns, broken friendships, writs, constables, sheriffs and court costs. We buy this or that, of A. B. or C., and we propose to pay him in a week, a month, three months, and so on, the common rule of credit not running beyond six months—for which credit we have to pay advance prices and interest—why not, even at some brave sacrifice, contrive to get so far the start of custom as to pass by this perpetual credit season, and from that point beginning with the world anew and even, keep even by paying as we go. It would be infinitely cheaper, better and more independent for us all. If we can ever pay, why not at once—now? Will it be easier when interest is added to principal?

The rich have no excuse for not paying as they go, though, to their shame be it said, they are oftenest the ones to decree misery and ruin by the credit they use—or rather, abuse, in their business intercourse with the world. They, by withholding the honest dues of the laborer, the mechanic, the merchant and the professional man, all poor comparatively, force these classes into indebtedness until communities become a tangled net, whose threads of affiliation are standing accounts, notes, bonds and mortgages, suit at law, judgments and executions. If those who are eminently able to pay as they go, were to be just and pay thus, the credit system which now makes one-half of society dependents and slaves, would be mainly swept away. The middle man and the poor man are driven to the wall by the system, they can be pushed and pursued under obligation, with impunity; but your man of means, your rich man, who dares to remind him of a debt?—he "will pay when he gets ready."

No one who observes and reflects on this subject, can deny the truth of the picture we have drawn. The evils of the credit-system, which now pervades every department of business and all the trade intercourse of society, are great and overwhelming. The poorer classes most especially feel them so. The mechanic, the laborer, and the tradesman, with little or no capital—as is generally the case—how can they succeed in enterprise, or in living, even, if they are not paid as they go. If they are paid, they, too, can pay. The reform, therefore, must begin, not like most others at the bottom of the scale, but at the top—with the rich. Let them incur no debts to those whom they employ or with whom they trade, and all classes below them in means, can be free of debt. Debts are curses, and among the greatest under which society groans—the greatest under which nations suffer.

137.

Buying and selling are so well understood in Turkey, that Mohammedans make a practice of going to mosque, and having their goods marked with their several prices, and those who go bazaaring—not shopping—choose what they want, and leave the money to every fraction. What a sensure upon Christendom, where Falstaff's exclamation is so peculiarly applicable :—"How this world is given to lying." Think of the bare-faced assurance of a clerk, with confidential looks, assuring customers that he is actually selling at cost price ! The most profound adept in falsehood is sure of promotion, therefore it is no wonder so many lick-spittles turn the tables on their employers, when the devil is the father of lies, and lying the origin of all evil. The popular mania for bargains first caused these deceptions to be practised among traders in their own defense ; at least this is certainly a plausible excuse, under present circumstances, for buyers and sellers are foes rather than friends, and each one exults in turn, when laying the flattering unctions to their souls that one has overreached the other.

"''Tis nought,' saith the buyer, but after a while he boasteth ;" this shows that a similar system was carried on in the days of Solomon. David seems to intimate that the children, in his days, told lies as soon as they were born. This pernicious custom of romancing has become so general as to produce a countless race, whose ideality is immense; they imagine that the most notorious falsehoods are merely poetical licenses and flowers of rhetoric. Major Longbow would have made his fortune in a retail dry goods store, or a Jew's ready-made clothing establishment. "One fib is oft the cause of ten more," says the old spelling-book, and one who has the gift of the gab, and "lays it on with a trowel," is now considered a first-rate salesman. Is it possible, after such manifestations, that a good understanding can be maintained between employer and employed? Let us consider the essential qualities most likely to attract patronage and inspire respect.

The primary object is unqestionably to win the *confidence* of those likely to become purchasers, and for such a purpose, *truth* is our card of recommendation; all duplicity is recoiled at as derogatory to the character of probity. The cost price of wares is never referred to, supposing such a reference might only produce incredulity and suspicion. Having a general knowledge of human nature, a salesman adapts himself to the disposition of the buyer, and, by sedulous attention and courtesy, he is sure to please. Should an injudicious choice be made of a defective article, an honorable man will point it out, and produce only what he can warrant. Such undeviating, straight-forward transactions are the sure methods of building up a business that will endure.

"Discretion in speech is more than eloquence," while sincerity and affability are passports that carry merchants through the world like winged Mercuries. An impertinent coxcomb is avoided, especially by ladies; and unmeaning tittle tattle—

foreign to the subject—is out of place, and resembles the trickery of a juggler, to divert attention. Every one has an indubitable right to make all the profits he possibly can—but honorably. "The worth of a thing depends on the want of it. The value of a thing is the market price of it. This is the only intelligible idea of *value,* and the only reasonable adjustment of *price.*" On competition depends the market price and its fluctuations. With these necessary causes, still, honor and truth need never be infringed. The public know how to discriminate between genuine and fictitious trading, which accounts for the failures so frequent in our cities; once imposed on, the rogue's store is shunned, and finally closed. Honesty is the best policy all the world over, and that accounts for the unprecedented prosperity enjoyed by the Gold Pen Company, whose commendable motto is "ONE PRICE AND NO DEVIATION."

138.

MANY traders and mechanics are in the habit of making their original charges, during the day, on slate, and having them at night, or at some convenient opportunity, transcribed on the day-book. It is a very unsafe practice. A decision directly in point was made a few years since in the Suffolk Court of Common Pleas.

"In the case of Buckley *vs.* Pillsbury, the defendant offered to make oath to his books of account, in which it appeared that the entries were made once a week, or oftener, by his clerk, who transcribed them from a slate, on which they were entered by the defendant himself; the clerk not being able to testify to the items charged any further than that they were correctly transcribed. The court ruled that the defendant could not be permitted to swear to the correctness of his books."

139.

"I TELL you, my dear, it is utterly impossible! Save three hundred dollars a year out of my salary? You don't understand it," said Charles Converse to his young wife.

"Perhaps I do not, replied Mrs. Converse, "but my opinion is very decided."

"Women don't understand these things. You think my salary of eight hundred dollars a year, a fortune."

"No such a thing, Charles."

"But eight hundred dollars, let me tell you, won't buy all the world."

"I had no idea that it would; yet, if you only had the habit of saving what you spend for things that you can get along without, you would be able to build a house in a few years."

"Build a house?"

"Yes, build a house, Charles."

"Well, that's a good one."

The young man laughed heartily at the idea—too chimerical, too absurd to be harbored for a moment.

"How much do you suppose it cost us to live last year?"

"Why, eight hundred dollars, of course. It took all my salary—there is none of it left."

The young wife smiled mischievously as she took from her work-table drawer a small account-book.

"You did not know that I kept account of all these things, did you."

"No; but how much is it?" And Charles was a little disturbed by the cool way in which his wife proceeded to argue the question.

"Four hundred and ninety-two dollars," answered Mrs. Converse.

"Oh, but, my dear, you have not got half of it down."

"Yes, I have—everything."

"My tailor's bill was sixty-five dollars."

"I have it here."

"Hats, boots, and—"

"I have them all."

"The deuce you have."

"When you had any new thing, you know I always asked you what you gave for it."

"I know you did; but I will bet five dollars I can name a dozen things that you have not got down."

"Done!" said the lady with a laugh, as she took from her drawer a five dollar bill, and placed it on the table.

Charles Converse covered the money.

"Capital idea for you to bet against me with my money!" said he good humoredly.

"If I lose, I will do without that new barege I am to have."

"Nay, my dear, I don't want you to do that."

"But go on."

"Pew-rent, six dollars," said the husband promptly.

"Here it is," answered she, pointing to the entry in the book. "Try again."

"Season ticket on the railroad—twenty."

"I have it."

"Sawing the wood."

"Entered."

Charles reflected a moment; the case began to look desperate.

"New linings for the cooking-stove."

"Here—two dollars."

"Cleaning the clock."

"One dollar—here it is."

Mr. Converse began to look hopeless.

"My taxes."

"Well, I have not got that."

But that was the only thing he could mention of these necessary expenses, that was not found to be regularly entered on his wife's book. Still Mr. Converse was not satisfied.

"Your figures cannot be correct, Mary," said he.

"Why not?"

"My salary is all used up, and you can account for only four hundred and ninety-two dollars of it."

"You must explain the balance."

"I! Why, Mary, I have not been extravagant. It is true, I buy a great many little things in the course of the year, but they are hardly worth the mention."

"Ah! there's the mischief. That is where the money goes, you may depend upon it."

"Nonsense! You women don't understand these things."

"Of course, we don't!"

"Well, your figures show that you don't.—Where has the three hundred dollars gone to, then?"

"I don't know, Charley. I haven't the least idea. I am sure that I have got down all the items that came within my knowledge. I am positive that you have brought home no article of any description that has not been entered upon the book—I mean the articles of food and clothing, and things for the house."

"But just look at it a moment. You don't mean to say that I have spent three hundred dollars over and above our necessary expenses?" said Charles, a little warmly.

"I don't mean to say anything about it, for I don't know anything about it."

"Now I think of it, there's my life insurance, have you got that down?"

"I have not."

"There is forty of the three hundred."

"But it leaves two hundred and sixty-eight dollars unaccounted for."

"It would take a great while to collect money enough to build a house, even if the whole of this sum were saved."

"Not a great while, Charles. You know my father has promised to give you the land when you have the means to build a house upon it."

"It will be a long while," laughed the husband.

"Five or six years, perhaps, if you are prudent. Hasn't the President of your bank promised you a thousand dollars a year?"

"Yes."

"Then you can certainly save four hundred dollars a year."

"There is a thousand things we want when my salary is raised."

"But we can do without them."

"I suppose we can."

"Just look here, Charles."

Mrs. Converse took from her pocket a circular issued by the "People's Saving's Bank," in which the accumulation of several small sums deposited weekly and quarterly, were arranged in a table.

"Fifty dollars deposited every quarter will net in five years, one thousand one hundred and forty-one dollars twenty-five cents!" continued she, reading from the circular.

"Bah!" added Mr. Converse.

"That sum would build a very comfortable house; and when your salary is a thousand dollars a year you can save more than fifty dollars a quarter."

"A five per cent. institution, isn't it?" asked the young man.

But he was much impressed by the reasoning of his wife, and in the course of the evening he carefully read the circular of the "People's Saving's Bank."

Certainly he had every inducement for being saving and economical. He had lived very cheaply in a small house belonging to his father-in-law, for which he paid a merely nominal rent.

His wife's father was a wealthy farmer, or rather he had been a farmer, before his domain was invaded by the march of improvement, and his pastures and mowing lots laid out into house lots. As it was, he still, from the force of habit, improved a few acres, kept a couple of cows, a "henery," and half a dozen pigs.

Charles Converse found this proximity to the "old folks at home," rather satisfactory, in a pecuniary as well as a social point of view, for his larder was partly stocked from the farm; and, of course, no account was ever made of half a pig, a barrel of apples or potatoes, or a pair of chickens. Milk and eggs were so much better and fresher from "pa's," that of course the young couple never desired to obtain them from any other source.

They lived cheaply and lived in clover besides. Charles never liked to talk about financial matters with "pa," because the worthy old gentleman used to tell him how he lived on a hundred and fifty dollars a year after he was married—thought he had a fat salary, and supposed, of course, he saved four hundred dollars a year out of it—and always wound up by saying that he would give him a lot—might take his pick of all he owned—whenever he got ready to build.

All these things rather worked upon Charles Converse. He

hadn't saved a dollar, and what was more, there was no present prospect that he ever would do so. The promised advance in salary was already appropriated to sundry luxuries. The idea of taking Mary to the opera, or a pleasant trip to Niagara, and other amiabilities, had taken possession of him.

But the reasoning of his wife had produced a strong impression upon his mind. She had been brought up in the strictest habits of economy. Her father, though rich, had an army of children; but they were all wealthy in their thrifty habits.

Charles read over and over the circular of the Saving's Bank in the evening, figured up the statistics, and wondered what had become of that two hundred and sixty-eight dollars.

Before he went to bed he had matured a resolution, though he did not say a word to his wife about it.

The next day, Charles Converse received a quarter's salary, and his first step, after receiving it, was to visit the People's Saving's Bank, where he deposited fifty dollars.

But the hundred and fifty dollars which he had left burned in his pockets. It was all he had to carry him through the ensuing three months. There were a dozen little things that he wanted, and a dozen big ones, for that matter. Against the latter he resolutely set his face, though, in consideration of the fact that his salary would be a thousand dollars a year, after the next pay-day, he had a week before made up his mind to have them.

Among other things his segar-case was empty, and he stepped into Seavy's, in Congress street, to have it replenished. Segars were a great luxury—in fact, a necessity to him, in his own opinion.

The gentlemanly proprietor of the establishment placed a box of the fragrant rolls upon the counter.

"Something new," said he.

Charles took up a handful and smelt them.

"Best segars in the market," continued the vender.

"Tip-top," replied Charles, inhaling the grateful odor. "How do you sell them?"

"Four cents apiece."

Six of them were transferred to the case, a quarter thrown down, and, as it was not magnanimous to pick up a copper's change, he left the store. But then, a little fellow inside seemed to say:

"Charley, you can't afford to smoke such segars as those. They will hardly last you two days. If you must smoke, buy a cheaper segar than that. You will not be able to build your house in ten years at this rate."

He did not pay much attention to the monitorial voice, however, and as he passed along he drank a sherry cobbler himself and paid for three friends, whom he could not help asking to drink with him, at Barton's.

At Vinton's, a Charlotte Russe was disposed of, and so on to the end of the chapter. And these were his daily habits. It was only a sixpence or a quarter at a time, and these were so ridiculously small, that they never caused him a thought. The idea that they absorbed any considerable portion of his salary, never occurred to him. He had always gratified his appetite or inclination in these matters, as they had come to be regarded as necessities.

Still, Charles Converse had turned over a new leaf. He refrained from purchasing a great many articles which he had intended to get when he received his quarter's salary, and as he seated himself in the cars, he congratulated himself on the firmness with which he had carried out the resolution of the previous evening.

"You are late, Charles," said Mary, when he reached his sunny little cottage.

"I have been paying my quarter bills," replied he, with a smile. "Here they are, my sweet accountant."

He threw the bills upon the table, and while she was examining them, he threw his bank-book in her face.

"What!" exclaimed she, in astonishment, as she saw the book. "Fifty dollars!"

"Yes, my dear, female influence—the influence of a wife," and the husband playfully kissed her. "I am convicted of sin, and converted, too, which is better still. I am resolved to be prudent, economical, saving, even parsimonious."

"I am glad to hear it."

"And the house will be built in just five years, according to the programme of the Saving's Bank."

As he spoke, he took from his pockets three of the city evening papers.

"Not quite cured, Charles," said Mary with a smile.

"What do you mean?"

"*Journal*, *Transcript*, and *Traveler*, two cents each," laughed Mary. "You are determined the publishers shall live."

"Why, Mary, you wouldn't have me live without a newspaper, would you? That would be a depth of barbarism to which I would never descend," replied Charles, with a look of astonishment, at the interesting mentor.

"Certainly not; but is not one paper a day enough?"

"That is but a trifle."

"The rain falls in drops, but washes the whole earth. Four cents a day, for a year, amounts to about twelve dollars."

Charles scratched his head. It was a most astounding revelation to him.

"You are right, Mary, one paper is enough."

Charles eat his supper, but was moody and abstracted. A new idea was penetrating his brain, which, he began to think, had been rather muddy on financial affairs.

As he rose from his table he took out his segar case, and as he did so, the little fellow within, who had spoken to him when he came out of the segar shop, began to upbraid him pretty sharply. He burned his fingers in attempting to light the fragrant roll, and then relapsed into a fit of deep musing.

"What are you thinking about, Charles?" asked Mary, after she had cleared away the table.

"Eh! Oh, I was thinking how much twelve times three hundred and sixty-five are."

"Twelve means twelve cents, I suppose?" said she, performing the problem on the margin of one of the newspapers. "Here it is, forty-three dollars and eighty cents."

"For segars," added he, blankly.

"Which added to the sum paid for superfluous newspapers, makes fifty-six dollars and twenty-eight cents."

"And twenty for shaving, which I may do myself, are seventy-six dollars and twenty-eight cents," continued he, taking the pencil and ciphering away with all his might for a few moments.

"*Gleason's Pictorial*, *Home Journal*, *Saturday Courier*, and your county paper come to——"

"But, my dear, we can't do without our county paper," exclaimed Charles, looking with amazement into the face of his wife.

"I don't want you to do without that," said his wife

"Sherry cobblers, ice creams, and oysters, over a hundred dollars, by thunder!" continued he, turning to his figures again.

"Indeed!"

"I begin to see where the two hundred and sixty-eight dollars have gone to," said he.

"And sherry cobblers are worse than useless. I had no idea you *drank*, Charles."

"Say no more, Mary, I am done."

And he was done. The idea of "saving up" something took complete possession of him—not so far as to make him niggardly—but for enough to make him abandon the four cent segars, three evening papers, Vinton's compounds, and especially sherry cobblers.

On the next quarter day one hundred dollars was added to his deposit at the Saving's Bank, and as his habits improved afterward, and his salary still further increased, much greater sums were added.

In four years the house was built, new furniture bought and paid for, and Charles is considered one of the most thrifty young men in the town—all of which propitious events, we honestly believe, had their origin in the beneficent influence of the Saving's Bank, whose circular had opened his eyes, and stimulated him to carry out his resolution.

40.

HAVE your property at all times fully insured. From a neglect of this caution, thousands are annually ruined. Insure at those offices that have the reputation of paying claims honorably and punctually; even if you give a higher premium. It would be judicious to show your policies to some experienced and disinterested person well versed in the subject of insurance, in order to be sure that all is right.

141.

It is related of Girard, that when a young tradesman, having bought and paid for a bag of coffee, proceeded to wheel it home himself, the shrewd old merchant immediately offered to trust his new customer to as many more bags as the latter might desire. The trait of character revealed by the young man in being his own porter, had given the millionaire confidence in him at once. His reputation was made with Girard. He became a favored dealer with the enterprising merchant, throve rapidly, and in the end amassed a fortune.

No mere capital will do so much for young men as character. Nor will always even capital and connection combined. In our own experience, we have known many beginners who have utterly failed, though backed by ample means, and assisted by the influence of a large circle of friends. In some cases, indeed, considerable experience, as well as industry and perseverance, have been added to these advantages, yet without securing success. We have known such persons, after a failure in their first pursuit, to try a second, and even a third, yet with no better result, although still assisted by capital, by friends, and even by their own activity. The secret was that they had missed, somehow, making a character for themselves.

On the other hand, it is a common occurence to see young men begin without a cent, yet rapidly rise to fortune. They achieve this triumph by establishing, at the outset, a reputation for being competent business men. Few are so fortunate as to do this by a single characteristic act, like the purchaser who won Girard's good will by wheeling home the bag ; for generally neither veteran merchants are as shrewd as the famous millionaire, nor young dealers as energetic as his customer. But a consistent life of sagacity, economy and industry, invariably establishes the right kind of reputation in the end. Confidence grows up in influential quarters, towards the young beginner. Old merchants shake their heads approvingly, and say, "he is of the right stuff, and will get along." Credit comes, as it were, unsought. Connection follows. The reputation of the new aspirant widens and deepens; his transactions begin to be quoted as authority; trade flows in on him from every quarter; and in a few years he retires with a competence, or remains to become a millionaire. All this is the result of establishing, at the outset, a character of the right sort.

We may say to every young man, about to start in life, make a character for yourself as soon as possible. Let it also be a distinctive one. It is better to have a name for excelling all others in some one thing than to enjoy simply a notoriety for merely general merit. Are you a mechanic?—outstrip your fellows in skill. Are you a young lawyer?—become superior in a particular branch. Are you a clerk?—be the best book-keeper your employers have. Are you in a store?—make yourself acquainted with the various buyers. In short, become known for an excellence peculiar to yourself; acquire a speciality, as it is called; and success is certain, because you will have, as it were, a monopoly, and can dictate your own terms.

Money may be lost, without fault of our own, by some one or another of the accidents of life. Connections may be broken up, by death, or failure, or change of interests. But character remains through all. It belongs to the individual, and is above the chances of fate. Thousands who have lost all else, have recovered themselves, by having a character to start anew with; but no man, without a business character, has even risen from the ruin caused by the loss of capital, or the destruction of connection.

142.

In the vicinity of B—— lived a poor but industrious man, depending for support upon his daily labor. His wife fell sick, and not being able to hire a nurse, he was obliged to confine himself to the sick bed and family. His means of support being thus cut off, he found himself in need. Having a wealthy neighbor near, he determined to go ask for two bushels of wheat, with a promise to pay as soon as his wife became well enough to leave, that he could return to his work. Accordingly he took his bag, went to his neighbor's, and arrived when they were at family prayers.

As he sat on the door-stone he heard the man pray very earnestly that God would clothe the naked, feed the hungry, relieve the needy, comfort all that mourn. The prayer concluded, the the poor man stepped in and made known his business, promising to pay with the avails of his labor. The farmer was very sorry he could not accommodate him, but he had promised to lend a large sum of money, and had depended upon his wheat to make it out; but he presumed neighbor A—— would let him have it.

With a tearful eye and a sad heart, the poor man turned away. As soon as he left the house the farmer's little son stepped up and said:—

"Father, did you not pray that God would clothe the naked, and feed the hungry, relieve the distressed, and comfort the mourners?"

"Yes—why?"

"Because, father, if I had your wheat I would answer that prayer." It is needless to add that the Christian father called back his suffering neighbor, and gave him as much wheat as he needed.

Now, Christian readers, do you answer your own prayers?

143.

It is astonishing how many people there are who neglect punctuality. Thousands have failed in life from this cause alone. It is not only a serious vice in itself, but it is the fruitful parent of numerous other vices, so that he who becomes the victim of it gets involved in toils from which it is almost impossible to escape. It makes the merchant wasteful of time; it saps the business reputation of the lawyer, and it injures the prospects of mechanics who might otherwise rise to fortune: in a word, there is not a profession, nor a station in life, which is not liable to the canker of this destructive habit.

It is a fact not always remembered, that Napoleon's great victories were won by infusing into his subordinates the necessity of punctuality to the minute. It was his plan to maneuver over large spaces of country, so as to render the enemy uncertain where he was about to strike a blow, and then suddenly to concentrate his forces and fall with irresistible force on some weak point of the extended lines of the foe. The execution of this system demanded that each division of the army should arrive at the specified spot punctually; for, if any part failed to come up, the battle was lost. It was by imitating this plan that the allies finally succeeded in overthrowing the emperor. The whole Waterloo campaign turned on these tactics. At Mount St. Jean, Blucher was punctual, while Grouchy was not; and the result was that Napoleon fell and Wellington triumphed.

In mercantile affairs, punctuality is as important as in military. Many are the instances in which the neglect to renew an insurance punctually has led to a serious loss. Hundreds of city merchants are now suffering in consequence of the want of punctuality among their western customers in paying up accounts. With sound policy do the banks insist, under the penalty of a protest, on the punctual payment of notes; for, were they to do otherwise, commercial transactions would fall into inextricable confusion. Many and many a time has the failure of one man to meet his obligations brought on the ruin of a score of others, just as the toppling down, in a line of bricks, of the master brick, causes the fall of all the rest.

Perhaps there is no one class of men less punctual than mechanics. Do you want an upholsterer? He rarely comes when he agrees. So with carpenters, painters, and nearly all others. Tailors and shoemakers often do not have their articles home in time. The consequence is that thousands remain poor all their lives, who, if they were more faithful in their word, would secure a large run of custom, and so make their fortunes. What would become of the *Ledger* if it was not punctual in going to press? or if our paper-makers were not punctual in delivering paper? or if our compositors were not punctual in coming to work? Be punctual, if you would succeed.

144.

WHILE journeying one day from London to Oxford, before railroads were in use, in the good old-fashioned stage-coach, I chanced to meet a fine, hearty, hale specimen of an Englishman, who was as good a stage-coach companion as one ever meets. He had a joke to crack at every mile-stone, and his laugh drove all *ennui* out of the way. At every stopping-place he was sure to draw a laugh from the bar-maid by some innocent piece of wit, and in the twinkle of his small black eye was a mingled expression of cunning and acuteness. An opposition coach came along, and for a little way we were side by side—the horses partaking of the spirit of the drivers, who seemed determined that it should be their last race, at the break-neck speed we were going. The old gentleman entered into the sport with great glee; and, with his head out of the window, he shouted first at the horses, and then at the opposition driver, till we finally outstripped them, when the old gentleman laid back and declared that "Opposition was the life of everything."

"When I was a young man," said he, "I set up in the hat trade, and took a store in London, where there was not a hat store within a quarter of a mile, thinking I should do more where there were no others; but I found that, at the end of the year, all that I made might have been put into the corner of my small eye, and not have injured its sight. I sat down one day, and, after thinking that my lot was a mighty hard one, told my boy that I was going out awhile, and that he must keep a sharp look-out for customers. I went down town, and, looking around, found that two or three hatters were driving a very good trade very near together, and passing into one store, I found its owner quite a talkative man. We put our heads together, and, in the course of a week, the store directly opposite his received my stock in trade, and a coat of blue paint on the outside, while his received a coat of green.

"The first day I did nothing but stand at the door and look pouty at the green store, and my friend Blake stood on his steps looking ditto at me. As people came in, I commenced running down the green store, and Blake always run the blue, so between us both, we built up a trade that way quite respectable. People having taken sides, and new comers always purchasing of one or the other, we gradually grew rich, and, at the end of some dozen years, we settled up, and I found that opposition, or apparently so, had made my fortune."

145.

"To depart from regular business is to lose money."

No maxim in life is more strictly true than the above quotation. How often do we see men who, in the pursuit of their regular business, were daily gaining in respect and credit, (lured away by the *ignis fautus* of sudden wealth,) embark in speculations and enterprises of which they know nothing. They continue on until serious embarrassment, and oftentimes positive ruin, open their eyes to the fact that in all descriptions of trade or commercial pursuit *toll must* be paid either by apprenticeship or money. We have frequently had occasion to notice the truth of this somewhat trite remark. We have seen the retailer striving hard to connect jobbing with his retailing ; and the jobber, in his turn, grown envious of the importer, seek to range out of his appropriate sphere, and in *nine* cases in *ten* these departures from legitimate trade have been *failures* in their results, and upon a calm analysis it will be found that quite as much success has been attained as could have been rationally expected. We see, in the first place, that the country merchant has the same sources open to him for the supply of his wants as the city retailer. If the purchaser is doing business in the country, the jobber takes into consideration that competition is less, and the risk consequently lessened. His offers in prices are quite as low, at least, to the country merchant as to the city retailer, and thus the purchases made of a smaller concern must have some extra inducement either in lower prices or length of time. If goods are sold without these inducements, we think it would be safe to conclude that a want of credit among jobbers is one reason for his seeking to make purchases among his equals. But even were this barrier removed, would it be sound policy for a man (whose main dependence is on the retail trade) to allow the gems to be selected at about cost from his stock, and goods of inferior qualities and more ordinary styles left, from which he *must* suit the taste of fastidious women. Generally a stock selected from in this way is injured vastly more than the profit made could benefit, even were there no risk in the credit.

The position of the jobber and importer can be illustrated better by an anecdote, which we heard from undoubted authority. A jobber who, one year since, was afflicted with the importing mania, and followed the business successfully during the year 1847, realizing therefrom over two thousand dollars, says he would willingly give all the money he made in '47, and five hundred dollars added thereto, to be rid of his imports for '48. Many will say this was all owing to circumstances, which probably might not happen again in years, and that the importers are all in the same boat. Softly, man! this is not exactly so. Upon inquiry you will find that but few of the present quantities of excess goods *belong* to our importers. They are merely the *factors*, the *ownership* rests elsewhere; and the heavy loss (for a heavy loss must be sustained on this spring's imports) will fall upon Europe, and not be sustained here.

Importers who are pecuniarily interested in the price at which goods are sold in this country, have some connection, branch, or resident partner in Europe, whose duty it is to watch the market there. The exports from thence is the barometer; and when such times as the present are upon us, we find that, although they seemingly and in reality have goods enough on hand, they belong to other parties, and in many instances have been shipped against their advice. So sensitively alive are these resident partners in Europe to the exports, that we have heard of five pounds having been paid for the outward manifest of a ship bound to the United States.

We have been frequently amused at the quaint remarks of Zadock Pratt, Esq., ex-member of Congress, (a man of strong common sense,) who was originally a tanner by trade. A speculator was showing him a new method of tanning, by which he represented great quantities of money could be made. Pratt told him he did not doubt it, but he was making money enough; that he (the speculator) had better find some one who was not doing so well. He has resisted all attempts to allure him from his legitimate business, and by close application has amassed a quarter of a million.

Our advice is, to the retailer, do not attempt to job; to the jobber, leave importing alone; and to the importer, allow not the offer of an extra price to induce you to break a package, for it is as completely unjust for you to rob the jobber of his legitimate profit as it would be for the jobber to retail goods. We say most emphatically, stick to your regular business.

146.

We know not who may be the author of the following maxims; but experience, the greatest human teacher, has long since satisfied us of their soundness. Our worthy friend, Zadock Pratt, of Prattsville, and many more, will bear cheerful testimony as to their efficacy in effecting the objects proposed.

Be Industrious.—Everybody knows that industry is a fundamental virtue in a man of business. But it is not every sort of industry which tends to wealth. Many men work hard to do a great deal of business, and, after all, make less money than they would if they did less. Industry should be expended in seeing to all the details of business; in carefully finishing up each separate undertaking, and in the maintenance of such a system as will keep everything under control.

Be Economical.—This rule, also, is familiar to everybody. Economy is a virtue to be practised every hour in a great city. It is to be practised in pence as well as in pounds. A shilling a day saved, amounts to an estate in the course of a life. Economy is especially important in the outset of life, until the foundation of an estate is laid. Many men are poor all their days, because, when their necessary expenditures were light, they did not seize the opportunity to save a small capital, which would have changed their fortunes for the whole of their lives.

Stick to your own Business.—Let speculators make their thousands in a year or a day; mind your own regular trade, never turning from it, to the right hand nor to the left. If you are a merchant, a professional man, or a mechanic, never buy lots nor stocks, unless you have surplus money, which you wish to invest. Your own business you understand as well as other men; but other people's business you do not understand. Let your business be something which is useful to the commnnity. All occupations possess the elements of profit in themselves, while mere speculation has no such elements.

Never trade at great hazard.—Such hazards are seldom well-balanced by the prospects of profit; and, if they were, the habits of mind which are introduced are unfavorable, and generally the result is bad. To keep what you have should be the first rule; to get what you can fairly, the second.

Do not love money extravagantly.—We speak here merely with reference to being rich. In morals, the inordinate love of money is one of the most degrading vices. But the extravagant desire of accumulation induces an eagerness, many times, which is imprudent, and so misses its object from too much haste to grasp it.

Don't be in a hurry to get rich.—Gradual gains are the

only natural gains; and they who are in haste to get rich, break through sound rules, fall into temptations and distress of various sorts, and generally fail of their object. There is no use in getting rich suddenly. The man who keeps his business under his control, and saves something from year to year, is always rich. At any rate, he possesses the highest enjoyment which riches are able to afford.

NEVER DO BUSINESS FOR THE SAKE OF DOING IT, AND BEING COUNTED A GREAT MERCHANT.—There is often more money to be made by a small business than a large one; and that business will be, in the end, most respectable which is most successful. Do not get deeply in debt; but so manage as always, if possible, to have your financial position easy, so that you can turn any way you please.

147.

HAMBURGH witnessed a curious proceeding on the 8th of November, 1847, as we find it stated in the "London *Sun*." The scaffold was erected, as for an execution, before the principal front of the Exchange, and at noon a large furnace filled with resinous wood was placed on it. The wood having been set on fire, the bell of the Town Hall was rung violently, as is usual during the execution of decrees inflicting infamous penalties. At the hour at which merchants are assembled on the Exchange, the public executioner ascended the scaffold, and, after having caused a drum to be beat, proclaimed, in a loud voice, the name of a merchant who had been declared guilty of a fraudulent bankruptcy, and who had taken to flight. He then displayed to the spectators an enormous placard, bearing the name of the culprit in gigantic letters. He next caused the drum to be beat a second time, after which he tossed the placard in the flames.

148.

We rejoice at every indication of life from the pulpit. The pulpit is never more divine in its ministrations, than when it applies its teachings to the wants of the age, or fearlessly points out the dangers that beset us in the ordinary, every-day walks of life. This simple remark is suggested to our mind, by the publication of a sermon, preached in Brooklyn, in September, 1847, by the Rev. Frederick A. Farley, in the ordinary course of his ministerial duties. The object of the reverend gentleman is, to point out some of the dangers of a business life. In the text, or motto selected for the occasion, "*be not slothful in business, but be fervent in spirit,*" etc., the preacher does not deprecate the importance of activity or industry, in the business of life, but the burthen of his discourse is rather to show the dangers peculiar to a too eager pursuit of gain. The first danger in commercial life noticed, is the continual, ever-present tendency to selfishness. On this head, Mr. F. remarks :—

"No matter how similar or how different your occupations, my brethren, you are all exerting yourselves for yourselves ; or, which is the same thing for all practical purposes, for those whose claims on you for support are always strengthened by a sense of duty, and in most cases by the ties of affection. There is a constant struggle going on for the greatest share of patronage and emolument—an unintermitted search for means and opportunities of peculiar and unwonted profits—a shifting of expedients to build up and magnify one's fortune—and an anxious, and almost literally a sleepless vigilance, to secure whatever advantages have been gained, or whatever success is promised. There is a direct and incessant conflict and competition between your own concerns, interests, advancement, and those of others, ever bringing into action, and encouraging and indulging the selfish passions. Now these passions, thus powerfully addressed and excited, may become tyrants over your better nature—swaying every part of your conduct—rendering you envious, narrow-minded, morose, meanly and grossly avaricious—changing the fair and noble enterprise of business, into a spirit of low cunning, chicanery, and intrigue—leading you to throw every possible obstacle in the way of your neighbor's success—tempting you to rejoice, or at least to feel very complacent, in his failure or embarrassment, and to stray from the course of strict and high-minded integrity, whenever, by so doing, you think you can gain some personal advantage, or avert some apparently threatening loss. How resolutely should every honorable and Christian man guard himself against the encroachments of this most despicable and dangerous temper! Be active—I would say, in the name of all that is holy, to each one of you, brethren, be active—industrious—enterprising; but O, be above any unworthy jealousy of others. Set the example on all occasions, under all circumstances, of a large, liberal, generous spirit. Let the world see that whatever success you attain, it is only by the legitimate exercise of the talents, means, and opportunities you can honestly command; taking no unfair advantages of others' straits or calamities, but, on the contrary, showing a readiness, as far as you have ability, to relieve rather than crush them."

The second danger adverted to, is the mistake of supposing that religion may be safely and entirely separated from any of the common occupations in which business men are engaged. He was not very far off from the truth, who somewhere said, that "work was worship." But let us hear the substance of Mr. F.'s reflections on this point, as expressed in the following passage:—

"Religion is designed to reach the minutest things which we do, to control even our thoughts, to become indeed the dominant principle of our characters. Who, then, is the religious man, in the highest, the Christian sense? Not he, surely, who appears to be religious on great occasions, when the eyes or ears of hundreds or thousands are observing or listening to him, but who, in the family retreat, is a source of grief or pain or mortification to the few, and as they ought to be, the beloved few around him. Character is not so tried or judged in regard to anything else—why should it be in regard to this? The little things in a man's conduct, as they are thoughtlessly called—the prevailing air of generous and high-souled virtue—the constant and delicate respect for the feelings, wishes, even, I am ready to say, the prejudices of others—the habitual love of excellence in any sphere or walk of life—the uniform mildness, serenity, benevolence of the disposition—the unshaken trust in, and loyality to God, and reverence for his being and perfections—in a word, the kindness, generosity, integrity, and piety of his demeanor, shown always, and everywhere, at home and abroad, not for the sake of display, but simply and obviously as the result of deeply laid principle ever operative within; these things I take to be among the strongest proofs that the man is a religious man. Men are very apt to think, nevertheless, engaged so constantly, not to say engrossed in their business, that they have nothing to do with religion, except on set occasions and in a special and prescribed way; and too often that it belongs to particular persons who may be religious in their behalf. So far from the truth is all this, that under the light and instruction of the Gospel, you ought to carry religion with you to the office, the factory, the warehouse, the workshop, the exchange. I do not mean that you are to carry there long and sad faces, a constrained air and manner, or the formal exercises of devotion. None of these alone, nor all of them put together, would prove you religious. No. But an inflexible love of honest, generous, upright dealing between man and man ; an humble, forbearing, forgiving, conciliating disposition ; showing you ever, in that crowded and exciting arena, to be superior to the world ; not absorbed in its pursuits, not wholly fascinated by its charms, not willing on any occasion, or for any temporal bribe, to compromise your conscientious sense of what, in the strictest sense, is right in the sight of God. This it is, to be religious in one's business ; to refer all that you do, in every business transaction and engagement, always and alone, to that moral standard which God himself has set up."

The preacher is right in affirming, that the standard of character among business men is in danger of being lowered. A single passage from this portion of the homily, will, perhaps, give the reader some idea of a danger that every one must feel him self exposed to.

"Amid the excitement of business, where each man is apt exclusively to seek his own, and not another's welfare, the lowest rather than the highest standard of moral obligation will prevail and be followed. It is not the future so much as the present, which is thought of. An individual will be far more likely to ask himself, in some great exigency, what is the law, the public law of the land—rather than what is right, strictly, unqualifiedly, truly right, by the law of God. Accordingly, such a man will, without the slightest compunction or uneasiness, transgress the Christian law of equity and of kindness. In the transaction of business, some men are daily and hourly manifesting an unwillingness to accommodate each other, a want of regard to the welfare of others, a reluctance to sacrifice the slightest personal convevience or profit, and a readiness to seize on every little petty circumstance which may result to their own benefit, even though, by so doing, they may essentially injure others;—things which, in the intercourse of private and social life, even they would condemn as breaches of the commonest charities and courtesies of life. Beware, brethren, of this! Let the unadulterated spirit and principles of the Gospel, in all their fullness and strictness of requisition, go with and guide you in every concern in which you engage. In the event, sooner or later, you will find you have gained much—much every way, for the want of which nothing could compensate; much in peace of conscience—in its silent, but deeply-felt approval—in the assurance which that makes doubly sure of the favor of God."

The preacher closes his rather generalizing view of the dangers of a business life, with a brief reference to the tendency to forget that life, the present life, is not the whole of existence. It seems to us, that we should view the life that now is, as the commencement of a conscious eternity of being; and, without taking anxious thought for the future, develop, no matter at what cost, those faculties of mind and body that must enhance the blessedness of the unfathomable and never-ending future. The kingdom of heaven is within us, now and forever, and should be as much so in the body as out of it.

149.

Ascertain the whole state of your affairs. Learn exactly how much you owe. Be not guilty of deceiving yourself. You may thus awaken suspicions of dishonesty, when your intentions were far otherwise. Deliberately and fully make up your mind, that come what will, you will practice no concealment, or trick, which might have the appearance of fraud. Openness and candor command respect among all good men.

150.

It is a peculiar vice of our age and country to put a false estimate on the mere acquisition of riches. I do not either undervalue wealth or the diligence and enterprise so often exercised in its attainment. I would not say a word to throw a doubt on the importance of acquiring such a measure of this world's goods as to render one independent, and able to assist others. The young man who thinks he can amuse or employ himself as he sees fit, at the same time throwing the burden of his support on others, or leading a precarious life on the verge of debt and bankruptcy, is a dishonor to his species. But I assert that the too common mistake, which makes men look upon the acquisition of a fortune, or having a fine and fashionable house, as constituting success in life, as pernicious. Success in life consists in the proper and harmonious development of those faculties which God has given us. Now we have faculties more important to our welfare than that of making money—faculties more conducive to our happiness, and our health of body and soul. There are higher and better modes of activity than those which are exhibited in multiplying dollars. Men can leave to their children a better patrimony than money; they can leave them the worth of a good example, good habits, a religious faith, a true estimate of the desirable things of this life ; resources of mind and a heart which will shed sunshine on adversity, and give a grace to prosperous fortune. "It is not wealth which is deserving of homage, but the virtues which a man exercises in the slow pursuit of wealth—the abilities so called forth, the self-denials so imposed."

I have heard of two brothers, whose father died, leaving them five hundred dollars apiece.

"I will take this money and make myself a rich man," said Henry, the younger brother. "I will take this money and make myself a good man," said George, the elder. Henry, who knew the multiplication table only, abandoned all thoughts of going to school, and began by peddling in a small way, over the country. He was shrewd, and quick to learn whatever he gave his attention to; and he gave all his attention to making money. He succeeded. In one year his five hundred dollars had become a thousand. In five years it had grown to be twenty thousand; and at the age of fifty he was worth a million. George remembered the words of the wise man: "With thy gettings get understanding." He spent two-thirds of his money in going to school, and acquiring a taste for solid knowledge. He then spent the remainder of his patrimony in purchasing a few acres of land in the neighborhood of a thriving city. He resolved on being a farmer.

After a lapse of thirty-five years the two brothers met. It was at George's house. A bright, vigorous, alert man was George, though upwards of fifty-five years old. Henry, though several years younger was very infirm. He had kept in the counting-room long after the doctors had warned him to give up business, and now he found himself stricken in healthiness beyond repair. But this was not the worst. He was out of his element when not making money. George took him into the library and showed him a fine collection of books. Poor Henry had never cultivated a taste for reading. He looked upon the books with no more interest than he would have looked on so many bricks. George took him into his garden, but Henry began to cough, and said he was afraid of the east wind. When George pointed out to him a beautiful elm, he only cried "Pshaw!" George took him into his green-house and talked with enthusiasm of some flowers, which seemed to give the farmer great pleasure. Henry shrugged his shoulders and yawned, saying, "Ah! I don't care for these things." George asked him if he was fond of paintings and engravings. "No, no! don't trouble yourself," said Henry, "I cant tell one daub from another." "Well, you shall hear my daughter Edith play upon the piano; she is no ordinary performer, I assure you." "Now don't, brother, don't, if you love me," said Henry, beseechingly; "I never could endure music." "But what can I do to amuse you? Will you take a ride?" "I am afraid of a horse. But if you will drive me carefully down to your village Bank, I will stop and have a chat with the President." Poor Henry! Money was uppermost in his mind. To it he sacrificed every other good thing. When, a few days afterwards he parted from his farmer brother, he laid his hand on his shoulder, and said:—"George, you can just snpport yourself comfortably on the interest of your money, and I have got enough to buy up the whole of your town, bank and all—and yet, your life has been a success, and mine a dead failure!" Sad but true words.

151.

THE personal accomplishments and public spirit, by which the higher class of mercantile pursuits would be greatly ennobled as a department of human life, and made more influential, must be built of many important qualifications.

The great merchant should be half a statesman. His occupation of itself, when conducted on the broadest scale, demands the exercise of that wide and comprehensive vision requisite for the operations of a chief minister, or a general, whose plans of campaigns cover half a continent. If, in addition to his own fortunes, he would understand and advance the great interests of his country, his qualities and acquirements must be much ampler To give him such capacities, what and how great training is necessary. For our own part, we would advocate the establishment, in our schools and colleges, of a distinct branch of commercial studies, with its own professorships, by which those designing to follow the more enterprising pursuits of trade should have their grasp of mind enlarged, and their views rendered more liberal and enlightened. We do not know why commercial knowledge—a knowledge embracing the products and essential interests of different countries, their relations to each other, together with the principles of maritime and international law—why a pursuit, thus covering the world with its observations and its action, is not a *science* as much as any other, and to be mastered with as severe and regular study.

This much for his department of life as an occupation; but the merchant should have more than this would argue. He should be accomplished in many things, like any other person, in the community, of cultivated mind. His pursuits must necessarily be very engrossing; but they need not be so to the exclusion of those gentlemanly tastes and acquirements which would place the mercantile business, in its more general departments, on a level, intellectually and socially, with the learned professions. Why should not a merchant have cultivated a very thorough knowledge of literature, a taste in architecture—one of the noblest of studies—a love for sculpture and paintings, a delight in landscape and garden ornation? These things should form a part of his education; and they need not afterwards interfere with the full prosecution of business. He has wealth to support his tastes, which many, if not most, professional and sedentary men have not; why should the sense of the beautiful slumber in him? Not many, perhaps, are formed to have a taste for all these ; but some part of them must appeal to the perceptions of every one ; and why should the man of traffic pour away the wine of life, satisfying himself with the dregs, though they be of gold ?

If, to this statesman-like scope of vision, and these refinements of mind, he add an understanding of the great moral and social interests of his country and the world, and the abiding disposition to help them forward, what one of all the professions which men follow, would be more worthy of honor, or of envy, than the profession of THE MERCHANT ?

152.

NOTHING is more common than to hear men complain that the chances of success lessen every day ; that every avenue of business is overcrowded, and unless a man be a perfect Hercules of talent he is elbowed out of the way and prevented from "getting on," in life, to languish in obscurity and pine in neglect ; to grow old, in short, before his time, and die at last of disappointment and heart-sickness. Undoubtedly there are many instances in which society is to blame, many sad instances of capacity overlooked, and talents slighted ; but the complaint, as a general thing, is false and foolish, and the evil is in the complainer, and not in society. Men often miscalculate their own powers and mistake their line. The speech of a wealthy citizen, when asked how he made his money, is the answer to all such railers against society. "Sir," said he, "I understood my business and attended to it, and if I were poor again to-morrow, I could commence as an ashman and make a fortune if God spared me life and health to work." A knowledge of our own capacities, and fixed and steady aim, in short, steadiness of purpose and steady consistent effort are the conditions of success, and almost invariably command it.

153.

It was the custom of the Rev. Rowland Hill, at the commencement of a new year, to preach an annual sermon for the "Benevolent Society of Surrey Chapel, for visiting and relieving the Sick Poor at their own Habitations," selecting, at the same time, a few of the most remarkable cases to read to his congregation, that had been visited during the preceding year. On one of these occasions, he narrated the afflictive circumstances of a lady, formerly of property and respectability, who had been plunged into the depths of poverty and want, in a time of sickness, through having imprudently become security for some relation or friend; and Mr. Hill took this opportunity of publicly warning and entreating all present to be on their guard against committing so fatal an error. "I would advise all my friends," said he, "to do the same as I do myself, when any request of this kind comes to me. I just walk out of one room into another, and consider what I can afford to *give*, and what I *ought* to *give* to the applicant; then I return and say—'Here, my friend, I make you a present of this sum, and if you can get a few others to help you in the same way, perhaps you will get over your difficulty.' Then," said Mr. Hill, with emphasis, "I know the *end* of it; but were I to lend my name, or become surety, I know not *how* that might end."

Strange as it may appear, he was waited on, a few months after this, by one of the members of the church, soliciting his kind assistance in procuring him a lucrative situation, then vacant in that parish and district, viz: a collector of the king's taxes; the person urged that it would be the making of him and his family, but that he must have two bondsmen for one thousand pounds each. Mr. Hill said he would consider of it. This petitioner was well known to Mr. Hill; he had long held a confidential situation in his chapel, and was, besides, in a good trade and connection of business, with his friends. There was no reason to doubt his integrity; and he was one that Mr. Hill was desirous to oblige. The result was, he became one of his securities, and prevailed on a gentleman, at Clapham, to be the other; and the situation was obtained. Alas! alas! for poor Mr. Hill and his brother bondsman! In three or four years, the collector was a defaulter to the amount of thousands. The securities were obliged to pay.

154.

In the year 1805, a small tradesman, in a country-town in Somersetshire, became so much embarrassed, that he thought it no more than an honest part to make known the situation of his affairs to his creditors. The consequent investigation which took place, terminated in an assignment of his effects, which, when sold, produced a dividend of nine shillings and fourpence in the pound, and he received a discharge from all further claims. But, although thus legally acquitted, and with little prospect of realizing his intention, this honest man formed the honorable resolution of, at least, attempting what appeared to him the obligations of unalterable justice, by making up the deficiency to all his creditors. It is true, the sum required was small, not quite ninety pounds; but his means were proportionably inadequate, having now nothing but his daily labor from which it could be obtained, after defraying the necessary expenses; and his wages were discouragingly low, not averaging more than twelve shillings per week. Mean accommodations and clothing, hard fare, and hard work, at length enabled him, through the Divine blessing, to accomplish his purpose. The creditors were all paid in full, and they esteemed his integrity so highly, that they thought proper to acknowledge their sense of it by a handsome present.

155.

A GENTLEMAN of Boston, says a religious journal, who was unfortunate in business thirty years ago, and consequently unable at that time to meet his engagements with his creditors, after more than twenty years of toil, succeeded in paying every creditor (except one whose residence could not be ascertained) the whole amount due them. He has in that twenty years brought up and educated a large family—but still he owed one of his former creditors; he was not satisfied to keep another's property; he made inquiry, and received information that the party had died some years since. He again pursued his inquiry respecting the administrator, and ascertained his name and residence, wrote to him, acknowledged the debt, and requested him to inform him of the manner he would receive the money. A few days since he remitted the whole amount, principal and interest.

156.

Dr. FRANKLIN relates the following anecdote of Mr. Denham, an American merchant, with whom he once went a passenger to England. "He had formerly," he says, "been in business at Bristol, had failed, in debt to a number of people, compounded, and went to America; there, by a close application to business as a merchant, he acquired a plentiful fortune in a few years. Returning to England in the ship with me, he invited his old creditors to an entertainment, at which he thanked them for the easy compensation they had favored him with; and, when they expected nothing but the treat, every man, at the first remove, found under his plate an order on a banker for the full amount of the unpaid remainder, with interest.

157.

A PERSON of the Quaker profession, says a London paper, having, through misfortune, become insolvent, and not being able to pay more than eleven shillings to the pound, formed a resolution, if Providence smiled on his future endeavors, to pay the whole amount, and, in case of death, he ordered his sons to liquidate his debts by their joint exertions. It pleased God, however, to spare his life, and, after struggling with a variety of difficulties, (for his livelihood chiefly depended on his own labor,) he at length saved sufficient to satify every demand. One day the old man went with a considerable sum to the surviving son of one of his creditors, who had been dead thirty years, and insisted on paying him the money he owed his father, which he accordingly did with heartfelt satisfaction.

158.

IRVING, in his life of Washington, dwells on the particularity with which the great hero attended to the minutest affairs. The Father of his Country, as his correspondence and account books show, was "careful of small things," as well as of great, not disdaining to scrutinize the most petty expense of his household; and this even while acting as the first magistrate of the first republic in the world. In private circles in this city, tradition preserves numerous anecdotes of this characteristic, which, if necessary, we could quote.

The example of Washington, in this respect, might teach an instructive lesson to those who scorn what they call "petty" details. There are thousands of such individuals in every community. We all know more or less of them. Nothing is worthy of attention, in their opinion, unless it can be conducted on a grand scale. They will not condescend to the pennies, it is only the dollars to which they will attend. They spurn a small business. They talk superciliously of those who overlook the little leakages that waste so much money in every concern. To hear them, one might think they were above the ordinary affairs of life, and that nothing was worthy of their time, except discovering a California or conquering a kingdom.

Yet no man ever made a fortune, or rose to greatness in any department, without being "careful of small things." As the beach is composed of grains of sand, as the ocean is made up of drops of water, so the millionaire is the aggregation of the profits of single ventures, often inconsiderable in amount. Every eminent merchant, from Girard and Astor down, has been noted for his attention to details. Few distinguished lawyers have ever practiced in the courts, who have not been remarkable for a similar characteristic. It was one of the most striking peculiarities of the first Napoleon's mind. The most petty details of his household expenses, the most trivial facts relating to his troops, were, in his opinion, as worthy of his attention, as the tactic of a battle, the plan of a campaign, or the revision of a code. Demosthenes, the world's unrivalled orator, was as anxious about gestures or his intonation, as about the texture of his argument or its garniture of words. Before such great examples, and in the very highest walks of intellect, how contemptible the conduct of the small minds who despise small things.

159.

It is said that, by a statute of King Athelstane, grandson of Alfred, it was provided that any merchant who made three voyages, on his own account, beyond the British channel, should be entitled to the privilege of a thane, or gentleman.

160.

Every workman will tell you that a good tool requires a good man, and that, unless a man either understands a tool, or takes kindly to it, he had better not be permitted to touch it. All the vast facilities afforded to us by our command of the sea, the use of steam, and such a fleet as the world never saw, are lost on men who imagine themselves waging war in the interior of Spain, and have settled in their minds that dysentery, half-rations, incessant exposure, nakedness, abandonment of baggage, frightful mortality, the utter absence of roads, and general disorganization are the normal conditions of war, and need excite no concern at head-quarters. Great generals have ever been men in advance of their times. Alexander was not a mere ingredient of the Macedonian phalanx; he was one of the first gentlemen of his day, literary and accomplished, surrounded by philosophers and *savans*, and always ready to profit by their suggestions. Hannibal's versatility and ingenuity are notorious. Cæsar was always in advance of his foes, and made a point of arriving earlier than even his friends expected. With twenty days' notice he made an earthwork as many miles long, which answered its purpose, and survives to this day. He was always looking to his commissariat in time, detecting conspiracies long before they ripened. He was the best engineer of his time, no one knowing better the construction of such engines of war as were used in those days. He conquered a nation of pirates on their own element, and when they thought to steal a march on him by cutting the tackle of his ships, he disconcerted them by the use of chains, instead of ropes. Had he waged war only as Scipio Africanus, or Marius and Sylla, or even Pompey had done, he would soon have succumb to a world of foes and rivals. But he beat the age by being always in advance of it. That is still the only way.

161.

Bonds, Notes, Covenants, Contracts, and all the forms of carefully drawn, signed and sealed instruments, have their places in business life. No man's integrity is questioned by his being requested, in any transaction, to have appropriate papers drawn, obligations written, and copies exchanged. To take a bill, or to give a bill, is always right; and there cannot be, many times, too much attention given to put into a written form, business agreements, in view of the forgetfulness, misunderstanding, vicissitudes and death of the best of men. But allowing all this, and urging the obligations of honor which necessarily enter into all these transactions, there is another matter wholly covered by the sanctions of honor between man and man—transactions where written statements and expectations are excluded, and where the reliance is and must be entirely on the honor of the trusted party—his strength of principle in adhering to the understood confidence reposed in him, and without which confidence no business would have been done with him at all. To give a plain illustration, we will take a common case: A trader becomes suddenly embarrassed in his business; he desires to deal on just principles with all his creditors, and while looking about him for the best method of operation, he asks of a friend to become the receiver of some portion of his property. That friend accepts the trust. He knows what a degree of confidence is reposed in him by the other, and an obligation is assumed as clear and obvious as any where papers are drawn up with superior skill. If he has any suspicion of fraud, he has a perfect right to decline to receive the said property; he can properly state his suspicions and, if he feels morally impelled, he can justly administer a rebuke of any attempt to make him a party in a fraudulent transaction. But if without anything of this kind, he receives the property, he becomes his guardian on the score of honor, to return it to the owner. It would be dishonorable thus to hold property ; and, at the same time, to expose it to attachment by a creditor of its owner. If his interest in a creditor is such that he thinks no property should, for any length of time, be held back from said creditor, he can relinquish the guardianship thereof, and then govern himself according to the new relations he holds towards it. Obligations of honor may then impel him to expose the existence and the where-abouts of said property, because the relations of honor are changed. He has settled with the owner ; he is released entirely from him ; and his duty may now, in the way of honor, lie in the direction of the interest of the creditor only.

Now we heard this reasoning called "loose morality" the other day, but we maintain there is nothing loose about it. It is tight as true, manly honor. It is manifestly in harmony with the only principles on which society can exist. It is based on the honor which alone can give just rules of conduct in business life. The "loose morality" is where a man will assume to act, under the given circumstances, the guardian of a friend's property, with no more idea of honor, or no higher idea of honor, than is compatible with an exposure of that property to that friends' creditors. He knows that no confidence would have been reposed in him had the friend dreamed that such a course was regarded right by him. He therefore violates honor, the sanctity of which is worth a martyr's struggle to defend untarnished and complete.

We have used this illustration only to give force to our commendation of the principle involved—honor in business life. In mercantile circles we not unfrequently hear regrets expressed that many business men do not regard manly honor more, being governed by a low expediency, and resorting to shifts and turns that show they are to be kept straight only by that course of dealing which pre-supposes a slippery character is being dealt with. When, like Shylock, they are ready to draw some honest merchant's blood, their hope, while they tremble at the fear of loss is, that they may, by some oversight, have admitted much "in the bond." Shakespeare pictures, too, the Jew trembling as he has been told to take his "pound of flesh," but to draw not one drop of blood! He is not on his own ground, and hastily grasping the written contract on which he lent his gold, he exclaims, "*Is it in the bond?*" and his eye scans the document with fearful intensity. No! "in the bond" was not written what *he* was bent on having—a merchant's life; and "in the bond" was not the place to look for the eternal law that forbade his drawing, for mercenary purposes, human blood. He was baffled, and humanity applauded the result of woman's wit against a Jew-broker's cunning. So in society about us—there is always a real satisfaction when those are foiled who discard all obligations of honor.

No more splendid compliment is possible, it seems to us, than that which the Hon. Horace Binney once gave to the character of Philadelphia business men, in reference to this matter of honor, he being himself one of those men who show us that

"Rightly to be great,
Is, not to stir without great argument,
But greatly to find quarrel in a straw
When honor's at the stake."

On one occasion Mr. Binney said: "In the course of an active professional life, I had constant opportunities to observe how vastly the cases of good faith among merchants and men of business in this city, outnumbered the cases of an opposite description, where at the same time there was neither formal security, nor competent proof to insure fidelity. I should say the proportion was greater than a thousand to one."

What a tribute is this to the faithful regard to manly honor on the part of the business men of this city. It is good to read it, to remember it, to cherish the spirit it expresses, and so to be governed by it, that illustrations of its beauty and dignity may never be wanting in our community.

162.

WHEN a man of limited means, undertakes any important project, requiring energy, skill and dexterous management, and succeeds, not only in accomplishing the object undertaken, but derives therefrom a fair competence, and amasses a tolerable fortune from his small beginnings, the world at large call the individual fortunate, and ascribe his success to good look ; but in general terms, if there is any luck in the matter, it is the luck of possessing an active temperament, and a liberal disposition. It is an awkward thing to launch into business without the usual allowance of capital, but this is not the thing most needed by a young man about engaging in commercial or mercantile pursuits. A liberal, but daring disposition, with a thorough knowledge of ones business, are indispensible requisites, and these in time, conquer capital ; but money will never purchase a business character.

We would not refer to extreme cases of beggars becoming millionairs, or of some suicidal miser, who from a paltry shilling had raised a hundred thousand ; fixed principles, fixed habits—a stern and unflinching character, yet honest, familiar, good natured and agreeable. These are some of the characteristics of the business man. These are the tools with which multitudes have carved out their fortunes, and with which multitudes have constructed a highway to fame.

We like the advice of Mr. John McDonough, late a merchant in New Orleans:

"Remember always, that labor is one of the conditions of our existence. Time is gold; throw not one minute away, but place each one to account. Do unto all men as you would be done by. Never put off till to-morrow what you can do to-day. Never bid another to do what you can do yourself. Never covet what is not your own. Never think any matter so trifling as not to deserve notice. Never give out that which does not first come in. Never spend but to produce. Let the greatest order regulate the transactions of your life. Study in your course of life to do the greatest amount of good. Deprive yourself of nothing necessary to your comfort, but live in honorable simplicity and frugality. Labor then, to the last moment of your existence.

163.

A correspondent writes to the Editor of the *Merchants Magazinc*, after this manner, March, 1848:—

"Success in business is usually the result of intelligent and well-directed efforts.

"Many of the failures in mercantile life, as well as in other pursuits, arise from a want of proper knowledge of the *principles* upon which success is based.

"The uncertainty of mercantile business has become a proverb; and from estimates made, and publicly proclaimed on various occasions, the proportion of those engaged in that employment, who are evidently successful, has been extremely small.

"But is this a *necessary* result? The writer thinks not. Men who have been successful, and who have been successful as a consequence of their practical knowledge and their prudent management, know to the contrary. And yet failure follows failure. Why is it thus? Need we continue in the dark upon this subject? Are there not minds, engaged in the pursuit of business, competent to enlighten us, and whose feelings would prompt them to the task if their attention was suitably turned to it?

"It is a subject of grave importance, and the remedy, as far as possible, should be provided; as, for want of it, the integrity of worthy men is constantly placed in jeopardy, and when laid waste, destruction of character and happiness is the usual consequence. This frequently occurs with persons who desire to do right, but, for want of a proper knowledge of the *land-marks*, get into a false position, and thereby involve themselves and others without intending it.

"The young and inexperienced, who are pressing forward confident of success, and yet without that knowledge that would insure it; and successful men, who stand in the position of creditors, are alike interested;—indeed, the whole community has a deep and an abiding interest in all measures that will promote good morals, and lead to happy and successful results.

"A portion of the evil arises from defective business training—partly from the indolence or inattention of the learner, and partly from the incompetency or disinclination of the instructor. The obligations mutually existing between master and apprentice are therefore not faithfully discharged, and loss is sustained by both parties.

"The more strictly methodical a business is conducted, provided it insures correctness and proper despatch, the nearer it will approach success, and the more those engaged in it will become fond of its details; and, as a consequence, the more willingly they will devote themselves to those duties which they feel at the same time promotes their pleasure and advances their interests.

"Why may not the profession of the merchant be reduced to a science?

"There *are* principles, that lie at its foundation, which are as true as those applicable to any other pursuit; and it needs but their development and arrangement, to enable those engaged in its duties to be equally successful.

"The attention of intelligent aud philanthropic merchants is in this manner invited to the subject, in the hope that some one, competent to the task, will accomplish it, and thereby confer a lasting benefit upon an extensive and valuable class in society; so that, while young men are acquiring a knowledge of their business practically, they may also study its principles, and thus become fitted not only to secure advantages to themselves, but useful in training others, and eventually be ornaments to their profession.

"In the mean time let each one interested in the subject, whether merchant, mechanic, or manufacturer, provide a book, and accustom himself to noting every important *fact*, *precept*, *principle*, or *illustration*, having a bearing upon his particular occupation, classified under suitable heads. By adopting this course, it will in time be found that he has not only improved his own mind and his own habits, and collected a mass of information important to himself and to those in his employ, but that he has provided a valuable legacy for his children, or for those who may succeed him in his line of business."

164.

It is always better to raise a person who has fallen than to trample him in the dust—to speak the words of hope and consolation than to express the feelings of contempt and scorn. We were led to this reflection the other day upon learning the circumstances attending the misfortunes of a merchant whom we know to be a man of honor and probity. B—— had, what is commonly termed, failed; that is, a series of misfortunes unlooked-for, and against which it was impossible to provide, had reduced his means so that he was unable to meet his engagements. With a gloom of heart which was natural under the circumstances, B—— prepared to meet his creditors and give them satisfaction as far as he was able. The day on which they assembled at his counting-room was rainy and dreary—a day on which a single gleaming ray of the sun would have been a blessing. The creditors were gathered around a table, and with gloomy brows they awaited the announcement of the amount they were to expect upon each dollar they had advanced to the broken merchant. B—— appeared, with an expression of resignation upon his countenance, and yet it was occasionally clearly seen that there was a suppressed agony in his heart. For a time there was a silent examination of books and papers, as each creditor sought to ascertain the amount for which he would suffer. Then, a man of keen sympathies, to whom this silence was painful, remarked, "It is a rainy day." "Yes," replied B——, and there was a beam of light on his countenance, "but it will not always be rainy." The tone and nature of the expression struck the sympathizing merchant, and he almost immediately arose, and proposed that an extension should be granted, to allow B—— to recover from his disaster. There was but little discussion. The proposition was received with general favor, and unanimously agreed to. B—— returned to his business with a light heart, labored earnestly and devotedly, and, in a surprisingly short time was, enabled to pay all to whom he was indebted, to the fraction of a cent.

The lesson of this anecdote is one that should be taken to the heart of every merchant. It is a lesson of duty, of humanity, and of profit, which no considerate and conscientious man will neglect. In the first and highest place—in the most religious sense—it is a lesson of duty. "Do unto others as you would have others do unto you," is the plain precept to be followed as a pillar of cloud by day and of fire by night. Consider the circumstances that have brought about this disaster to a brother merchant's business. Imagine yourself surrounded by the same gloomy attendants—the keen apprehension of the ills of sudden poverty, and, with the imputation of dishonesty—

"The general scorn of men—which who can bear?"

Then, and then only, can you appreciate in full the terrors of the broken merchant's position, and feel intensely that it is your duty to reach forth a helping hand.

In the second place, the anecdote teaches a lesson of humanity. How many fall never to rise again! How many who have failed like Mr. B—— have despaired of ever regaining their credit and position in the commercial world, and have given themselves to idleness and dissipation, till their families have hungered and shivered beside the cold hearth! It is true that their creditors are not to be held responsible for the evils consequent upon a weakness of will. They may plead they were not their brother's keeper. But would it not have been better to have allowed the broken merchant some ground to stand upon?—to have let at least one ray of hope shine upon him in his hour of gloom, in order to encourage him for another effort in business, and save his wife and children from the perils of starvation? We think that such would have been the plain path of humanity, and that the prayers and blessings of the rescued family would have been a reward beyond all Golconda's wealth.

Lastly, the anecdote teaches a lesson of profit, using the word in the mercantile sense. If B——'s creditors had taken their few cents on the dollar at the meeting we have described, that would probably have been all they would ever have received of the money due them. By the extension, they obtained every cent, and this might be the happy result in a hundred cases where it now occurs in one, if the value of an extension were but properly appreciated. If the few cents could be spared for the time to enable those who are trembling on the verge of a precipice, to recover their balance and continue the prosecution of their business, we are satisfied that in very many cases the full amount advanced could be regained.

While thus urging upon the mercantile class their duty to their unfortunate brethren, we would also caution them to inquire always, whether a failure is the consequence of a series of misfortunes, or of continued dishonesty or neglect; or, metaphorically, whether the farm has gone to ruin because of the farmer's neglect or fraudulent speculation, or because of opposing elements or disease. An extension to one convicted of dishonesty would be but a fresh impulse to fraud; and, granted to one of habitual neglect, would be but to consign the money to a deeper grave. It is always possible to gain a knowledge of the principal causes of a failure in time, if we go about the investigation in time. Upon the result of that investigation let the creditor's course of action be founded. To the neglectful or dishonest, let there be awarded a speedy settlement and a rapid riddance of all business connection. But in behalf of many families who have been condemned to ruin and poverty, and in behalf of many of the honest and industrious who may be unfortunate and by unrelieved misfortunes, driven to vicious courses, we plead for an extension when it is deserved.

165.

Sir Edward Bulwer Lytton, in a lecture, in England, gave the following history of his literary habits: Many persons seeing me so much engaged in active life, and as much about the world as if I had never been a student, have said to me, "When do you get time to write all your books? How on earth do you contrive to do so much work?" I shall surprise you by the answer I make. The answer is this: "I contrive to do so much, by never doing too much at a time. A man to get through work well, must not overwork himself—or, if he do too much to-day, the reaction of fatigue will come, and he will be obliged to do too little to-morrow. Now since I began really and earnestly to study, which was not till I had left college and was actually in the world, I may perhaps, say, that I have gone through as large a course of general reading as most men of my time. I have traveled much, and I have seen much—I have mixed much in politics and in the various business of life, and in addition to all this, I have published somewhere about sixty volumes, some upon subjects requiring much special research. And what time do you think, as a general rule, I have devoted to study—to reading and writing? Not more than three hours a day; and when Parliament is sitting, not always that. But, then, during those hours, I have given my attention to what I was about."

166.

THE great characteristic of the young men of the present day is an over ambitious desire to become suddenly rich, or masters of their profession, whatsoever they may be; in every class we find the same anxiety, the same disposition to get gain and reputation. The students at their books, either in "Law," "Theology," or "Physic," in their unwise haste to become as it were, Lawyers, Priests, or Doctors, forget what are the essentials to make them truly eminent, and so hurry over their studies: looking only to the time when they shall be invested with a title, which neither their neglected opportunities of study nor the natural talent with which they are are endowed, entitle them; if they can but pass their examinations they rest content, each one presuming that he has but to receive the title, and all the honors and profits must necessarily ensue. We would say to them, however, that such things do not necessarily ensue; far from it, we could point them at this moment to many in our own city, who, it is true, enjoy the title, but few of either the honors or profits—young men who started with the best advantages, whose parents gratified every wish, who in their early days gave evidences of becoming distinguished men, but who are now idling away their hours throughout the thoroughfares of our city, satisfied only with the titles they have so unworthily received, and of no use to themselves or the community around them.

And the same failing exists in other quarters to quite as great an extent; among our mercantile and business classes we find the same results: young men who have become clerks from boys, without acquiring a full and thorough knowledge of every branch of the business in which they are engaged, without scrutinizing faithfully the methods by which a successful and honorable eminence are acquired, imagine too often that they are engaged in a service in which their labors are not requited, that they are capable of conducting business on their own account, that they possess all those habits upon which the success of a business in a great measure depends, and, accordingly, they branch out for themselves, and become competitors, as it were, of those from whom they are receiving their business education, and against whom, in most cases, they can neither command a sufficient capital or credit to compete successfully. And what, generally speaking, are the final consequences of such a course? A premature failure, or a series of embarrassments, which utterly dishearten and cripple them, and render it almost impossible, ever after, for them to acquire the confidence of those around them or be successful in business; few, very few of those who enter upon business under such circumstances can expect to succeed: it is only by a perfect knowledge of business, by an exercise of tact, judgment, and cautious discrimination, coupled with habits of industry, close application to business, and a diligent observation of the laws of trade and manners of men, that the young man can ever hope to become a merchant of honorable eminence: without these qualifications, which can only be obtained by years of labor and toil, in the capacity of clerk, capital will avail but little, practical ignorance and the want of proper business habits most generally gain the preponderance, even where capital has been invested, and the fatal result is too often shown by a complete failure and subsequent insolvency, the haste of the young man to be master, instead of clerk, has thus led him on inevitably to his own ruin, and when he should be enjoying the ease and comfort attendant upon a salary prudently and safely managed, and the prospect of entering into business with those he has so faithfully served, he has by his undue haste, wasted his capital, tarnished his reputation, failed in business, and is seeking once more the humble employment of a clerk. Such examples are too common in every business community, they are not imaginary, but as true as that the sun shines at noon-day ; let every young man who reads these suggestions ponder upon them, their future welfare and happiness may depend thereon; let them not suppose for one moment, that it is either humiliating or degrading to be a clerk or subordinate, or that they will lose time by devoting a series of years to a faithful acquiring of the details of the business which they hope to pursue. If there is anything either humiliating or degrading, it is in neglecting to improve the opportunities given us in our early days, and, by so doing, having jeoparded our right to a future honorable standing among men whose names are mentioned with respect, and who are looked to as examples of what a truly just and honorable merchant should be.

167.

It has been supposed by those who have long observed the course of things, says an intelligent writer, that to take forty lads, divide them, all things considered, into two equal companies, place half of them in the professions and merchandise, the other half in agricultural pursuits, the result will be, after a lapse of years, the latter will have the greatest aggregate wealth diffused among the whole ; while, perhaps a fourth of the former may make large acquisitions, and the families of the other three-fourths may be found in rather straightened circumstances. It is the opinion of those who have long held situations favorable to such observations as to enable them to come to correct couclusions on this subject, that only one in four of the trading classes, perhaps from causes beyond their control, escape insolvency, or are successful in the professions.

168.

There is no more honorable title on earth than that of the upright merchant. In these days of mercantile degeneracy and mercantile recklessness, it is profitable for us to pause in our career, and look back to other days, to the period when mercantile honor existed in fact, as well as in name—when our merchants were above princes, and our traffickers the honorable of the earth.

We want a great example to hold up before the rising generation, which shall deeply impress upon their minds the great truth that industry, unfaltering rectitude, scrupulous exactness in all the affairs of business, and honorable and upright dealings with our fellow men, form the only true basis for mercantile success, and are the only sure principles upon which mercantile character can be builded.

In looking over the list of merchants whose names are borne on the scroll of our history, whose virtues adorn their lives, whose patriotism burned with a pure and hallowed flame, whose rectitude of purpose was a deep seated principle, whose love of truth was dearer, far, than life, whose honor shone brightly as the sun in mid-day; we sigh for the days that were. To the patriot merchants of Boston, we owe a debt of lasting gratitude. Theirs were the first impulses that grew into a revolution, out of which a nation sprang into existence—the freest nation on the face of the earth. To them we owe no small share of our ancient renown. Hancock, who sacrificed more than one hundred thousand dollars, and devoted his life to the cause of liberty, was a true type of the Boston merchants in the era of the revolution. To them, and their influence, we owe no small share of our high consideration abroad. Our noble institutions of learning, our well endowed benevolent organizations, are monuments of their zeal in behalf cf education, sound morals, and all Christian charities.

Amos Lawrence was born in Groton, Mass., on the 22d of April, 1786. His constitution was feeble, and he suffered much in early life from sickness. With a natural quickness of apprehension, and a fondness for books, he made commendable progress in spite of his disadvantages. His only education was received at the District School and the Groton Academy, to which institution he afterwards made liberal benefactions. In the fall of 1799, at the age of fourteen, he commenced his apprenticeship in a country variety-store, where he remained until the 22d of April, 1807, when he became of age.

Being now released from his indentures, he resolved to seek a wider sphere for his energies and the business talents which he was conscious of possessing. Accordingly, on the 29th of the same month, he took his father's horse and chaise, and engaged a man to drive him to Boston, with, as he says many years afterwards, —"Twenty dollars in my pocket, but feeling richer than I ever felt before, or have felt since."

A few days after his arrival in Boston, he secured a clerkship in a respectable house. His employers were so well satisfied with the capacity of their new clerk, that, in the course of a few months, they made a proposition to admit him into partnership; but to their surprise he declined their offer. In a few months they failed, and young Amos was appointed by the creditors to settle up their affairs.

On the 17th of December, 1807, Mr. Lawrence commenced business in a small store in Cornhill. In a memorandum in one of his account books, he alluded to his condition at that time, by the remark, "I was then, in the matter of property, not worth a dollar." But his industry and habits of regularity had secured him friends and credit.

I a letter written in later life he says: "I practiced upon the maxim—'*Business before friends*' from the commencement of my course. During the first seven years of my business, I never allowed a bill against me to stand unsettled over the Sabbath. If the purchase of goods was made at auction on Saturday, and delivered to me, I always examined and settled the bill by note or crediting it, so that in case I was not on duty on Monday, there would be no trouble for my boys; thus keeping my business *before* me, instead of allowing it to *drive* me."

Further, Mr. Lawrence remarks. "I made fifteen hundred dollars the first year, and more than four thousand the second. Probably had I made four thousand the first year, I should have failed the second or third year. I practiced a system of rigid economy, and never allowed myself to spend a fourpence for unnecessary objects until I had acquired it."

Having become fairly established in business, he took his brother Abbott, then fifteen years of age, as an apprentice. Abbott came to the city bringing his bundle under his arm, with less than three dollars in his pocket, and this was his fortune.

Mr. Lawrence was married on the 6th of June, 1811; to Miss Sarah Richards, daughter of Silas Richards, who resided in Boston at the close of the revolutionary war. This union, which was one of unalloyed happiness, continued until January 14th, 1819, when it was severed by the death of her who was to him the most beloved of all earthly objects.

On the 1st of January, 1814, the celebrated firm of A. & A. Lawrence was formed. Abbott entered the partnership on equal shares, Amos putting fifty thousand dollars that he had then earned into the concern. Abbott was called off to do duty as a soldier through most of that year. Writing in 1849, Mr Lawrence says: "We still continue mercantile business under the first set of indentures, and under the same firm, merely adding, '& Co.,' as new partners have been admitted."

In 1815, Abbott visited England, and Amos improved this opportunity to impart useful instruction to his younger brother, both in relation to the course of business, as well as for his future moral guidance. What was useful then, will be no less useful now, to younger brothers just entering upon life.

"As a first and leading principle, let every transaction be of that pure and honest character that you would not be ashamed to have appear before the whole world as clearly as to yourself. It is of the highest consequence that you should not only cultivate correct principles, but that you should place your standard so high as to require great vigilance in living up to it."

Mr. Lawrence was an advocate of early marriages, but was strenuously opposed to any man's marrying a fortune. Speaking of a desirable match for a friend, he says, "My only objection to her is, she has a few thousand dollars in cash. This, however, might be remedied; for, after purchasing a house, the balance might be given to near connections, or to some public institution."

In April, 1821, Mr. Lawrence was again married to Mrs. Nancy Ellis, widow of Judge Ellis, of Claremont, New Hampshire. The same year he was elected to the Massachusetts Legislature, and this was the only occasion on which he ever served in a public legislative body.

On the first of January in each year, he was in the habit of noting down an accurate account of all his property, in order that he might have a clear view of his own affairs, and also a guide to his executors, in case of his death. This annual statement commences in 1814, and is continued, with the exception of 1819, every year until his death, in 1852. On the 1st of January, 1828, he remarked, after taking an account of his affairs :—

"This amount of property is great for a young man under forty-two years of age, who came to this town when he was twenty-one years old, with no other possession than a common country education, a sincere love for his own family, and habits of industry, economy and sobriety. Under God, it is these same self-denying habits, and a desire I always had to please, so far as I could without sinful compliance, that I can now look back upon and see as the true ground of my success."

The subsequent life of Mr. Lawrence is known and read by all men. His bountiful and systematic benevolence to institutions of learning, and of religion; his readiness to further and encourage a spirit of unselfish patriotism, his unostentatious private charities are now deeds of which the world knows, made public by no act of his, but necessarily public, in order that the world might have the full benefit of his noble example.

Mr. Lawrence peacefully yielded up his spirit to his Creator on the last day of the year 1852. Death found him not unprepared. And to him we may apply, with eminent appropriateness, the beautiful and oft repeated lines of Bryant,

> "—— sustained and soothed
> By an unfaltering trust, approach thy grave,
> Like one that draws the drapery of his couch
> About him, and lies down to pleasant dreams."

On the morning of his death, his son found upon the father's table the following lines, which had been copied by him a few days previous, and which are the more interesting from being a part of the same hymn containing the lines repeated by his wife on her death bed, thirty-three years before :

> "Vital spark of heavenly flame,
> Quit, O, quit this mortal frame!
> Trembling, hoping, lingering, flying—
> O, the pain, the bliss, of dying!
> Cease, fond nature, cease thy strife,
> And let me languish into life.
> Hark! ———"

It would almost seem that a vision of the angel messenger had been afforded, and that the sound of his distant footsteps had fallen upon his ear; for, with the unfinished line, the pen thus abruptly stops.

169.

THE City of Barcelona, in Spain, posesses a peculiar pawnbroking establishment—where loans are made without interest to necessitous persons, on the deposit of any articles. Two-thirds of the value of the deposit are at once advanced, and the loan is made for six months and a day; but if at the expiration of that period the depositer should declare himself unable to redeem it, another period of six months is allowed. At the end of the second six months the pledges are sold, but if they yield more than the amount advanced, the difference is given to the original owner. The Marquis de Llio is president of this charitable establishment, and he has just addressed a letter to the clergy of the diocese, praying them to make its advantages known. It bears the name of the Pawnbroking Establishment of Our Lady of Hope. In the year 1849, five thousand six hundred and eighty-six persons availed themselves of its generosity.

170.

Nothing is more common in the mercantile experience of this country than for men to start in life poor, but, overcoming all obstacles, to rise into high credit and affluence. It is unhappily quite common also for the same men, when arrived at this elevation, to put everything at hazard in the hope of more rapid gains, and, missing their object, to lose all. Strange that men should do so, the spectators say, and yet if they ever reach the same point of elevation they will very likely pursue the same course. It is not very strange perhaps in such a community as this that it should be so. Our merchants are pressed so severely with business that they have time for little else. Their thoughts are engrossed constantly with business and its gains, and in this way the desire of acquisition, which is implanted in every bosom for useful purposes, is nourished into a passion, and breaks away from reason. For its improper action there is always at hand a ready gratification. Besides, a man who has by steady application obtained property and credit, gets to feel as if it would always be so with him. He comes to think more of his own sagacity and less of his steady plodding than he ought; and, having more credit, and perhaps more money, than his present business requires, spreads out his plans in a disproportionate enlargement. Men so situated do not really expect to be materially happier or better for the large increase of wealth which they strive for. It is the passion for *acquisition* which urges them on. Some may indeed hope to set up a carriage and enter the fashionable world, and so become the slaves of postillions and the *bon ton*. But in general it is *acquisition* which fills and controls the mind. In sober seriousness, men all know that they want but little here below, nor want that little long. They know that such an amount of property as makes them easy in their affairs, and leaves them to labor steadily for the maintenance of their families and the performance of other duties, is enough, and that more will but increase care and perplexity, without any compensating enjoyment. If their thoughts are accustomed to reach on to the end of life and beyond it, and to cherish the feeling that some heart-work is to be done by way of preparation for the future, they confess to themselves that more property would rather be a hindrance than a help in that matter. Yet they love to *make money*. One says, I wish I had five hundred thousand dollars. What would you do with it? No matter; I should like to *have* it.

Most men believe that the possession of *some* property is very desirable as a means of rational enjoyment and usefulnesss. They would think that the first thousand dollars which a man should acquire would be worth more to him than the next *two* thousand; and that all his additional gains sink proportionably in value. Some would run along by this rule until they would at no distant point pass by the summit of increase, and count further gain nothing but loss. It is, any how, a remarkable fact, staring us all in the face continually, that very rich men are seldom reputed happy; though others will continue to think if *they* could gain the wealth they would contrive to avoid the anxiety.

How shall business men protect themselves from the danger we are considering? Certainly, it is a great danger. The danger is evidently not to be avoided by simple reliance upon one's own superior wisdom and prudence. It is among those who have been longest in the exercise of prudence that the most conspicuous examples of imprudence are to be found.

If we may be allowed to suggest remedies for so great a danger, we would say that in the first place every business man should feel that he *is in danger*. Then he should cultivate other faculties besides that of acquisitiveness. *That* will cultivate itself. Then he should set bounds to his desires from the outset of his acquisitions. Not by fixing a definite sum perhaps beyond which he will not accumulate, but so far at least as not to allow the fact that he has reached the point to which he first aimed to be merely a new starting point for new plans much larger than the first. Then dwell much upon the inestimable value of *peace* of mind. Think how dearly millions are earned at the expense of anxious days and restless nights. Think how short life is; too short for its days to be eaten out by useless distress. Put in practice the adage "keep what you've got," and only act upon the other part of it, "get what you can" in a way consistent with the first. Give away money freely if you are prosperous. This may not cure the passion of acquisitiveness, but it will counteract and tame it, and if done in true benevolence will be a source of more true happiness than wealth can buy in any other way.

Consider that in truth the surest way of arriving at great wealth is never to be in a hurry. Set it down as a fixed principle that you will *never* depart from your regular business unless it be by the mere use of surplus funds. Study the book of the Proverbs of Solomon until your mind is full of those old truths; truths which live in constant youth and beauty, though they be six thousand years old. Go fully into the considerations drawn from morality and religion, and you may find more powerful motive than any we have presented.

171.

Guarantees should only be taken in writing, and a consideration always expressed therein.

172.

THE *aim* makes the man—the spirit, the energy, the greatness or bitterness of the character and life. When the Merchant's Aim is right, he will have something that shall survive defeat and glorify even poverty ; and when accumulating prosperity is his, it shall not undermine his principles, nor make him insensible to the uses of wealth.

A short time since, two merchants in the same line of business in our city, were conversing on the method to be adopted to make a fortune.

The one remarked, "I have been working fifteen years to establish a quality of goods and to fix a reputation, and I shall hold to the reputation I have gained, and shall carefully keep up the quality of my manufactures."

"Pooh!" answered the other, "I shall do no such thing. I'm not a going to *work* as long as that, but am determined to make a fortune in a few years and let the reputation go."

Here are the representatives of the two classes in the mercantile community ; the one to whom character and conscience are unspeakable wealth, the other to whom they are nothing.

It is easy to go through the histories of our prominent merchants, and see the wisdom of the one class, and the folly of the other ; for the aim of the man is not something he can always keep covered up and out of sight. It will gleam out to shame or dignify; and shrewd business men soon discover on what principle trade is conducted by those with whom they are brought in contact. They are repelled by the discernment of the low and mean aim, as they are attracted by the noble and generous spirit of the true merchant. Hence, though now and then to test man's regard for lofty principle, some flashy adventurer may amass a fortune speedily, yet the greater amount of success will be found, as it is found in the department of science and discovery, with the men of generous purposes, dignifying aims, cautious and unpresuming, addressing themselves to what is right as well as to what promises immediate success.

A man who goes on the policy of deception and cheating, *begins* by deceiving and cheating *himself;* and he is distinguished from the upright by the inward experience, which has more to do with the enjoyment of life, than wealth or poverty;—by the regard in which he is held in the community—by his influence on the young and those connected with him in business, and by the chances of recovery from disaster should that overtake him. "My misfortune," said a good merchant, "was made almost sweet to me by the kind expressions drawn out by it from so many of my fellow citizens." *That* is the reward of a Right Aim.

173.

Studying mankind from the point of view afforded by a gig; waging unflinching war with knavish ostlers; ogling buxom chamber-maids; eloquent in praise of full-bodied port,—more eloquent in eulogy of their master's wares; great in whisker and loud in voice; good-natured, vulgar, jocular, overwhelming, persevering, and industrious to the last degree; the commercial traveler of old was a very different personage to his easy-going, locomotive succeessor. His journeys were long and his visits infrequent. Say that he came out of Nottingham, with lace and stockings, and, in a gig well stocked with samples and patterns, perambulated the length and breadth of the land during six long months. Making some great commercial inn his head-quarters, he would drive about from village to village, until all the district was exhausted of its orders, and enough goods were sold to supply the vicinity with hosiery and lace for years to come; this done, he would move off to some other centre, driving, drinking, swearing, puffing his wares, and making love as only a bagman could. How different the mode of the modern "commercial!" A clerk, or possibly a partner in the house which he represents, he travels about with nothing but a black leathern portmanteau, well strapped down, and filled with patterns of his wares. With this, a railway-rug, a small carpet-bag, and a Bradshaw, he contrives to be everywhere, and whips off what used to be a six months' circuit, within the space of a single day. Breakfasting at home in London, he lunches in Manchester, and, after doing a good stroke of business there, passes on to York, whence, after a cozy dinner and a satisfactory interview with his principal customers, he is whisked back by the night train to London, where he arrives in good time for the morning-meal. He is the only man who knows Bradshaw. He is great upon three fifties, fourteens, and one-forty-five. He takes his seat with his back to the engine, by instinct. He is tolerably well-read; thanks to the railway literature. He has no time for driving, or drinking, or swearing, or puffing, or even for making love. He has not, in fact, one single characteristic for which the commercial traveler used to be distinguished.

174

THE two closing paragraphs of a speech, made by the HON. WILLIAM H. SEWARD, on the Claims of American Merchants for Indemnity for French Spoilations, delivered in the Senate of the United States, January 21st, 1850, contain sentiments appropriately and eloquently expressed, that should find a response in the bosom of every honest and patriotic statesman in the Union.

The tribute to Commerce is as just in morality, as it is comprehensive and beautiful in expression :—

"Commerce is one of the great occupations of this nation. It is the fountain of its revenues, as it is the chief agent of its advancement in civilization and enlargement of empire. It is exclusively the care of the federal authorities. It is for the protection of Commerce that they pass laws, make treaties, build fortifications, and maintain navies upon all the seas. But justice and good faith are surer defences than treaties, fortifications, or naval armaments. Justice and good faith constitute true national honor which feels a stain more keenly than a wound. The nation that lives in wealth, and in the enjoyment of power, and yet under unpaid obligations, lives in dishonor and in danger. The nation that would be truly great, or even merely safe, must practice an austere and self-denying morality.

"The faith of canonized ancestors, whose fame now belongs to mankind, is pledged to the payment of these debts. 'Let the merchants send hither well-authenticated evidence of their claims, and proper measures shall be taken for their relief.' This was the promise of Washington. The evidence is here. Let us redeem the sacred and venerable engagement. Through his sagacity and virtue, we have inherited with it ample and abundant resources, and to them we ourselves have added the newly discovered wealth of Southern plains, and the hidden treasures of the Western coasts. With the opening of the half-century, we are entering upon new and profitable intercourse with the ancient Oriental States and races, while we are grappling more closely to us the new states on our own Continent.

"Let us signalize an epoch so important in Commerce and politics by justly discharging ourselves forever from the yet remaining obligations of the first and most sacred of all our national engagements. While we are growing over all lands, let us be rigorously just to other nations, just to the several States, and just to every class and to every citizen ; in short, just in all our administrations, and just towards all mankind. So shall prosperity crown all our enterprises—nor shall any disturbance within, nor danger from abroad, come nigh unto us, nor alarm us for the safety of Fireside, or Fane, or Capitol.

175.

THE Boston *Traveler* relates the following shrewd and successful method of restoring to the paths of honesty and rectitude a young man who had been tempted into dishonest acts, and who might, under any other course of treatment, have been confirmed in fraud, and reckless of the esteem of society. One such successful stroke is worth far more than the recovery of all the goods purloined. The merchant who adopts such a course deserves to take rank among the moral and social reformers of the day; and we would say to the readers of this volume who may, unfortunately, be placed in similar circumstances—"Do LIKEWISE." Pay your clerks an adequate compensation for their services, and lead them "not into temptation" by withholding the means of supplying their every reasonable want.

"Some months ago, one of our city constables traced a large quantity of stolen goods to a young clerk in one of the large wholesale stores in the vicinity of Milk street, where business to the amount perhaps of a million or more is carried on during the year. The officer in the first place informed the young man of his discovery, and he acknowledged his crime. He then went to a member of the firm, and informed him also of what had taken place. The merchant seemed troubled, said that the boy had for some time been with him, and to all appearance was a faithful clerk; that he had sole control of a room containing one hundred thousand dollars worth of goods, with several lads under him, etc., and further stated that he paid him for his services three dollars and fifty cents per week. The officer asked if the young man did not pay nearly that amount for board, washing, etc. The merchant acknowledged that he probably did. He then called the boy down, and asked him to confess the whole truth, which he did, with tears in his eyes, and promises of reformation. The merchant then told the officer that he wished time to consider as to his course. When the officer called again, the young man still continued at his old employment, with this difference, that he had increased his pay to six dollars per week. The officer asked how the boy got along, to which his master replied, 'Admirably, admirably; I have not a better servant in the store.' Thus ended the matter, and the young man still continues at his said stand, with a firm intention to deserve, by his future good conduct, the confidence which, perhaps, he so little deserved by his previous course."

176.

In the first place, it is abused by the creditor, who, in consequence of an overweening anxiety to sell, when he meets what he considers a good customer, more goods than that customer can pay for without depending upon a great many contingencies. But the consideration is too often, is he good for it? when it should be, Will his legitimate business enable him to make prompt payments? The bills receivable of those who cannot conveniently pay them, but whose property it will be necessary to sacrifice to collect them—having to go through all the glorious uncertainty of the law—are most certainly what we would call the poorest possible description of available funds.

Again, the credit system is abused by the buyer, when he is tempted to buy more goods than his regular trade will call for, under ordinary circumstances. It is not all that can be sold to the consumer is well sold, no matter how good he may be for it, but only what he can pay for conveniently.

Again, the credit system is abused by men who have a moderate capital and a good credit, and who are tempted to open a mercantile house in a certain location because it is considered a good place for business, and some of those who have grown up with it have become rich; and in order to make a show, and thereby build up a business at once, as they call it, they are tempted to tax their capital and their credit to the utmost extent; and the consequence is, that before the foundation is laid, their capital and their credit are both swept from under them.

Again, the credit system is abused by those who sell merchandise which they have bought on time, and which virtually belongs to their creditors, for anything but cash down, or at a stipulated time. The man who finds he has bought more goods in this way than he can find a ready sale for, and gives them in exchange for houses or lands, is not only abusing the system, but is doing his creditor a great injustice—a decided injury.

The facility offered by this system to embark in mercantile life, induces hundreds to accept of it, who are either incapable of conducting business successfully, or who attempt to carry it on in locations already full—where there are already more business houses than the trade of the place demands; and this is another most ruinous abuse of the credit system.

But there is another way in which this system is abused, or rather used, which is by far the most ruinous of all others—we mean, where it is used by dishonest men to make grand speculations out of. An individual, possessed of a moderate amount of money, commences business in some thriving town. He comes to one of our wholesale marts, and with one or two commendatory letters, but particularly with his money, he soon becomes acquainted; at first but limited, but he has only to manage his trumps (his money) with a little tact, and his acquaintance will very soon extend. At first he purchases cautiously and meets his obligations promptly, always managing to have his goods packed carefully and marked scientifically, and placed on the street several days before he removes them—

"Like books and money
Laid in show,
As nest-eggs,
To make clients lay."

And he succeeds. He soon becomes known as a man of promptness and capital, and doing a dashing business; and such a business he does do; for the motto at home is, "Sell low for cash—never mind profits." His acquaintance is courted; he is bedrammed, bedinnered and besuppered; everything goes on swimmingly, and finally he buys largely, goes in deeply, makes one grand maneuver, a most prodigious swell, and then judiciously and profitably explodes.

Finally, the farmer or mechanic, who buys beyond his available means, is a bad customer. The merchant who is continually selling at cost, or under, in order to undersell his more judicious neighbor, is a bad customer; and the dealer who buys goods to swell with, is a bad customer. The man who does business altogether on credit, is a bad customer; and lastly, the man who does not own the one-half of his stock in trade, at least, is not a safe customer.

177.

"EVERYTHING," says an old proverb, "is bought with a price;" and all, we may add, who are able and willing to pay the price, will, sooner or later, possess the object of their pursuits. ASTOR, GIRARD, and McDONOGH paid the price, and obtained their reward; they became rich in this world's goods, but died with stinted, impoverished souls, in their insane desire of accumulation. They denied the world those kindnesses of heart, which are, after all, the chief glory of humanity. The desire of a competence is, doubtless, very laudable; but great wealth is not the "one thing needful." "Contentment with godliness," says Holy Writ, endorsed by Human Experience, "is great gain." But not the gain which the Astors, the Girards, and the McDonoghs, have obtained. These reflections were suggested to our mind, on reading a conversation among several distinguished lawyers of New Orleans, during "some idle moments," (?) in a court room, in that city, when one of them, as we learn from a New Orleans cotemporary, related the following reminiscence of an interview with McDonogh. The moral of the story, and the conclusion, which the narrator of this anecdote arrived at, we commend to the serious consideration of our readers.

"I said to Mr. McDonogh, 'You are a very rich man, and I know that you intend to leave all your property to be expended in charitable purposes. I have been thinking over your singular life, and I want you to give me some advice in regard to the great success which has attended you, for I, too, would like to become very rich, having a family, so as to leave my heirs very wealthy.' 'Well,' said he, 'get up sir;' and as I rose from my arm-chair, he took my seat, and turning to me as if he was the proprietor and I his clerk, said, pointing to a common chair in which he had been sitting, 'Sit down, sir, and I will tell you how I became a rich man, and how, by following three rules, you can become as rich as myself.

"'I first came to Louisiana,' continued Mr. McDonogh, 'when it was a Spanish colony, as the agent for a house in Baltimore, and a house in Boston, to dispose of certain cargoes of goods. After I had settled up their accounts and finished their agency, I set up to do business for myself. I had become acquainted with the Spanish Governor, who had taken a fancy to me, although I had never so much as flattered him, and through his influence I obtained a contract for the army, by which I made ten thousand dollars. After this, I gave a splendid dinner to the principal officers of the army and the Governor, and by it obtained another contract, by which I made thirty thousand dollars.

"'This is what the Creoles and French do not understand. I mean the spending of money judiciously. They are afraid of spending money. A man who wishes to make a fortune, must first make a show of liberality, and spend money in order to obtain it. By that dinner which I gave to the Spanish authorities, I obtained their good will and esteem; and by this I was enabled to make a large sum of money. To succeed in life, then, you must obtain the favor and influence of the opulent, and the authorities of the country in which you live. This is the first rule.'

"'The natural span of a man's life,' observed Mr. McDonogh, "is too short, if he is abandoned to his own resources, to acquire great wealth, and, therefore, in order to realize a fortune, you must exercise your influence and power over those who, in point of wealth, are inferior to you, and by availing yourself of their talents, knowledge, and information, turn them to your own advantage. This is the second rule.' Here the old man made a long pause, as if lost in thought, and seeing him remaining silent I asked, 'And is this all?' 'No,' said he, 'there is a third and last rule, which it is all-essential for you to observe, in order that success may attend your efforts." 'And what is that?' I inquired.

"'Why, sir,' said he, 'it is prayer. You must pray to the Almighty with fervor and zeal, and you will be sustained in all your desires. I never prayed sincerely to God in all my life, without having my prayer answered satisfactorily.' He stopped, and I said, 'Is this all?' He answered, 'Yes, sir;' follow my advice, and you will become a rich man.' And he arose and left me."

"Well," asked one of the company, "have you followed his advice?"

"No," said the counsellor, "I have not for certain reasons; I do not wish to be considered harsh in drawing the conclusion I did from Mr. McDonogh's advice. They were, that when a man desires to become rich, he must corrupt the high, oppress the poor, and look to God to sustain him."

178.

IN extracting, from *Dickens' Household Words*, the following description of a shipwreck, it has occured to us to suggest to our Life Insurance companies, who issue policies on the lives of travelers, emigrants, etc., the propriety of adopting a system of salvage:—

"The crew of the first life-boat managed to reach the vessel; and by the numbers that crowded the deck, all crying out and praying to be saved, the boatmen immediately saw that there was a good deal more rough work chalked out for them. Two or three "trips," and the co-operation of their mates ashore, would be necessary to save so many lives. They made up their minds to the task, and at once took as many as they could—landed them safely at Broadstairs, and then buffeted their way back to the same vessel again—the sea often running clean over men and boat. This they repeated—a second life-boat from Broadstairs joining them in the exploit—and in the course of the day they succeeded in taking off every soul on board and bringing them safely ashore. The vessel also had a number of casks of butter and lard in the hold, which the captain had ordered upon deck, all ready; but if the boatmen had taken these they must have saved two or three lives less for each cask, according to weight, so the butter and lard were left to perish. The crew of the boat that made its way to the other vessel, at the furthermost end of the sands, found that, although there were but few lives to save, (only the captain, mate, and two "hands,") there was a much better thing—a valuable cargo. No wild and unmanageable passengers, desperate men, half frantic women, screaming children, all very difficult to get into the boat, and yet more difficult to prevent from leaping down into her in a crowd that would capsize or sink her,—but four seamen, who assisted them in getting out of the hold cases of placid sheet tin, patient tiles of copper, imperturbable solid cakes and docile pigs of lead. They also found a mine of penny-pieces in the shape of casks of copper nails and a thousand copper bolts. They made their way back with as much as they could safely carry, and shortly afterwards returned with two other boats. They persevered in this "labor of love" till they had got out nearly all the cargo and carried it safely on shore. Now comes the question of remuneration for these two parties of bold sailors, and the wise condition of maritime laws in these very important cases. The sailors who had assisted in moving the sheet tin, the tiles and cakes, and casks and bolts of copper, and the pigs of lead, received each man twenty pounds in the current coin of the realm; and the sailors who had risked their lives in saving the crowd of passengers in the other vessel (having no lawful claim to anything for only saving human lives) received, by special subscription and consideration, half-a-crown each! Had they saved the casks of butter and lard, that would have given them a legitimate claim to salvage; but as it was, they had no claim at all. It should be added that the sailors knew this at the time."

179.

We commend to the citizens of every State in the Union, the statesman-like views contained in the subjoined extract of a letter written by the Hon. Luther Bradish, of New York, while the question of allowing the Ogdensburgh Railroad Company to bridge Lake Champlain, was pending in the Legislature of New York:—

"As to the objection, (that it would divert trade from the market of New York,) it rests upon a basis too narrow, and an apprehension too little flattering to the capacities of the great State of New York, to form a principle in her public policy. Even conceding, that to some small extent the supposed result should take place, and that an occasional barrel of flour, or other provisions, should leave the broad and deep current of trade with New York, and stray across the Green Mountains, to feed the factories of New England, they would constitute only the very limited exceptions to the general rule, and would be too few and inconsiderable to form a basis of legislation for the Empire State.

"The laws of trade are paramount to all human legislation.

They will work out for themselves their own channels, and carry the products, which constitute its elements, to those marts, both of consumption and supply, which are more alluring, and which hold out to them the strongest inducements. New York, in this regard, has nothing to fear, and should adopt and pursue a policy as liberal as her resources, and as broad as her power.

"But even upon the ground of interest, and supposing that those occasional drippings from the great current of trade with New York, in finding their way across the mountains, should have the effect of increasing the wealth of our good neighbors of the East, the consequence would only be that it would increase, in a corresponding degree, the ability and desire in them to purchase and consume such things as we must forever supply. New York would, therefore, after many days, receive back again, with large increase, the bread that she had thus trustfully cast upon the waters. Trade and Commerce have in themselves wonderful compensating power, and never fail to promote reciprocal advantage if they be not diverted, crippled, or restrained by narrow policy, or local legislation."

180.

We have noticed in the *Merchant's Magazine* various methods of adulterating different articles of commerce and consumption, brought to light by the investigations of the London *Lancet*, a medical journal of high repute. The last investigations of that journal, on the subject of adulterations, have been directed to mustard, flour, and bread. With regard to mustard it has been ascertained that the article is scarcely ever to be obtained genuine, whatever may be the price paid for it.

Out of forty-two samples purchased indiscriminately, the whole were adulterated with immense quantities of wheaten flour, highly colored with turmeric, the specimens in tinfoil packages, and labeled "Fine Durham Mustard," or "double superfine," containing, with the exception of much husk, scarcely anything else. In connection with bread and flour the conclusions arrived at were unexpected. Out of forty-four samples of wheat flour, (including several of French and American,) purchased in all quarters of the metropolis, not a single instance was detected of admixture with any other farina, or of the presence of spurious matters of any kind. It is admitted, therefore, that millers and corn-dealers are somewhat maligned. As respects bread, the results were not so favorable. Although its adulteration with alum is an offense liable to a penalty of twenty pounds, this material was found in every one of the samples examined, the objects for which it is used being to give bad flour the white appearance of the best, and to enable the bread made from it to retain a large proportion of water, so as to gain in weight. The number of samples was twenty-four, and in ten of these the quantity was very considerable, while in all cases it was such as to be injurious to health, the operation of the drug being to interfere with the activity of the digestive functions. This article of adulteration, however, appears to be the only one generally employed in bread, neither potato, nor any other inferior farinaceous matter, nor carbonate or sulphate of lime being found—an improved state of affairs, which is most probably owing to the cheapness of flour caused by free trade. At the same time an examination of the weight of bread, as delivered at houses, shows that, upon an average, there is a deficiency of from two and a half to three ounces in every quartern loaf.

181.

CREDIT should be sparingly given, and integrity be the basis of it.

182.

All classes, with us, are connected with Commerce, and are, in some way, interested in its welfare. There is gloom over society when the ship stops too long at the wharf, and the prices current manifest depression. Anxiety is not confined to faces on "'change." There are haggard looks among laboring men wanting work, and the stillness in the shop of the mechanic denotes the state of trade. The mill wheel groans at half speed; the mule works lazily; the crowded warehouse will not admit another yard, and the stockholder consoles himself for no dividends by abusing government. But the ship has hauled into the stream, and the sailor heaves cheerily at the anchor. The merchant moves briskly, and looks as though chancery had always been a mythical conception. The hard-featured bank smiles grimly as it loosens its stringent gripe, and the original phrase of "tightness in the money market" is dropped for a season. There is stir and bustle in the street; the sound of the saw and the hammer is heard again; manufacturing stock looks up at the broker's board, and the government is not so bad, after all.

The American merchant is a type of this restless, adventurous, onward-going race and people. He sends his merchandise all over the earth; stocks every market; makes wants that he may supply them; covers the New Zealander with Southern cotton woven in Northern looms; builds blocks of stores in the Sandwich Islands; swaps with the Feejee cannibal; sends the whale-ship among the icebergs of the poles, or to wander in solitary seas, till the log-book tells the tedious sameness of years, and boys become men; gives the ice of the northern winter to the torrid zone, piles up Fresh Pond on the banks of the Hoogly, gladdens the sunny savannahs of the dreamy South, and makes life tolerable in the bungalow of an Indian jungle. The lakes of New England awake to life by the rivers of the sultry East, and the antipodes of the earth come in contact at this "meeting of the waters." The white canvas of the American ship glances in every nook of every ocean. Scarcely has the slightest intimation come of some obscure, unknown corner of a remote sea, when the captain is consulting his charts, in full career for the "terra incognita."

The American shipmaster is an able coadjutor of the merchant. He is as intelligent in trade as in navigation, and combines all the requisites of seaman and commercial agent. He serves his rough apprenticeship in the forecastle, and enters the cabin door through many a hard gale and weary night watch. His anxieties commence with his promotion. Responsibility is upon him. Life, and character, and fortune depend on his skill and vigilance. He mingles with men of all nations, gathers information in all climes, maintains the maritime reputation of his country, and shows his model of naval architecture wherever there is sunshine and salt sea. He has books, and he reads them. He hears strange languages, and he learns them. His hours of leisure are given to cultivation, and prepare him for well earned ease and respectability, in those halcyon days to come, so earnestly looked for, when he shall hear the roaring wind and pelting rain about his rural home, and shall not feel called upon to watch the storm.

183.

WHAT has Commerce done for the world, that its history should be explored, philosophy illustrated, its claim advanced among the influences which impel civilization?

It has enabled man to avail himself of the peculiarities of

climate or position, to make that division of labor which tends to equalize society, to distribute the productions of earth, and to teach the benefit of kindly dependence. It unites distant branches of the human family, cultivates the relation between them, encourages an interest in each other, and promotes that brotherly feeling which is the strongest guarantee of permanent friendship. People differing in creed, in language, in dress, in customs, are brought in contact, to find how much there is universal to them all, and to improve their condition, by supplying the wants of one from the abundance of the other. The friendly intercourse, created by Commerce, is slowly, but surely, revolutionizing the earth. There was a time when men met only on the field of battle, and there was but one name for stranger and enemy. Now, wherever a ship can float, the various emblems of sovereignty intermingle in harmony, and the sons of Commerce, the wide world through, in consulting their own interests, advance the cause of Humanity and Peace.

In looking for the mighty influences that control the progress of the human race, the vision of man ranges with the scope of his own ephemeral existence, and he censures the justice which is steadfastly pursuing its course through the countless ages. We turn away bewildered by the calamities, which extinguish nationality in blood, and give to the iron hand, fetters forged for the patriot. Let him who desponds for humanity, and mourns for faith misplaced, for hopes betrayed, for expectations unrealized, look back. Has revolution and change done nothing? Is there no advance from kingly prerogative, and priestly intolerance; no improvement on feudal tenure? The end is not yet. Let the downcast be cheered, for the Eternal Right watches over all, and it moves onward, to overcome in its good time.

184.

What the poor expend in tobacco we lament, forgetting that men labor by only the coercion of wants, and that Diogenes, who disciplined himself to live without wants, lived without labor also.

Tobacco, and other coarse superfluities, perform for the poor what equipages and gorgeous furniture perform for the rich. Our organization is so admirably adapted to keep us active, by the coercion of wants, that new wants arise in every man spontaneously, as fast as he can satisfy old ones. Napoleon, in the zenith of his prosperity, craved more dominion, with an intensity augmented by his present possessions, instead of being thereby mitigated. The design of Providence, to thus keep men active by the pressure of wants, life insurance and assistance clubs, counteract. All sumptuary laws contain the same error, and all Malthusian restraints on marriage. Railroads would never have been invented, had we coercively limited the operations of every man to his local neighborhood, as a means of obviating the disadvantages of distance. To evolve good out of apparent evil, is one of the most striking characteristics of Providence; and one which man's short-sightedness is continually endeavoring to counteract, by diminishing his wants instead of gratifying them by increasing efforts.

185.

Gambling lures men from industry, frugality, and accumulation, by hopes of gain, through processes less slow than these, and less self-denying ; and in this result, also, life insurance assimilates with gambling. "Eat, drink, and be merry, for to-morrow we die," and a life insurance will provide for our family, is the tendency of life insurance, whether conducted by corporations which catch large adventurers, or by clubs that catch humble people, or by health societies, that wring from manual labors their pettiest surplus earnings. To paralyze a man's efforts, no surer means can be devised, than companies and clubs which shall care for him in sickness, bury him when dead, and provide for his widow and orphans. By like influences, the heirs of rich men rarely exhibit self-denial in expenditures, or energy in business, and become drones in society. Necessity is nature's expedient to vanquish man's love of ease. Providence intends that we shall take care of the future by taking care of the present, and take care of our descendants by taking care of ourselves; just as a horse takes care of his hind steps, by taking heed where he places his fore feet.

186.

To become fonder of accumulation than of expenditure, is the first step towards wealth. An agriculturist will receive a few grains of an improved species of corn, which he will not eat, but will plant them, and replant the product from year to year, till his few grains will become hundreds of bushels. Money is increasable by analogous processes, and success is within the power of every man who shall attain to ordinary longevity. If a man at the age of twenty years can save from his earnings twenty-six cents every working day, and annually invest the aggregate at compound legal seven per cent. interest, he will, at the age of seventy, possess thirty-two thousand dollars. Many men who resort to life insuranee can save several times twenty-six cents daily, and thus accumulate several times the above sum, long before the age of seventy. Nearly all large fortunes are the result of such accumulations; hence the men who amass great fortunes are usually those only who live long. The last few years of GIRARD'S and ASTOR'S lives increased their wealth more than scores of early years. To be in haste to become rich by a few great operations, is a direct road to eventual poverty. We cannot, however, command long life, but we can approximate thereto by commencing early the process of accumulation—an elongation by extending backward being as efficacious as an elongation forward. Every hundred dollars expended by a man of the age of twenty years, is an expenditure of what, at our legal rate of interest, would, by compounding it annually, become three thousand dollars, should he live to the age of seventy. This lesson is taught practically by savings banks, and well counteracts the fatal notion of the young that old age is the period for accumulation, and youth the period for expenditure. By like principles, a young man who pays annually a premium for life insurance, loses not the premiums only, but the immense increase which the money would produce, should he invest it at compound interest, and live to the ordinary limit of man's life. Extremely old men, who have no length of life in prospect, are the only persons, if any, who should insure their lives, for the expense of their insurance would be but little more than the annual premiums.

187.

THE highest value of affluence is the social influence which it confers, whereby the possessor may become useful to society by his example and precept. Many persons keep themselves poor by lavish expenditures, in the hope of being deemed rich, and enjoying the superiority which riches confer. The deception is necessarily of short duration ; but had the party carefully saved and accumulated, he might soon have become permanently rich. The mental anguish which a man feels when he loses part of a large fortune, proceeds from an imagined diminution of his influence and power, not from any physical privations that the lost wealth will create. Nor is such a notion fanciful; men who have been esteemed wise counsellors while rich, lose commonly their reputed wisdom, if they lose their property. This phenomenon was observed by Shakspeare, who accounts for it by saying—

> "Men's judgments are
> A parcel of their fortunes; and things outward
> Do draw the inward quality after them,
> To suffer all alike."

That money is useless except for the physical enjoyments which its expenditure will produce, is the error of the poor; while persons who have experienced the intellectual gratifications which result from the retention of money, gain a better estimate of its value. The respect that attends wealth is as old as the Bible, which says—"If a man come unto your assembly with a gold ring and goodly apparel; and there come in also a poor man in vile apparel, and ye have respect to him that weareth the gay clothing, and say unto him, Sit thou here in a good place; and say to the poor, Stand thou there, are ye not partial?" If two men arrive at the Astor House, where the charge for board and lodging is the same for both, yet the man who is known to possess the most property will be lodged in a better room than the other, and receive, in every way, a preference. If the two take passage in a steamboat, the like preference will be accorded to the man of superior wealth; and these instances are but exemplifications of a general custom.

188.

As savings banks are the laboring man's only mode of accumulation, they should pay depositors as high rate of interest as practicable; for the more productive a poor man's mite can be made, the stronger will be his motive for frugality and industry. Some savings banks in Connecticut pay depositors five and a half per cent. interest, while our banks pay only five per cent., though our legal interest is one per cent. more than Connecticut; consequently, our long-established city savings banks have accumulated enormously large surplus profits which exist without a legal owner or a legitimate object. These banks are required by their charters "to regulate the rate of interest so that depositors shall receive *a rateable* proportion of all the profits, after deducting the necessary expenses;" but the provision fails to effect its object, (as is manifested by the accrued surplus profits,) though portions thereof have in some cases been invested in the erection of expensive banking-houses, and the purchase of valuable city grounds. The depositors from whose hard earnings these costly investments were abstracted, have received their stipulated five per cent. interest, drawn out their deposits, and are heard of no more forever. Like other property for whom no owner exists, erections of the above character belong to the state, and are subject to legislative disposals, together with all other surplus profits posessed by these institutions. Why, then, should not all savings banks be compelled to honestly divide annually (as a bonus) among its depositors the total amount of its net earnings, beyond the stipulated five per cent? The surplus which any bank may own at the time of the enactment of the law, can be reserved from distribution, except the income which may thereafter be annually earned therefrom. Every savings bank possessing a surplus, will thus present to new depositors an inducement which will be salutary to the thrifty poor who may avail themselves of the common benefit; and as the existing large surpluses are owned mostly in cities, the inducement will be presented to the class of poor persons who are locally (by reason of surrounding temptatations) most in need of inducements to self-denying accumulations. The law will be beneficial to depositors also, who reside where new savings banks are located, by reason that the depositors will receive more than five per cent. interest, as soon as the bank shall possess deposits enough to neutralize the contingent expenses, and thus every depositor will become a quasi bank stockholder to the amount of his deposits, and feel a common interest in increasing the number of depositors so as to diminish rateably the per centage of contingent expenses.

189.

THE idea, and even name, of a Mercantile Biography originated with the editor of the *Merchant's Magazine* shortly after its establishment in 1839; and since that time, we have occasionally given sketches of men who have commanded success in the varied walks of commercial life by their integrity, sagacity, industry and frugality, and we have reason to believe that these sketches have not been without their influence on a portion, at least, of the rising generation of American merchants.

These remarks have been suggested by Mr. ARTHUR, the editor of the "*Home Gazette*," who, in republishing our biography of Mr. Grigg, prefaces it with a few pertinent observations on the subject indicated in the title at the head of this article, as follows :—

"Biography, to have its true value, should present the history of men whose talents, industry and perseverance have elevated them above the dead level of society. Especially is this true in regard to American Biography. The use of this species of writing is to furnish youth and young men the experience of the energetic and successful who have gone before them. In this country, the most prominent and efficient men are not those who were born to wealth and eminent social positions, but those who have won both by the force of untiring personal energy. It is to them that the country is indebted for unbounded prosperity. Invaluable, therefore, are the lives of such men to the rising generation, and those who furnish a history of the progressive steps by which they arose from obscurity into high and useful positions, so far make themselves public benefactors. Hitherto, American Biography has confined itself too closely to men who have won political or literary distinction, and has been exceedingly careful to trace the genealogy of the individual back to some old English or aristocratic family, as if birth could give one jot of true merit to the individual—to the true American citizen. Limited to the perusal of such biographies, our youth must, of necessity, receive erroneous impressions of the true construction of our society, and fail to perceive wherein the progressive vigor of the nation lies.

"What we have most wanted is industrial (so to speak) and mercantile biography; or the histories of those men who have arisen by patient industry, united to strong and untiring energy, from poverty to wealth; who have built our ships, established vast manufactories, carried on our Commerce, erected our cities, and spread our vast country with railroads, canals, and telegraphs, like a very net-work. We want the histories of our self-made men spread out before us, that we may know the ways by which they came up from the ranks of the people.

"Of late more of this kind of biography has been given, and we regard it as a good indication. *Hunt's Merchant's Magazine* presents us with a brief and very interesting sketch of the life of John Grigg, Esq., of Philadelphia, (recently of the bookselling firm of Grigg & Elliot,) once a poor, uneducated, friendless boy, but now one of the wealthiest of our retired merchants. This sketch, which we transfer to the columns of the *Home Gazette*, contains many of Mr. Grigg's experiences and opinions on business matters, which young men in this too eager, 'go-ahead' age, would do well to lay to heart. There is such a thing as going too fast, and this is the evil of the present time. Thousands make shipwreck of their prospects in life for want of patience. They are neither willing to rise by slow degrees, nor to give to business the untiring devotion that creates success. To all such, as well as to those who are looking for the true ways and means of mercantile prosperity, the history of Mr. Grigg's business life will be of great value."

190.

A MAN's self-respect, and the respect of his wife and children for him and themselves, will increase continually as his savings augment. The gradual increase of wealth which attends the accumulation of a man's savings, is also more favorable to its preservation and to the possessor's equanimity than any sudden accumulation of prosperity. The upstart is a well-known genus of repulsive and pernicious peculiarities. A family who succeeds to the slowly accumulated savings of a deceased father, know his modes of investment, (a knowledge almost as valuable as the property he may leave them,) and the family will be more likely to retain the property permanently, than a widow or orphans suddenly enriched by a life insurance, which will be paid them in money, of whose proper uses and safe investment they will be ignorant. Besides, the parent whose savings are safely accumulated in a savings bank feels not the anxiety which sometimes attends life insurance, lest he may be incapacitated by sickness, inadvertence or disappointment, from paying his burdensome and insidious renewal premium. He is, on the contrary, master at all times of his deposits, and can recall them all or a part, as his necessities may require, or as more lucrative investments may become known to him—savings banks being a school to teach the art of accumulation to the poor, rather than a resort for experienced capitalists. Nor is a savings bank depositor a sort of prisoner under bonds not to travel into foreign countries without the consent of some life insurance company; his freedom nor his money is lost to him; nor, in case of his death, are his deposits liable to be wrested from his family by any quibble such as life insurance companies occasionally will and always can interpose, where the company happens to believe that the insured person was not so robust as he or some physician represented at the commencement of his insurance.

191.

WHAT perturbation of mind! What struggling, and scratching, and shifting, and lying, and cheating, is practiced every day by mammon worshipers to make money! What a comparison between the successful and unsuccessful! Of the millions who embark in business to make money, how few succeed! And why! Because but few know the secret of success. Most think it chance, or good fortune, but they are sadly mistaken; and if such as are now pining to get rich would only strictly mind the following advice and be guided by it, there would be no doubt of their realizing their golden dreams:—

"Let the business of every body else alone, and attend to your own; don't buy what you don't want; use every hour to advantage, and study to make even leisure hours useful; think twice before you throw away a shilling, remember you will have another to make for it; find recreation in looking after your business ; buy low, sell fair, and take care of the profits ; look over your books regularly, and if you find an error, trace it out ; should a stroke of misfortune come upon you in trade, retrench, work harder, but never fly the track ; confront difficulties with unflinching perseverance, and they will disappear at last ; though you should fail in the struggle, you will be honored—but shrink from the task, and you will be despised."

192.

Among the dishonorable tricks, practiced by many publishers, is the re-printing of foreign novels, by unknown, or indifferent writers, as works of the first geniuses of the age. Another equally miserable cheat is the publication of conclusions of serials, when the real conclusion has not yet even appeared in England : in this case some unprincipled hack writing the spurious conclusion. These are tricks, to play which temptation is great, for the public generally does not detect the fraud till too late, and the press, from ignorance or indifference, fails frequently to expose the deception. The country is deluged with bad novels enough, without having them increased in this manner. Thousands are often induced, by the announcement of a great name, to peruse a trashy or immoral book, when, if the cheat is discovered, the knowledge comes too late, and if not, the author suffers in reputation. Can there be no protection for the victims in such cases? A publisher, who filches a reader's cash in this way, is morally guilty of obtaining money under false pretenses, even though some legal quibble may shield him from the law. We allude to no recent or special case in these remarks. Sometimes publishers charge each other unjustly with tricks of this kind ; and it is well to be sure of the evidence, before making a direct charge. Nevertheless, people should be on their guard.

193.

THAT ever busy and mischievous old dame, Madam RUMOR, has been even more than usually industrious during the past week in circulating reports of the financial condition of certain houses. It has been gravely announced that several large establishments had refused to meet their liabilities, and were compelled to wind up their business; still these identical establishments keep their doors open, receive their customers, pay all demands, and go through the whole routine of their business operations as usual, Madam Rumor's fabrication to the contrary notwithstanding. Now, why this attempt to injure the reputation of some of our leading merchants?—Is it for the purpose of increasing the business of one man at the expense of a rival neighbor? These rumors, by the way, are circulated in an exceedingly confidential way (!) manner at the start—they are at first imparted to you as secrets,—as something that is not generally known; and which the informer (if you are verdant enough to believe him) would impress on your mind, he would not have mentioned to another party for any consideration. In this way, he succeeds in getting his story pretty well circulated; for it is well known that an injunction to keep anything secret is tantamount to advertising it in the papers—it is then bound to spread.

It is true, there have been several failures in New York and other cities recently—but they are too unimportant to notice, or to excite distrust, when it is remembered how small a proportion they bear to the thousands of sound and well-tried houses in our great, growing, and prosperous city. The stringency of the money market has, we know, somewhat incommoded a large number of business men, but nothing serious, we imagine, is likely to grow out of it.

194.

We have great pleasure in copying the subjoined notice of an accomplished American merchant residing in London, from the *Home Journal*, and transferring it to this volume. It furnishes an example of mercantile character worthy of imitation, and therefore entitled to a wider circulation, and a more permanent record, than it would secure in the elegant and unique, but necessarily ephemeral "folio of four," from which it is taken:—

"The fame of the princely spirit and splendid hospitality of George Peabody, has now gone abroad into all lands, and the distinction with which he caused the Fourth of July to be publicly honored in London, by a commemoration which involved an English tribute, as well as an American one, to the dignity of the anniversary, has gained for him the respect and esteem of his countrymen in every part of the Union. But to those who have visited London within the last few years, there is nothing in the least new in this manifestation of Mr. Peabody's noble liberality or warm national feeling. Socially, though not politically, and at his own cost, not the nation's, he has long performed in London a ministerial function; receiving all respectable Americans who appeared in that city, whether they presented any claims upon his notice or not, showing them substantial kindness; and affording them valuable facilities for seeing and enjoying all that was most worthy of regard. His frequent entertainments to his countrymen have been the most luxurious and delightful banquets that the most generous and skilful host ever arranged. He has not only been accustomed to render important social services to Americans, who, but for him, might have lacked all assistance in the metropolis, but he has, on more than one occasion, protected and promoted American interests in the most signal and effective way. His intervention in aid of American credit, at the time our securities became depreciated in England, is well remembered; and in a late instance his prompt and generous self-exposure and expenditure for the national benefit, rescued the country from open disgrace, and presented an example of patriotic conduct with which the niggardliness, public and private, displayed in this country, stands in a dismal contrast. It is to Mr. George Peabody that our productions are indebted for being in the Exhibition at all. When they were landed there from the St. Lawrence, no pecuniary provision whatever had been made for the expenses of setting them up in the building. Mr. Peabody called at the place, and finding that nothing was done to establish the American Articles in their places, inquired the reason, and was told that there were no funds for the purpose. He replied, that he would himself advance whatever amount might be necessary for the object; and at once furnished two thousand pounds, without any security at all; trusting to the decency of Congress to take proper action in the matter, and choosing to pay the money from his own pocket rather than allow the country to be disgraced. The restitution of this sum, accompanied by some appropriate acknowledgement of the national respect, should form one of the first duties of Congress."

195

By the former we would intend everything that excites to commendable action with a view of obtaining the means of enjoyment. By the latter we would designate that state of the mind and heart that leads us to distribute these accumulations with a view of promoting the happiness of others. These two are the great reforming influences that will ameliorate and advance the condition of mankind. We are commanded to be diligent in business, to be active, to contrive, to invent, to waken up intellect, to render the material world tributary and subservient, and to accumulate the products of art and nature. All this is to be done for rational purposes, compatible with the dignity and end of man, creation and destiny. Do we need any other organization of society than that which gives and secures to every individual the full and free exercise of all his powers? Do we wish to implant any other motive in the heart than a desire to spread and diffuse accumulations, to promote present and eternal enjoyment? Does not common sense, universal experience, point out these two simple laws as the ones on which all our hopes of progress depend? What more can we wish than to see our fellow-creatures industrious, enterprising, economical, striving to accumulate for their own and others' happiness, remembering that the earth and the fulness thereof is the Lord's? Liberty and encouragement to act, and increasing benevolence to distribute, are the hopeful signs of the times.

196.

The following forcible remarks on the moral effect of the usury laws, are from a lecture delivered in 1848, before the New York Mercantile Library Association. How professed moralists and philanthropists can, with any show of reason, support such laws, is a problem that we cannot solve on any principle of common sense:—

"The usury law invites and encourages the borrower to become a downright and shameless knave. Either he was ignorant of the usury, or else the loan was taken upon his honor; and his plea of usury is a denial of that last attribute of character which makes even a barbarian to be trusted. The man who pleads usury never after respects himself. Before he makes his plea he must pass through the several stages of loss, vexation, mortification, and despair of regaining his position in society. He feels that he is disgraced, and society enters heartily into his feelings. And this disgrace the legislature has invited, and strongly encourages him to bring on himself.

"When his case comes on in court, the judge blushes as he charges the jury in favor of the borrower, and the jury despise him at the moment of returning a reluctant verdict in his favor. The only difference in public estimation between the maker of this plea and a certain other character, is this:—The one finds his neighbor's property, and keeps it, and the other takes it by stealth. Truly we may say, 'The law entered, that offence might abound.'"

197.

The *North Western Gazette* gives its readers, in the shape of a leader, a brief but sensible lecture on the tendency of the public mind to inflation, which we here re-produce for the special benefit of our readers, whose temptations to "inflation" are peculiarly great:—

"There is a strong disposition in the public mind to inflation. Men are discontented and restless. Are not as contented as they should be with a plain and economical way of living, with small but sure gains and moderate fortunes. They must get *very* rich, and that *very soon*, or be miserable. Happiness does not consist in great wealth, and that acquired without patient thought and laborious toil. Neither is it the surest way to attain it, to embark in bold speculations, to blow up bubbles, to turn sharper, to rely on brazen impudence for stock in trade, pay no regard to justice, and run just as near as possible to the line of violated law as will keep one out of the penitentiary. Men seldom get wealth in that way, though for a time they may have the *name* of it. We ask the humble, hard working man, who pursues his honest calling, yet it may be with too little patience for his highest peace, to point out to himself and name the number of those, who, within the last ten years, have relied on the above false means for success, that are not now poor? Again we ask the same humble man to point out to himself and name over all those within his knowledge, who have pursued an honest calling, been content with small gains, who have placed their claim to success on their own intrinsic merits, and not on the demerits, the downfall and destruction of others,—who have lived peaceably, economically, prudently, in the faith of a clear conscience,—how many of such men do you find who have *not* acquired a competence? Fortune, in most cases, is not won by unfair means; when it is so won, it cankers the heart that hugs it.

"We have said, there is a disposition in the public mind to inflate itself. There are great prospective speculations in the dreams of men. There are crude longings for indulgence in the pleasant fancies of 1836. Still we trust the country will escape such a disaster. While the California idea has had much to do in bringing about this impatience to acquire sudden wealth, it likewise operates as a safety valve to let off the extra steam. As a man becomes disposed for California, he becomes indisposed to work for reasonable gains here. He sells what he has got for what he can get for it, and as the property goes almost always below its true value, it tends to keep down the prices for similar property in the vicinity. The man goes to California. The prescription usually makes thorough work—it kills or cures. Those who take it and live through it, come back wiser, if not richer men. A large proportion of them grasp the bubble, and it vanishes in their hand. A few find therein visible substance. The powerful California attraction keeps down unhealthy irritation here, precisely as a blister drawn on the back of the neck sometimes relieves an inflammation of the brain. So our readers will bear us testimony, that we have at last found or imagined some use for California. The over excitement there, may keep those who stay at home cool and sensible. That they may be so kept free from nightmare, water-lot speculations, wild-cat fortunes and the itch, we trust."

198.

SOME few years ago, a lad who was left without father or mother, of good natural abilities, went to New York, alone and friendless, to get a situation in a store as errand-boy, or otherwise, till he could command a higher position; but this boy had got in bad company, and had got in the habit of calling for his "bitters" occasionally, because he thought it looked *manly*. He smoked cheap cigars also.

He had a pretty good education, and on looking over the papers, he noticed that a merchant in Pearl street wanted a lad of his age, and he called there, and made his business known.

"Walk into the office, my lad," said the merchant. "I'll attend to you soon."

When he had waited on his customer, he took a seat near the lad, and he espied a cigar in his hat. This was enough. "My boy," said he, "I want a smart, honest, faithful lad; but I see that you smoke cigars, and in my experience of many years, I have ever found cigar-smoking in lads to be connected with various other evil habits, and, if I am not mistaken, your breath is an evidence that you are not an exception. You can leave; you will not suit me."

John—this was his name—held down his head, and left the store; and as he walked along the street, a stranger and friendless, the counsel of his poor mother came forcibly to his mind, who, upon her death-bed, called him to her side, and placing her emaciated hand upon his head, said, "Johnny, my dear boy, I'm going to leave you. You well know what disgrace and misery your father brought on us before his death, and I want you to promise me before I die that you will never taste one drop of the accursed poison that killed your father. Promise me this, and be a good boy, Johnny, and I shall die in peace." The scalding tears trickled down Johnny's cheeks, and he promised ever to remember the dying words of his mother, and never to drink any spirituous liquors; but he soon forgot his promise, and when he received the rebuke from the merchant, he remembered what his mother said, and what he had promised her, and he cried aloud, and people gazed at him as he passed along, and boys railed at him. He went to his lodgings, and, throwing himself upon his bed, gave vent to his feelings in sobs that were heard all over the house.

But John had moral courage. He had energy and determination, and ere an hour had passed, he made up his mind never to taste another drop of liquor, nor smoke another cigar, as long as he lived. He went straight back to the merchant. Said he, "Sir, you very properly sent me away this morning for habits that I have been guilty of; but, sir, I have neither father nor mother, and though I have occasionally done what I ought not to do, and have not followed the good advice of my poor mother on her death-bed, nor done as I promised her I would do, yet I have *now* made a solemn vow never to drink another drop of liquor, nor smoke another cigar; and if you, sir, will only *try* me, it is all I ask."

The merchant was struck with the decision and energy of the boy, and at once employed him. At the expiration of five years, this lad was a partner in the business, and is now worth ten thousand dollars. He has faithfully kept his pledge, to which he owes his elevation.

Boys, think of this circumstance, as you enter upon the duties of life, and remember upon what points of character your destiny for good or for evil depends.

199.

Credit to a man is what cream is to a nice cup of coffee—what loaf sugar is to Old Hyson tea—it mollifies and enriches him, makes a smooth face, a pair of beaming eyes, a pleasant smile, a cheerful tone of conversation, a sally of wit, and a steady, quick gait. A man with good credit never runs after patent medicines; he keeps a tonic in his stomach every day. He cannot pass his butcher's cart but the very horse seems sensible of his presence, and stops short to receive orders. His grocer runs with the "pass book," and from a cent's worth of yeast, to a box of Havana or a basket of champagne, he cheerfully "items" till quarter-day. His creditors had as lief take his note as the money, for there is no trouble in getting a discount; and his tailor slaps him on the shoulder, and says he "has a piece of broadcloth about the finest," and begs him to give him a call.

The man of credit walks up State-street, not with a strut, but a sense of self-respect, which the feeling "I owe no man" gives to every one; for he knows his money is on deposit and waiting orders. You would tell in an instant that he is no herb-tea drinker—no sarsaparilla and dock-root man—his pulse is regular, and he sits down in arm-chairs in insurance offices as self-satisfied as President Fillmore in the chair of State. He never was asked "if it would be convenient to pay that little bill to-day?" in his life, for the plain reason, the man of good credit most generally anticipates his bills; consequently he is not so sympathetic to those who inquire, "Any thing over to-day?"

And then what a rush the brokers make after him! The "bears and bulls" are all ready to seize him, and just before the "Board" meets, are sharpened to victimize him. "Canton is rising"—"Edgeworth tending upward"—"buoyancy in dividend-paying stocks"—"any orders to-day, Mr. Godey?" Once in a while he makes a purchase, but with great caution, and always when such a degree of certainty seems to hang over his operation as to leave him no chance for a bad dream at night.

The man of credit never has long standing accounts. He always squares up when he receives his dividends; pays for his wife's bonnet when the milliner sends it home, for he knows it must be a convenience to work-women to receive cash on the spot. He acts up to the rule that "honesty is the best policy," and his religion seems to influence his every-day affairs—for he always contends, a man troubled about meeting worldly payments, is very apt to rob his Maker of his dues. He therefore never subscribes more than he is willing to pay on the spot—for he is worldly-wise, and can narrate to you how he attained his present experience. He informs you that a heavy debt sorely disturbs the peace of a religious society; consequently he never worships in a church burdened with a debt. He knows statistics, and can compute interest; pities men who are obliged to mortgage their *homes*, but condemns those who owe for *Churches*. Moreover, he has a large acquaintance, and freely gives his advice to lone women and orphan children.

Whether the man of credit has many trials is quite uncertain. His family are cheerful, and his home is hospitable, but he does not always live on turtle-soup nor water-fowls. Beef is digestible and nutritious, and beef he enjoys. He eats only the food that keeps the mind clear and the purse in a well condition. He does not choose to go to Europe, because it is "fashionable;" nor to "Cuba," because his daughter has a slight cough; he keeps a thermometer, and makes a southern climate at home.

Easterly winds, and the trying month of March, strangely affect those whose credit is impaired. Imports have been too great; exports too small; trade does not show a healthful activity, and a certain "blue" look settles on his countenance. This man drinks his coffee strong, and occasionally indulges in late hours and high wines. His wife wears a velvet cloak and gay bonnet, but she has the "blues" prodigiously. No woman can be happy where the husband has an empty pocket, and she depends on him to fill her own. His credit is not good, and this entails misery on all his family affairs.

The woman of good credit likewise carries with her an immense advantage. She can wear what she pleases, and every body knows she can have better if she desires—she can stay at home because every one knows she can afford to go abroad—in fine, it is not half as hard work to live and be a Christian, as to be straining after unattainable goods, fretted how to pay for them, lying down to bad dreams, and rising with a bunch in one's throat. The best recipe in such cases is to wrap a flannel tightly over our superfluous wants, never let them go abroad, and we shall soon be able to swallow with ease.

200.

WE extract the following passage from the report of a discourse delivered in the Plymouth Church, Brooklyn, by HENRY WARD BEECHER :—

"There is not a single provision for the moral conduct of men, which does not bind commercial firms. Evasion, falsehood, fraud, robbery, dishonesty and dishonor of every kind, are just the same before God in a commercial firm, as they would be in a single member of it. Nor can any man be allowed to charge it upon an *abstraction*, and say, I did not do it—the firm did it. If the firm did it, that is only euphemism —a soft way of saying that three men agreed together that each and all of them would defraud, or in any way do wrong, and divide the profits between them. Yes, the profits will be divided; but the *whole* villany, unparceled and undivided, will be charged up to *each man!* Nor will God be mocked; the miserable subterfuges which men employ to bribe their consciences, will not bribe God. All the sideway paths, by which men come at last to a wickedness, are just as bad as the broad way itself. If you procure an agent to deal fraudulently, or to lie; if your clerk performs your will; or if, with a seeming ignorance, but a real knowledge of the whole, a partner does the wrong, God will hold each one of the whole to be a principal.

"Let one case of subtile connivance suffice:—Two men engaged in a neighboring village in traffic. The one had been a sterling temperance man—the other not. The second partner insisted upon trading in liquors, and drove a large and lucrative business at it. The temperance partner would not sell it, nor handle it, but continued the partnership, and received *an equal division of profits!* He scorned the imputation of partnership guilt! But when God confronts him in judgment, he will require of him not only as much as of his partner, but the added guilt of duplicity and hypocrisy. And he will be held responsible for all the mischiefs which he set on foot by distributing that inevitable destroyer of man. God will burn him with every dollar got by making good men, bad; and bad men, worse; and rich men, poor; and poor men, poorer. God will draw from his eye a tear for every tear which his avarice has wrung out; a groan for every sigh he has made; a pang for every heart-string which he has broken; and for all the heart-brokenness and despair, and wild frenzy, or sullen and immovable insanity which his liquor has sent upon man—*God shall give him double.*

"*Reward her! even as she rewarded you, and double unto her double according to her works; in the cup which she hath filled, fill to her double.*"—*Rev.* 18 : 6.

201.

Give us the straight-forward, fearless, enterprising man for business—one who is worth a dozen of those who, when anything is to be done, stop, falter and hesitate, and are never ready to take a decided stand! One turns everything within his reach into *gold*—the other tarnishes even what is bright; the one will succeed in life, and no adventitious circumstances will hinder him—the other will be a continual *drawling* moth, never rising above mediocrity, but rather falling below. Make up your mind to be firm, resolute and industrious, if you desire prosperity. There is good in that saying of the Apostle, "Whatsoever your hands find to do, do it with all thy might."

202.

ONE of the greatest difficulties in the way of elevating the sailor, says the *Sailor's Magazine*, grows out of the bearing of his officers. The latter in most cases, seem to think that their dignity or influence will be compromised by talking familiarly with their crews, even on subjects of acknowledged importance. This erroneous idea should be assailed, until masters and mates are convinced that kind words and needed counsel will do more to secure obedience and respect than haughty reserve or rigid discipline. Officers, by neglect of manifesting interest in the personal welfare of their crews, check their aspirations and crush their better feelings, thus aiding other formative influences towards a degraded character. There is no danger that a sailor will think he has a right to cabin privileges because the master talks with him about his plans, and urges him to a course that may secure his promotion. Such treatment will elicit gratitude and stimulate to good conduct.

203.

A WRITER in the Boston *Post*, alluding to several merchants who have recently died, thus mentions the living. Mr. —— has since deceased :—

"We believe that ROBERT G. SHAW, Esq., is now the oldest active merchant in this city, as he is the most opulent one. We remember him from our boyhood, as a stirring, enterprising and successful man; and he has probably done as much for the city —has contributed as largely, by his wealth and liberal feeling, towards its growth, prosperity and business facilities, as any other citizen. We think we should be safe in saying that he has done more. Next in age to Mr. Shaw, we should name the venerable THOMAS B. WALES, a gentleman who is universally respected by the commercial classes of Boston, where he has been engaged iu business for half a century. And then there is his brother-in-law, JOSIAH BRADLEE, Esq., whose sign on Long Wharf—No. 8, we think—we remember to have read, when a boy, some fifty-six years ago. He has ever been an industrious, active merchant, and, like the others that we have named, has accumulated, by a close devotion to trade, and strict integrity, a large fortune. We might mention a few others, who are some years their juniors in mercantile business, but who have amassed large fortunes, and are as much respected for their generous qualities as those we have named. It is painful to think, as we have said before, that they are all going, going, the same way that thousands have gone before them.

"We have an anecdote to tell about Mr. Shaw, which was never before in print, and which, we think, will amuse our mercantile readers, and not give offense to our venerable friend. We happened to be present when the occurrence took place. A gentleman met him in the street, and, upon a brief conversation, asked him to lend him ten dollars, as he was short—not an uncommon thing for him at the time. It was many months ago. Mr. S., raising his spectacles, replied :—'Yes, sir, with pleasure, on one condition.' 'What is that, sir?' 'Why, that when we next meet, you will turn your face towards me, look pleasant, and not turn it away! I lent Mr. —— a small sum of money about a month ago, and ever since that time he has *cut* me most decidedly. Meet him where I will, on State-street, Commercial-street, or in the Exchange, and he always turns his head away. When I lend a man money, and he is owing me, I want him to look me full in the face, as though nothing had happened. And then I shall be willing to lend him again. There is a veritable story."

204.

Debt is a perfect bore. How it haunts a man from pillar to post—lurking in his breakfast cup—poisoning his dinner—embitters his tea!—now it stalks from him like a living, moving skeleton, seeming to announce his presence by recounting the amount of liabilities. How it poisons his domestic joys, by introducing its infernal "balance" into the calculation of madam respecting the price of a new carpet, or a new dress! How it hinders dreamy plans for speculations and accumulations. Botheration! How it hampers useless energies, cripples resolutions too good to be fulfilled.

At bed and board, by night or by day, in joy or grief, in health or sickness, at home or abroad—debt, grim, gaunt and shadowy, falls as an incumbrance. As no presence is too sacred, no ground is too holy to deter the memory of "bills and notes payable" from taking immediate possession, so no record is so enlivening, no reminiscence more delicious than the consciousness that debt has fallen like a January morning, twenty-nine degrees below zero

205.

Beware of thinking all your own that you possess, and of living accordingly. This is a mistake that many people who have credit fall into. To prevent this, keep an exact account for some time, both of your expenses and your income. If you take the pains at first to enumerate particulars, it will have this good effect: you will discover how wonderfully small trifling expenses mount up to large sums; and will discern what might have been, and may for the future be saved, without occasioning any great inconvenience.

206.

The fraternal association of rag-gatherers (*chiffoniers*) gave a grand banquet in Paris, in June, 1851. It took place at a public house called the Pot Trincolore, near the Barriere de Fontainebleau, which is frequented by the rag-gathering fraternity. In this house there are three rooms, each of which is specially devoted to the use of different classes of rag-gatherers: one, the least dirty, is called the "Chamber of Peers," and is occupied by the first class; that is, those who possess a basket in a good state and a crook ornamented with copper; the second, called the "Chamber of Deputies," belonging to the second class, is much less comfortable, and those who attend it have baskets and crooks —not of first rate quality; the third room is in a dilapidated condition, and is frequented by the lowest order of rag-gatherers, who have no basket or crook, and who place what they find in the streets in a piece of sackcloth; they call themselves the "Re-union des Vrais Proletaires." The name of each room is written in chalk above the door, and generally such strict etiquette is observed among the rag-gatherers that no one goes into the apartment not occupied by his own class. At the banquet, however, all distinctions of rank were set aside, and delegates of each class united fraternally. The president was the oldest rag-gatherer of Paris; his age is eighty-eight, and he is called the Emperor. The banquet consisted of a sort of *olla podrida*, which the master of the establishment pompously called a *gibelotte*, though of what animal it is mainly composed it was impossible to say. It was served up in huge earthen dishes, and before it was allowed to be touched payment was demanded and obtained. The other articles were also paid for as soon as they were brought in, and a deposit was exacted as security for the plates, knives, and forks. The wine, or what did duty as such, was contained in an earthen pot, called the Petit Père Noir, and was filled from a gigantic vessel named Le Moricaud. The dinner was concluded by each guest taking a small glass of brandy. Business was then proceeded to. It consisted in the reading and adoption of the statutes of the association, followed by the drinking of numerous toasts to the president, to the prosperity of rag-gathering, to the union of rag-gatherers, &c. A collection, amounting to f 6 c 75 was raised for sick members of the fraternity. The guests then dispersed, but several of them remained at the counter until they had consumed, in brandy, the amount deposited as security for the crockery, knives, and spoons.

207.

In copying the following remarks from an exchange, we do not wish to be understood as endorsing all the writer says on the subject of "Men-Milliners," for the simple reason that we love freedom in everything that is right. If a man has a taste for the pursuit of a milliner, or a woman for that of a carpenter, let them adopt it. Occupation is everything; and they only give dignity to it, who excel in perfecting whatever is undertaken.

"When we see stout, able-bodied men, monopolizing the business and calling for which women are peculiarly adapted, and of the two so much better qualified, to the serious disadvantage, and perhaps eventual starvation of the latter, we feel like applying the thumb and fore-finger of our right hand to their nasal organs, and inflicting a 'twinge' severe enough to make them sneeze for a fortnight thereafter. A man has no business whatever in a milliner shop, and when he attempts to assume the duties of such an establishment, he should be waited upon by a martialed corps of *real* milliners, and compelled, with a loud and clamorous salutation of groans and hisses, to vacate instanter. Of late, females have been almost entirely driven out of this kind of business, save, only, in the capacity of half-paid employees. Manufacturers have also got to getting up different styles of bonnets for every change of season, so that hundreds of industrious females who formerly earned a living by 'doing up' that article of dress, are now, for the most part, thrown out of employment, unless they accept of it in the 'down town' work-shops, and perform men's labor for a few shillings a week. Men-milliners are a nuisance, and should be ashamed of themselves for permitting their 'avarice' to starve poor women."

208.

Soon after my arrival, the sailors went to dinner. Rows of tables in symmetrical order were spread over the floor; and seated at these, I saw my old unmistakable friends, "the blue jackets," discussing their beef; generally, what a naval man would call a good set of men—strong, quiet, self-reliant looking men. One feels as if one was an intruder, and comforts oneself with thinking of one's good intentions—but don't be alarmed, visitor! That is all your conceit. Jack is nowise disturbed by *your* presence. He cuts his beef, looks at you casually as you pass in your inspection, and puts you quite at your ease! I really think that a sailor has as good manners as you ever see anybody with. There is such a calm, good-natured independence about him; a Neptunian politeness, which carries you along like a fine rolling wave. Manners being, however, the characteristic of a man "who feels the dignity of a man, and is conscious of his own"—as Carlyle has described it, and as Brummell never knew it to be! The fact is, that a sailor is generally in a true, real position—has certain work to do—certain people to obey. There are no false struggles, no sham pretensions, afloat. Every thing is determined by book and order. Jack will love a ruffian if he is an honest ruffian, and a barbarian if he is a well-meaning barbarian. It is the continual value set on reality at sea, that gives him independence and self-possession. The ocean knocks him about till he is rounded like a pebble. Salt water keeps character wholesome, as it preserves beef.

209.

One of our religious exchanges has the following strong remark on this subject. They drive the nail in to the head, and clinch it :—

"Men may sophisticate as they please; they can never make it right, and all the bankrupt laws in the universe cannot make it right, for them not to pay their debts. There is a sin in this neglect, as clear, and as deserving church discipline, as in stealing or false swearing. He who violates his promise to pay, or withholds the payment of a debt when it is in his power to meet his engagement, ought to be made to feel that in the sight of all honest men he is a swindler. Religion may be a very comfortable cloak under which to hide; but if religion does not make a man 'deal justly,' it is not worth having."

210.

Every body in the city of New York knows how active Mayor Kingsland has been since the first of January, 1851, in causing various nuisances to be abated. Among his other reforms he caused the boxes, bales, and barrels which have so long encumbered side-walks, in the business portion of the city, to be removed, and any merchant caught using the side-walk as a storehouse was forthwith made to pay a penalty for his violation of the city ordinances. Many were victims of the Mayor's unrelenting adherence to the laws; and a vast improvement was manifest in the regions of the old "burnt district." But the *Tribune* states that even the Mayor himself has been victimized to a large extent in this way. Not long since, while the persons employed by him at his oil store were engaged in receiving a large consignment of oil, his neighors were taking notes and entering comlpaints at the Mayor's Office for violations of the city laws. The complaints were well founded, the proofs abundant —and before the wrath of Kingsland, the Mayor, could be appeased, Kingsland, the merchant, enriched the city Treasury some three hundred dollars.

211.

WE have received a pamphlet, devoted to "*Thoughts on the subject of Influence*," a topic, as the author correctly remarks, considered in its entire length and breadth, of an infinite nature, and comprehending the universe. The title, which is learnedly explained in the preface, runs thus:—"A Sermon first delivered to various congregations in Massachusetts, and now preached from the Pulpit of Print to the 'Common People.' By David Fosdick, Jr., one of their 'Order,' and for several years Minister at large in Massachusetts." "Published by request," which also appears on the title page, Mr. Fosdick says, the reader is at liberty to suppose, as perhaps he does in other cases, that the most important request was from the author to the bookseller. Dropping the clerical character, the author retains the phases of the pulpit, with a sort of lay signification. Mr. Fosdick may be known to our readers, as the author of a series of essays on the "Interest of Money," which were originally published, at intervals, in the *Merchants' Magazine*. The "Sermon" before us contains so many capital "thoughts" on the subject of "influence," so forcibly and frankly expressed, that we should be glad to transfer the larger portion of it to our pages, but a single extract, and that not by any means the best, must suffice. It includes all that our "minister at large" has to say, or rather has said, in this instance, on a topic that falls within the province of our particular parish:—

"The idea of *trade* is a very comprehensive one. With a like sense to that in which Shakspeare says: 'All the world's a *stage*, and the men and women in it merely *players*,' we might say: All the world's a *shop*, and the men and women in it merely *traders*. It would appear that every body has something to sell. The spirit of trade, of Mammon, is certainly a very prevalent spirit of the day in these United States. It has made us so sharp, that confidence between man and man is sadly diminished. When we hear a person using his lungs in any wise whatever, we at once jump to the supposition that he has some sinister aim at the money in our pockets or something else that is ours. We regard all men as of one trade, that of auctioneer. If we hear a man explaining and defending lightning-rods, for example, we suppose he has lightning-rods to sell—and so of other wares.

"This business of Trade, in all its branches and bearings, much needs to be ransacked. Could we examine it thoroughly by what the Sacred Scriptures call 'the candle of the Lord,' we should undoubtedly find a great deal that ought to be altered. There is a good time coming, in which it will be. I by no means say, with some, that all trade must be inconsistent with pure religion. It can be amended, sanctified. Almost every wrong form of human action is but a corruption of what, properly applied, is useful. I know of but one thing in which the Bible prohibits free trade, and that is *the truth.* 'Buy the truth, (says the Bible,) and sell it not.'

"Trade, even in its imperfect state, has manifestly done much to help on human freedom: it had much to do with the settlement of this our land of liberty, as we fondly style it, and as it is, compared with other lands. Trade bears large sway at present in our politics. In some points of view this is not to be regretted. But the trading spirit involves some peculiar perils, from which we must soberly pray: 'Good Lord, deliver us!' The doctrine 'that all is fair in politics' is the doctrine of the sharper in trade. Get the advantage of your fellow man, what matter how, so the law cannot chastise you? Ah, my friends, all is *not* fair in politics; all is *not* fair in trade: that is not fair anywhere which is contrary to the eternal principle of honesty. Only think of *dishonest politics* in a land where it is a very prevalent principle that 'honesty is the best policy.' Prevalent, did I say? It is a principle honored with the lips while the heart is far from it. Duplicity is the sin of corrupt trade. It is a horrible sin throughout society. WHERE IS TRUTH? May we not say with Isaiah: 'Truth is fallen in the street, and equity cannot enter. Yea, truth faileth, and he that departeth from evil maketh himself a prey.' How our politicians

> 'Sigh and groan
> For public good, and mean their own.'

I think the sin of duplicity in politics has grown upon us since the days of our fathers. I think they were a more blunt, straightforward generation than we. If this be true, it is trade that has given us the infection.

212.

TRUTH is a restorative—it saves the conscience, and keeps up a glow of happiness under all the workings of life.

213.

THE yearly report of the Chamber of Commerce of Aix-la-Chapelle contains a statement of the extent to which smuggling prevails in that district. Within the jurisdiction of the circle of Aix-la-Chapelle alone, the collective sentences of imprisonment passed on smugglers apprehended, amount to 560 months 26 days, and the fines imposed to 6,796 thalers, although the sentences are generally light—a fact that shows the number of persons charged with the offense to be great. The chief article smuggled is coffee; the receipts from the duty on it have been for several years decreasing. In the custom-house of the district there are 3,000 centners less coffee annually passed than in 1843 and 1844, although it is known that the consumption has positively increased. The evasion of duty on this article is estimated as at least 20,000 thalers a year. In the course of last year 121 centners of coffee were seized and confiscated. It is not believed that this is more than five per cent. of the quantity smuggled. Most of the contraband coffee is introduced from Holland. The remedy proposed is a reduction of the import duty, from 6½ thalers (19s. 6d.) per centner to 4 thalers. The report states that the revenue would lose nothing by the change.

214.

THE disadvantages of life insurance and clubs proceed from our organization, and, therefore, are inevitable. The advantages of savings banks are equally organic. A boy who makes snow-balls will throw them away as fast as he makes them, but should he chance to roll up one of more than ordinary size, it will excite in him an ambition to enlarge it, instead of throwing it away; and the bigger it becomes under his efforts, the stronger will become his desire for its further increase. The principle applies to money. The day's earnings of a poor man are cast away as soon as earned, a man's recklessness being as great as his poverty; but should he deposit any of his earnings in a savings bank, an appetite, for accumulation is immediately produced by the usual possession of a surplus; and the appetite, growing by what it feeds on, will add an impulse to the industry and frugality of the depositor. "Eat, drink, and be merry, for to-morrow we die," is no longer the maxim of such a man; but rather, "refrain from *expenditure* to-day, that we may add to our deposites to-morrow."

215.

Our cotemporary of *Cumming's Evening Bulletin*, (a neutral and independent journal,) occasionally turns aside from the passing news of the day and treats his readers to an essay on some topic connected with the morals and manners of man and society. These essays are necessarily brief, and the better for that, because they are more likely to be read and remembered. As the subjoined editorial from the *Bulletin* touches upon a subject that should interest a part, at least, of our particular "parish," and as it embraces a homily too good to be lost, we take the liberty of giving it a more permanent record among our "*Maxims and Miscellanies*":—

"Faith and trustfulness lies at the foundation of trade and commercial intercourse, and business transactions of every kind. A community of known swindlers and knaves would try, in vain, to avail themselves of the advantages of traffic, or to gain access to those circles where honor and honesty are indispensable passports. The reason why savage hordes are suspected and shunned, is because they are deceitful and treacherous

We have no faith in their promises. If they manifest kindness and friendship, we apprehend it is for the sake of more successfully accomplishing their selfish and malicious purposes. So of cheats and knaves under whatever circumstances we may meet them. However fair may be their exterior, we know they are black at heart and we shrink from them as from the most deadly poison. Hence, the value which is attached, by all right-minded men, to purity of purpose and integrity of character. A man may be unfortunate, he may be poor and penniless, but if he is known to possess unbending integrity, an unwavering purpose to do what is honest and just, he will have friends and patrons whatever may be the embarrassments and exigencies into which he is thrown. The poor man may thus possess a capital of which none of the misfortunes and calamities of life can deprive him. We have known men who have suddenly been reduced from affluence to penury from some dispensation of Providence which they could neither forsee nor prevent. A fire has swept away the acuumulation of years, or misplaced confidence, or a flood, or some of the thousand casualties to which we are exposed, has stripped them of their possessions. To-day, they arc prosperous; to-morrow, every earthly prospect is blighted, and everything in its aspect is dark and dismal. Their business is gone, their property is gone, and they feel that all is gone. But they have a rich treasure which the fire cannot consume, which the flood cannot carry away. They have integrity of character, and this gives them influence, and raises up friends, and furnishes them with pecuniary aid.

"Young men, especially, should be deeply impressed with the vast importance of cherishing those principles, and of cultivating those habits which will secure for them the confidence and the esteem of the wise and the good. Let it be borne in mind, that no brilliancy of genius, no tact or talent in business, and no amount of success will compensate for duplicity, shuffling and trickery. There may be apparent advantage in the art of dissimulation, and in violating those great principles which lie at the foundation of truth and duty. But it will at length be seen, that a pound was lost where a penny was gained; that present successes are outweighed, a thousand fold, by the pains and penalties which result from loss of confidence and loss of character. It cannot be too strongly impressed upon our young men to abstain from every course, from every act, which shocks their moral sensibilities, wounds their consciences, and has a tendency to weaken that nice sense of honor and integrity so indispensable to character. The habit of concealment, of dissimulation, of telling "white lies," as Mrs. Opie calls them, is most disastrous in all its influences and issues. How many have become confirmed liars, and been consigned to dishonor and infamy, who began their career in this way! Language is utterly inadequate to describe the amazing, the infinite importance to our young men of forming their characters by the right models, and in accordance with the unchanging principles of truth. Who has not read with deep interest the incident in the life of Washington, who, when he had injured a favorite tree of his father's, frankly confessed his offense, because he 'could not tell a lie.' Here was manifest one of those essential elements of character which made Washington 'first in war, first in peace, and first in the heart's of his countrymen.'

"INTEGRITY OF CHARACTER! who ever possessed it, that did not derive untold advantages from it? It is better than the gold of Ophir; it is of more value than diamonds, 'and all precious stones.' And yet every man may possess it. The poorest may have it, and no power can wrest it from them. To young men, we say with earnestness and emphasis, look at integrity of character with the blessings it confers, and imbibe such principles and pursue such a course, that its benefits may be yours. It is a prize so rich, that it repays every sacrifice and every toil, necessary to secure it. Suppose a mercantile community could be found whose every individual was known and acknowledged to possess strict and uncompromising integrity; the representations of each one were in strict accordance with truth; 'his word as good as his bond!' Such a community would have a monopoly of the trade, so far as they had the means of supplying the demand. 'The tricks of trade,' whatever be their apparent advantages, impair confidence, and in the end, injure those who practice them far more than they benefit them. It is a short-sighted, as well as a guilty policy, to swerve, under any circumstances, from those great principles which are of universal and everlasting obligation. Let a man maintain his integrity at all times, and he will be satisfied there is a blessing in it, and a blessing flowing from it, and a blessing all around it."

216.

The following passage occurs in a lecture on Character, delivered by Henry Ward Beecher, first before the Mercantile Library Association of Boston, and afterwards at the Tabernacle in New York, at the instance of a number of conscientious merchants, who "liked to be preached to":—

"Commercial men do not love conscience. I speak of them not as men, but as commercial men. Practical commerce, at best, is as cold as a stone. *Business is business.* On Sunday, the exemplary merchant hears from the pulpit, 'Look not every man on his own things, but every man also on the things of others,' and he says amen to that. On Monday he hears the genius of Commerce say, 'Every man for himself,' and he says amen to that. He has one conscience for Sunday, and another conscience for Monday. If I wished to send consternation along the exchange, and panic to the tables of the money-changers, I would not send war nor pestilence, but I would bring down love's brightest angel, Benevolence, before the sweet splendor of whose face the financial men would flee away. Why! the Lord's Prayer would bring down fire from heaven if answered. '*Thy will be done on earth as it is in heaven,*' would be the death-knell of banks and offices; the caucus would vomit out its impurity; the slave go up; the master would go down; the crooked places would be made straight, and the rough places smooth. If every brick in every wall that had been laid in transgression, and every nail driven in sin, and every bale and box brought forth in iniquity, were to groan and sigh, how many articles around us would remain silent? How men would shriek and cry out, 'Art thou come to torment us before the time?' If every article of trade in *any* store, that was there through wrong, were to fly through the air to the rightful ownership, what a flight of bales and boxes and sugar casks should we see! The Lord's Prayer would be a very unsafe prayer to pray, *if it were answered.* But is not the wrong as much here, as if it were thus demon strated before our eyes?"

217.

RASCALS may flourish, but honest men will out-sleep them.

Lying won't stand while truth is truth.

Risk anything before you risk your reputation.

218.

A MAN who is furnished with arguments from the mint, will convince his antagonist much sooner than one who draws them from reason and philosophy. Gold is a wonderful clearer of the understanding; it dissipates every doubt and scruple in an instant; accommodates itself to the meanest capacities; silences the loud and clamorous; and brings over the most obstinate and inflexible. Philip of Macedon was a man of most invincible reason this way. He refuted by it all the wisdom of Athens, confounded their statesmen, struck their orators dumb, and, at length, argued them out of all their liberties.

219.

As in no department of life is success more earnestly desired, or more perseveringly sought, than in mercantile pursuits, it will not be out of place in a work like the present to exhibit all the aids and hindrances to a consummation so devoutly wished by the thousands that crowd the marts and thorougfares of commercial life. With this view we quote some sensible suggestions from the author of "*Companions of my Solitude*," which the reader is at liberty "to mark, learn, and inwardly digest" at his leisure:—

"One of the great aids, or hindrances, to success in anything lies in the temperament of a man. I do not know yours; but I venture to point out to you what is the best temperament; namely, a combination of the desponding and the resolute, or, as I had better express it, of the apprehensive and the resolute. Such is the temperament of great commanders. Secretly, they rely upon nothing and upon nobody. There is such a powerful element of failure in all human affairs, that a shrewd man is always saying to himself, What shall I do, if that which I count upon does not come out as I expect? This foresight dwarfs and crushes all but men of great resolution.

"Then, be not over choice in looking out for what may exactly suit you; but rather be ready to adopt any opportunities that occur. Fortune does not stoop often to take any one up. Favorable opportunities will not happen precisely in the way that you have imagined. Nothing does. Do not be discouraged, therefore, by a present detriment in any course which may lead to something good. Time is so precious here.

"Get, if you can, into one or other of the main grooves of human affairs. It is all the difference of going by railway, and walking over a ploughed field, whether you adopt common courses, or set up one for yourself. You will see, if your times are anything like ours, most inferior persons highly placed in the army, in the church, in office, at the bar. They have somehow got upon the line, and have moved on well with very little original motive power of their own. Do not let this make you talk as if merit were utterly neglected in these or any professions; only that getting well into the groove will frequently do instead of any great excellence.

* * * * *

"Whatever happens, do not be dissatisfied with your worldly fortunes, lest that speech be justly made to you, which was once made to a repining person much given to talk of how great she and hers had been. 'Yes, madam,' was the crushing reply, 'we all find our level at last.'

"Eternally that fable is true, of a choice being given to men on their entrance into life. Two majestic women stand before you: one in rich vesture, superb, with what seems like a mural crown on her head, and plenty in her hand, and something of triumph, I will not say of boldness, in her eye; and she, the queen of this world, can give you many things. The other is beautiful, but not alluring, nor rich, nor powerful; and there are traces of care, and shame, and sorrow in her face; and (marvelous to say) her look is downcast and yet noble. She can give you nothing, but she can make you somebody. If you cannot bear to part from her sweet, sublime countenance, which hardly veils with sorrow its infinity, follow her; follow her, I say, if you are really minded so to do; but do not, while you are on this track, look back with ill-concealed envy on the glittering things which fall in the path of those who prefer to follow the rich dame, and to pick up the riches and honors which fall from her cornucopia.

"This is, in substance, what a true artist said to me only the other day, impatient, as he told me, of the complaints of those who would pursue art, and yet would have fortune."

220.

WE love our upright-energetic men. Pull them this way, and then that way, and the other, and they only bend, but never break. Trip them down, and in a trice they are on their feet. Bury them in the mud, and in an hour they will be out and bright. They are not ever yawning away existence, or walking about the world as if they had come into it with only half their soul; you cannot keep them down—you cannot destroy them. But for these the world would soon degenerate. They are the salt of the earth. Who but they start any noble project? They build our cities and rear our manufactories. They whiten the ocean with their sails, and they blacken the heavens with the smoke of their steam-vessels and furnace fires. They draw treasures from the mine. They plow the earth. Blessings on them! Look to them, young men, and take courage; imitate their example, catch the spirit of their energy and enterprise, and study the pages of the *Merchants' Magazine*, and you will deserve and no doubt command success.

221.

A WRITER complains that the business hours of Boston close at 2 instead of 4 o'clock, as in New York, thus shortening the time for making purchases and cheapening goods. He says, very feelingly, that "there is a loss of precious time for business purposes." Our opinion is, if it is worth anything, that there is too much "precious time" lost *in* "business purposes," and too little expended for higher advantages than dollars and cents. As people live around us, it would seem as if there was nothing but money worth striving for; and every energy of mind and body must be exerted for its attainment. *Get rich!* appears to be the rule that men have written on their hearts, and it is a "waste of precious time" to turn aside for a moment from its direction.

222.

THE young man who leaves the farm-field for the merchant's desk or the lawyer's or doctor's office, thinking to dignify or ennoble his toil, makes a sad mistake. He passes, by that step, from independence to vassalage. He barters a natural for an artificial pursuit, and he must be the slave of the caprice of customers and the chicane of trade, either to support himself or to acquire fortune. The more artificial a man's pursuit, the more debasing is it morally and physically. To test it, contrast the merchant's clerk with the plowboy. The former may have the most exterior polish, but the latter, under his rough outside, possesses the truer stamina. He is the freer, franker, happier, and nobler man. Would that young men might judge of the dignity of labor by its usefulness and manliness, rather than by the superficial glosses it wears. Therefore, we never see a man's nobility in his kid gloves and toilet adornments, but in that sinewy arm, whose outlines, browned by the sun, betoken a hardy, honest toiler, under whose farmer's or mechanic's vest a kingliest heart may beat.

223.

PERHAPS the reader may have a *penchant*, as a friend of ours has, for buying things *cheap*. We say *perhaps*—for it is a weakness with which many are troubled, and it is a most expensive one. There are many who have been tempted to lay up goods where moth and rust doth corrupt, merely because they were obtained cheap; but it is a poor policy, and patronizing peddlers is a still poorer one. One of these wandering Jews stept into a counting room a few days since, and, after warming his hands, turned to the gentleman occupying the seat of authority, just then busily engaged in weighing the evidence regarding the true cause of the recent Whig defeat, so admirably and differently attributed by the *Atlas*, the *Daily Advertiser*, and the *Courier*, and politely inquired if he would like to look at a vest pattern?

"No, no! Don't bother me. Very busy just now."

"It is the best article and the neatest pattern that you ever saw."

"Don't want any vest patterns."

"But just look, sir,"—and the peddler had a piece of vesting unfolded, which was really quite neat, and the cogitator, unable to unravel the political web, determined to unravel the web of the fabric. "All silk, sir; warranted, and sufficient for two double-breasted vests, or three with rolling collars."

"What do you ask for it?"

"Twelve dollars. I bought it in Liverpool, and brought it over with me, and if you want it you shall have it for just what it cost me—twelve dollars."

"It is too much, sha'n't give any such a price—but will give you six dollars."

"Oh, my gracious," exclaimed the peddler, as if astonished at such an offer, "I can't think of it;" off he walked. In ten minutes the door was opened, and the peddler thrust in his head: "You may have it for ten dollars."

"No," was all the reply he got.

"I will say eight, as the very lowest."

"No, *sir*,"—and away went the peddler a second time. The gentleman was about relapsing into his revery upon the disputed question already mentioned, when the peddler re-entered boldly, and laid the vesting on the desk, exclaiming, "Well, give us six dollars, and it is yours." The money was paid, and the peddler was about leaving the door, when he turned round and took from his pocket another roll, and, undoing it, exposed to view a piece of vesting, as far preferable to the other as the new building on the corner of State-street exceeds in height all its neighbors.

The gentleman at once made a proposal to exchange. The peddler couldn't think of such a thing; he didn't mean to sell it on any account; he intended to keep it till he was able to have it made up for himself—but, after considerable trading and talking, he gave it up, received his first piece and two dollars, and walked off, making eight dollars for his piece of vesting. The gentleman, quite satisfied with the exchange, walked up to his tailor's at noon, threw down the piece, ordering him to cut off sufficient for one vest.

"How many vests do you expect it will make?" inquired the tailor.

"Three, of course," was the reply.

The yard stick went down, and looking up, he informed the purchaser that it would make two, by piecing out the collar with black silk. The idea of measuring the article had not occurred to him before, but at this piece of news, he felt a kind of film spread over his eyes, a lightness of pocket troubling his ribs, while the letters s-o-l-d, by a delusion of his optical nerves, appeared to be written on the outer walls of all adjacent buildings. He then inquired the probable worth, and was informed that such vesting could be purchased at about two and a quarter per yard. This was sufficient. He has resolved never to patronize a peddler, but to extend his patronage to those good tax-paying citizens who have a local habitation and a name.

224.

There are a good many merchants who think that honesty in every-day business matters is incompatible with success. They seem to think that in order to get along they must practice a certain degree of trickery and deception. They argue that the up-and-down honest man, who will not swerve from the path of rectitude, is sure to fail in whatever he undertakes; and hence they justify themselves in practicing petty as well as wholesale dissimulation, and in taking advantage of the verdancy of their customers, under the plea that *custom* and *necessity* compel them to adopt this course. The high-wayman might, with as good a degree of plausibility, advance a similar theory to justify his depredations, only that his "calling" is not quite as general as that of the merchant. There are not so many men who threaten your life, if you do not comply with their demands, as there are dealers who justify general imposition and fraud, and that makes the seeming difference between the *honesty* of the highway robber and that of the merchant who deliberately utters untruths, and misrepresents the value of an article in order that he may effect a sale of goods.

We firmly believe that the man who possesses the requisite business qualifications, can succeed better in the mercantile field by pursuing an honest straight-forward course, than if he were to deaden his conscience and disregard all moral obligations by amassing riches (to last for a brief period) at the expense of the unwary and inexperienced, and in defrauding people generally, not openly, but "*on the sly*," as the custom is. We frequently hear the expression made in reference to some good-natured, inactive, old-womanish man, "*Oh, he's too honest to get along.*" Now this is a false inference, for in nine cases out of ten the honest man's failure does not arise from the practice of an honest course, but from his unfitness for the business in which he is engaged. We do not by any means intend to convey the impression that *honesty* will cause a man who is not qualified for the business in which he is engaged to succeed. What we mean to assert, and the impression that we would leave on the minds of the readers of the *Ledger*, is that a man who is adapted for a certain pursuit *will* and *must* necessarily succeed better by dealing honestly and uprightly than by cheating and defrauding when he thinks he will not be detected.

But in addition to the matter of success, how cheerful and pleasant is the condition of the man who knows and feels that he is doing an honest business—a business which his conscience approves! This is of more value to him than the possession of millions. It is a source of happiness which the fashionable swindler never can realize nor appreciate. Let every honest merchant, then, be encouraged by these reflections, and if he does not amass wealth as rapidly as he could desire, he can find abundant consolation in the old version of the words of the "sweet singer of Israel:"—

"A little that a just man hath
Is more and better far,
Than is the wealth of many such
As false and wicked are.
* * * * *
"I have been young, but now am old,
Yet have I never seen
The just man left, nor that his seed
For bread have beggars been."

225.

A STRANGE old man is he, who may be seen any day, be it cold or hot, in the neighborhood of the Poydras Market, with a bundle of socks in his hand or on the banquette beside him. Selling socks is now his only business; yet time was when it was not so. Of the multiform mutations of human life, that old man has experienced more than mortal's share. See how he mutters to himself, and smiles, half insanely, as he praises his wares to his real or pretended customers! One eye is closed, and the lid is swollen, and the face of the sock seller is covered with scars. These are traces left in the old man's face by assassin burglars, who, some two years ago, robbed him of his goods, and left him as one dead, in his house on Circus-street. It was long before this old man recovered, and when he did, his intellect was a wreck, and nothing save his business habits were left to save him from total insanity. Since then he has followed the business of selling socks.

But it were unjust to the old man to give so imperfect an

abstract of his history. Let us roll back the tide of time some quarter of a century, and a tall, fine-looking gentleman may be observed walking down Broadway, in New York. Fair ladies ogle him as he passes, and feel flattered when he smiles on them. And is it strange?—for the smiler of that day is a wholesale merchant of princely fortune! After that, changes came. The merchant, broken in fortune, removed to New Orleans, and his remains may now be found in the muttering sock seller of the Poydras Market. There is a strange tale of love connected with the old man.

226.

"*A bird in the hand is worth two in the bush.*" The extreme caution ridiculed by this proverb is of a kind which one would hardly have expected to be popular in a commercial country. If this were acted upon, there would be an end of trade and Commerce, and all capital would lie dead at the banker's—as a bird who was held safe. The truth is, our whole practice is of a directly opposite kind. We regard a bird in the hand as worth only a bird; and we know there is no chance of making it worth two birds—not to speak of the hope of a dozen—without letting it out of the hand. Inasmuch, however, as the proverb also means to exhort us not to give up a good certainty for a tempting uncertainty, we do most fully coincide in its prudence and sound sense. It is identical with the French, "*Mieux vaut un* 'tiens' *que deux* 'tu l'auras,'"—one "take this" is better than two "thou shalt have it;" identical also with the Italian: "*E meglio un uovo oggi, che una gallina domani;*" an egg to-day is better than a hen to-morrow. It owes its origin to the Arabic—"A thousand cranes in the air are not worth one sparrow in the fist."

227.

On the 10th of March, 1852, a singular old custom was revived at Hamburg. When the Exchange was thronged at high noon, two of the city drummers appeared in uniform before the entrance and beat a roll ten minutes long. Then over the great door of the Exchange they suspended a black tablet inscribed with the name of a bankrupt merchant who had absconded. When this was done, the bell in one of the towers—the bell of shame—rang for two hours. The tablet remains for three months and a day. In many German cities the bankrupt, as a sign of his condition, is compelled to wear a straw hat for a year and a day.

228.

We have before us, says the Boston *Traveler*, a private letter from a *lady*, though a hard-working woman, in Calfornia. It would interest our readers, we have no doubt, as it has us, were we at liberty to publish it entire. The writer appears to keep a restaurant or eating-house, in a mining village. Among her visitors she accidentally discovers the son of an old Connecticut acquaintance, and finding he was endeavoring to induce his father and mother to visit California, she writes this letter to encourage them forward. After an introductory explanation of who she was, and where they became acquainted with each other, she goes on to say :—

"I have made about eighteen thousand dollars worth of pies —about one third of this has been clear profit. One year I dragged my own wood off the mountains and chopped it, and I have never had so much as a child to take a step for me in this country. Eleven thousand dollars I baked in one little iron skillet, a considerable portion by a camp fire, without the shelter of a tree from the broiling sun. But now I have a good cooking stove, in which I bake four pies at a time, a comfortable cabin, carpeted, and a good many 'Robinson Crusoe' comforts about me, which, though they have cost nothing, yet they make my place look habitable. I also hire my wood hauled and chopped. I bake on an average about twelve hundred pies per month, and clear two hundred dollars. This, in California, is not thought much, and yet, in reality, few in comparison are doing as well.

"I have been informed there are some women in our town clearing fifty dollars per week at washing, and I cannot doubt it. There is no labor so well paid as women's labor in California. It is hard work to apply one's self incessantly to toil, but a few years will place you above want with a handsome independency. I intend to leave off work the coming spring, and give my business into the hands of my sister-in-law. Not that I am rich, but I need little, and have none to toil for but myself. I expect to go home some time during the present year, for a short visit, but I could not be long content away from the sunny clime of this yellow land. A lovelier or more healthy climate could not be, and when I get a few friends about me, I think I shall be nearly happy again."

229.

A THIN, cadaverous-looking German, about fifty years of age, entered the office of a Health Insurance Company in Indiana, on the first day of May, 1852, says the *Daily Courier*, and inquired—

"Ish te man in vot inshures de people's helts?"

The agent politely answered, "I attend to that business, sir."

"Vell, I vants mine helts inshured; vot you charge?"

"Different prices," answered the agent, "from three to ten

dollars a year; pay ten dollars a year, and you get ten dollars a week in case of sickness."

"Vell," said Mynheer, "I vants ten dollar vort."

The agent inquired his state of health.

"Vell, I ish sick all the time. I'se shust out te bed too tree hours a tay, und te doctor says he can't do noting more goot for me."

"If that's the state of your health," returned the agent, "we can't insure it. We only insure persons who are in good health."

At this Mynheer bristled up in great anger.

"You must tink I'se a tam fool; vot you tink I come pay you ten dollar for inshure my helt, *ven I vos vell?*"

230.

Some are not honest in buying or selling. Their rule is, to buy at all times as cheap as they can, and sell as dear as they can. This is a wicked rule. We often trade with those who do not know the worth of the thing bought or sold. It is cheating them, to make the best bargain we can. Sometimes we trade with those who are in great want, and we fix our own prices, and make them much too high if we sell, or too low if we buy. There is a fair price for everything. Let that be paid or taken for everything. He who is just and true, and loves his nighbor as himself, will soon find out what a fair price is. Almost all men use too many words in buying and selling; and when too many words are used, there is almost always a lie somewhere.

231.

Closely upon the heels of the gambler came the "fast" man of business—in haste to be rich, impatient of labor, and, by his expenses, proving that if he did not make his own fortune, he understood as well how to spend another man's fortune as if he learned the art in our Common Council. Life to such a man was very like a Mississippi voyage to those on the lookout for a race, consoling themselves with the reflection that the chances of their rival's boiler bursting and blowing them to atoms would be as great as their own. The "fast man" thought the locomotive but a "slow coach," and that the telegraph "did very well for a beginning." The "fast man" of business also looked forward with confident expectation for the arrival of the period when all days of receipt would be brought very near, and all days of payment indefinitely postponed.

232.

Competition in trade is considered the life of business. We do not pretend to set up our opinions in opposition to the established and acknowledged proverbs of our fathers, but we do differ, in some particulars, with the spirit of the adage quoted above. It might be qualified and amended. Honorable competition is a means of creating trade, and develops the capacity of men. But that competition that seeks every means in its power to monopolize trade, by reducing prices, is far from the life of business, but is, in fact, its very death. Fair, upright, honorable dealing, will always be sure to meet its reward—although the returns may not be immediate, and it is better to compete fairly and openly, than secretly and covertly. We live in excitement, and life is a constant battle. In this country, where competition does not exist to the extent that it prevails in Europe, we have but a faint conception of its injurious tendency, when carried to excess, and know but little of the schemes, resorted to there, to secure trade. In the great battle of existence, as seen in the old world, men resort to every species of trick to secure success in business, and every device is used to obtain custom. This spirit is, unfortunately, on the increase in this country, and men undersell each other oftentimes, to the injury of themselves as well as those whose trade they seek to destroy. We are of those who hold to the sentiment, "Live, and let live;" and we consider it a golden rule. It is at variance with that motive which prompts a man to undersell his neighbor, for the purpose of obtaining his customers, and deserves to be practiced more than it is. There is no selfishness in it; but, on the contrary, a spirit of liberality and Christianity, worthy of our attention and adoption. If business men were to study their true interest, there would be less competition among us than there is at present, and there would be fewer complaints about dull times, and not so many failures as now. The spirit of competition, when carried to excess, tends to degrade men, and make tham heartless, selfish, and even cruel; and if not checked, leads to distrust, enmity, and uncharitableness. A disposition to fair dealing does much to destroy it, and makes our situation less irksome than if we engage in it with full determination to advance our own interests, to the injury of others. There is a living, and more, for all of us, without endeavoring to deprive each other of the means of livelihood, and if we throw aside that spirit of selfishness that prompts to excessive competition, we will benefit ourselves as well as others, and "do unto others as we would they should do unto us."

234.

WE are often entertained, says an English journalist, by the tone of sentiment adopted in advertising a death. There is frequently a facetious union of puff and despondency. We will give a specimen of a "death:"—"Died on the 11th ultimo, at the shop in Fleet-street, Mr. Edward Jones, much respected by all who knew and dealt with him. As a man he was amiable, as a hatter upright and moderate. His virtues were beyond all price, and his beaver hats were only one pound four shillings each. He has left a widow to deplore his loss, and a large stock to be sold cheap for the benefit of his family. He was snatched to the other world in the prime of life, and just as he had concluded an extensive purchase of felt, which he got so cheap that the widow can supply hats at a more reasonable charge than any house in London. His disconsolate family will carry on the business with punctuality."

235.

A FEW years since, a worthy hardware merchant, who had made his fortune at the business in the city of New York, determined to sell off his stock and retire. His goods were soon disposed of, and the shop empty. In sweeping out the store one day, he found in the crevices and corners a few shot (about twenty) of all sizes; he gathered them up in the hollow of his hand, and stood for some seconds gazing at them; at length, seizing his hat, he rushed into an adjoining liquor store, where they also sold shot, and thus addressed the proprietor:—"In cleaning my store I found a few shot; they are no use to me, but to you they are worth something. I don't value them very highly, but perhaps (here he lowered his voice) you would give me *half a glass of beer* for them." Reader, do you suppose this worthy, we should, perhaps, say mean, hardware merchant was either a patron or reader of the "*Merchants' Magazine?*"

235.

The Hon. Edward Everett, in one of his speeches at the dinner in Boston, given to Baring, the celebrated London Banker, argued in his felicitous style that there could be no antagonism between Capital and Labor.

The owner of capital, said Mr. Everett, in England or America, really reaps the smallest portion of the advantages which flow from its possession—he being but a kind of head book-keeper, or chief clerk to the business community. He may be as rich as Crœsus, but he can neither eat, drink, nor wear more than one man's portion. Mr. Everett said he remembered hearing a jest made about Mr. Astor's property, which contained, he thought, a great deal of meaning—a latent, practical philosophy. Some one was asked whether he would be willing to take care of all Mr. Astor's property—eight or ten millions of dollars—merely for his board and clothing.

"No," was the indignant answer; "do you think me a fool?"

"Well," rejoins the other, "that is all Mr. Astor himself gets for taking care of it; he's *found*, and that's all. The houses, the warehouses, the ships, the farms which he counts by the hundred, and is obliged to take care of, are for the accommodation of others."

"But then he has the income, the rents of all this mighty property, five or six hundred thousand dollars per annum."

"Yes, but he can do nothing with his income but build more houses, and warehouses, and ships, or loan more money on mortgages for the convenience of others. He's *found*, and you can make nothing else out of it."

236.

How pleasant 'tis when I can say,
My work is done, 'tis Saturday,
My cash is settled, letters done,
My duties finished, every one.
'Tis passing sweet to us cashiers,
Whose labor circles with the years,
To close the Bank and turn the keys,
Then close the week with books and ease.
We read of one, and him we thank,
Who years ago first closed a Bank;
Rebuked cashiers, their desks o'erthrew,
And drove them out with whip-cord too.
I often think of this in church,
When for my wandering thoughts I search,
I find them deep in moneyed schemes,
In dividends, or golden dreams.
I start! my sin is just the same
As that of old, though not in name;
I sin as much with moneyed thought,
As did the Jews of old, who brought
Their desks within the temple's range,
And shaved the green ones making change;
And should I suffer whips of cord,
I should but suffer just reward.
Yes, turn all thoughts of loss and gain
From out the place where God should reign;
Nor let such thoughts with footsteps rude
Upon your Sabbath hours intrude.

237.

Credit should be sparingly given, and integrity be the basis of it.

Prudence in promises is a fair guarantee in the redemption of them.

238.

A CORRESPONDENT of the London *Youth's Instructor* relates an anecdote, which we transfer to this book for the especial benefit of young men entering mercantile life:—

"I once new a young man," said an eminent preacher the other day, in a sermon to young men, "that was commencing life as a clerk. One day his employer said to him, 'Now, to-morrow, that cargo of cotton must be got out and weighed, and we must have a regular account of it.'

"He was a young man of energy. This was the first time he had been intrusted to superintend the execution of this work. He made his arrangements over night, spoke to the men about their carts and horses, and, resolved to begin very early in the morning, he instructed the laborers to be there at half-past four o'clock. His master comes in, and, seeing him sitting in the counting-house, looks very black, supposes that his commands had not been executed.

"'I thought,' said the master, 'you were requested to get out that cargo this morning.'

"'It is all done,' said the young man, 'and here is the account of it.'

"He never looked behind him from that moment—never! His character was fixed, confidence was established. He was found to be the man to do the thing with promptness. He very soon came to be one that could not be spared; he was as necessary to the firm as any of the partners. He was a religious man, and went through a life of great benevolence, and at his death was able to leave his children an ample fortune. He was not smoke to the eye nor vinegar to the teeth, but just the contrary."

239.

MONEY—*to get money*—let us frankly admit at the outset, is the aim, the paramount end of business, of retail and wholesale, of business on a large scale, of business on a small scale, of the peddler, of the merchant-prince, of him who trades under the open sky, at the corner of the street, of him who sends ships to the ends of the earth, whose calculations take in the fortunes of nations, and whose operations may determine peace and war, the happiness or misery of millions. MONEY! with what an intonation of contempt the word is sometimes uttered. The "accursed hunger for gold" is the standard subject of classical and philosophical anathema. Yet with what a secret charm the word falls on the mental ear! The theory of getting money is the theory of business, and is the topic of the interesting book whose title we give below.

Mr. Freedley's book is written with much liveliness of style, is full of anecdotes and illustrations, and abounds in practical suggestions, based upon the present business prospects and relations of the country. It may be read with profit not only by those who are entering upon business life, but by those also who would compare their own experience with that of others, and whose minds are open to new suggestions. We must needs like the book, yet find it difficult to quote from it—and for one and the same reason. Not only have the ideas been again and again inculcated in our pages, but Mr. Freedley has had the good taste to avail himself of our labors by liberal extracts. The merit of the work is, that it presents, in a compendious and convenient shape, the opinions of many experienced business men, and many hints and suggestions, either original or derived from reliable sources, relative to business management, the choice of business, habits of business, "getting money by farming," "getting money by merchandising," "how to get customers," "the true man of business," "how to get rich by speculation, banking, patent inventions," "how to become millionaires," and "the chances of success." So much has been said in our pages on all these topics, that by quoting we run the risk of repetition.

Getting money (we repeat the confession) is the chief end of business. But what is money? Money is bread. Money is raiment. Money is shelter. Money is education, refinement, books, pictures, music. Money is the society of the learned and accomplished. Is it less true than in Solomon's time, that "wealth maketh many friends; but the poor is separated from his neighbor?" Money is science, invention, discovery, enterprise. Money is the canal, the railroad, the telegraph, the steamship. In short, in modern society, under modern governments of law, the essence of which seems to consist in rigidly maintaining the distinction of *meum* and *tuum*, money takes the place of that arbitrary rule of the king, the baron, the aristocrat, which in old times commanded by power, what is now only to be obtained by wealth. "Commerce is king," it is said; say rather money, which is the end of Commerce. And here lies the danger. The danger is that a new power, more cruel, more heartless, than kingly or feudal power, shall, in the form of capital and monopoly, rise to crush the mass of men. For money is hardening to the heart. Money is selfish. Money is rivalry, competition, deceit. Money sends "the weak to the wall," and says, "Every man for himself." That mixture of good and evil, which we find everywhere in the world, has its acme and highest point in that greatest of merely earthly good, that "root of all earthly evil"—money. Not to be "taken from the world, but to be delivered from the evil that is in the world," must be the motto and the prayer of every true merchant. Let him feel that while he is laboring for the increase and distribution of wealth, he is working for the elevation and civilization of the masses. Let him feel that in pursuing trade for the purpose of acquiring wealth, the first object, the main object, he is never "delivered from temptation."

Franklin was the first, we think, to bring together in a somewhat formal way the maxims of business, and thus to do something to establish a theory of business life. By his essays, his biography, and the collection of sayings in "Poor Richard," he did more than any man before him, more than any man since, perhaps, to shape the business mind of America, to say nothing of the influence of his works in Europe. Some carp at the mercenary spirit, the low aims, which they are pleased to discover in Franklin's economical teachings. But to require of a writer, who is to teach us how to better our material condition, exalted views of our moral or intellectual nature or aims in life, is simply to wander from the question. There are, doubtless, things infinitely higher in life than money or physical well-being, but bread is *prior*, if other things are higher. *To live* is the previous question, which has to be settled before men can determine *how* they shall live, morally or sensually, wisely or foolishly.

The idea of Mr. Freedley's book appears to be to exhibit, in a formal treatise, the theory of business, developing thus Franklin's idea, and adapting it to the present state of business, and present physical, commercial, and industrial development of the country. We are not aware that this has ever been attempted before. And his execution of the plan is, in many respects, highly satisfactory. We say, theory of business. Why should it not have its theory as well as law or medicine? Every practice has its theory. There is a good way, there is a bad way of doing everything. The good way is the true, the bad way is the false theory of that thing, whatever it is, whether "playing on the stops" of a pipe or of the world, practicing a profession or "doing business."* There are rules and maxims of mercantile life, the observance of which is, as a general thing, as necessary to success as that of the rules of geometry to the engineer, or of the rules of war to the soldier. It is true some business men are less systematically and *consciously* governed by formal rules than others, but, we repeat, no man can act, without acting upon some rule, good or bad, the suggestion of the moment, or the result of previous thought.

This practical treatise contains a chapter of opinions of rich men as to the how, the mode of getting rich. "John Jacob Astor," says the author, "I am informed by his son, W. B. Astor, is not known to have had any fundamental rule or favorite maxim" of business life. Yet there can be no doubt that in this instance of colossal fortune, Mr. Astor's positive genius for money-making was aided by a sort of instinctive observance of the rules and habits suggested by the best mercantile experience.

The readers of the *Merchants' Magazine* will bear us witness that we have at all times endeavored to inculcate sound rules, a true theory of business. It has been a standing topic in these pages, which would but poorly exhibit the literature of Commerce if it neglected the theory of business. Our mercantile biography has furnished excellent illustrations of the best rules for the conduct of business life. Many of the maxims of most direct and practical bearing, are stated with much force, and

* The idea, in short, is that of Bacon, respecting the true mode of philosophical inquiry, enlarged and applied to all the pursuits of life—"*Nihil veniat in practicam cujus non fit etiam doctrina aliqua et theoria.*"

illustrated by example in the biography of John Grigg, the eminent bookseller of Philadelphia, which we gave in the number for July, 1851. That sketch has been so widely copied, and so often quoted, that we are encouraged to hope that the rules and maxims it contains, drawn from and illustrated by the rich and varied experience of that excellent man, will be of use to the young merchants of America. All men may not possess his business genius, but the business virtues of industry, punctuality, and honor, are within the reach of all. If the man of highest business capacity cannot dispense with these, how can others do without them?

The chapter of opinions, to which we have referred, contains rules for acquiring wealth, or, as Mr. Freedley expresses it, "how to become millionaires," attributed to Rothschild, David Ricardo, Girard, and others:—

Many of those who have risen to elevated positions by unlocking the golden gates of wealth, have favored the world with very valuable opinions which they regarded as the key to their success, and a recapitulation of them in a connected form, which was never done before, will afford us entertainment, and perhaps instruction.

Rothschild's Opinion. The founder of this world-renowned house, whose immense transactions we may subsequently notice, is said to have ascribed his early success to the following rules:—

1. "I combined three profits; I made the manufacturer my customer, and the one I bought of my customer; that is, I supplied the manufacturer with raw materials and dyes, on each of which I made a profit, and took his manufactured goods, which I sold at a profit; and thus combined three profits.

2. "Make a bargain at once. Be an off-hand man.

3. "*Never have anything to do with an unlucky man or place.*

I have seen," said he, "many clever men who had not shoes to their feet. I never act with them; their advice sounds very well, but fate is against them; they cannot get on themselves; how can they do good to me?

4. "*Be cautious and bold.* It requires a great deal of boldness and a great deal of caution to make a great fortune; and when you have got it, it requires ten times as much wit to keep it."

The continued prosperity of the eminent banking-house of the Rothschilds is ascribed, in the following biographical extract, to two principles:—"He who does not delay for casualties, and has knowledge enough to perceive that in all great affairs the success not only depends on the choice and use of the favorable moment, but *especially on the pursuit of an acknowledged fundamental maxim,* will soon perceive that particularly two principles were never neglected by this banking-house; to which, besides to a prudent performance of its business and to advantageous conjunctures, it owes the greatest part of its present wealth and respectability.

"The first of these principles was that which caused the five brothers to carry on their business in a perpetual and uninterrupted communion. This was the golden rule bequeathed to them by their dying father. Since his death, every proposition, let it come from whom it may, is the object of their common deliberations. Every important undertaking was carried on by a combined effort, after a plan agreed upon, and all had an equal share in the result. Though for several years their customary residences were very remote, this circumstance could never interrupt their harmony; it rather gave them this advantage, that they were always perfectly well instructed of the condition of things in the different capitals—that each of them, on his part, could the better prepare and initiate the affairs to be undertaken by the firm. The second principle in perpetual view of this house is, not to seek an excessive profit in any undertaking; to assign certain limits to every enterprise; and, as much as human caution and prudence can do, to make themselves independent of the play of accidents."

David Ricardo, the celebrated political economist, was born in London, of a Jewish family, in 1772. His character for probity, industry, and talent, early procured for him the means of support; and becoming a member of the Stock Exchange, he accumulated an immense property. He is author of many works on finance; and in 1819 was elected to Parliament. Died, 1823. He had what he called his own three golden rules; the observance of which he used to press on his private friends. These were:—

"Never to refuse an option when you can get it.

"Cut short your losses.

"Let your profits run on."

By cutting short one's losses, Mr. Ricardo meant that, when a member had made a purchase of stock, and prices were falling, he ought to resell immediately. And by letting one's profits run on, he meant that, when a member possessed stock, and the prices were rising, he ought not to sell until prices had reached their highest, and were beginning again to fall. These are indeed golden rules, and may be applied with advantage to innumerable transactions other than those connected with the Stock Exchange.

John Jacob Astor, I am informed by his son, W. B. Astor, is not known to have had any fundamental rule or favorite maxim, and the general outline of his career is too well known to need rehearsal.

NICHOLAS LONGWORTH, the millionaire of Cincinnati, was born in Newark, N. J., January 16th, 1783. Formerly a cobbler, as I have been informed, he removed to Cincinnati in 1804, studied law, and practiced for some fifteen years. His earnings and savings he invested in lots around Cincinnati, the rise of which was the foundation of his fortune. He then turned his attention entirely to land and lot speculations, which, in a rising market, as that has always been, is a business in which all is gain, and nothing loss. As an example of the facility with which small amounts, comparatively, secured what has since become of immense value, Mr. Cist, in his memoir of him, states that Mr. Longworth once received as a legal fee from a fellow who was accused of horse-stealing, and who had nothing else to give, two second-hand copper stills. The gentleman who had them in possession refused to give them up, but proposed to Mr. Longworth to give him a lot of thirty-three acres on Western Row, in lieu of them—a proposal which the latter, whose opinions of the value of such property were ahead of his time, gladly accepted. This transaction alone, taking into view the prodigious increase of real estate in that city, would have formed the basis for an immense fortune, the naked ground being now worth *two millions* of dollars.

What Mr. Longworth is worth is not known. The estimates vary greatly, and it is probable that after his death there will be considerable litigation. A gentleman recently has recovered land from him to the value of five hundred thousand dollars. In 1850, his taxes amounted to upwards of seventeen thousand dollars, which is the largest sum paid by any individual in the United States, William B. Astor excepted, whose taxes for the same year were twenty-three thousand one hundred and sixteen dollars. It must be remembered, however, that the taxes in Cincinnati are no trifle on any amount of property.

Mr. Longworth's opinion probably is, that speculating in real estate, in a constantly rising market, is a very good business. I am informed, by a friend in that city, that he holds it to be an indispensable requisite, that a man who desires to get rich should be from Jersey, where he himself hails from. I regard this as metaphorical language, meaning, probably, that he must have a *sandy* head and a stony heart.

John Freedley's never-varying motto was—self-dependence, self-reliance.

"It is a mistaken notion," he writes, "that capital alone is necessary to success in business. If a man has head and hands suited to his business, it will soon procure him capital. My observations through life satisfy me that at least nine-tenths of those most successful in business start in life without any reliance except upon their own head and hands—hoe their own row from the jump. All professions and occupations alike give the field for talent, perseverance, and industry; and these qualities, whether in the East, West, or South, sooner or later, will crown the aspirant with success. But to enable any new beginner to succeed, he must not be allured from his course by attractive appearances, nor be driven from it by trifling adverse gales. He must fit himself for the calling he adopts, and then pursue his course with a steady eye. The first and great object in business is to make yourself independent—to have the means of livelihood without being under obligations to any person; whatever more is acquired increases the power of doing good and extends influence."

Mr. Freedley's opinion of the value of our own labors is almost too flattering to quote, but his business reasons for subscribing for the *Merchants' Magazine* are so ingenious and excellent that we cannot resist giving ourselves the benefit of his commendation :—

"I cannot omit this opportunity, as an act of justice to Mr. Hunt, who has done as much as any man in America to raise the reputation of American books in England, and in justice to all who may favor this book with a persual, to commend Mr. Hunt's Magazine to their especial attention and patronage, as one of the most certainly profitable investments they can make. Every business man should as certainly subscribe for it as he should insure his property. In the case of insurance, if his property does not burn down, he loses his money, but in the case of subscription to that Magazine he will not lose his money in any event, and may reap an advantage as great as the restoration of property destroyed. In the first place, he will increase his stock of useful and practical ideas, which in itself is worth more than the cost; secondly, he will possess the most comprehensive work of the age for present and future reference; and thirdly, he will take the best possible means to put himself in the way of meeting with suggestions and ideas that may happen to just suit his circumstances, and which he may turn to his advantage to the tune of hundreds or thousands of dollars. Let every one be watchful, for he knows not the day nor the hour when the good idea may come."

By way of pendant to Mr. Freedley's flattering opinion of the *Merchants' Magazine*, we feel bound to give the opinion, freely and warmly expressed by an old and eminent merchant, whose experience is the best of commentaries on the practical rules of business given in this work, and whose well-known name, were we allowed to publish it, would add weight with every reader to the recommendation that "every father of a family should read it carefully, and then each of his sons. The book is calculated to do much good in this country, and should be widely circulated."

240.

From the able and eloquent speech of the Hon. David Seymour, of New York, on the River and Harbor Bill, delivered in the House of Representatives, July 21, 1852, we extract the following brief but comprehensive picture of our commercial progress :—

" Let us briefly survey the present position of our Republic, and see what it demands of us as wise and patriotic legislators. Our country is rapidly advancing in her career of greatness. Compare its situation in 1838, when the last general appropriations for the rivers and harbors were made, with its present condition, and we are astonished at the progress we have made. No other nation has achieved so much in the same period. We have peaceably annexed one empire, settled the boundaries of another, and conquered a third. Our Commerce, which, fourteen years ago, was found in three grand divisions—that of the western rivers, the northwestern lakes, and the Atlantic coast—has crossed the isthmus, and now covers the shores of the western ocean. To our two maritime fronts, the Atlantic and the Gulf, we have added the Pacific. And there, from a coast of sixteen hundred miles in extent, we look out upon the primeval habitations of our race—the seats of ancient empire—and the most inviting field ever opened to the moral or physical energies of man. Nor is the dominion thus gained a barren scepter. On the contrary, the precious metals found in abundance in California have placed in the hands of this Republic a monetary power which, ere long, will transfer commercial ascendency from Europe to America, and will adjust in our great commercial emporium the balance-sheet of the world. And can such a nation be longer held in the swaddling bands of its infancy or the leading-strings of its childhood? The enterprise of our country, always bold and restless, is already, by the liberal aids of an improved science and the vast accessions of capital, driven onward almost with maddening speed. Nothing can arrest the progress of individual effort in all the avenues of Commerce. You may excite the apprehensions of the timid, the doubts of the wavering, or the opposition of the enemies of progress, but all will be in vain. The mighty current of events, as they are ordained, will, in spite of our resistance, bear us onward and still onward to our destiny. It is, then, the part of wisdom, of exalted patriotism, to grasp the helm of the ship of State, and, with a strong and bold hand, guide it on its course by the chart of the Constitution."

241.

We occasionally see the announcement in the public prints, says the *Sachem*, that some individual, who had been unfortunate in business and compelled to avail himself of the lenity of his creditors, or the forms of law, to obtain a legal discharge from the payment of his debts, had again embarked on the dangerous sea of trade, been favored with prosperous gales, and had liquidated the old indebtedness, principal and interest. Such conduct is frequently lauded in most extravagant terms, as though the morality which impelled the act were of a higher order than could reasonably be expected from frail humanity. We see nothing in such an act beyond the performance of a duty which is demanded by the plain precepts of pure morality. We are not of the number who measure their duty to others by what the law prohibits and enforces. We acknowledge in the matter of paying debts, the higher law of conscience and fair dealing between man and man. We do not find fault with the statute which enables the honest debtor, upon a surrender of his property to his creditors, to obtain his discharge from his liabilities. Were there no such provision, a single unfeeling creditor might doom to helpless poverty and misery his unfortunate debtor, and those dependent on him for support. But we do find fault with, and most conscientiously condemn that lax morality which considers a debt paid by a release, voluntarily given, or a discharge obtained by operation of law. It is true that in such a case the law will not enforce payment, notwithstanding the individual thus discharged may afterwards have abundance and to spare, wherewith to cancel his debts. But the moral duty still remains, and, in our opinion, no one who has it in his power to pay his debts, and refuses to do so on the plea that the law will not compel him, is entitled to be considered an honest man.

242.

A BANKER, anxious about the rise and fall of stocks, came once to Talleyrand for information respecting the truth of a rumor that George III. had suddenly died, when the statesman replied in a confidential tone, "I shall be delighted if the information I have to give, be of any use to you." The banker was enchanted with the prospect of obtaining authentic intelligence from so high a source; and Talleyrand, with a mysterious air, continued, "Some say that the King of England is dead, others, that he is not dead; for my own part I believe neither the one nor the other. I tell you this in confidence, but do not commit me." No better parody on modern diplomacy could easily be written.

243.

The *Dutchman* very justly observes that the moment money becomes cheap, up goes the price of beef and potatoes, so that it makes but very little difference to anybody save gold diggers and borrowers, whether the yield of gold mines be one ton a year or one thousand tons. Since the discovery of gold in California, interest has fallen some forty per cent, while rents have gone up seventy-five. The idea that the quantity of comfort in the world depends on the quantity of money in it, is, therefore, all moonshine. Double the present supply of gold, and we would double the price of every article for which gold is given in exchange—so that it makes "no difference to nobody" whether half the mountains in California are composed of precious metals or not. Things will find their level, and if an hour's labor in California will produce an ounce of gold, the time will soon come when an ounce of gold will be given for an hour's cobbling. The quantity of labor necessary to produce an article determines its value. Make gold dust as common as gravel, and it would bring the same price per peck.

244.

THE Pittsburgh *Daily Dispatch* puts a question, and makes a statement in the following paragraph, which we are assured is supported by the most incontestable evidence.

"HOW IS THIS?—Can a Commission Merchant, in 'good and regular standing' in a Christian Church, go to a steamboat officer and bargain for the shipment of say four hundred bbls. of flour at *forty* cents per barrel, provided the steamboat officer will agree to fill up the bill at *fifty* cents per barrel,—so as to enable the merchant to make forty dollars over his legitimate commission, &c.,

off the confiding consignor or owner, who pays this forty dollars more than he need pay, if the whole transaction were straight forward and *bona fide?* Is this a 'fair business transaction?' Is it honorable or even honest? Is it not a mean fraud? We think so—yet it is done here, not occasionally, but constantly—by people affecting honor and even piety. A man who confides in them is made to suffer to the tune of five or ten cents per hundred on the freight which he intrusts to them for shipment, and steamboatmen must become parties to the fraud, or in case of refusal, give place to those who will. We may be told this is none of our business, but it *is*: all that demoralizes or depraves public sentiment, concerns every wise citizen; and it is our duty to see that neither steamboatmen nor other men are tempted or compelled to do what they feel and acknowledge to be wrong, by those who profess to be moral *Christian* men. We have a host of witnesses to support our statements, if anybody doubts."

245.

LUNDY FOOT, the celebrated snuff manufacturer of Dublin, originally kept a small tobacconist's shop at Limerick, Ireland. One night his house, which was uninsured, was burnt to the ground. As he contemplated the smoking ruins on the following morning, in a state bordering on despair, some of the poor neighbors, groping among the embers for what they could find, stumbled upon several canisters of unconsumed but half-baked snuff, which they tried, and found so grateful to their noses, that they loaded their waistcoat pockets with the spoil.

Lundy Foot, roused from his stupor, at length imitated their example, and took a pinch of his own property, when he was instantly struck by the superior pungency and flavor it had acquired from the great heat to which it had been exposed. Treasuring up this valuable hint, he took another house, in a place called "Black Yard," and preparing a large oven for the purpose, set diligently about the manufacture of that high-dried commodity, which soon became known as "Black Yard Snuff"—a term subsequently corrupted into the more familiar word "Blackguard."

Lundy Foot, making his customers pay liberally through the nose for one of the most "distinguished" kinds of snuff in the world, soon raised the price of his production, took a larger house in the city of Dublin, and was often heard to say—"I made a very handsome fortune by being, as I supposed, utterly ruined!"

When he was rich enough to own and use a carriage, he applied to Lord Norbury for an appropriate motto for its panels. The wily Judge suggested the Latin phrase, "*Quid rides.*"

246.

Some men devote themselves so exclusively to their business, as to almost entirely neglect their domestic and social relations. A gentleman of this class having failed, was asked what he intended to do. "I am going home to get acquainted with my wife and children," said he.

247.

Do not, like a foolish mariner, always calcutate on fair weather.—Commerce, as well as life, has its auspicious ebbs and flows, that baffle human sagacity, and defeat the most rational arrangement of systems, and all the calculations of ordinary prudence. Be prepared, therefore, at all times, for commercial revulsions and financial difficulties, by which thousands have been reduced to beggary, who before had rioted in opulence, and thought they might bid defiance to misfortune.

248.

A GENTLEMAN from Paris writes the following:—I saw through one of the windows of the Mayor's office, in the twelfth arrondissement, the body of a negro hanging by the neck. At the first glance, and even at the second, I took it for a human being, whom disappointed love, or perhaps an expeditious judge, had disposed of so suddenly; but I soon ascertained that the ebony gentleman in question was only a large doll, as large as life. What to think of this I did not know, so I asked the door-keeper the meaning of it.

"This is the Contraband Museum," was the answer: and on my showing a curiosity to examine it, he was kind enough to act as my cicerone.

In a huge dirty room are scattered over the floor, along the walls and on the ceiling, all the inventions of roguery which had been confiscated from time to time by those guardians of the law, the revenue officers.

It is a complete arsenal of the weapons of smuggling, all, unfortunately, in complete confusion.

Look before you: there is a hogshead dressed up for a nurse, with a child that holds two quarts and a half. On the other side are logs hollow as the Trojan horse, and filled with armies of cigars. On the floor lies a huge boa constrictor, gorged with China silks; and just beyond it, a pile of coal curiously perforated with spools of cotton.

The colored gentleman who excited my sympathy at first, met with his fate under the following circumstances:—He was built of tin, painted black, and stood like a heyduck, or Ethiopean chasseur, on the foot-board of a carriage, fastened by his feet and hands. He had frequently passed through the gates, and was well known by sight to the soldiers, who noticed he was always showing his teeth, which they supposed to be the custom of his country.

One day the carriage he belonged to was stopped by a crowd at the gate. There was, as usual, a grand chorus of yells and oaths, the vocal part being performed by the drivers and cartmen, and the instrumental by the whips.

The negro, however, never spoke a single word. His good behavior delighted the soldiers, who held him up as an example to the crowd.

"Look at that black fellow," they cried, "see how well he behaves! Bravo, nigger, bravo!"

He showed a perfect indifference to their applause.

"My friend," said a clerk at a barrier, jumping up on the foot-board, and slapping our sable friend on the shoulder, "we are very much obliged to you."

Oh, surprise! the shoulder rattled. The officer was bewildered, he sounded the footman all over, and found he was made of metal, and as full as his skin could hold of the very best contraband liquor drawn out of his foot.

The juicy mortal was seized at once, and carried off in triumph.

The first night the revenue people drank up one of his shoulders, and he was soon bled to death. It is now six years since he lost all the moisture of his system, and was reduced to a dry skeleton.

249.

An old gentleman had owed a firm for years; at last, after everybody's patience and temper were exhausted, a clerk named Frank undertook to get the money.

Frank called upon the gentleman, and met with a polite

reception, and the usual answer, with the addition, "You need not trouble yourself, young man, about the matter; I will make it all right."

"Oh, no," replied Frank, "I could not think for a moment of compelling you to call at the store for a few dollars. It will not be the slightest inconvenience for me to stop in, as I pass your place of business six times a day, to and from my meals, and I can call every time I go by."

"Here," said the old fellow to his book-keeper, alarmed at the prospect of being dunned six times a day for the next six months, "pay this impertinent rascal. He can beat me in politeness, and, if he wants a situation, I will give him two thousand dollars a year."

250.

In learning, concentrate the energy of mind principally on the study; the attention divided among several studies is weakened by the division; besides, it is not given to man to excel in many things. But while one study claims your main attention, make occasional excursions into the fields of literature and science, and collect materials for the improvement of your favorite pursuit.

The union of contemplative habits constructs the most useful and perfect character; contemplation gives relief to action; action gives relief to contemplation. A man unaccustomed to speculation is confined to a narrow routine of action; a man of more speculation constructs visionary theories, which have no practical utility.

Excellence in a profession, and success in business, are to be obtained only by persevering industry. None who thinks himself above his vocation can succeed in it, for we cannot give our attention to what our self-importance despises. None can be eminent in his vocation who devotes his mental energy to a pursuit foreign to it, for success in what we love, is failure in what we neglect.

251.

A RAILROAD train was rushing along at almost lightning speed. A curve was just ahead, beyond which was a station at which the cars usually passed each other. The conductor was late, so late that the period during which the down-train was to wait had nearly elapsed : but he hoped yet to pass the curve safely. Suddenly a locomotive dashed into sight right ahead. In an instant there was a collision. A shriek, a shock, and fifty souls were in eternity ; and all because an engineer had been *behind time.*

A great battle was being fought. Column after column had been precipitated for eight mortal hours on the enemy posted along the ridge of a hill. The summer sun was sinking to the west ; reinforcements for the obstinate defenders were already in sight ; it was necessary to carry the position with one final charge, or every thing would be lost. A powerful corps had been summoned from across the country, and if it came up in season all would yet be right. The great conqueror, confident in its arrival, formed his reserve into an attacking column, and led them down the hill. The whole world knows the result. Grouchy failed to appear ; the imperial guard was beaten back ; Waterloo was lost. Napoleon died a prisoner at St. Helena because one of his marshals was *behind time.*

A leading firm in commercial circles had long struggled against bankruptcy. As it had enormous assets in California, it expected remittances by a certain day, and if the sums promised arrived, its credit, its honor, and its future prosperity would be preserved. But week after week elapsed without bringing the gold. At last came the fatal day on which the firm had bills maturing to enormous amounts. The steamer was telegraphed at daybreak ; but it was found on inquiry that she brought no funds ; and the house failed. The next arrival brought nearly half a million to the insolvents, but it was too late ; they were ruined because their agent, in remitting, had been *behind time.*

A condemned man was being led out for execution. He had taken human life, but under circumstances of the greatest provocation, and public sympathy was active in his behalf. Thousands had signed petitions for a reprieve, a favorable answer had been expected the night before, and though it had not come, even the sheriff felt confident that it would yet arrive in season. Thus the morning passed without the appearance of the messenger. The last moment was up. The prisoner took his place on the drop, the cap was drawn over his eyes, the bolt was drawn, and a lifeless body swung revolving in the wind. Just at that moment a horseman came into sight, galloping down hill, his steed covered with foam. He carried a packet in his right hand, which he waved partially to the crowd. He was the express rider with the reprieve. But he had come too late. A comparatively innocent man had died an ignominious death because a watch had been five minutes too slow, making its bearer arrive *behind time.*

It is continually so in life. The best laid plans, the most important affairs, the fortunes of individuals, the weal of nations, honor, happiness, life itself, are daily sacrificed because somebody is "behind time." There are men who always fail in whatever they undertake, simply because they are "behind time." There are others who put off reformation year by year, till death seizes them, and they perish unrepentant, because for ever "behind time." The Allies have lost nearly a year at Sebastopol, because they delayed a superfluous day after the battle of Alma, and came up too late for a *coup de main*, just twenty-four hours "behind time." Five minutes in a crisis is worth years. It is but a little period, yet it has often saved a fortune or redeemed a people. If there is one virtue that should be cultivated more than another by him who would succeed in life, it is punctuality; if there is one error that should be avoided, it is being *behind time.*

252.

There is nothing which should be more frequently impressed upon the minds of young men than the importance of steadily pursuing some *one* business. The frequent changing from one employment to another is one of the most common errors committed, and to it may be traced more than half the failures of men in business, and much of the discontent and disappointment that render life uncomfortable. It is a very common thing for a man to be dissatisfied with his business, and to desire to change it for some other, and what seems to him will prove a more lucrative employment; but in nine cases out of ten it is a mistake. Look round you, and you will find among your acquaintances abundant verification of our assertion.

Here is a young man who commenced life as a mechanic, but from some cause imagined that he ought to have been a doctor; and after a hasty and shallow preparation has taken up the saddle-bags only to find that work is still work, and that his patients are no more profitable than his work-bench, and the occupation not a whit more agreeable.

Here are two young men, clerks; one of them is content, when his first term of service is over, to continue a clerk till he shall have saved enough to commence business on his own account; the other can't wait, but starts off without capital and with a limited experience, and brings up after a few years in a court of insolvency, while his former comrade by patient perseverance comes out at last with a fortune.

That young lawyer who became disheartened because briefs and cases did not crowd upon him while he was yet redolent of calf-bound volumes, and had small use for red tape, who concluded that he had mistaken his calling and so plunged into politics, finally settled down into the character of a middling pettifogger, scrambling for his daily bread.

There is an honest farmer who has toiled a few years, got his farm paid for, but does not grow rich very rapidly, as much for lack of contentment mingled with his industry as any thing, though he is not aware of it—he hears the wonderful stories of California, and how fortunes may be had for the trouble of picking them up; mortgages his farm to raise money, goes away to the land of gold, and after many months of hard toil, comes home to commence again at the bottom of the hill for a more weary and less successful climbing up again.

Mark the men in every community, who are notorious for ability and equally notorious for never getting ahead, and you will usually find them to be those who never stick to any one business long, but are always forsaking their occupation just when it begins to be profitable.

Young man, stick to your business. It may be you have mistaken your calling,—if so, find it out as quick as possible and change it; but don't let any uneasy desire to get along fast, or a dislike of your honest calling, lead you to abandon it. Have some honest occupation and then *stick to it:* if you are sticking type, stick away at them; if you are selling oysters, keep on selling them; if you are at the law, hold fast to that profession: pursue the business you have chosen, persistently, industriously, and hopefully, and if there is any thing of you it will appear and turn to account in that as well or better than in any other calling; only if you are a loafer, forsake that line of life as speedily as possible, for the longer you stick to it, the worse it will "stick" to you.

253.

The most splendid prizes offered to resolute ambition are presented in the United States. The unexampled vigor of thought, quickness of apprehension, promptitude of action, and indomitable effort arise from this fact; and this affords a grand reason why we should aim for the diffusion of general intelligence, as only intelligent labor can achieve the results towards which we look. The young man feels the influence of the mighty activity about him in the great city, as the swimmer feels the pressure and heaving of the sea, and he longs to put forth new efforts for the grand results which he sees others achieving. He sees all around him men who began life without a dollar, and with no more credit than honesty, skill and industry may call to his aid at any time; and as he glances at their greatness of achievement, he asks himself, "Why cannot I also be rich and influential?" To such an one a few thoughts may be useful touching Capital and Enterprise, by which alone the splendid prizes of mercantile life are to be secured.

And first, many persons suppose that success is mainly dependent on having a good "set out" in youth, and the winning of legislative favors in behalf of one's business. These are common fallacies, but by a belief in them thousands are kept from making any vigorous effort, saying, "It's too late for me to try," and, "I can't get political influence to help me." Now in reference to the first idea, take the nearest illustration—Stephen Girard. We walk through a splendid square, and find it the "Girard Property." Here is a Bank, there stately edifices, and elsewhere a magnificent College with its imposing companion buildings, and it is all "Girard Property." When did this man begin to accumulate? Hon. Edward Everett says Girard told him that at the age of forty his circumstances were so narrow that he was employed as commander of his own sloop, engaged in the coasting trade between New York or Philadelphia and New Orleans, adding that he was once forty-five days in working his way up the Balize to the city. And surely legislation did not help Girard. By no favor of politicians was his labor secured as profitable; and nothing is more foolish than to take away attention from steady, prudent, heroic effort, and try to find some political magic to account for the golden product.

Many persons are kept from securing the aid of Capital by the false or low views entertained of it, as those views prompt them to think meanly of capitalists, and to doubt more than they should the disposition of capitalists to aid the enterprising. The young merchant should be cautious of dealing with those who make great pretensions of disinterested aid, who stimulate ambition by encouraging hopes of an immediate fortune; for such is not the method of the really generous. A bubbling stream may make more noise than a deep and strong river; and when the summer heat has dried up the brook, the river may roll on still mighty and strong; and so there is more noise in unloading than in loading the cart. A man who really means to aid a young merchant, is a man of cautious dealing; he wants to impart not only the capital of gold, but also of that wisdom and direction which are better than gold, as by the sagacity which they impart gold is best secured, best used, and best enjoyed.

When declamation is made against Capital, the declaimer generally has in view gigantic corporations, the consolidation of many interests into one. But this is wrong. Whatever a man has beyond what is necessary to supply his immediate wants, is Capital. The story of many an opulent merchant is, "Having, when I began life, a little capital, I bought a few articles and opened a little store." The few dollars of that man were as truly capital as his hundreds of thousands afterwards; and he was trading on his capital no less when he paid fifty dollars rental per annum, than when he paid five thousand dollars. Such men are now in our city, who owe their great change to nothing but what is available to every young man who will patiently and thoroughly educate himself for the business for which he has an aptitude. Capital is property, be the amount small or great; as the perseverance, industry and talent of the young merchant is as really the essential of success when united with small means, as when it is applied to the accumulated success of years, and helps on the commerce of a great city by aiding railroads and the establishment of lines of steamships and packets, making the humblest citizen the better off by the increase of business thus induced. Capital is the mainspring of business operations. Enterprise keeps up the motion imparted by Capital, and accumulates forces as it moves on. Capital builds the ship, and Enterprise works it. Enterprise talks, imagines, projects: Capital affords the means to do. And nothing is more important than that there should be a good understanding between the two: for true Enterprise will no more recklessly give its talent and energy, than true Capital will enter into Quixotic fights with a windmill.

The inventive complain that Capital will not help them: but they never think they are wronging Capital when by some improvement on an invention which Capital has aided, they make the property in their first invention valueless. A man's money is as much his own as a man's talent; and Capital may as well complain that Enterprise will not help it as Capital desires, as Enterprise complain that Capital will not listen to its voice and make the experiment proposed. If, as every one allows, Capital is requisite to the most advantageous employment of labor, talent, genius, why cast any odium on capitalists as a class? Why not seek for a better understanding between the classes who need each other? Capital can no more afford this war than Enterprise, and the American should cautiously guard himself against cherishing the traditions of Europeans respecting the accumulation of property, for we have laws which forbid the existence of the principal causes that pile up wealth in the old world in a manner that renders it destructive to the ambition of the lowly. He who scorns poverty, because he possesses riches, is scorning his father or grandfather; and he who despises wealth, is despising that to which he is secretly aspiring, and to which he is looking for the good of his children and country. Capital must be honored; for it is, in general, the representative of arduous toil, sobriety, frugality, promptitude of action, and it speaks of the successful treading in paths open to all—to the feeblest foot, as well as to the most gigantic. Capital builds our wharves; erects our factories: creates a sphere for the noblest efforts of the mechanic arts; feeds the fires of the furnaces that separate the ore of the iron and melt the material which takes ten thousand forms, all symbolizing what united energies can achieve. Capital in the vast merchant keeps the small capital invested in each of the hundreds of drays moving and productive;

and the success of Capital in its vastness is felt no less in the price of eggs in the market than in the price of bales of cotton on the wharves. The American who cherishes the generous principles which are allied to the real prosperity of his country, will scorn the thrusts at Capital—will regard the sacredness of property in the mass as in the minutia—will never lend his tongue to the disorganizing shout, "*Down* with Capital!" but give a bugle's tone to the shout, "*Up* with Capital and Enterprise!"

But let us not fail to qualify the common idea of Enterprise Enterprise is not simply a steam engine, but a steam engine with a good engineer. It remembers draw-bridges, and looks ahead to see if they are down or up. It remembers that the reverse movement is as essential as the advance. It is the grand thought of deathless Crockett, "*Be sure you're right*—THEN *go ahead.*" It is not that rash extravagance which pushes effort to the very verge of ruin so that the least disaster is fatal. It deals with Capital, when it wants its favor, as the Irishman dealt with the gentleman who wanted a coachman, and who asked each applicant how near he thought he could drive to the edge of a certain precipice without going over? Some declared they could drive to within half a foot or less, but Patrick more prudently answered, "And faith I'd keep away as far as I could." *That* was the man desired; and he was impelled not only by regard to the safety of his master, but also the safety of himself. But there are many who are like the rash engineer, who pushed on in his recklessness by the idea that when the train must go over the precipice, he can safely jump off from the engine. True Enterprise will neither risk Capital of others, nor its own character. It builds on a real foundation. It is no less practical than speculative. It keeps before its vision the whole field of operation; and while it talks large, it has facts to justify even a broader expression. It knows the philosophy of common sense: it asks for what is known, not for what is fancied; and while it has a wonderful impressibility, quick to see and understand, it has also a reserve power of all-controlling energy. Its perturbations are only as those in the heavens by which the new planet was discovered; and when its grand projects, its magnificent schemes seem to be but as the river covered with mist, when there is no sign of a ship on the waters, the result will show something as real and grand as the sight of the steamships and the sail ships moving up the river, when the mist has departed and the fresh winds are favorable.

Honor, then, to Capital! as the representative of Enterprise which has wrought in adaptation to other times and other modes of business operations than are now about us. Honor to Enterprise! now in the field, with energies fresh for the work of to-day, with keen eyes to see all the relations of commerce, and with a brain affluent in resources to baffle the perplexities of the present, and prepare for the possible emergencies of the future. Honor to Capital *and* Enterprise! hand clasping hand in the amenities of commerce, and mind working with mind to build up the waste places, to restore the breach, to develop the resources which make shuttles fly and hammers ring on the anvil—that light up the mines and send the loaded car of "black diamonds" over the shining rail—and that fill the mighty city with the accumulated evidences of the Art and Energy, the Industry and Thrift of the nation, and with the tributes of the world to youthful America.

254.

Take care of your business, when young, and it will take care of you when old.—Follow your business closely, and it will lead you to honor and wealth.

255.

WHEN Prince Talleyrand was in office, he always had agents who visited the coffee-houses, and all other places of resort in Paris, who reported to him what ordinary people said of all public measures and public men. While he was dressing in the morning, these agents were admitted, and thus informed him of the state of current opinions upon all important affairs. From these sources he obtained the idea of many of those measures which made him the most renowned diplomatist of the day. When asked the secret of that sagacity which had surprised all Europe, he replied that his rule was to keep his watch ten minutes faster than those around him. That is, anticipating those changes which public feeling had rendered certain, he always placed himself at their head, and thus appeared to be a leader, while others appeared to be led. This is the great secret of all success in life. The wise man waits not to be the sport of men or of measures but anticipates the inevitable.

In the choice of associates and friends, if a man will keep his watch ten minutes fast, it will save him many a troublesome and disreputable acquaintance. Two wealthy men of the Southern States visited a city together. They were brothers-in-law. Both had speculated largely, and they frequently endorsed each other's paper. They strolled into a billiard saloon, and one of them was soon engaged in play, and won a thousand dollars that night. It was not to either of them a large sum, either to win or lose. Nothing was said at the time, but next morning the fortunate player bought a valuable property, on time, and requested his brother-in-law to become his security. The other replied, that had he applied the previous day, he should of course have done it at once, but after what had happened the night before he saw he would soon be ruined and would endorse for him no more. In a few years the successful player was ruined, and law-suits probably not yet decided had grown out of that very purchase. The other became immensely wealthy, speculated largely in cotton, and once related this anecdote as a proof of his sagacity. He, however, himself became addicted to intemperance, and not long afterwards a large planter refused to send him cotton, lest his affairs might get into confusion, owing to his habits. Thus each man tries to set his watch ten minutes faster than his neighbor, and he who succeeds wins.

Character is the essence of destiny, and habits soon form and fix character. All men have in the circle of their acquaintances many whose habits will cause them to rise, while others for the same reason must sink. If misfortune overtake a friend, or if injustice be done him, abhorred be the man who will not stick to his companion, and do his best to see him through.

But for that very reason, if he knows beforehand that his associate be a man of unprincipled habits, let him not cultivate his acquaintance, but keep his watch ten minutes fast. So he who helps forward an industrious, well-principled man, however poor at the time, is but anticipating the judgment of the world; leading public opinion, instead of following it, making a friend who is sure to rise.

In the government of himself especially, let every man strive to set his watch faster than other people. Habits good in themselves may increase until they become injurious to health or character. Some need keeping in check, some stimulating, some pruning, and some are downright weeds, pulling right up, root and branch, without mercy. If taken in time and with daily care, it will be a pleasant duty thus to keep in order the garden of the mind. But if the weeds once get the upper hand, a man will find his task one of increasing difficulty! The richest lands are most troubled with weeds. In the cotton fields of the South, if the grass once gets a fair start and a little wet weather sets in, the whole field may be rendered unproductive. Idleness is a very common weed, but is easily kept under, if industrious habits be only formed in time, and he whose day begins only ten minutes earlier than those around him, will find the benefit of Talleyrand's maxim. A good name is not difficult to obtain, by simply observing the same rule. Let a man only keep a little in advance of all that can be reasonably expected of him in every department, and reputation is certain. But once get a little behind, and it will be almost impossible ever again to take the lead.

No man illustrates the truth of the diplomatist's saying more completely than "the fast young man." His watch has lost the balance-wheel. It goes round and round with erratic useless violence, tearing all the works to pieces with the force of its own motions, rushing through a hundred hours in one, but keeping no time for a second.

Earnest moral principle is the balance-wheel of character. It regulates and keeps the whole man in order. Each man has in him the germs of habits that may become his ruin. If indulged to excess, his very best qualities may do this. Even a warm, generous and impulsive heart is the ruin of many a man, if its impulses are not held in check, and balanced by a lofty sense of immediate duty to God and man. He will never regret it, who occupies a short portion of each day in adjusting and quickening conscience, the regulator of his actions, by communion with the Father of Spirits.

256.

Live up to your engagements. Keep your own secrets, if you have any.

257.

THERE is not only no necessity, but no propriety in a man's making a slave of himself. Men enough there are to do the work of society without imposing double duty upon any. Indeed, many are standing idle, who might find occupation, if others did not insist on monopolizing more than their share of work. It is a pity, if, after so many boasted inventions of labor-saving machines, the inventor himself is to derive no benefit from them in some relief from work. But it really seems that the more powers of mechanics, steam, and electricity are brought into play, the more men and horses are obliged to work.

There are two evils that require to be corrected: one is laziness; the other, overwork. The world has about enough of labor to be done easily and with comfort. All that seems requisite to accomplish it agreeably, is, to make each person do his share and no more. Moderate labor is the virtue; indolence and slavery the opposite vices. The complete man is he who has not sold himself to any calling or profession, who plays and works by turns, keeps a corner of his heart for friendship, the affections and humanity; and, through and over all, consecrates his activity, capacities and powers to the great Invisible, from whom he has derived them, and to whom he is accountable for their use or their abuse.

258.

Appearances not always to be trusted.—Trust to no man's appearances; they are deceptive,—perhaps assumed for the purpose of obtaining credit. Beware of a gaudy exterior. The rich and prudent are plain men. Rogues usually dress well. Never deal with a man who flies in a passion on being dunned.

259.

What a glorious thing is occupation for the human heart! Those who work hard seldom yield themselves entirely up to fancied or real sorrow. When grief sits down, folds its hands, and mournfully feeds upon its own tears, weaving the dim shadows, that a little exertion might sweep away, into a funeral pall, the strong spirit is shorn of its might, and sorrows became our master. When troubles flow upon you dark and heavy, toil not with the waves, wrestle not with the torrent; rather seek, by occupation, to divert the dark waters that threaten to overwhelm you into a thousand channels which the duties of life always present. Before you dream of it those waters will fertilize the present and give birth to fresh flowers that may brighten the future—flowers that will become pure and holy in the sunshine which penetrates to the path of duty in spite of every obstacle. Grief, after all, is but a selfish feeling, and most selfish is the man who yields himself to the indulgence of any passion which brings no joy to his fellow-man.

260.

If you want to learn the value of money, says the "*Knickerbocker*," go and labor for a day or two as a hod-carrier, beneath the scorching rays of a summer sun. This is an excellent idea, and if many of our young gentlemen had to earn their dollars in that way, how much less dissipation and crime we would witness every day! So of our fashionable young ladies, if they, like some of the poor seamstresses of our large cities, had to earn their dollars by making shirts at ten cents apiece, how much less finery should we see about them, and how much more truthful notions would they have of their duties of life and their obligations to the rest of the world.

261.

One day, as Mr. Lawson, a merchant tailor, stood at his cutting board, a poorly dressed woman entered his shop, and approaching him, asked, with some embarrassment and timidity, if he had any work to give out.

"What can you do?" asked the tailor, looking rather coldly upon his visitor.

"I can make pantaloons and vests," replied the girl.

"Have you ever worked for a merchant tailor?"

"Yes, sir, I have worked for Mr. Wright."

"Has he nothing for you to do?"

"No; not just now. He has regular hands who always get the preference."

"Did your work suit him?"

"He never found fault with it."

"Where do you live?"

"In Cherry street at No —."

Mr. Lawson stood and mused for a short time. "I have a vest here," he at length said, taking a small bundle from the shelf, "which I want by to-morrow evening at the latest. If you think you can do it very neatly, and have it done in time, you can take it."

"It shall be done in time," said the young woman, reaching out eagerly for the bundle.

"And remember, I shall expect it made well. If I like your work, I will give you more."

"I will try to please you," returned the young girl.

"To-morrow evening, recollect."

"Yes, sir; I will have it done."

The girl turned and went quickly away. In a back room in

the third story of an old house in Cherry street, was the home of the poor sewing girl. As she entered, she said in a cheerful voice to her sick sister, "Mary, I have got work; it is a vest, and I must have it done by to-morrow evening."

"Can you finish it in time?" inquired the invalid in a feeble voice.

"Oh, yes; easily."

It proved to be a white Marseilles. As soon as the invalid sister saw this, she said, "I am afraid you will not be able to get it done in time, Ellen. You are not very fast with the needle, and besides, you are very far from being well."

"Don't fear in the least, Mary; I will do all I engaged to do."

It was after dark the next night when Ellen finished the garment. She was weary and faint, having taken no food since morning. The want of everything, and particularly for herself and sister, made seventy-five cents, the sum which she expected to receive for making the garment, a treasure in her imagination. She hurried off with the vest the moment it was finished, saying to her sister, "I will be back as soon as possible, and bring you some cordial, and something for our supper and breakfast."

"Here it is half-past eight o'clock, and the vest is not yet in," said Mr. Lawson, in a fretful tone. "I had my doubts about the girl when I gave it to her. But she looked so poor, and seemed so earnest about the work, that I was weak enough to intrust her with the garment." At this moment Ellen came in and laid the vest on the counter, where Mr. Lawson was standing. She said nothing, neither did he. Taking the vest, he unfolded it in a manner which plainly showed him not to be in a very placid frame of mind.

"Goodness!" he ejaculated, turning over the garment, and

looking at the girl. She shrunk back from the counter and looked frightened.

"Well, this is a pretty job for one to bring in!" said the tailor in an excited tone of voice; "a pretty job indeed!" at the same time tossing the vest away from him in angry contempt, and walking off to another part of the store.

Ellen remained at the counter. At length he said to her, "You need not stand there, Miss, thinking I am going to pay you for ruining a job. It is bad enough to lose my material and customer. In justice you should pay me for the vest; but there is no hope for that; so take yourself off, and never let me set eyes on you again."

Ellen made no reply; she turned round, raised her hands to her forehead, and bursting into tears, walked slowly away.

After Ellen had gone, Mr. Lawson returned to the front part of the store, and taking up the vest brought it back to where an elderly man was sitting, and holding it towards him, said, by way of apology for the part he had taken in the little scene, "That is a beautiful article for a gentleman to wear, isn't it?." The man made no reply, and the tailor after a pause, added, "I refused to pay her as a matter of principle. She knew she could not make the garment, when she took it away. She will be more careful how she tries to impose herself upon customer tailors as a good vest-maker."

"Perhaps," said the elderly gentleman in a mild way, "necessity drove her to undertake a job that required greater skill than she possessed. She certainly looked very poor."

"It was because she appeared so poor and miserable that I was weak enough to place the vest in her hands," replied Mr. Lawson, in a less severe tone of voice. "But it was an imposition for her to ask for work she did not know how to make."

"Mr. Lawson," said the old gentleman, who was known as a pious and good man, "we should not blame with too much severity the person who, in extreme want, undertakes to perform a piece of work for which she lacks the skill. The fact that a young girl, like the one who was just here, is willing, in her extreme poverty, to labor instead of sinking into vice and idleness, shows her to possess true virtue and integrity of character; and that we should be willing to encourage, even at some sacrifice. Work is slack now, as you are aware, and there is but little doubt that she had been to many places seeking employment before she came to you. It may be that she and others are dependent upon the receipt of the money that was expected to be paid for the making of the vest you hold in your hand. The expression as she turned away, her lingering steps, her drooping form, and her whole demeanor, had in them a language which told me all this, and even more."

A change came over the tailor's countenance. "I didn't think of that," fell in a low tone from his lips.

"I did not think you did, brother Lawson," said his monitor; "we are all more apt to think of ourselves than others. The girl promised the vest this evening, and so far as that was concerned she performed her contract. Is the vest made very badly?"

Mr. Lawson took up the garment and examined it more closely. "Well, I can't say that it is badly done. But it is dreadfully soiled and rumpled; and it is not as neat a job as it should be, nor at all such as I wished it."

"All this is very annoying, of course; but still, we should be willing to make some excuse for the shortcoming of others. The poor girl may have a sick mother or sister to attend to, which constantly interrupted her, and under such circumstances, you could hardly wonder if the garment should come somewhat soiled from under her hands. All this may be the case ; and if so, you could not find it in your heart to speak unkindly to the poor creature, much less turn her away angrily, and without the money she had toiled for so earnestly."

"I didn't think of that," was murmured in a low, suppressed tone of voice.

Ellen, on returning home, entered the room, and without uttering a word, threw herself upon the bed by the side of her sick sister, and burying her face in a pillow, endeavored to smother the sobs that came up convulsively from her bosom.

Mary asked no questions. She understood the cause of Ellen's agitation. It told her that she had been disappointed in her expectation of receiving the money for the work.

Just at that moment there was a knock at the door, but no voice bade the applicant for admission enter. It was repeated, but it met with no response. Then the latch was lifted, the door swung open, and the tailor stepped into the room.

The sound of feet aroused the distressed sisters, and Ellen raised herself up, and looked at Mr. Lawson, with a countenance suffused with tears.

"I felt that I did wrong in speaking to you in the way that I did," said Mr. Lawson, advancing towards the bed, and holding out to Ellen the money she had earned. "Here is the price of the vest. It was better made than I first thought it was. To-morrow I will send you more work. Try to cheer up."

Mr. Lawson, finding that his presence was embarrassing, withdrew, leaving the two sisters so deeply affected that they could but look at him with thankfulness. Shortly after they received a basket, in which was a supply of nourishing food, and a sum of money to procure such articles as might be necessary for the sick sister. Though no one's name was sent with it, they were not in any doubt as to the individual who sent it. Mr. Lawson was not an unfeeling man, but like too many others in the world, HE DID NOT ALWAYS THINK.

262.

LEISURE may be a very pleasant garment to look at, but it is a very bad one to wear. The ruin of millions may be traced to it. Who of our readers who is out of business and poor, or troubled in some other respect, will not agree with us? How many, with too much leisure, take too much of something else, thus making gloom deeper and misfortunes more. The truth is that the condition of man is at the best but a lamentable piece of patchwork, and the less we ponder upon it the less we are inclined to the blues. Drink will never drive it off. If we rely on drinking solely, the sure return of mental activity brings horror back increased. Business of some kind that will employ us constantly is the better remedy. You that are sick of the rascalities of men, depressed by reverses, discouraged by lack of sympathy, though you go to employment like a child to an emetic, or a horse to a second quid of tobacco, persevere in labor, and you will soon be more cheerful, life will be less of a trouble, its enjoyments keener, and thoughts of death will not so often crowd upon the brain. Shun leisure, that treacherous abyss whose brink is crowned with flowers. Shun all that may tend to alienate your inclinations from that industry which is and has been the doom and duty of all men since Cain. Shun all that tends to encrust your energies with the rust of sloth, for sorrow and sloth are the handmaids of despair. Better toil for little profit, or die, than to drag on that miserable existence which is passed in the demoralizing hours of a desponding leisure. Look to it.

The rich indolent finds that the wheels of life run heavily, slowly with him ; but the sluggard who is poor has nothing to console him. The rich drone, though he lives to no purpose, keeps wealth between him and the wrongs and contempt of the world ; but he who is poor and idle too, may well account himself a wretch. He hath need of the intercession of all good angels to keep him from the webs of vice, the tyranny of the heartless, and a grave of frightful associations.

263.

A SHOEMAKER of Dublin had a longing desire to work for Dean Swift. He was recommended by Mr. James Swing, the banker, and Mr. Sican, a merchant. The Dean gave him an order for a pair of boots, adding, "When shall I have them?"

"On Saturday next," said the shoemaker.

"I have no appointments," said the Dean, "nor would I have you disappoint others: set your own time, and keep to it."

"I thank your reverence," said Bamerick, (for that was his name;) "I desire no longer than Saturday e'en, when you will be sure to have them without fail."

They parted. The boots were finished at the time; but through the hurry of business, Mr. Bamerick forgot to carry them home till Monday evening. When the Dean drew the boots on and found them to his mind, he said:

"Mr. Bamerick, you have answered to the commands of your friends, but you have disappointed me, for I was to have been at Sir Arthur Axhoson's, in the county of Armagh, on this day."

"Indeed, and indeed, sir," said Bamerick, "the boots were finished at the time, but I forgot to bring them home."

The Dean gave him one of his stern looks; and after a pause

asked him whether he understood gardening as well as bootmaking. Bamerick answered:

"No, sir; but I have seen some very fine gardens in England."

"Come," said the Dean, in a good-humored tone, "I will show you some improvements I have made in the deanery garden."

They walked through the garden to the further end, when the Dean started as if recollecting something. "I must step in," said he; "stay here till I come back." Then he ran out of the garden, locked the door, and put the key in his pocket. Bamerick walked about till it grew dark, and not seeing the Dean, he at last ventured to follow him, but found the door locked. He knocked and called several times to no purpose; he perceived himself confined between high walls, the night dark and cold in the month of March. However, he had not the least suspicion of his being intentionally confined.

The deanery servants went to bed at the usual hour, and the Dean remained in his study until two o'clock in the morning. He then went into the hall and drew the charge out of a blunderbus and other fire-arms, then returned and rang his bell. He was immediately attended by one of his servants.

"Robert," said he, "I have been much disturbed with a noise in the garden side; I fear some robbers have entered; give me a lantern, and call up Saunders." Then the Dean took the lantern, and stayed by the arms until the men came. "Arm yourselves," said he, "and follow me." He led them into the garden, where the light soon attracted poor Bamerick, who came running up to them. Upon his approach the Dean roared out, "There is the robber; shoot him!" Saunders presented, and Bamerick, terrified to death, fell on his knees and begged his life. The Dean held the lantern up to the man's face, and gravely said:

"Mercy on us! Mr. Bamerick, how came you here?"

"Lord, sir," said Bamerick, "don't you remember you left me here last evening?"

"Ah, friend," said the Dean, "I forgot it as you did the boots;" then turning round to Robert, who was the butler, he said, "Give the man some warm wine and see him safe home."

264.

About ten years ago there was a little newsboy—very little for his age, which was fourteen years, who sold papers at the corner now occupied by the Tribune building and its adjuncts. The boy, owing to his cheerful countenance, his proverbial integrity, his industry—in brief, his good qualities generally, (and very good qualities are rarely found among the peripatetic venders of the dailies and weeklies,) manufactured friends for himself everywhere, and particularly among publishers. He did a very good business as a newsboy, but his position did not suit him, as he one day confidentially informed us, and he was determined to abandon it.

"That you can easily do," said we. "Go into a store."

"I can neither read nor write," responded he, mournfully.

"Apprentice yourself to some trade, then," was our advice.

"I think I will," he exclaimed, with a brightening eye and a flushed cheek; "I think I will," and off he bounded.

We lost sight of him a short time after this conference was held, and finally forgot that such a being existed.

About a week ago, an athletic, well-dressed young man, with a ferocious—a regular brigandish pair of whiskers, and a brace of merry, twinkling optics, that betokened a good heart and the best of health, stopped us in the street, and, extending his hand, called us by name.

Not recognizing him, we had recourse to the phrase of "Really, sir, you have the advantage of me."

"Not know ——, the little newsboy!" he cried, astonished.

Truly, it was our little newsboy. He had taken our early advice, and apprenticed himself to a machinist.

"Where are you working?" we inquired.

"Oh, I don't work now," was his proud answer. "I own a saw-mill on Long Island, and am now doing business for myself. I have been my own boss a year now. I bought the concern with the savings of eight years. I have a wife and two children, and my own cottage-house and garden for them to live and delve in, and am as happy as the day is long. I can read and write, too," he continued, smilingly, but with an air of triumph.

That man will be somebody besides a boss yet. If we dared to tell his name, hundreds would at once hail with rapture the news of the good fortune of their persevering little friend, who once supplied them with the *Sun* and *Herald* every morning.

Perseverance—it is the grand lever by which the most astounding results may be accomplished. George Borrow, the author of "Lavengro," says: "Perseverance, and a determination to conquer all difficulties, will invariably make a man of the veriest dolt."

Do you hear that, boys? No matter how poor or how ignorant you may be, perseverance, conjoined with virtue, will gain you both wealth and education.

265.

The life of a man of business gives his character a pretty hard trial. Not only does it exercise his sagacity and prudence, but it puts his integrity to the severest test. He is surrounded by the selfishness of trade; he sees men profit by cunning and fraud, and he is tempted to try his skill in artifice and deception.

Every day his honesty is tried in some way. He is thrown back upon his inward principle, and if his heart is hollow and deceitful, he will be sure to show it. And that man has reason to thank God who has gone through a long course of business, through times of wild speculation and general bankruptcy, and goes down to the grave with the never shaken consciousness of being *an honest man.* He who can see others making money by false representations, and never stoop to these tricks of trade, is fitting his own pure mind for a world that is more worthy of him.

And yet a man cannot wholly escape these temptations. To do that, he must needs go out of the world, or retire into solitude. He might, indeed, avoid all danger, by shutting himself within the walls of a convent, to pass a life of outward sanctity and lazy contemplation. But the piety that is nursed in cloisters is of a sickly growth, compared with that which maintains its integrity amid strong inducements to evil. It is not the will of God that we should retire apart to keep from contamination. Not in deserts, but in cities; not in the hermit's cell, but among men, sharing the common lot, meeting temptation as it comes, are we to form our characters for eternity. Men ought to rejoice in a rigid discipline. Whenever assailed by temptation, an opportunity is given to conquer themselves, and so to become nobler beings.

The most heroic virtues of the human character are brought out in the struggle with inborn selfishness, and with the cowardly examples of the world. Men of brave hearts ought to welcome the conflicts and buffetings of life. Every victory they gain will make them stronger, as the tempest, which rocks and tears the mountain oak, causes it to strike its roots down deeper in the earth, and to lift higher its majestic arms toward heaven.

266.

One morning at breakfast, Mr. Howard said to his children, "Now, I should like you to tell me, how many nations have contributed to our breakfast table, and then you will see what a great blessing Commerce has been to the world. Try if you cannot find something from all the quarters of the globe to begin with?"

"Asia!" shouted Arthur; "there is tea from China."

"Africa!" exclaimed Edith; "there are the ivory handles from Africa."

"America!" said George; "there's the mahogany of the table from America."

And for Europe they had twenty things to speak about.

"Now, see if you cannot go another round; and you, Edith, for Africa first."

"The gold with which the sugar basin is lined."

"That may be, for gold, in greater or less quantities, is the produce of all the four quarters of the globe. But for Asia, Arthur?"

"Coffee—is it not Mocha coffee, mamma? And then there are the table mats, which came, you know, from Calcutta."

"Are the napkins of cotton, mamma?—for that comes from America?" "No! George, but of linen, which is made of flax. Do you know where the finest flax comes from?" "Is it not from the Netherlands?" "Yes," answered Mr. Howard; "but you have not made your American discovery, George."

"The tea urn—is not copper an American product?" "Yes! but it is more likely that this copper was furnished by English mines," was his father's answer.

"Oh, papa! I see America in the scarlet of the urn-rug—it

must have been dyed with cochineal." "Perhaps with lac-lake, boy, which is an Asiatic production, and which has nearly superseded the use of cochineal. However, you have answered well."

It is not necessary to go on with the conversation. One after another the origin and adventures of the different articles on the table were traced. One topic led to another, and Mr. Howard talked to his children of the effects of commerce, as a means of making people better and happier.

"Every one who makes an exchange," said Mr. Howard, "if he acts wisely, obtains something of greater value than that which he gives; and this is the case with both parties—each supplies some want or some desire of the other. Thus, the two virtues of prudence and benevolence are exercised—prudence, inasmuch as an addition is made to your own enjoyment—benevolence, inasmuch as an addition is made to the enjoyment of others. And the infinite variety of production with which the world is covered, the boundless differences of climate and soil, and national habits and education, give to every part of the earth some means of exchange with others, the exchange being a mutual benefit. Some lands have their riches on the surface, others buried deep below. In some, agriculture is the great source of wealth—in others, manufactures; in some, mines—in others, navigation. Out of their peculiar facilities, commercial relations grow. They are infinitely happier, infinitely wealthier by their intercourse than they could possibly be by being isolated and separated. The notion of every nation being sufficient to itself is as foolish and far more mischievous than the notion that every individual should be sufficient to himself. It is but selfishness on a large scale, calling itself by some name as false as fine—'patriotism,' for instance, or 'national independence.' The dependence of nations upon one another affords the true security for peace and common prosperity. As a wisely calculating self-interest would add necessarily to the well-being of others, if it were only because their well-being would increase our own, so a wise and generous patriotism would see in the strength, wealth, felicity, and industry of another nation a reason of confidence, and a subject of rejoicing. It is the destiny of commerce to undo what hatred and war have done. Out of the very selfishness of man it will extract benevolence. It will make nationality itself subservient to philanthropy. I know no profession more honorable than that of the instructed merchant—his history is the history of contributions to human pleasures. He brings nations into contact which are placed by nature far apart. He brings to the frozen north the productions of the burning tropics, and makes the whole world contribute to the daily happiness of every home. He has given to the meanest enjoyments formerly denied to the mightiest, and the portions of the world are small and few which have not been benefited by the foreign trader. Into the obscurest villages of Europe, Asia, and America, commerce has penetrated, accompanied by its novelties and its attractions; and in the very heart of Africa, at the court of one of the petty princes of the country, a French traveler informed me that he himself had seen very considerable quantities of European manufacture, and had been able to clothe himself as he would have done in London or Paris. The desire of gain, in itself a laudable and even a virtuous feeling, when controlled by prudence and kindness, is thus by commerce made subservient to the happiness of man. But this leads me to tell you the history of a little boy, who became a great merchant.

"Tom Traffic was the most active lad of the small town in

which he was born. When sent on an errand nobody ran so fast as he ; nobody rose earlier in the morning ; nobody washed and dressed more expeditiously ; nobody was more regular at school, more sharp at his lessons, or more ready and active at play. Everybody liked Tom, who was brisk as a bee, and playful as a grasshoper ; his whistle was well known in the streets, and his hands were always ready to do service to others.

"Tom was the only child of an aged mariner—a pensioner—whose pittance just enabled himself to live in decency; and Tom was the son of his old age ; for he had married at the end of a long service, and the boy was born to him when he had passed sixty years. You may believe he was proud and fond of Tom, which, indeed, he was ; and having little else to do, his time was almost wholly devoted to the boy. He rocked him in his cradle, whether he lay down at morning, noon, or night ; carried him about in his arms almost wherever he went. As soon as the boy ran alone, the old mariner seemed to grow young again, so did he share in all the boy's sports and pleasure. He taught him to play at marbles, to trundle a hoop, to 'follow my leader :' in a word, the father was the son's playfellow, and they were a very happy pair.

"The first time Tom had ever known real sorrow was when his mother died. He was then six years old ; and her death was the last real sorrow that the old mariner knew. Tom's mother had always been an affectionate mother, and did not like her husband the less for all the care and attention he bestowed on their only son. She told him often that he would spoil the boy, but said so between jest and earnest. But the old mariner's indulgences were not of a sort to do Tom any harm. On her deathbed, however, she said to her husband, 'You will always be kind to Tom!' and to Tom the said, 'You will always be kind to your father!' She did not speak to either as if she doubted; or as if she meant to give them lessons which really they did not need; but she spoke as if foretelling that they would be kind to each other.

"The living and the dying of the poor is for the most part a short and simple history. Duties to the poor as to others come daily to be done, and are as honorable to the poor who do them, as the more influential virtues of the opulent are honorable to the opulent. Through the years in which Tom's mother had managed her little household, she had managed it well and prudently; and when death removed her from her husband and her child, many there were to praise and none to blame her. And no one can aspire to a higher privilege among survivors than this—to be thought of with nothing but affection.

"There was some danger, indeed, that the death of his mother might have a baneful influence upon Tom, in whom all his father's cares and thoughts were now centered, and who was little disposed to check any of his son's impulses. But Tom had been gifted by nature with a happy temper, and he did not give way to unavailing grief: such grief would not have brought back his mother, and have only distressed his father; so the tears he shed were soon dried—not that he forgot his mother—not that he failed to think of her, and remember her kindness to him, and her affection for him; but he thought that she herself would not have wished him to be less busy, less useful than before. So he indulged himself in the habit of talking about his mother; and, though at first the subject was painful, it became, by and by, the sweetest of all subjects to him and his father; and, by frequently conversing, his memory became impressed with a thousand little circumstances, that he would otherwise have forgotten, and the recollection was a delight to him through the remainder of his life.

"One day the old mariner said to Tom, 'I am unusually out of spirits. I have been thinking, my boy, of what your future fate may be, and that it is time for you to be thinking about it too, for I am growing old, and fear I shall not last long; and I shall not die in peace, unless I know that you have some business and some prospects in life.'

"Now, Tom had himself often thought of this, for he was nearly twelve years old, but did not like to speak to his father, lest he should give him pain, by appearing desirous of leaving one he loved so well; but as his father now mentioned the matter, Tom said, 'Father, I am glad you have spoken of this. If I knew your wishes, perhaps I might be doing something to fit myself for some honest trade.'

"The old man hoped that Tom would have hinted at some line of life that he preferred; and Tom wished that his father should speak out. Their thoughts and wishes were indeed the same; but each feared to suggest what might be unacceptable to the other. 'When you were at sea,' said Tom, 'did you ever carry on any trade with the natives of foreign countries?' The inquiry showed the bent of Tom's mind; and the old mariner answered, 'Oh yes, my boy, and have turned many an honest penny in that way. Should you like to go to sea, Tom?' 'Indeed should I, if I could establish a little business with the natives of distant countries.'

"After this the subject was often talked of, and the old man told Tom how barter was conducted with people of various lands. He taught him, too, all he knew of the art of navigation; explained to him, as far as he was able, the trade winds, and the ocean currents, and the equinoctial gales. He loved to recount the dangers he had seen and the risks he had run; he spoke of the different moneys used in different countries, and taught Tom many a foreign word which he had picked up when abroad. Tom listened with great attention, and stored in his mind every thing that was likely to be useful; and his father's conversation became more and more interesting, as it became more and more instructive. Sometimes, indeed, the old man felt that by these conversations he was preparing Tom for his early departure; and even when Tom was most excited by an account of the way in which, when a young sailor, he had exchanged with a naked negro a string of beads for a noisy parrot, the old man suddenly stopped; he thought of dangerous climates, and the shipmates he had buried on the African coast—he stopped suddenly, and told Tom that he would end the story some other day.

"A short time after this, while Tom was reading to his father from the Bible, as he was used to do, the old man's face grew pale, and he fell back in his chair. Tom fanned his cheeks with the book he held in his hands; and, after a few minutes, his father was able to say, faintly and feebly, 'To bed, Tom! to bed!' Tom helped him in, ran to the neighbors for help, but soon perceived, by their countenances, that matters were in a sad way. And so indeed they were. The old mariner became speechless. Once he stretched his hand to Tom; Tom seized it and kissed it. In a few hours the mariner was dead; in a few days his body was laid in the churchyard by the side of his wife, and a small white grave-stone was raised over it, on which Tom had engraved, with his own hands, the initials of his father's and his mother's name.

"Tom had many friends: they came and offered their services, and would have kept him among them, but Tom's thoughts were wandering through the wide world. The neighbors bought the little furniture at its value, for Tom had told them he had determined to seek his fortune afar off. About eight or nine pounds he received for the small possessions of his parents. He said to himself, 'I hope the people will not forget me, if I should come back again; I have nothing now left me to care for. The wind may blow from what quarter it will, all ports are alike to me.' Tom paid one visit to his parents' grave; it was then he took leave of the place of his birth.

"He went to Liverpool, and lost no time in inquiring out a respectable ship-broker, to whom he told his short but simple story. It was his good luck to fall in with a kind-hearted and clever man, who said he would give him a berth on a vessel bound for the coast of Africa. Tom remembered how suddenly his father had stopped when telling him of his own African adventures; but Tom was not superstitious: the climate, he said, he did not fear. The bargain was made. Tom felt as if his life and history were now begun; and, as the kind ship-broker had offered to assist him in investing his little capital, Tom fancied himself the luckiest, as he was then one of the proudest of mortals.

"On the voyage Tom obtained the good opinion of the captain, and the confidence of all the crew. The adventure was successful, and when he arrived in England, he had doubled his wealth. He had got experience, too; and, as the vessel was to return to Africa, Tom's observations were of great value to the ship-broker, and to the owners, to whom the captain had reported the cleverness and activity of young Tom.

"Tom remained on board the vessel during three voyages. He was now nearly nineteen years old, and his fortune was accumulated to somewhat more than £160. A favorite with everybody, because willing to be a friend to everybody, there was nobody on board whose good fortune was witnessed with so much pleasure. On returning from the third voyage, the captain told Tom that the owner had been talking of him, that he desired to see him, and he believed would make to him an agreeable communication. Tom went—it was at the time when the supplies of timber were checked by the war—and the merchant, after many inquiries about Tom's success, reminded him that he had once spoken of the vast forests on the shores of the African rivers, and expressed an opinion that the negroes might be induced to fell the trees and barter them with Europeans. 'The idea has often occurred again to my mind,' said the merchant, 'and if you still think so, we will make the experiment; we will find ships and capital, and you shall have an interest in it.' In truth it was a favorite project of Tom's; he was delighted to see it adopted, and soon after a vessel was fitted out, of which Tom had the charge.

"He sailed for Africa; and I have often heard Tom describe the toil and trouble which it cost him to teach the Africans how best to fell and saw the trees, and bring them to the river's edge. But Tom succeeded, and the speculation succeeded. At first only a few straggling blacks came to cut down the forest trees; but, as they were liberally recompensed, they afterwards came in great numbers, and built their huts in the neighborhood of the place where Tom fixed his own habitation, and where he dwelt for many years. The trade became a very large one, and Tom dwelt like a prince, surrounded by his subjects. He taught them many arts, and reclaimed them from many barbarous and savage habits. He administered justice among them, settled their misunderstandings, and, though so young, was always called by them their father.

"Six years Tom lived in Africa. He had become wealthy, and the desire to visit his native country grew stronger and stronger. He fancied, too, that he was beginning to feel the effects of the climate; so, having made arrangements for supplying his place, he returned to England, and visited the spot where he had seen his father and mother buried. He ordered the grave to be surrounded by iron railings, and a stone to be erected to the memory of his parents, with their names and ages at length; but he would not allow the stone to be removed on which he himself had cut the first letters of their names.

"It is the beginning of a successful career that is most difficult, not its progress. Mr. Thomas Traffic is still living, a rich and honorable merchant and magistrate. He has not forgotten, nor is he likely to forget, that he was the son of a poor old mariner. He often speaks of it, not for the purpose of pride and parade, but for the encouragement of others, and the young especially, showing them that they must learn to conquer difficulty, and that those who endeavor to gain the good opinion and confidence of others, seldom fail to obtain them."

267.

KIND words cost but little. Any one but a confirmed cynic ought to be able to dispense them at pleasure. They make nobody the poorer. Like the widow's cruse, the stock need not be exhausted even by constant using—yea, better than the widow's cruse, the stock increases the more it is drawn from the fountain. A kind heart, which is the only true source of kind words, is a perennial stream. No winter's cold can freeze it, no summer's drouth can dry it up. Through all seasons it pours out its life-giving flood, making glad and green whatever it touches, gurgling and eddying round with inward joy, because of its offices of love. One would think that kind words, diffusing gladness, as they do, through the hearts of both donors and receivers, would be the common currency in life's intercourse. Even the employer, who has hundreds at his beck and call, might afford to lay aside his oriental majesty, sufficient to speak to his underlings a word of recognition; journeymen and apprentices would not render themselves menials and abjects by putting off their reserved-rights attitude, so as to speak to their employer with deference and respect; clerks and salesmen need not consider dumb solemnity or waspish rudeness essential to their calling; and last, but not least, their high mightinesses, steamboat and hotel clerks, and railroad conductors, might, perhaps, occasionally, without too much condescension, afford to give a civil answer. We are a great people in this country, certainly. Every body is so oppressed with a consciousness of his inherent dignity, that he fears to compromise it by the exercise of common courtesy.

> "A little word in kindness spoken,
> A motion, or a tear,
> Has often healed the heart that's broken,
> And made a friend sincere."

268.

Will Young Bullion ever be Rich?—It has become very much the fashion, now-a-days, to say, "Oh, young Bullion will be rich when his father dies;" and to understand thereby that young Bullion is sure to be rich one of these days.

But the proverb concerning a "slip between the cup and the lip" holds good in this case as in all others, and young Bullion may die before old Bullion does, in which case he would never become rich—in this world's goods, at any rate. Nor is his chance of living so much greater than the governor's (as he terms him) as may be at the first glance imagined.

Suppose old Bullion to be fifty-five years of age, young Bullion twenty-five. Old Bullion is a bank director—young Bullion is "one of the b'hoys;" old Bullion turns in every night at ten—young Bullion is "on a time" till 4 A. M. Balance of health is in favor of old Bullion.

Old Bullion takes a glass of brandy and water, and don't eat any thing going to bed—young Bullion devours oysters, woodcock, broiled chicken, at horribly indigestible hours, and drinks champagne, champagne brandy, and Scotch ale, till he blesses the man that invented soda water, when he wakes up next morning. Balance of health in favor of old Bullion again.

Old Bullion goes down to the bank in an omnibus about 10 A. M. About the same time young Bullion is going it with a fast horse to "the great race," incurring the danger of being run over, of being run away with, or of running over somebody else and getting spilt. Balance of safety in favor of old Bullion.

You don't find old Bullion promenading very often—the gout won't allow it; young Bullion is all the time on a tramp, over sidewalks under which are steam engines, across streets where runnings over are frequent. Old Bullion don't go traveling—young Bullion is on the move all summer; and the steamboat blowings up and railroad collisions are frequent now-a-days. Balance of safety still in favor of old Bullion.

Old Bullion is never out after dark—young Bullion, like cats, travels principally at night, and stands a very fair chance, in the present state of society, of having his head and a slung shot acquainted some dark night.

Old Bullion has against him thirty years and the gout—young

Bullion has the risk of late hours, champagne suppers, fast horses, "pistols and coffee for two," street-crossings, boiler-burstings, railroad smash-ups, and fractured craniums.

So the chances, you see, are not so very much in young Bullion's favor, after all.

269.

INTEGRITY of character and truth in the inner man are the prerequisites for success in any calling, and especially so in that of the merchant. These are attributes of the man which never fail to command respect and win admiration. No one fails to appreciate them; and if they "do not pay," in the vulgar sense of this phrase, they bring an amount of satisfaction and peace to the owner, that all the wealth of Crœsus could not yield. There is no better stock in trade than these commodities; no capital goes so far, or pays so well, or is so exempt from bankruptcy and loss. When known, it gives credit and confidence, and in the hardest of times will honor your paper in bank. It gives you an unlimited capital to do business on, and every body will endorse your paper, and the general faith of mankind will be your guaranty that you will not fail. Let every young man in commencing business look well to these iudispensable elements of success, and guard and defend them as he would the apple of his eye. If inattentive and reckless here, he will imperil every thing. Bankruptcy in character is seldom repaired in an ordinary lifetime. A man may suffer in reputation and recover—not so the man who suffers in character. Be just and truthful. Let these be the ruling and predominating principles of your life, and the rewards will be certain, either in the happiness they bring to your own bosom, or the success which will attend upon all your business operations in life—or both.

270.

Getting along Slowly.—Such is the answer frequently given to inquiries respecting the worldly prosperity of our friends. "How are you getting along?" "Well, I don't know—*getting along slowly!*" This question and the answer may be set down as among the most familar phrases, asked and answered, over and over again, just as unthinkingly and unmeaningly as the salutations given in passing, "Good day—How d'ye do?"

But without stopping to quarrel with custom, we will suppose that the answer is made, as in many cases it may be, in all soberness and truth, and see if we cannot draw from it some lessons of practical utility. "*Getting along slowly.*" This is generally spoken, whenever earnestly uttered, in a regretful, fault-finding tone, and yet contains an admission for which the individual should feel grateful. It is something, yea, it is a great thing—it is decidedly a meritorious achievement to be *getting along* at all in this busy, crowding, selfish world of trade. Do you say, reader, that you are *getting along slowly?* Then, you have much to be thankful for. By *getting along* you mean that you are advancing in your worldly interests—that you are increasing in prosperity, gaining riches; but you say, *slowly.* Very well, "slow and sure" has been the maxim of the wisest and wealthiest men.

Getting along. Let the man who feels that he is "just getting along" look round him, and scan closely the condition and circumstances of many whom he knows. Here is Mr. A. and Mr. B., with others, who had before seemed to him as model business men—who he supposed were getting along rapidly. Now, he penetrates beneath the glittering surface, and finds them, instead of being firmly planted upon the high rounds of the ladder of fortune, merely held suspended by specious *promises to pay*, and in momentary dread of dropping into ruin. And still others, whom he had once known as *eminently* successful merchants, he sees already suffering in the lowest vale of poverty. Let him go out from the circle of his own acquaintance, and look upon thousands in the city who are *trying* to get along in the world. He will see that the large majority of them are incessantly wrestling against seeming fate. They try, and strive, and contrive, and study ; struggle hard at one thing, then another ; fail ; begin again ; work early, late ; in fact, enter into a perfect warfare against body, mind, and life itself, in order, as they term it, to get along. And they can't get along. Fate is against them, friends are against them, fortune is against them, society is against them—every thing is against them—and they can't get along. These toiling, struggling, unfortunate thousands would feel that a new life had come to them, and rejoice with unspeakable joy if they were afforded the least cause for saying, we are *getting along slowly.* While contemplating the two extremes, the ruin that is likely to fall upon those who make haste to get rich, and the suffering condition of those who, by misfortune or incapacity, vainly strive for the necessities of life, do you not feel reproved for murmuring because of your slow progress in wealth ?

Getting along slowly. If you really are getting along slowly in worldly prosperity, and in honorable reputation, then you have abundant reason for rejoicing. All great, grand, and most dur able things are of slow growth. The grand old trees of the forests require centuries to perfect their majestic proportions. The noblest animals are of long life and slow development ; and from twenty-five to thirty years are requisite for the mature growth of man in his physical and mental being. Gradual development is the great law of nature, and is applicable to almost every thing pertaining to human society. Speed either debilitates or insures danger. Hot-house plants are comparatively puny, fragile things; and he who rides astride the locomotive may glory in the speed with which he passes the poor pedestrian by the wayside, and at the same time meditate on the chances of having his name in print among the *list of killed and wounded.*

Let no one infer that we would favor idleness, or discourage proper effort in business men. We utter not a word against the most strenuous, constant exertions after wealth, when attended by a cheerful disposition, thankfulness of heart, and guided by a soul of noble charity and of moral integrity. But that spirit of fault-finding, that murmuring ungrateful spirit so frequently manifested by those of moderate business success, we most heartily condemn; and we say, instead of complaining because they are *getting along slowly*, they should rejoice in the fact that they are getting along at all. No man is worthy of an abundance who is not thankful for even the smallest degree of prosperity.

And now, if we have any readers of the get-along-slowly order, we will say to them: Get along, *slowly*, if you must, but get along *honestly*. Neither sit down supinely in despair of success, nor enter into any hazardous speculation in hope of sudden gain. Better patiently learn the great life-lesson, "to labor and wait," with the prayer of Hagar ever on your lips and in your heart—"Give me neither poverty nor riches"—so that, whether getting along slowly, or in the full tide of prosperity, you may have the same heart of thankfulness, the same generosity of purpose, and be distinguished by the same nobleness of character.

271.

SMUGGLING is no new thing in China. Nothing in all the land seems better regulated, or to be conducted more systematically than this branch of business. How far its tariff of duties has been reduced to writing no one can tell; indeed, every tariff in China is merely nominal, as different from the reality as can well be imagined. One of these new features, the only one I will allude to, seems to have resulted from the stolidity of the functionaries connected with the native custom-house department. Because a foreign vessel happened to be furnished with a certain kind of machinery, her owners must be subjected to any amount of annoyance the custom-house people might see fit to impose. The managers of the steamer were not to be wronged in this way, nor were those who wished to ship cargo by her; and accordingly they arranged their own business. The amount of duties lost on the one side, and saved on the other, by this measure, must, some persons say, be reckoned by thousands of dollars.

272.

THERE is a class of men who rail at fortune, and accuse her of being blind in her gifts. They say that dull, plodding men succeed, while men of brilliant attainments fail; but they never pause to ask why it is so. To the end of their days they continue to murmur at fickle fortune, whereas they would be far wiser to complain of fickle self. There is a simple truth, too, often lost sight of by the world, which we shall now seek to demonstrate; it is that the lesser virtues win.

Alpha and Omega begin life together as clerks in a merchant's counting-room. Alpha has more varied talents than Omega and gains more favor in the eyes of their employer during the first few months. There is no denying that Alpha is smart, and Omega comparatively slow. Alpha can accomplish more work in a given time ; but Omega is more painstaking. It occurs to Alpha that all his duties can be perfomed in less time than he now gives to them, and he determines to come to business a little later, and leave a little earlier. Omega is always punctual. One evening their employer stays late in town, and wanting the services of Alpha, finds him not at his books, and has to ask Omega to do his work. Again and again this occurs, but Alpha is always ready with excuses, and his employer is of an indulgent nature.

The dissipations of the world have strong allurements for Alpha, and he often comes to business with feverish brow and nervous hand. His thoughts are then how to dissemble his sufferings, not how to fulfil his duties. His books are carelessly kept, and he is told to imitate Omega. Then Alpha begins to murmur at life. The plodding Omega preferred to him ; why, he "could talk and write down such a fellow any day." "Very true, Alpha, but you forget that Omega does much more useful work in a year." Omega is persevering, and is continually surmounting difficulties over which Alpha stumbles, until at last Omega's painstaking, punctual and persevering habits are known to insure reliability in every business transaction, and he is rewarded by being made a partner in the firm, while Alpha remains a clerk on sufferance.

Shall we pursue the story further, and see Omega rising to the topmost pinnacle of fortune, and Alpha sinking lower into the gulf of dissipation? Shall we hearken to the latter railing at fortune, while in his every action he courts misfortune? Shall we view him willfully perverting his talents, and yet blaming society for not seeing him as he might have been instead of as he is? Shall we gaze on him, when, an utterly ruined and disappointed man, he falls into a premature grave, self-deluded to the last; the cruel world and not the cruel self his final theme?

We prefer to dwell for a moment on a more pleasing subject —the moral to be gathered from the life of Omega. We have said that the lesser virtues win, and it ever must be so, for they lead to the higher virtues. Painstaking perseverance lead to strict probity. Omega was engaged to do his very best for his employer, and he scrupulously did so. To dissipate is not alone to trifle with health and reputation, but to rob the employer of a portion of the time for which he pays. It is not enough for a young man to say he will be in business during the hours specified, but he should come calm and collected, so as to perform his duties well; and to insure this he must be as regular in his habits away from business as when in business. The punctual man becomes the honorable man, for in saving moments he preserves his good faith with the world. His word rises in public estimation, for it is known to be the word of a truly honest man. Prize then the lesser virtues, young men, on the threshhold of life, and then in the meridian of your days the higher virtues will be your solace and reward.

273.

JOHN DOE is a man of large possessions. He has houses, lands, stocks, and all the appurtenances of a man of wealth. He is industrious, shrewd, and successful. His neighbors and the money-changers say he is *worth* a great deal, and so he is, if a man's worth must be measured by the length of his purse. But a real man is something else, and more than the gold and silver he happens to own; and therefore the gospel of Mammon, and its credulous dupes, err in opinion and lie against the truth, when they pronounce John Doe *worth* a great deal, merely because he is rich. For worth and wealth are not synonymous or convertible terms; and a very rich man may be a very worthless one.

None are really worth any more or less than the characters they possess, and their fitness for doing good to others. If one be ignorant, selfish, and miserly, he may sport a carriage in Broadway, yawn at the opera, lodge in the Fifth Avenue, and create a great sensation in Wall street, where

> *Money* "makes the man, the want of it the fellow;
> And all the rest is leather and prunella."

But if it be asked, to what purpose does this man live? what is he worth to his fellow-men? what good does he do in the world? echo answers, *What?* Like a sponge he grows distended and dropsical with borrowed matter; and if he be thoroughly squeezed, and made to part with his fictitious weight, he becomes as light and worthless as gossamer, for he has no internal solidity of character. He has transmuted himself into gold, and when that is gone, the man is gone too.

There are some every where, in our prosperous country, of great possessions, who resemble nothing else so much as the receiving vault of a cemetery, which locks up in darkness and death all that comes within its dreary precincts. No appeal of sorrow, no cry for aid, no glorious promise of future good, no prophetic voice, nor angel whisper of love, can penetrate or dispel the putrid composure that reigns within.

And thus Mr. John Doe may fill up his coffers and increase his personal resources; but if his heart be pitiless, devoid of generous sympathies and humane desires ; if riches are with him the end of existence ; if he can find no other use for his money than to employ it in purchasing base indulgences, or laying it by for uncertain and perhaps profligate heirs ; if he finds not pleasure in sustaining the charities of life, or institutions devoted to human weal ; if he is always a greedy receiver, and never a liberal dispenser ; alas ! then, for the so-called rich, but actually *poor* John Doe. His penury is worse than that of a Lazarus. He is more worthless than the beggar child, who shares her crust with others, remembering and feeling that "it is more blessed to give than to receive."

"What is a man worth ?" He is worth precisely just so much as he has capacity and inclination to be useful. He is to be estimated by the good he attempts or accomplishes. Not the tax-gatherer, but the word of God can decide his true value. Neither polished marble nor lying epitaph can ever preserve the memory or ennoble the life of him who, dying, leaves behind no monument of mercy, and no remembrancers of generous and benevolent worthiness.

"Oh, brother man! fold to thy heart thy brother ;
Where pity dwells, the peace of God is there.
To worship rightly is to love each other ;
Each smile a hymn, each kindly deed a prayer.

"Follow with reverent steps the great example
Of Him whose holy work was 'doing good ;'
So shall the wide earth seem our Father's temple
Each loving life, a psalm of gratitude."

274.

In business, the keeping close to the matter procureth dispatch ; and true dispatch is a rich thing.

275.

A MERCHANT very extensively engaged in commerce, and located upon Long Wharf, died February 18th, 1806, at the age of 79, intestate. His eldest son administered upon the estate. This old gentleman used pleasantly to say, that for many years he had fed a large number of Catholics on the shores of the Mediterranean during Lent—referring to his very extensive connection with the fishing business. In his day he was certainly well known: and to the present time is well remembered by some of the 'old ones down along shore,' from the Gurnet's Nose to Race Point.

Among his papers, a package of considerable size was found after his death, carefully tied up, and labelled as follows: "Notes, due bills, and accounts against sundry persons down along shore. Some of these may be got by a suit or severe dunning. But the people are poor; most of them have had fisherman's luck. My children will do as they think best. Perhaps they will think with me, that it is best to burn this package entire."

"About a month," said my informant, "after our father died, the sons met together, and, after some general remarks, our eldest brother, the administrator, produced this package, of whose existence we were already apprised, read the superscription, and asked what course should be taken in regard to it. Another brother, a few years younger than the eldest, a man of strong, impulsive temperament, unable at the moment to express his feeling by words, while he brushed the tears from his eyes with one hand, by a spasmodic jerk of the other toward the fire-place, indicated his desire to have the paper put into the flames. It was suggested by another of our number, that 't might be well first to make a list of debtors' names, and of the dates and accounts, that we might be enabled, as the intended discharge was for all, to inform such as might offer payment, that their debts were forgiven. On the following day we again assembled, the list had been prepared, and all the notes, due bills, and accounts, whose amount, including interest, exceeded thirty-two thousand dollars, were committed to the flames.

"It was about four months after our father's death, in the month of June, that, as I was sitting in my eldest brother's counting-room, waiting for an opportunity to speak to him, there came in a hard-favored, little old man, who looked as if time and rough weather had been to the windward of him for seventy years. He asked if my brother was not the executor. He replied that he was administrator, as our father died intestate. 'Well,' said the stranger, 'I have come up from the Cape to pay a debt I owed the old gentleman.' My brother," continued my informant, "requested him to be seated, being at the moment engaged.

"The old man sat down, and putting on his glasses, drew out a very ancient leather wallet. When he had done, and there was quite a parcel of notes, as he sat, waiting his turn, slowly twisting his thumbs, with his old gray meditative eyes upon the floor, he sighed; and I well supposed the money, as the phrase runs, came hard, and secretly wished the old man's name might be found upon the forgiven list. My brother was soon at leisure, and asked him the common question, his name, etc. The original debt was four hundred and forty dollars; it had stood a long time, and, with the interest, amounted to a sum between seven and eight hundred dollars. My brother went to his table, and after examining the forgiven list attentively, a sudden smile lighted up his countenance, and told me the truth at a glance—the old man's name was there! My brother quietly took a chair by his side, and a conversation ensued between them, which I shall never forget. 'Your note is outlawed,' said my brother, 'it was dated twelve years ago, payable in two years; there is no witness, and no interest has ever been paid; you are not bound to pay this note: we cannot recover the amount.'

"'Sir,' said the old man, 'I wish to pay it. It is the only heavy debt I have in the world. I should like to pay it,' and he laid the bank notes before my brother, and requested him to count them over.

"'I cannot take this money,' said my brother.

"The old man became alarmed. 'I have cast simple interest for twelve years and a little over,' said the old man. 'I will pay you compound interest if you say so. That debt ought to have been paid long ago, but your father, sir, was very indulgent,—he knew I had been unfortunate, and told me not to worry about it.'

"My brother then set the whole matter plainly before him, and, taking the bills, returned them to the old man, telling him, that although our father left no formal will, he had recommended to his children to destroy certain notes, due bills, and other evidences of debt, and release those who might be legally bound to pay them. For a moment the worthy old man seemed to be stupified. After he had collected himself, and wiped a few tears from his eyes, he stated, that from the time he had heard of our father's death, he had raked and scraped, and pinched and spared, to get the money together for the payment of this debt. 'About ten days ago,' said he, 'I had made up the sum within twenty dollars. My wife knew how much the payment of this debt lay upon my spirits, and advised me to sell a cow, and make up the difference, and get the heavy burden off my spirits. I did so—and now what will my old woman say? I must get home to the Cape and tell her this good news. She'll probably say over the very words she said when she put her hands on my shoulder as we parted—'I have never seen the righteous man forsaken, nor his seed begging bread.' After a hearty shake of the hand, and a blessing upon our father's memory, he went upon his way rejoicing.

"After a short silence, seizing his pencil and making a cast—'There,' exclaimed my brother, 'your part of the amount would be so much—contrive a plan to convey to me your share of the pleasure derived from this operation, and the money is at your service."

Such is the simple tale, which I have told you as it was told to me.

276.

WE rail at Trade, and the philosopher and lover of man will have much harm to say of it; but the historian of the world will see that Trade was the principle of Liberty; that Trade planted America and destroyed Feudalism; that it makes peace and it keeps peace, and it will abolish slavery. We complain of the grievous oppression of the poor, and of its building up a new aristocracy on the ruins of the aristocracy it destroyed. But there is this immense difference, that the aristocracy of trade has no permanence, is not entailed, was the result of toil and talent, the result of merit of some kind, and is continually falling, like the waves of the sea, before new claims of the same sort. Trade is an instrument in the hands of that friendly Power which works for us in our despite. We design it thus and thus; but it turns out otherwise and far better. This beneficent tendency, omnipotent without violence, exists and works.

277.

"WHEN you were showing us, papa," said George, "that a great many of the virtues, commonly so-called, are not virtues unless they are under the control of other virtues, I thought Perseverance, too, might be sometimes a *false* virtue,—for that a man might *persevere* in doing wrong."

"That is most true, George, and I am glad that you are learning how to distinguish between what are real virtues and what are not; between what are virtues sometimes, and what are virtues always. And as I remember two cases, one of vicious, and another of virtuous perseverance, they will serve to explain what is good and what is evil in persevering conduct.

"A quarrel had taken place between two clerks in a merchant's counting-house—Jonas and Jonathan. The quarrel was of little importance in itself, for it was merely as to the quantity of work that each had to do. The merchant has given six letters to be copied: Jonas said that each should copy three; Jonathan said, that as they were not of the same length, one should copy four and the other two. They disputed violently about it. and from words came to blows. Jonas beat Jonathan severely. and Jonathan vowed that he would be revenged. In this determination he *persevered,* and it was a part of every day's thoughts how he could injure Jonas.

"Jonas kept what is called the petty cash in the merchant's counting-house, that is, he was charged with the payment of all the small sums for the ordinary expenses of the business, and was settled with by the merchant every week, on his producing the accounts, and the vouchers for payment when any receipts were given. Jonas was particularly careful to keep his documents in order, and Jonathan, who knew Jonas's pride in having his cash-book right, determined to do all that he could to embarrass and confuse him. Whenever Jonathan could lay his hands upon any voucher that Jonas wanted to show that his payments were regular, Jonathan took the opportunity, when nobody was present, either to burn or otherwise destroy it. This made Jonas very miserable, who never fancied that his companion would have been so wicked; but Jonas was bitterly distressed, when, on three following Saturdays, instead of receiving the merchant's accustomed praise, he was reprimanded for negligence. Jonas protested that he had been as careful as usual, but could not conceive how the documents had disappeared. He determined, in future, to lock them up, instead of leaving them under the leads of the desk, as he had hitherto done. The next week all Jonas's accounts were as correct as usual, and all the vouchers in order, and his tranquillity returned.

"But it did not last long; for Jonathan, finding that he had not succeeded in his ill-natured attempt, was resolved to injure Jonas even more seriously; and one day, when Jonas had gone to the docks, and had by accident left the key in his desk, Jonathan took a five-pound note out of the cash-box which Jonas had kept there, and concealed it in another part of the desk. He did not dare to steal it; he would have been afraid of detection; but he knew how much Jonas would suffer, and he *persevered* in making him suffer.

"Jonas came home, and put the keys in his pocket; he did not even recollect that he had left them in the desk; but the next day, when he opened his desk to count the money in the cash-box, a five-pound note was missing. This was, indeed, a sad discovery; he racked his brains to remember whether he had made any payments that he had not entered. He inquired of Jonathan whether he had seen him pay any money away. Jonathan professed to feel for his distress, while, in fact, he was rejoicing in it; and he was even much delighted (wicked lad!) when he heard the merchant, in his private room, severely reproaching Jonas for his carelessness.

"A few weeks after, Jonas having occasion to ransack his desk for some papers, found the five-pound note. It never occurred to him that any body could have been so spiteful as to hide it, in order to give him pain; and he supposed that he himself had, by accident, stowed it away with other papers. But his joy at finding it was even greater than his distress at losing it. He ran to the merchant, and told him of his good fortune. The merchant recommended more caution in future.

"Still Jonathan *persevered* in persecuting Jonas; and having been hitherto undetected, became bolder. It was Jonas's duty to take the letters to the post-office. One day a letter of great importance, containing a bill of exchange for a large amount, was missing. The merchant had, as usual, intrusted the correspondence to Jonas's care, and had left the city for his country abode. Next day the first inquiry, when the merchant came, was whether the letters had been dispatched. Jonas burst into tears, and said that the letter with the remittance was not to be found. 'What!' said the merchant, with extreme displeasure; '*that* letter missing!' And, looking on the ground, he saw the letter at Jonas's feet, wet and dirty, as if it had been trampled on. This had been also Jonathan's doing. He had concealed the letter the night before. He had flung it unperceived—having himself trodden upon it—under Jonas's desk.

"In this way many months passed. All Jonathan's conduct was the *persevering* annoyance of Jonas; but he generally managed with so much cunning as to be undiscovered in his malice; but things went on so ill, that the merchant dismissed them both.

"Years rolled by, in which they had little intercourse with one another. Jonas and Jonathan, in the progress of time, became merchants themselves, but nothing could eradicate from Jonathan's mind the determination to injure, and, if possible, to ruin Jonas. And he at last accomplished it, though his own ruin was at hand. He undermined the credit of Jonas by *persevering*, indirect insinuations as to the state of his affairs, by doubts and innuendos, and shrugs of the shoulder, by a succession of unfounded reports and malevolently expressed suspicions, Jonas's reputation as a merchant suffered, and bankruptcy took place. Some of the statements by which Jonas had been injured were, however, traced to Jonathan. He was prosecuted for damages, convicted, and his own insolvency soon followed.

"But of perseverance—vicious perseverance—he was a striking example.

"It is not long ago, that I went to visit an interesting old man, who lives by the side of the Rhone, at a short distance from Lyons. Have you ever heard of the Jacquard machine, one of the most ingenious of modern discoveries, by which the most complicated patterns can be woven with the same ease as the plainest; a machine which enables an ordinary weaver to produce all those many-colored oriental shawls, fashionable silks, and variegated ribbons, which formerly required a dexterity possessed only by a very few, and a continuous labor that made them costly and inaccessible to any but the rich? Now-a-days, silk stuffs, exquisitely tasteful and beautiful, can be purchased for a small sum of money, and are worn by hundreds of thousands of the classes whose garments were formerly made of coarse wool or hemp. The old man I speak of was Jacquard, and he was one of the great causes of this diffusion of enjoyment. As I happened to be near the place of his abode, I determined to visit him, and did so, accompanied by several friends.

"It was a sunshiny day, I remember, and we had a delightful walk along the margin of the rapid Rhone, a river renowned in history, and whose banks are still crowded with the ruins of past time, calling to mind the days when every feudal chief was obliged to shut himself up in high and embattled towers, built often upon dangerous crags, in order to be secure from the attacks of some neighboring lord. The petty sovereigns and the petty feuds have passed away together. Every thing now bears the face of security, of industry, of peace. Talking of the delightful contrast, and hoping that nations would one day harmonize, as the once contending peasantry of the Rhone *now* harmonize, we reached old Jacquard's abode.

"He welcomed us with heartiness. 'But come forth into my vineyard,' he said; 'let us get among the grapes and the sunshine;' so he led the way with a tottering step. 'Hither, hither,' he called out; 'come with me to the arbor.' We followed him there. 'Let me sit in the centre, and let me tell you how glad I am to see you, my friends!' We sat down around him; the clematis was blended with the vine, and together they made the roof and the walls of the quiet retreat, where, every day, the venerable old man was used to sit, and to recall the events of his much chequered life. Some of those events you shall hear as he himself related them, and you will see what perseverance—virtuous perseverance—is, and what virtuous perseverance can do.

"I told Jacquard that I was an Englishman, and as he had been one of the benefactors of my country, I was come to thank him. 'How proud I am,' said he, 'to be visited by an Englishman. If I have ever done any good, I owe the very first suggestion to England. It was an English newspaper that led me to occupy my thoughts with mechanical improvements. But for that, perhaps, I should still have been a poor straw-hat maker in an obscure street at Lyons, instead of the happy man you see me, honored by my native town, recompensed by the government, (pointing to the red ribbon which he wore at his button-hole,) and pensioned by the state.' 'But how,' I inquired, 'did you owe to England your first success?' It was,' he answered, 'during the peace of Amiens, that we were accustomed to meet, in order to talk politics, at a friend's house, on the quay. It was there a translated extract from an English newspaper met my eye, stating that a premium was offered by a society in London, to any one who would apply machinery to the manufacture of nets. I meditated long upon the matter, and after many attempts, I made a machine by which nets could be produced. It was the first of my mechanical experiments, and I will tell you, if you have the patience and the desire to hear me, how that trifling affair was the beginning of my good fortune and my fame.' Nothing, we assured him, could gratify us more than to continue his history. 'Well, then,' said he, 'I contrived a machine and made a net by it, and thought no more of the matter. I carried the net about in my pocket, and one day, meeting with a friend who had heard the paragraph of the English paper read, I threw it to him, saying, "There is the difficulty got over, and the net made!" And the matter passed out of my mind. I had persevered until I had succeeded, and there was an end of it. Some time afterwards, I was much surprised at getting an order from the Prefect to appear at the Prefectal palace. I went, and the Prefect said he had only lately heard of my proficiency in the mechanical arts. It was a great mystery to me; I really did not comprehend his meaning, and I stammered out a sort of an apology for not understanding him. My net, and the machine that made it, had gone quite out of my head. The Prefect expressed surprise that I should deny my own abilities, but at last he produced the very net that I had made, and which to me had seemed a very trifling affair, as it was in reality. "I have orders from the Emperor to send the machine to Paris," said the Prefect. "From the Emperor! That's strange indeed; but you must give me time to make it." So I set about it, and in a few weeks I completed it, and trudged away with my machine and a half manufactured net in it to the Prefect. He was very impatient to see it work, so I bid him count the number of loops, and then strike the bar with his foot; he did so, and another loop was added to the number. Great was the delight that he expressed, and he told me that no doubt I should hear from him again. I heard from him again, in truth, very soon, and in a way that perplexed me not a little; for his first greeting was—"You must go to Paris, M. Jacquard, by his Majesty's orders." "To Paris, sir! how can that be? What have I done? How can I leave my affairs here?" "Not only must you go to Paris, but you must go to-day—you must go immediately!" These were not times in which there was any resisting the orders of authority; so I said, "If it must be so, it must; I will go home and pack up my baggage, and I shall be ready to obey your commands." "No! M. Jacquard," said the Prefect, "you cannot go home; a carriage is waiting to take you to Paris." "Not go home!—not say adieu to my wife!—not make up my luggage for a journey of 150 leagues!" "I have orders," said the Prefect, "to dispatch you instantly; you may send to your wife; you may tell her to give to my messenger any thing you desire to take—I will provide you with money; but there must be no delay." There was no argument about the matter, so I sent to my wife, got a small bundle of clothes, jumped into the carriage, and away! away! we were off, full gallop towards Paris! When we reached the first station, I opened the door, and I found myself stopped by a gendarme, who said to me, "Sir, if you please, you are not to go out of my sight." I found I was a prisoner, and escorted by military force to the capital; things were so managed at that time; there was, however, no use in complaining, so I made the best of my fate, and submitted in good humor.

"'I reached Paris for the first time in my life, and strange was my introduction there. I was escorted to the Conservatory, and whom should I see there but Napoleon and Carnot. Carnot said to me suddenly, "Are you the man that can do what Omnipotence cannot do? Can you tie a knot in a string on the stretch?" I was overwhelmed with the presence of the Emperor, and the abruptness of his minister, and knew not what to answer. But Napoleon spoke very condescendingly to me about my discovery; told me he would protect me, and urged me to go on with my mechanical pursuits.

"'Materials were brought me, and I was directed to make a net-producing machine in the Conservatory, which I did.

"'At that time, a superb shawl was being woven for the Empress Josephine, and for its production they were employing a very costly and complicated loom—a loom upon which more than twenty thousand francs had been expended. It appeared to me that the same effect might be produced by a less perplexing machinery, and I recollected having seen a model by Vaucauson, in which I thought a principle was developed which I could apply to the desired purpose. Long thought and perseverance enabled me to produce the mechanism that bears my name. When I had succeeded, the Emperor conferred this decoration upon me, and granted me a pension of one thousand crowns.

"'But on returning to Lyons, far different was my destiny. When I endeavored to introduce my machine, the workmen broke out into open revolt. I was every where denounced as the enemy of the people, as the man who had been scheming the destruction of their trade, and the starvation of themselves and their families. Three plots were laid to assassinate me, and twice I had great difficulty in escaping with my life. So strong was the tide of prejudice and indignation, that my machine was ordered to be openly destroyed by the public authorities. It was broken to pieces in the great square of the city. The iron was sold for old iron ; the wood for fire-wood. Think what a shipwreck of all my hopes !

"'I did not quite lose courage. The successful competition of foreigners, and the consequent decline of trade in France, led some intelligent manufacturers, a few years after, to think of the man whose discovery might, perhaps, bring some relief to that depression under which they labored. They found strength of mind to make another experiment. It succeeded. Silks of greater beauty were introduced, at a lower cost. There was a dawn of prosperity, and it has continued to shine. Of that machine which had been devoted to ignominy and destruction, I have now seen thousands introduced, and there is now scarcely any man so blind, or so ignorant, as not to acknowledge that its introduction has been a great blessing. It has given labor to tens of thousands, and I have had a complete recompense for all I have gone through.'

"We talked of these and other matters till the shades of coming twilight bid us depart. The happy old man is still in my memory ; a striking instance of virtuous perseverance, crowned with fit reward."

278.

If there is any symptom of another commercial crisis in the United States, similar to that of 1837, it is to be found in the really wicked personal extravagance, which at present forms the most prominent social feature of our Eastern cities. Such ruinous wastefulness has always hitherto been among the immediate antecedents of great revulsions, serving both as an index and a cause of coming disaster.

The reader will scarcely credit the following revelation in regard to this matter, which we take from the Philadelphia *Ledger*:—

"A fashionable dry goods dealer advertises a lace scarf, worth fifteen hundred dollars. Another has a bridal dress, for which he asks twelve hundred dollars. Bonnets at two hundred dollars are not unfrequently sold. Cashmeres from three hundred dollars and upwards are seen by dozens in a walk along Broadway. A hundred dollars is quite a common price for a silk gown. In a word, extravagance in dress has reached a height which would have frightened our prudent grandmothers, and appalled their husbands. A fashionable lady spends annually on her mantua-maker and lace-dealer, a sum that would have supported an entire household, even in her own rank in life, in the days of Mrs. Washington. A thousand dollars a year is considered, we are told, quite a narrow income for such purposes among those pretending to be 'in society' in some of our cities. Add to this the expenditure for opera tickets, for a trip to the

Springs, and for a score of little inevitable *et ceteras*, and the reader gets some idea of the comparatively wanton waste of money, carried on year after year, by thousands, if not tens of thousands of American women.

And for what end? Do these human butterflies improve their intellect, enlarge their culture, or elevate their characters by this spendthrift system? On the contrary, they deteriorate all. Do they bestow additional happiness on their husbands and fathers? The very reverse: for to sustain these extravagances, the father or husband, as the case may be, toils late and early, consumes his health, and often is driven into wild speculations that end in utter ruin. Do they win the approval of the other sex? Never was the esteem of any worthy man secured by a costly, reckless style of dress. All that this perilous extravagance effects is, to gratify miserable, personal vanity. The fostering of one of the most petty of human vices is the only result of these spendthrift habits. Mrs. Potiphar plumes herself on having outshone her rival in laces, at some grand soirée, or in having worn more jewels; and that is the single, barren harvest which she reaps by the expenditure of thousands. Can the pampering of such vanity benefit her or others? Alas! the women who live for such triumphs as these, whose whole souls are given to diamonds and dress, are little fitted to be wives or mothers, to be companions for men or educators of children. When the Roman matrons sunk to a similar condition, Rome commenced to decline.

Fortunately for our country, however, such painted triflers form but a small minority of the women of America. Unfortunately, however, their influence on society is greater than their numbers, for to their extravagance and vanity is united a presumption, which asserts for themselves socially a superiority over the rest of their countrywomen; and this superiority, so undeserved, is conceded to them, partly because of their apparent wealth. They are thus enabled practically to give a tone to society at large. In city circles less ostentatious, in country villages, and even in farm houses, their extravagance and vanity is copied, till in half the families in the land females spend upon their dress more than they can afford. With too many, happily we need not say with all, adorning the person takes the place of mental culture. To be showily dressed is often considered to be of more moment than to be graceful, amiable, and intelligent Where will this end? If this continues for another generation, where will we be?

279.

Politeness is the distinctive attribute of a gentleman—rudeness, of a boor. The bear growls its characteristic utterances. The man who is addressed with civility, and replies with rudeness, gives utterance to his innate brutality.

True politeness is the natural exponent of a well-regulated mind. It is inseparable from good breeding, self-respect, and a high sense of honor. The gentleman is consequently courteous in all his intercourse. But the ill-bred man, regarding politeness as an occasional advantage or *necessity*, fancies that he may exercise it or not, to suit his convenience. In his view, courtesy is simply matter of traffic. Thus, in a degree, he makes himself merchantable, although he cannot make himself a gentleman.

Universal politeness has become a primary law in all eminent mercantile houses. It characterizes the intercourse of the Barings, Rothschilds, Laboucheres, and all the most highly respected American houses. Every Boston merchant remembers with pleasure the genial urbanity which graced the energy, success, grand beneficence, and important public services of Abbott Lawrence, the distinguished merchant and statesman. The feelings and courtesies of a true gentleman marked his eminent character.

Whoever enters the counting-rooms of a Baring, Labouchere, or a Lawrence, whether his proposals are accepted or declined, is sure to meet with civility. In the offices of such merchants, the visitor might as soon be expected to be greeted with the whoop of a wild Pawnee, brandishing a scalping knife at his head, as to hear a polite request repelled with snobbish incivility, graced perhaps with a characteristic "*What the devil do you suppose I care?*" Their urbanity, self-respect, and dignity are not occasional appliances, hence they cannot descend to vulgar arrogance. Happily the latter is reserved to that class of hybrid magnates who readily mistake their native rudeness for mercantile dignity.

280.

We hear very much of political economists, but very little of life economists. Demand and supply are synonymous terms, say the former; and yet the latter would have very little difficulty in proving that the demand upon the strength and energies of man is, in many cases, more than equal to the supply. In nothing are we so prodigal as in the waste of human life. The majority of men die prematurely through overtaxing their mental and physical powers. Unrest is a prominent characteristic of modern times. Food hastily swallowed; work hastily done; money hastily made; health carelessly sacrificed; life wilfully robbed of its peace and sanctity: such are some of the errors almost peculiar to this age.

A moment's reflection will show how much treasure is sacrificed by this prodigality of life. It is stated by Dr. Lyon Playfair—a man of great scientific attainments—that in England's largest manufacturing city, Manchester, the average length of life among her one million of inhabitants is eleven years less than in other parts of the country. He attributes this fearful result to child labor in factories, imperfect ventilation, and over toil among adults. Eleven million years wasted in every generation! Take only a momentary view of the matter, and reckon the average worth of each year at but fifty dollars, and we have the enormous sum of five hundred and fifty millions of dollars wasted in one city in every thirty years. If we take a philanthropical view of the question, and consider the sacredness of human life, and the duty confided to man of leaving the world better than he found it, how terrible must be the neglect of those who thus bequeath to posterity, debility and sorrow.

Are there no Manchesters in this country? Do we not find in our midst, youth robbed of its sunshine and taught to ape manhood; and early manhood forced to suffer premature age, in consequence of the violation of the laws of nature? If we take from childhood its joy, we inevitably denude old age of its venerable character. Live fast means too often die fast.

In a scientific age like the present the value of life-economy should be fully appreciated. Excess of work or excess of care is sure to curtail the life and diminsh the strength of man. With the aid of machinery, labor might lose much of its severity. Every day the inventive faculties of man are introducing labor-saving machines, and yet people toil as unremittingly as ever. Medical science has not been able to remove one disease from the prolific vocabulary of human ills, because man perversely thwarts science, by drawing too largely on his powers of endurance. Thus he may become rich in money, but be bankrupt in health and happiness.

Let recreation be part of the business of life. By recruiting the frame we husband our strength and energies, and are enabled to accomplish more than by spasmodic effort. Nature will ever come triumphant out of the contest, if we only resolve to be faithful to her laws.

281.

"*I have lived too fast.*"—Such was the exclamation of the young man, Caldwell, who was convicted of embezzling money while acting as a conductor on the Burlington railroad, when he was arrested and told that he had been detected. There are volumes in that sentence, and it reveals the secret of his fall. He is a man of fine address, was one of the most popular of conductors, had once a good character and good habits, and was readily trusted, and had occupied positions of considerable responsibility. But he indulged his appetites and passions too freely. He was extravagant, associated with worthless and dissipated companions, and if he did not gamble, was compelled to exceed his income in his expenditure, to preserve appearances, and to defray his share of the expenses of the company he kept; and alas! in an evil hour, to meet these drafts upon his purse, he ventured on the experiment of appropriating to himself a portion of the funds of the Company which were intrusted to him, and as the result was discovered, arrested, tried, convicted, and sentenced to the penitentiary. Disgrace and ruin followed hard upon his sin. His case is but another illustration of the text of Scripture, "The way of transgressors is hard."

Alluding to the phrase we have quoted, the eloquent counsel for the prosecution, in his concluding plea, said to the jury:

"Ah, gentlemen, the pivot on which all this sad drama turns, is condensed into that single expression, '*I have lived too fast!*' Pregnant words!—they should fall from this court-room like a tocsin, on the giddy whirl of young men below; the multitude that has watched, with varied emotions, but all with intense interest, the progress of this trial, should carry it forth and spread it in the saloons and in all the popular resorts of youth. *I have lived too fast!* It is the most forcible, as it is the most graphic expression of the unhealthy life that characterizes —I shall be allowed to say—a multitude of young men in this beautiful city. In no town in the world do the centers of allurement and temptation bear such a proportion to the population. Extravagance in dress, extravagance in living, dangerous extravagance every where, is apparent to the observer, nor need that observer wear Puritanical glasses to see what I allude to. Perhaps it is the inseparable incident of the marvellous growth of this great city; and that when things become settled, and the more conservative institutions of society become established, their superior moral force will cause all other elements and tendencies to revolve around the true central influences of society."

Will not young men take warning from this melancholy case, and avoid the rock on which Caldwell made shipwreck? They should realize that character is worth more than money, and that pleasures purchased at the sacrifice of morals and honor, are bought too dear. Let those who would escape the danger of dishonesty, avoid saloons and gambling-houses, and the company of those whose ways take hold on hell. Let clerks and others who are intrusted with money never yield for a moment to the temptation to fraud; for one dishonest act paves the way for another; and no one, who takes the first step, knows where his career will end, what disgrace and suffering he will bring on himself, and what anguish he will cause to friends who are deeply interested in his welfare. "He," and he only, "who walketh uprightly, walketh surely." The dangers of a city life for young men are appalling; but he who acknowledges God in all his ways will find the promise fulfilled, that *He* will direct his paths.

282.

"The wild, the reckless, and the indiscreet—
His word was always doubted."

It not unfrequently happens that young men damage themselves for life, or at least for many years, by what to them appear as trifling or unimportant errors. They violate the truth, form reckless associations, and neglect positive engagements. Thus, at the very beginning, they impair confidence, excite suspicion, and create distrust. Character is a jewel of priceless value, and yet it is easily impaired or tarnished. The young, generally speaking, do not appreciate its importance, because they lack experience, and know but little of the world and its severity. An individual, for example, who is in the habit of repeating all sorts of wild and improbable stories, who boasts, exults, and magnifies, is at first looked upon with surprise and caution by the intelligent and discerning, and then, detected in some monstrous fabrication, he is distrusted and avoided. Thus, in an effort to appear what he is not, and to occupy a position to which he is not entitled, he destroys his character, and loses friends who otherwise would prove useful to him.

The young and indiscreet do not appreciate the realities of life, but permit fancy and folly to mislead them. They do not remember that character is, to a certain extent, like an edifice that is intended not for a day or an hour, but for years, and hence its foundation should be of the best material. The advanced in life are, perhaps, too severe and too critical. They do not make sufficient allowance for the indiscretions and the impulses of youth. Hence they are often disposed to consider as vices, what are in fact merely foibles—foibles, too, which might readily be modified and amended, if not wholly cured. When, however, the habit of exaggeration and falsehood becomes so fixed that it forms a feature of character—when engagements are made, pecuniary or otherwise, without any intention of fulfilling them, the reputation soon becomes damaged to so serious an extent, that it can never be redeemed or re-established.

Not a few individuals among the young indulge in the error, that by extravagance of speech, recklessness of sentiment, and insolence of manners, they make themselves important, and excite envy and astonishment. The mistake is a fearful one. The only feelings produced among the sensible and observing, are those of pity and contempt. If, in brief, a statement cannot be relied upon, because of the known habit of the person who makes it to falsify and exaggerate thereafter, his career in life and society will be disreputable and downward, and at the most rapid rate. The beginnings of character cannot be too carefully attended to. Temptations beset the young on all sides. In the first place, they have to resist their own evil passions and weaknesses, as well as their inexperience, and in the second, the evil associations with which society abounds, and the many allurements which pleasure and profligacy hold out. This is especially the case in great cities. The chief peril may be said to exist within the ages of eighteen and twenty-five. It is at that period that the character and the reputation are more fully developed than at any other. The habits then become fixed, the tone of the mind settled, the disposition regulated. But if a false step be taken, and a false system be adopted, it will be difficult, nay, almost impossible to recover in after life.

Only a short time since, a young man paid a visit to a neighboring city, as well for relaxation as for pleasure. Before he left the place of his abode, his standing was every way creditable. He had grown up under the eyes of watchful parents, had received a good education, possessed a fine mind, and was addicted to no vice. It so happened, that on the way, he formed an acquaintance with a dashing man of the world as he described himself, who, in fact, was nothing more than a polished sharper and gambler. The youth was led on from step to step, until all his funds were exhausted, and he was compelled to write home to his parents for a sufficient sum to pay his hotel bill and passage back. Meantime he had been seen in one of the streets of New York partially intoxicated. Fortunately he was recalled to a sense of propriety in time, but not before his character had received a shock, from the effects of which it took months of good conduct to recover. Naturally kind of heart and correct of deportment, he intended nothing of the kind, but was led on gradually by an evil associate. How many are ruined in a similar manner! How many forget the little proprieties of life, commit some excess, and then discover, to their mortification and shame, that they have disgraced themselves. The young cannot be too watchful. They cannot guard too vigilantly against bad habits and evil associations. They cannot be too careful to protect themselves from the vice of falsehood. Character, to many of them, is all they possess; it is the only inheritance that has been left to them by their parents, and it should be cherished accordingly. No young man, who has a just sense of his own value, will trifle with his reputation. It should be as precious to him as the breath of his nostrils. But, like the down of the peach, or the fragrance of the rose, when once gone, it can never be replaced. According to the poet, "all's well that ends well," but there is seldom a good end that has not a good beginning.

283.

Moral Courage.—A virtue, and great as it is rare. We remember when we thought the courage of the field everything, the charge—the word of command, high-sounding and clear amid the battle's fury—the clash of arms, the roar of artillery, the thrill of the bugle's note, as with more than magic sound, it bids the soldier dare all for victory—the banner of your country in front—planted there to stand amid victory or defeat. Oh! how young hearts beat to be actors in such a scene—calling it glorious to mingle in, and fighting nobly, to lie down and die.

But what is the courage of the battle-field compared with the moral courage of every-day life? Stand alone, see friends scowl, hear distrust speak its foul suspicion, watch enemies take advantage of the occasion, laboring to destroy—who would not rather encounter the shock of a hundred battle-fields, and lead a forlorn hope, than bear and brave these things? Why, the one is as the summer breeze on the ocean to winter's stormiest blast. The common spirit may summon courage enough to play the soldier well. Use quickly fits him for it. But it requires a man to speak out his thoughts as he thinks them—to do, when, like that stormy blast in winter on old ocean, peace, honor, security, and life are threatened to be swept away. Yet who can look back to the page of history, or forward to the hope of the future, and hesitate which of the two to chose? The martyrs, what are they? Chronicled names in all hearts. The patriots who died for liberty ignominiously, and on the scaffold, how fares it with them? Cherished as earth's honored sons. The good who spoke the truth and suffered, where are they? The best and brightest—first in our thoughts and love. And yet, what did they? Like men, they spoke the truth that was in them. This was their courage. If they had been silent, if trembling before tyrants or mobs, they had feared to tell what they knew, to speak what they felt, they would have lived and died like other men. But they had the courage to do all this, and through their suffering and truth, lighted it up with new glory and power.

Give us moral courage before every thing else! It is the only bravery on which humanity may count for any real blessing. Give us moral courage! For while it nerves a man for duty, it roots out of his heart hate and revenge, and all bad passions, making him wise amid danger, calm amid excitement, just amid lawlessness, and pure amid corruption. It is the crowning beauty of manhood.

284.

We met, in our reading, with a fresh word spoken by the editor of the *North American Review*, in a "Charge" at the installation of a minister—a word which has as forcible an application to business men as to ministers. It was on the momentum of character—the force which a man's character, if high and good, imparts to his doing. Dr. Peabody said:—

"It is a fundamental law of mechanics, that quantity and

velocity together make up momentum. A feather might dance about throughout all eternity, or might move with the swiftness of a sunbeam, without acquiring any appreciable momentum The same law holds good in spiritual dynamics. To insure valuable results, there must be, not only activity, but quantity of character. Our own souls, such as they are, are our chief instruments of usefulness; and what we accomplish can never transcend the measure of what we are. Your public and private ministrations, my brother—the words you utter, the offices you perform—are but small multiplicands, of which your own mass of spiritual experience, your weight of character, is the much larger multiplier in producing the amount of good you bring to pass. You put your whole soul into whatever you do; and, if that soul be small, and lean, and low, a century of the most active industry would leave no mark; but if your soul be pure and true, rich and full, devout and lofty, there is an intense spiritual momentum in all that you do; your strokes are all blows; your notes all staccato; your words, as was said of Luther's, 'half-battles.'"

This was a happy illustration; and we are sure that scores of business men who heard it felt the application of the sentiment to business character; many a one instantly calling to mind some illustration of the best talents vainly applied, because of the want of this moral momentum—the character of the man was nothing; and however men might wish to have the benefit of the talents they admired, the man was really but a floating feather. In contrast with this, they doubtless thought of some one whose only wealth, at some time, had been this spiritual momentum, who, victimized by fraud, or overwhelmed by some unavoidable mercantile disaster, had kept on, leaving the past as a wreck to be deserted, and pressing forward to new voyages and fresh adventures, building up fortunes again with youtnful vigor and elastic spirits.

It is a grand sight to behold such a man—to not only see that he has power when stripped of fortune, but to witness the respect paid to his character, manifesting that those whose good opinion is worth having, value, most of all, the forces in a man's life which are independent of exterior circumstances, and which flow out of the moral qualities of character. And why will not young men more readily see the bearing of this fact on their hopes of success in business life? Why will they not aim to be "fast men" in this respect, seeking that momentum, which comes from the activity of mental talents and the quantity of moral principle and purpose.

285.

Every day shows us how men fail for want of a proper self-reliance. Here was our neighbor Mr. Faintheart, we all knew that he might make a respectable and useful man; he had an average amount of talent, a good figure, a pleasant manner, sufficient education, and many friends,—yet he could never get above a subordinate place. What doomed him to such inferiority? His lack of courage. A salutary law took effect; we could not hold up him who would not stand upon his feet. Our neighbor on the other side, young Mr. Resolute, how different his history. He said, "I can," and like the word in the Arabian tale, that affirmation lays open the hidden treasures of the world. He says, "I will," and the prophecy secures its own fulfillment. The consciousness of strength was the soul's encouragement to itself; it was the support of enterprise, the main spring of independence.

286.

"PLEASE, *sir*, *don't* you want a cabin-boy?"

"I *do* want a cabin-boy, my lad, but what's that to you? A little chap like you ain't fit for the berth."

"Oh! sir, I'm real strong. I can do a great deal of work, if I ain't so very old."

"But what are you here for? You don't look like a city boy. Run away from home, hey?"

"Oh! no, indeed, sir; my father died, and my mother is very poor, and I want to do something to help her. She let me come."

"Well, sonny, where are your letters of recommendation? Can't take any boy without those."

Here was a damper. Willie had never thought of its being necessary to have letters from his minister, or his teacher, or from some proper person, to prove to strangers that he was an honest and good boy. Now, what *should* he do? He stood in deep thought, the captain meanwhile curiously watching the workings of his expressive face. At length he put his hand into his bosom and drew out his little Bible, and without one word put it into the captain's hand. The captain opened to the blank page and read:—

"Willie Graham, presented as a reward for regular and punctual attendance at Sabbath School, and for his blameless conduct there and elsewhere. From his Sunday School Teacher."

Captain McLeod was not a pious man, but he could not consider the case before him with a heart unmoved. The little fatherless child, standing humbly before him, referring him to the testimony of his Sunday School teacher, as it was given in his little Bible, touched a tender spot in the breast of the noble seaman, and clapping Willie heartily on the shoulder, he said :—" You are the boy for me ; you shall sail with me ; and, if you are as good a lad as I think you are, your pockets shan't be empty when you go back to your good mother."

287.

One might suppose, that parsimony and economy in trade, would require but a few words of explanation to the reader. To some, the bare announcement is sufficient to indicate the difference, but to others the clearest reasoning will not avail. This may be owing to the fact that they have been accustomed to confound the one with the other in all the affairs of life—in the family and in business, in pleasure and in profit.

A person of this stamp wishes to go into business ; he has some little capital, but not much experience. He chooses the profession of a grocer or a merchant, and, supposing that parsimony is economy, in order to save rent, he commences business in the outskirts of the city, or in some obscure alley or unfrequented street, and fails to succeed, and wonders why it is, with all his industry and economy, he cannot make both ends meet, much less thrive! His parsimony is the chief cause of his failure. But you can't convince him of it, and he will live and die in the little nest which his own hands created, and grieve to think that fortune has not been more gracious in the bestowment of her favors upon him.

Another person opens an establishment on Chesnut-street ; he has but recently come to the city, having been a successful merchant in one of the towns in the interior of the State, where he was known by every one, as he was born and raised in the county. Neither he, nor his father before him, had ever availed themselves of the facilities of advertising in the county papers, and yet they got along, and in process of time amassed what in that region was considered to be quite a fortune. He now opens a fine stock of goods in a commodious house on Chesnut-street, and thinks that every body knows him, and of course will trade with him. Was he not known in Buncombe? Did he not come from Lancaster? He has fallen into the delusion that, because he was known in the town and county that gave him birth, that certainly he must be known here.

On the score of economy, as he deems it, he refuses to advertise. It costs too much, he never did it before, why do it now? He has a good house, he has good stock, he has competent clerks; he himself is a pleasant and accommodating merchant —why does he not succeed? Nobody knows him or cares to know him. The competition in the market does not permit Mr. Fogy to become a necessity. Chesnut-street can do without him, and the city would not miss him any more than she would a fly, if he was to move to parts unknown. Now, what does economy of rent require? What of clerk's hire? What of interest on capital? What of time? They all require that he should invest something in advertising, and that, too, on a liberal scale. Not in one paper only, but in many; not occasionally, but constantly. And he will soon find the benefit of so doing. Parsimony may say, No—it will be too expensive; you can't stand it. But Economy replies, You are mistaken; I must advertise to be known, to be felt, to be appreciated. If I feel interested in my own success, my neighbors will sympathize with me, and if they see me helping myself, they will cheerfully and promptly come to my aid.

Take the following illustration of the difference between parsimony and economy. Sir Walter Scott tells of a near kinsman, who, having been informed that a family vault of his was decaying and like to fall in, and that ten pounds would make the repairs, proffered only five pounds. It would not do. Two years after he proffered the full sum. He was assured that twenty pounds would scarce serve. He hesitated, hemmed and hawed for three years more, then offered twenty pounds. The wind and rain had not waited for his decision, and not less than fifty pounds would now suffice. A year afterwards he sent a check for fifty pounds, which was returned by post, with the intelligence that the aisle had fallen the preceding week. The reader will make the application.

288.

The employment of ladies as clerks in stores, especially in retail dry goods stores, is becoming very general in America.

The New York *Times* is earnestly advocating the employment of females as clerks in stores—particularly in all retail dry goods stores. It is an employment for which they are well fitted, and would properly enlarge their sphere of action and occupation. And it is a business that they can do better than men. They are more active and expert at handling dry goods, more tasteful in folding and arranging them, more polite and conciliatory to customers, and have better judgment in all matters of taste in relation to dress. On the other hand, young men should be employed in more active and manly labor. Measuring off calicoes and tape is too light a task for their physical strength, and is usurping a place and occupation that properly belongs to women.

We are decidedly in favor of this branch of women's rights being conceded to them. It would give employment at good wages to a great many young ladies, and would be degrading to no one willing to earn a living. If the ladies generally preferred those stores where females are employed to sell goods, a change would soon be effected, and women employed in all the stores.

The employments of females are becoming more numerous and remunerative every year, and it is right that it should be so. In the New England States and in New York, nearly all the public schools are taught by ladies both in summer and winter. This enlargement of the sphere of woman's activity and usefulness is a matter of public economy. It gives them work that they can do as well as men, and it diverts the labor of men into other channels, and to more athletic and useful employments. In this active age and country, there is no difficulty in men finding useful and lucrative employment—work, too, better suited to their physical nature than measuring off tape and calico.

289.

In the *Merchants' Magazine*, for June, 1855,* we gave a sketch of the life of Peter C. Brooks, from the pen of that accomplished statesman and scholar, the Hon. Edward Everett, and we have since noticed with pleasure the comments it has elicited from our contemporaries of the press in our own and other lands. The Philadelphia *Merchant* thus illustrates, by a brief abstract from the memoir of Mr. Brooks, in the Magazine, the "power of integrity":—

"When from a balcony that overlooked the tumultuous populace of Paris, in 1848, Lamartine introduced the venerable De l'Eure to the multitude, he said, 'Listen, citizens! it is sixty years of a pure life that is about to address you.' His rising was like that of the full moon on the dark waters, and

* See also "Lives of American Merchants," published in 1856.

every soul felt his influence as each wave is tipped with the radiance of the moonlight. It was the power of integrity—the potential influence of a man who had been a consistent republican, and who, by obedience to the great laws of justice and truth, had proved himself worthy of being heard in an hour of peril.

"But to impress the populace is not always the greatest evidence of the power of integrity, for there are other occasions when the elements to be impressed are of a less passionate nature. Such an instance is given in the late memoir of one of the truest 'Boston merchants,' Peter C. Brooks, by his son-in-law, Hon. Edward Everett, which we find in Hunt's *Merchants' Magazine* for June, 1855. It seems that at the death of a confidential partner of Mr. Brooks, a final settlement in full was made with the adminstrators, by Mr. Brooks paying sixty thousand dollars. This was in 1808; but in 1829, an action at law was brought against Mr. Brooks, to set aside this settlement, on the ground that important items had been omitted in the summing up of accounts—nearly one hundred thousand dollars being claimed by the parties who instituted the suit. When the case was tried, William Wirt, then in the zenith of his fame, was called to Boston in behalf of the plaintiffs, to combat the power of Daniel Webster, as Wirt himself wrote, 'on his own arena.' Webster, in a speech of six hours, made a grand and splendid effort; and Wirt acknowledged that he never went to a court, as he did the next day, with such a sinking heart. But he did mightily, and never satisfied himself better than on that occasion. The impression made by both speakers was powerful; and says Mr. Everett, 'The most arid details of account, and the abstrusest doctrines of equity, were clothed by them with living interest.' The court-room was densely crowded, and after the close of the argument of Mr. Webster, Mr. Brooks himself obtained permission to ad dress a few words to the court in explanation. There he stood, at the age of sixty-two, in the dignifying consciousness of stainless integrity. By his side lay the old account-books, drawn from an obscurity of thirty years, and which the court pronounced the most perfect set of books that had ever been brought into their presence—the penmanship as plain as print, and order and exactness evinced on every page. Laying his hand on those old account-books, Mr. Brooks stood up before the court, and, with a voice slightly tremulous, he uttered, in the simple language of plain truth, a few sentences of explanation, which had great weight with all who heard him. 'The transparent clearness,' says Mr. Everett, 'the simplicity, the unmistakable air of conscious integrity with which he briefly restated the turning points of the case, produced an effect on the minds of those who heard him beyond that of the highest professional power and skill.'

"The court decided that no evidence at all had been given of any fraud, nor even of the least impropriety, on the part of Mr. Brooks, and the only item allowed to the plaintiffs was one of two thousand three hundred and fifty-eight dollars, Mr. Brooks having from the first agitation of the claim avowed his readiness to meet any such error, notwithstanding the closing of the account in full—a settlement which was intended to cover the possibility of any such error. The suit terminated to Mr. Brooks's 'entire satisfaction,' as he wrote in his journal; and Mr. Wirt recorded in a letter, that when he had finished, Mr. Brooks came to him, took his hand at the bar, and spoke in the kindest terms, expressing his high satisfaction at Mr. Wirt's demeanor toward him during the trial.

"Such is the nobility of Conscious Integrity. Such a man as Mr. Brooks needs no patent from royalty.

"'For the rank is but the guinea's stamp,
The man's the gold for all that.'"

290.

THERE is a class of men whose patronage of art has been princely in its munificence, as their wealth has equalled that of princes, whose interests have become a chief concern of statesmen, and have involved the issues of peace and war; whose affairs afford a leading subject of the legislation of States, and fill the largest space in the volumes of modern jurists. This class has produced men who have combined a vast comprehensiveness with a most minute grasp of details, and whose force of mind and will in other situations would have commanded armies and ruled States; they are men whose plans and combinations take in every continent, and the islands and the waters of every sea; whose pursuits, though peaceful, occupy people enough to fill armies and man navies; who have placed science and invention under contribution, and made use of their most ingenious instruments and marvellous discoveries in aid of their enterprises; who are covering continents with railroads and oceans with steamships; who can boast the magnificence of the Medici, and the philanthropy of Gresham and of Amos Lawrence; and whose zeal for science and zeal for philanthropy have penetrated to the highest latitude of the Arctic seas, ever reached by civilized man, in the ships of Grinnell.

Modern scholars have seen the important bearing of the history of commerce upon the history of the world; have seen, rather,—as who, in this most commercial of all eras, can fail to see?—how large a chapter it forms in the history of the world, although crowded out of the space it ought to fill by the wars and crimes which destroy what it creates. Hume was among the first to call attention to this branch of historical inquiry, and Heeren has investigated with much learning the commerce of the ancients. If we were in possession of lives of the great merchants of antiquity, what light would they not throw upon the origin of States, the foundation of cities, and inventions and discoveries, of which we now do not even know the dates?

Trade planted Tyre, Carthage, Marseilles, London, and all the Ionic colonies of Greece. Plato was for a while a merchant; Herodotus, they say, was a merchant. Trade was honorable at Athens, as among all nations of original and vigorous thought; when we find discredit attached to it, it is among nations of a secondary and less original civilization, like the Romans.

But if commerce forms so large a chapter in the history of the world, what would the history of America be if commerce and men of commerce were left out? Trade discovered America in the vessels of adventurers, seeking new channels to the old marts of India; trade planted the American colonies, and made them flourish, even in New England, say what we please about Plymouth Rock; our colonial growth was the growth of trade—revolution and independence were the results of measures of trade and commercial legislation, although they undoubtedly involved the first principles of free government: the history of the country, its politics and policy, has ever since turned chiefly upon questions of trade and of finance, sailor's rights, protection, banks, and cotton.

www.ingramcontent.com/pod-product-compliance
Lightning Source LLC
LaVergne TN
LVHW020914110826
845150LV00004B/673

* 9 7 8 1 4 2 5 5 5 5 7 0 2 *